Utilizing Big Data Paradigms for Business Intelligence

Jérôme Darmont
Université Lumière Lyon 2, France

Sabine Loudcher
Université Lumière Lyon 2, France

A volume in the Advances in Business Information Systems and Analytics (ABISA) Book Series

IGI Global
DISSEMINATOR OF KNOWLEDGE

Published in the United States of America by
IGI Global
Business Science Reference (an imprint of IGI Global)
701 E. Chocolate Avenue
Hershey PA, USA 17033
Tel: 717-533-8845
Fax: 717-533-8661
E-mail: cust@igi-global.com
Web site: http://www.igi-global.com

Library of Congress Cataloging-in-Publication Data

Names: Darmont, Jerome, 1972- editor. | Loudcher, Sabine, 1969- editor.
Title: Utilizing big data paradigms for business intelligence / Jerome Darmont and Sabine Loudcher, editors.
Description: Hershey : Business Science Reference, [2018] | Includes index.
Identifiers: LCCN 2017032931| ISBN 9781522549635 (hardcover) | ISBN 9781522549642 (ebook)
Subjects: LCSH: Business intelligence--Data processing. | Big data.
Classification: LCC HD38.7 .U75 2018 | DDC 658.4/72028557--dc23 LC record available at https://lccn.loc.gov/2017032931

This book is published in the IGI Global book series Advances in Business Information Systems and Analytics (ABISA) (ISSN: 2327-3275; eISSN: 2327-3283)

British Cataloguing in Publication Data
A Cataloguing in Publication record for this book is available from the British Library.

Advances in Business Information Systems and Analytics (ABISA) Book Series

ISSN:2327-3275
EISSN:2327-3283

Editor-in-Chief: Madjid Tavana, La Salle University, USA

MISSION

The successful development and management of information systems and business analytics is crucial to the success of an organization. New technological developments and methods for data analysis have allowed organizations to not only improve their processes and allow for greater productivity, but have also provided businesses with a venue through which to cut costs, plan for the future, and maintain competitive advantage in the information age.

The **Advances in Business Information Systems and Analytics (ABISA) Book Series** aims to present diverse and timely research in the development, deployment, and management of business information systems and business analytics for continued organizational development and improved business value.

COVERAGE

- Business Intelligence
- Performance Metrics
- Business Models
- Decision Support Systems
- Business Decision Making
- Business Systems Engineering
- Big Data
- Data Management
- Legal information systems
- Geo-BIS

The Advances in Business Information Systems and Analytics (ABISA) Book Series (ISSN 2327-3275) is published by IGI Global, 701 E. Chocolate Avenue, Hershey, PA 17033-1240, USA, www.igi-global.com. This series is composed of titles available for purchase individually; each title is edited to be contextually exclusive from any other title within the series. For pricing and ordering information please visit http://www.igi-global.com/book-series/advances-business-information-systems-analytics/37155. Postmaster: Send all address changes to above address.

Titles in this Series

For a list of additional titles in this series, please visit:
https://www.igi-global.com/book-series/advances-business-information-systems-analytics/37155

Protocols and Applications for the Industrial Internet of Things
Cristian González García (University of Oviedo, Spain) Vicente García-Díaz (University of Oviedo, Spain) B. Cristina Pelayo García-Bustelo (University of Oviedo, Spain) and Juan Manuel Cueva Lovelle (University of Oviedo, Spain)
Business Science Reference • ©2018 • 356pp • H/C (ISBN: 9781522538059) • US $215.00

Social Network Analytics for Contemporary Business Organizations
Himani Bansal (Jaypee Institute of Information Technology, India) Gulshan Shrivastava (National Institute of Technology Patna, India) Gia Nhu Nguyen (Duy Tan University, Vietnam) and Loredana-Mihaela Stanciu (University Timisoara, Romania)
Business Science Reference • ©2018 • 321pp • H/C (ISBN: 9781522550976) • US $215.00

Harnessing Human Capital Analytics for Competitive Advantage
Mohit Yadav (BML Munjal University, India) Shrawan Kumar Trivedi (Indian Institute of Management Sirmaur, India) Anil Kumar (BML Munjal University, India) and Santosh Rangnekar (Indian Institute of Technology Roorkee, India)
Business Science Reference • ©2018 • 367pp • H/C (ISBN: 9781522540380) • US $215.00

Corporate Social Responsibility for Valorization of Cultural Organizations
María del Pilar Muñoz Dueñas (University of Vigo, Spain) Lucia Aiello (Sapienza University of Rome, Italy) Rosario Cabrita (University Nova de Lisboa, Portugal) and Mauro Gatti (Sapienza University of Rome, Italy)
Business Science Reference • ©2018 • 328pp • H/C (ISBN: 9781522535515) • US $215.00

Contemporary Identity and Access Management Architectures Emerging Research...
Alex Chi Keung Ng (Federation University, Australia)
Business Science Reference • ©2018 • 241pp • H/C (ISBN: 9781522548287) • US $175.00

For an entire list of titles in this series, please visit:
https://www.igi-global.com/book-series/advances-business-information-systems-analytics/37155

IGI Global
DISSEMINATOR OF KNOWLEDGE

701 East Chocolate Avenue, Hershey, PA 17033, USA
Tel: 717-533-8845 x100 • Fax: 717-533-8661
E-Mail: cust@igi-global.com • www.igi-global.com

Editorial Advisory Board

Table of Contents

Detailed Table of Contents

The field of life imaging spans a large spectrum of scientific study from mathematics and computer science to medical, passing by physics, biology, etc. The challenge of IDV project is to enrich a multi-parametrized, quantitative, qualitative, integrative, and correlative life imaging in health. It deals with linking the current research developments and applications of life imaging in medicine and biology to develop computational models and methods for imaging and quantitative image analysis and validate the added diagnostic and therapeutic value of new imaging methods and biomarkers.

A moving object database is a database that tracks the movements of objects. As such, these databases have business intelligence applications in areas like trajectory-based advertising, disease control and prediction, hurricane path prediction, and drunk-driver detection. However, in order to extract knowledge from these objects, it is necessary to efficiently query these databases. To this end, databases incorporate special data structures called indexes. Multiple indexing techniques for moving object databases have been proposed. Nonetheless, indexing large sets of objects poses significant computational challenges. To cope with these challenges, some moving object indexes are designed to work with parallel architectures, such as multicore CPUs and GPUs (graphics processing units), which can execute multiple instructions simultaneously. This chapter discusses business intelligence applications of parallel moving object indexes, identifies issues and features of these techniques, surveys existing parallel indexes, and concludes with possible future research directions.

A wide range of smart mobility technologies are being deployed within urban environment. These technologies generate huge quantities of data, much of them in real-time and at a highly granular scale. Such data about mobility, transport, and citizens can be put to many beneficial uses and, if shared, for uses beyond the system and purposes for which they were generated. Jointly, these data create the evidence base to run mobility services more efficiently, effectively, and sustainably. However, generating, processing, analyzing, sharing, and storing vast amounts of actionable data also raises several concerns and challenges. For example, data privacy, data protection, and data security issues arise from the creation of smart mobility. This chapter highlights the various privacy and security concerns and harms related to the deployment and use of smart mobility technologies and initiatives, and makes suggestions for addressing apprehensions about and harms arising from data privacy, protection, and security issues.

Discovering trend reversals between two data cubes provides users with novel and interesting knowledge when the real-world context fluctuates: What is new? Which trends appear or emerge? With the concept of emerging cube, the authors capture such trend reversals by enforcing an emergence constraint. In a big data context, trend reversal predictions promote a just-in-time reaction to these strategic phenomena. In addition to prediction, a business intelligence approach aids to understand observed phenomena origins. In order to exhibit them, the proposal must be as fast as possible, without redundancy but with ideally an incremental computation. Moreover, the authors propose an algorithm called C-Idea to compute reduced and lossless representations of the emerging cube by using the concept of cube closure. This approach aims to improve efficiency and scalability while preserving integration capability. The C-Idea algorithm works à la Buc and takes the specific features of emerging cubes into account. The proposals are validated by various experiments for which we measure the size of representations.

Research on the analysis of time series has gained momentum in recent years, as knowledge derived from time series analysis can improve the decision-making process for industrial and scientific fields. Furthermore, time series analysis is often an essential part of business intelligence systems. With the growing interest in this topic, a novel set of challenges emerges. Utilizing forecasting models that can handle a large number of predictors is a popular approach that can improve results compared to univariate models. However, issues arise for high dimensional data. Not all variables will have direct impact on the target variable and adding unrelated variables may make the forecasts less accurate. Thus, the authors explore methods that can effectively deal with time series with many predictors. The authors discuss state-of-the-art methods for optimizing the selection, dimension reduction, and shrinkage of predictors. While similar research exists, it exclusively targets small and medium datasets, and thus, the research aims to fill the knowledge gap in the context of big data applications.

This chapter discusses concepts and tools for the exploration and visualization of computer-mediated communication (CMC), especially communication involving multiple users and taking place asynchronously. The work presented here is based on experimentally validated social networks (SN) extraction methods and consists of a diverse number of techniques for conveying the data to a business analyst. The chapter explores a large number of contexts ranging from direct social network graphs to more complex geographical, hierarchical, and conversation-centric approaches. User validation studies were conducted for the most representative techniques, centered both on extracting and on conveying of CMC data. The chapter examines methods for automatically extracting social networks, which is determining who is

Foreword

Business intelligence is a mature topic within the computer science and data analysis literature. In fact, to the surprise of many, IBM coined the term as far back as 1958. With the advent of data warehousing and data mining research in the late 1990's, business intelligence technologies became a research topic within the data management and data mining communities, focusing mainly on "business" data like sales and costs. In the last decade, "Big Data" term and paradigm appeared, supported by new technologies and tools, but first and foremost by new, much larger and more diverse datasets. These come from radically new data sources, often produced by novels sensors or specialized equipment, marking a shift from human-generated to machine-generated data.

But what is the relationship between business intelligence and big data really? Is it just more of the same, something really different, or rather more of a logical progression?

This book was put together to answer this question. The editors, Jérôme Darmont and Sabine Loudcher, both professors at Université de Lyon, Lyon 2, and highly respected researchers, tackled the question by putting out a broad Call for Papers, and carefully selecting among the submitted papers. The chapters in the book show that the answer to this question is not simple, but rather structured into different categories.

The first chapter, "Applications of Artificial Intelligence in the Realm of Business Intelligence," by P. Mehrotra, tackles the question from a top-down perspective, concluding that AI, applied on Big Data, can significantly enhance BI, i.e., AI and Big Data is seen as an embedded component of (traditional) BI systems.

The second chapter, "A Big Data Platform for Enhancing Life Imaging Activities," by L. Abidi et al., takes a very different, bottom-up, approach, focusing on a specific analytics solution for the huge volume of machine-generated medical imaging data. Here, Big Data is key, and a dedicated BI solution is built for one type of Big Data.

The third chapter, "A Survey of Parallel Indexing Techniques for Large-Scale Moving Object Databases," by E. Leal et al., considers location-sensor data, e.g., from GPS, but focusing on a specific orthogonal technical aspect, namely indexing.

The fourth chapter, “Privacy and Security in Data-Driven Urban Mobility,” by R. Akerkar, also considers the wider class of big mobility data, but consider another orthogonal technical aspect, namely privacy, and security.

The fifth chapter, “C-Idea: A Fast Algorithm for Computing Emerging Closed Datacubes,” by M. Martin-Nevot et al., changes the focus yet again, now to a specific type of technique for mining the big data, specifically so-called closed datacubes.

The sixth chapter, “Large Multivariate Time Series Forecasting: Survey on Methods and Scalability,” by Y. Hmamouche et al., also looks at a specific type of techniques, but a different one, namely time series forecasting.

The seventh chapter, “Exploring Multiple Dynamic Social Networks in Computer-Mediated Communications: An Experimentally Validated Ecosystem,” by I. Osesina et al., combines the above perspectives, looking at a novel type of data, social networks, but also considering specific techniques and a specific experimental application.

Finally, the eighth chapter, “Analysis of Operation Performance of Blast Furnace With Machine Learning Methods,” by K.-W. Hsu and Y.C. Ko, closes the circle by again considering a deep, specific application, namely that of machine learning to furnace data.

So, the answer to the question is: *it depends: on the type of data you have, on what you want to do with it (the techniques), and what you want to use it for (the applications).*

To get the full details, read this interesting book on an essential topic for any enterprise or organization in the twenty-first century.

Torben Bach Pedersen
Aalborg University, Denmark

Torben Bach Pedersen *is a Professor of Computer Science at Aalborg University, Denmark where he co-directs the Center for Data-intensive Systems (Daisy), the largest Big Data group in Denmark. His research interests include many aspects of Big Data analytics, with a focus on technologies for “Big Multidimensional Data” - the integration and analysis of large amounts of complex and highly dynamic multidimensional data in domains such as logistics (indoor/outdoor moving objects), smart grids (energy data management), transport (GPS data), and Linked Open Data. He is an ACM Distinguished Scientist, and a member of the Danish Academy of Technical Sciences, the SSTD Endowment, and the SSDBM Steering Committee. He serves/has served as Area Editor for IEEE Transactions on Big Data, Information Systems and Springer EDBS, PC Chair for DaWaK, DOLAP, SSDBM, and DASFAA, and regularly serves on the PCs of the major database conferences like SIGMOD, (P)VLDB, ICDE, and EDBT.*

Foreword

The Big Data paradigm requires a new way of thinking in how data is stored, processed, and analyzed. This paradigm shift is crucially needed in all aspects of data processing, including data warehousing and business intelligence. Big Data paradigms offer researchers and practitioners opportunities to explore new techniques to address Big Data challenges.

It is often to address Big Data paradigms by addressing many different "V"s of Big Data. The main ones are Volume, Variety, Velocity, and Veracity. These will be outlined in the context of data processing, especially in business intelligence.

VOLUME

Big Data certainly has large volume of data. Data retrieval techniques that have been used to efficiently retrieve smaller volume of data might not be effective to retrieve data from Big Data. It is then natural to apply some parallelism techniques in Big Data Retrieval. Therefore, parallel operators must be specifically designed for big data retrieval, including the use of parallel indexing.

Traditionally, parallel data retrieval relies on horizontal data partitioning of relational tables. In other words, data parallelism is due to parallel I/O scans. Challenges occur in regard to parallelism of indexes, where indexes are not implemented as flat tables, but as indexing trees. Consequently, index tree partitioning is a new level of challenge in parallel data retrieval. The issue becomes more complex when the data is moving objects which is dynamic and frequently updates.

Parallelism in data warehousing and business intelligence to process big data volume is even more important, as building and processing data cubes is more complex than relational database processing. Data cubes are multi-dimensional, and this creates similar complexities to parallel indexing.

VARIETY

The data Big Data exists in a variety of data formats; not only flat relational tables. This new data format raises new challenges not only in data storage, but also data modelling and processing. In the past, there had been waves in different data formats and modelling, including object-oriented data format and modelling, object-relational, temporal databases, multimedia databases, etc. Although these waves are passing, many more new data format requirements have emerged. This is due to many raising and emerging applications, such as social networks, sensors, IoT, etc., which have become big data producers in many applications. Consequently, Big Data must accommodate this new wave of data formats. This raises challenges in both processing, as well as data design and modelling.

This new data format trends give even more impact to data warehousing and business intelligence, as business analysis must take into account the large volume of non-traditional data, especially social network data, and time-series data, both of which are highly dynamic.

VELOCITY

Data in the Big Data era is coming faster than ever. It is not about time-series data and how to handle or to process time-series data. It is even bigger than this. As data is ubiquitous, and ubiquitous data producers produce high-speed data, it is critical for the data repository be able to absorb the data as quickly as they are being produced. Data ingestion in Big Data is literally a big problem. New techniques to load and to ingest the data must be used in order to keep up with the high velocity of data being produced by data producers. Handling time-series data is more challenging than ever.

Traditionally data warehousing and business intelligence handle more static data. High velocity of data raises new requirements in how data warehousing and business intelligence operates. It is crucial for businesses to provide a faster feedback looks, and business intelligence must be able to cope with this when high velocity of data is concerned.

VERACITY

Veracity, which is often described as data quality and governance, is an important aspect in Big Data, as data not only comes from everywhere, but belongs to everyone.

Data quality traditionally is an important problem; it becomes even more important when Big Data is concerned, as there are many different data producers, as well as data ubiquitous which may not belong to one organization, and is often a public data source. Therefore, veracity is a new complexity, which does not naturally exist previously.

This book contains a rich collection of knowledge in Big Data especially in the context of business intelligence and its applications, including those in artificial intelligence, machine learning, imaging, etc. This book provides a good source of emerging techniques and applications in utilizing Big Data paradigm in business intelligence, as the title states.

Happy reading, and keep learning.

David Taniar
Monash University, Australia

David Taniar *is an Associate Professor at the Faculty of Information Technology, Monash University, Australia. His research is in the area of data management, particularly big data processing, parallel database processing, spatial and Geographical Information Systems, data warehousing and mining. He has authored two books on databases ("High Performance Parallel Database Processing and Grid Databases", Wiley 2008, and "Object-Oriented Oracle", 2006), and has received four best paper awards (from three IEEE conferences and one international journal). He is the founding editor-in-chief of three Science Citation Index Expanded (SCI-E) journals (Mobile Information Systems, Intl. J. of Data Warehousing and Mining, and Intl. J. of Web and Grid Services), a PC chair and a General chair of a number of international conferences, and has been invited to deliver keynote speeches and tutorials at various international events.*

Preface

Business intelligence (BI) aims to support decisions, not only in the business area *stricto sensu*, but also in the domains of health, environment, energy, transportation, science, and so on. BI provides a transverse vision of an organization's data and allows accessing quickly and simply to strategic information. For this sake, data must be extracted, grouped, organized, aggregated and correlated with methods and techniques such as data integration (ETL), data warehousing, online analytical processing (OLAP), reporting, data mining and machine learning. BI is nowadays casually used both in large companies and organizations, and small and middle-sized enterprises, thanks to the advent of cloud computing and cheap BI-as-a-service. The development of BI in the 1990's has also sparkled vivid research that currently addresses new challenges in big data.

Mashing up an organization's internal data with external data (e.g., open data) is acknowledged as the best way to provide the most complete view for decision-making. Yet, tackling data heterogeneity has always been an issue. With big data coming into play, benefits from processing external data look even better, but issues are also more complex. Data volume challenges even warehouses that were tailored for large amounts of data. Velocity challenges the very idea of materializing historicized data. Variety and veracity issues remain, but at a much greater extent. Thence, actually extracting intelligible information from big data (data value) requires novel methods. Eventually, new technologies such as cloud computing, distributed and parallel computing on frameworks such as Hadoop, Spark and Flink, and NoSQL and NewSQL database management systems also question classical BI.

This book gathers a collection of chapters of high scientific quality that address various research and practical issues related to the five "Vs" of big data in the BI field. After issuing calls for contributions from 2017 to early 2018, we received nineteen chapter proposals from Africa, Asia, Europe and North America. Eighteen fell within the scope of the book. Fifteen full chapters were actually submitted. Each chapter received at least two reviews in a double-blind process, by an international scientific committee consisting of twenty-six leading researchers, with most papers (thirteen) receiving three reviews. Eventually, we accepted eight chapters for revision and, ultimately, publication.

Chapter 1, "Applications of Artificial Intelligence in the Realm of Business Intelligence", by Prakhar Mehrotra, nicely introduces this book by giving an overview of basic concepts in BI and artificial intelligence, respectively. Then, the author reviews the integration of artificial intelligence in BI, discusses the many open issues and challenges related to the big data "Vs" in this context, and finally presents current and most probable applications of artificial intelligence in BI, as well as actual industrial examples.

Chapter 2, "A Big Data Platform for Enhancing Life Imaging Activities", by Leila Abidi, Hanene Azzag, Salima Benbernou, Mehdi Bentounsi, Christophe Cérin, Tarn Duong, Philippe Garteiser, Mustapha Lebbah, Mourad Ouziri, Soror Sahri and Michel Smadja, opens the first part of the book, which mainly focuses on big data management architectures and methods. This chapter accounts for a large-scale, interdisciplinary life imaging project, Atlas IDV, which aims at supporting cooperation between scientists and extracting of new knowledge from big multi-modal and multi-scale clinical images. Images are stored in a private cloud, as a data lake that enforces data quality and privacy and allows intra and inter-site collaborative research. To enhance image retrieval, native metadata from imaging equipment are enriched, notably by crowdsourcing and resorting to semantic resources such as linked open data and medical ontologies. Eventually, the authors discuss image analytics in Atlas IDV's context.

Chapter 3, "A Survey of Parallel Indexing Techniques for Large-Scale Moving Object Databases", by Eleazar Leal, Le Gruenwald and Jianting Zhang, introduces moving objects (constituting trajectories), which come in high volume, velocity and uncertainty from various applications such as meteorology and mobile advertising. Extracting spatiotemporal patterns for decision making from such data requires efficiently indexing moving objects, and scaling up to big data requirements necessitates parallelizing the indexes. The authors first discuss the main research challenges in designing such parallel moving object indexes, and then extensively survey existing methods through the prism of a taxonomy they propose.

Chapter 4, "Privacy and Security in Data-Driven Urban Mobility", by Rajendra Akerkar, also relates to data and mobility, from a data privacy, protection and security point of view, in case of either user mismanagement or malign access. The chapter first introduces the context of big urban data and smart mobility, before listing privacy and security threats, as well as current and prospective solutions, whether technical, legal or governmental. In conclusion, the author advocates for an ethical approach that cares for the interests of citizens.

Chapter 5, "C-Idea: A Fast Algorithm for Computing Emerging Closed Datacubes", by Mickaël Martin-Nevot, Sébastien Nedjar, Lotfi Lakhal and Rosine Cicchetti, makes a good transition from big data management to big data analytics, which is the focus of the second part of the book. The authors address the issue of detecting trends, and more precisely trend reversals, in data warehouses viewed as unions of cubes. So-called emerging cubes do the job, but require the (costly) computation of the compared cubes and cannot scale up to big data volumes. Thus, the authors propose emerging *closed* cubes, which are compact representations of cubes on which OLAP queries can still be executed. The data structures used, the C-Idea algorithm that computes emerging closed cubes, and an experimental comparison of the respective size of emerging and emerging closed cubes, are then thoroughfully detailed.

Chapter 6, "Large Multivariate Time Series Forecasting: Survey on Methods and Scalability", by Youssef Hmamouche, Piotr Marian Przymus, Hana Alouaoui, Alain Casali and Lotfi Lakhal, addresses the time series forecasting methods that are extensively used in BI systems. Today's big data applications require high dimensional time series that induce two main issues: selecting predictors for a target variable and assessing how the number of variables affects prediction accuracy. Thus, the authors review how three recent families of time series forecasting methods from the literature address these two issues; and discuss their respective merits and flaws when facing massive datasets.

Chapter 7, "Exploring Multiple, Dynamic Social Networks in Computer-Mediated Communications: An Experimentally Validated Ecosystem", by Isaac Osesina, Eduard Tudoreanu, John P. McIntire, Paul R. Havig and Eric E. Geiselman, addresses the challenges of analyzing and visualizing data from computer-mediated communication (CMC), i.e., microblogging, chatting, messaging and online social networking, which are exploited in various domains. The authors first review social network extraction and visualization from CMC data. Then, they present wide-ranging experiments for comparing both extraction and visualization methods on realistic data, with actual users giving feedback on visualizations.

Eventually, Chapter 8, "Analysis of Operation Performance of Blast Furnace with Machine Learning Methods", by Kuo-Wei Hsu and Yung-Chang Ko, presents an application of machine learning to analyze the operation of a blast furnace, which is very complex. The authors first use clustering to determine class labels. Then, domain knowledge-driven feature selection helps connect variables to economic and technical performance indices. Finally, predicting the operation performance of the blast furnace is achieved by classification. Moreover, beyond the proposed methodology, the originality of the approach lies in the use of real data (vs. simulated or experimental lab data typically addressed by the literature) notably bearing hundreds of variables.

In conclusion, our ambition when deciding to edit this book was to make it one of the first foundation references in the field of big data processing for business intelligence. We hope that our intended targets, i.e., researchers, practitioners from the industry and graduate students in the fields of computer science, data science and business intelligence, will enjoy this book and find it valuable.

Jérôme Darmont
Université Lumière Lyon 2, France

Sabine Loudcher
Université Lumière Lyon 2, France

Acknowledgment

As editors of this book, we would like to thank all chapter authors and scientific committee members for their careful and dedicated work. We also particularly thank Torben Bach Pedersen and David Taniar, who made us the honor to write insightful forewords. We would also like to thank Jordan Tepper from IGI Global, who supported us all along the editing process.

Jérôme Darmont
Université Lumière Lyon 2, France

Sabine Loudcher
Université Lumière Lyon 2, France

Chapter 1
Applications of Artificial Intelligence in the Realm of Business Intelligence

Prakhar Mehrotra
Uber Technologies, USA

ABSTRACT

The objective of this chapter is to discuss the integration of advancements made in the field of artificial intelligence into the existing business intelligence tools. Specifically, it discusses how the business intelligence tool can integrate time series analysis, supervised and unsupervised machine learning techniques and natural language processing in it and unlock deeper insights, make predictions, and execute strategic business action from within the tool itself. This chapter also provides a high-level overview of current state of the art AI techniques and provides examples in the realm of business intelligence. The eventual goal of this chapter is to leave readers thinking about what the future of business intelligence would look like and how enterprise can benefit by integrating AI in it.

0. INTRODUCTION

The purpose of this chapter is to provide an overview into how recent advances in Artificial Intelligence (AI) can be applied to Business Intelligence (BI) systems thereby making the latter truly intelligent. This chapter is divided into five main sections: (1) the first section defines BI and AI, discusses their pros & cons, and how they are used in industry today, (2) the second section provides a high-level introduction of the fundamental concepts in AI. Readers who are well versed with

DOI: 10.4018/978-1-5225-4963-5.ch001

the basics of AI can skip this section. (3) the third section discuss the technical considerations of integrating AI systems into existing BI systems, (4) next section discusses open issues and challenges related to learning, storage, processing and organizational structure of big data, and (5) the last section discusses the applications of AI combined with BI, some current examples from industry and direction of future research.

1. DEFINING BUSINESS AND ARTIFICIAL INTELLIGENCE

1.1 Business Intelligence

The term "Business Intelligence" first appeared in the year 1865 in the context of gathering data (Devens, 1865). However, it was not until the technological advancements in 20th century that the BI gained traction. In fact, it was a seminal paper by IBM that described BI as an "automatic system" designed to share information to various parts of an organization (Luhn, 1958). Since then the term BI has been defined as an engineering product with a set of software applications that aim to organize the raw data into meaningful information to be used in decision making (Sabherwal, 2007). It has also been defined as a set of processes, methodologies and technologies that leverages information to aid in analysis and decision making (Evelson & Norman, 2008). Thus, the main objective of a BI system is to aggregate the vast amount of structured and unstructured data in an automated fashion so as to provide the following:

- Continuous reporting of the metrics that define the health of a company,
- Aid in both tactical and strategic decision making by surfacing descriptive statistics from the data,
- Report on observed anomalies in the data, and
- Provide Online Analytical Processing (OLAP) support to enable quick and customized insights from the aggregated data

The ever-increasing quantity, multitude of sources, and access to cheaper technologies to log raw data implies that BI systems need to continuously evolve to distill any meaningful actionable information from big data. In order to describe the so called "Big Data", Gartner defined 3 essential aspects of the data using 3 V's namely: Volume, Velocity and Variety. The fourth dimension (Veracity) was added later on to denote uncertainty in the data.

- **Volume:** Refers to the amount of data. We are living in a world of ever increasing data sets
- **Velocity:** Refers to the speed/frequency at which data comes in.
- **Variety:** Refers to the sources and types of data. Is there one source or multiple sources? Today, in a complex competitive environment, decision makers often look at multiple sources and types of aggregated data to reach a decision.
- **Veracity:** Refers to uncertainty in the data. Uncertainty here implies uncertainty about the quality of the data. In other words, whether the data that is collected is accurate or not?

The BI system needs to take into account the above four dimensions of the data to deliver a product. It needs to be flexible enough to accommodate increasing Volume, changing Variety, different Velocities and while taking into account the data's Veracity. To do so, most of the BI tools focus on Extract, Transform and Load (ETL) processes and converting the raw data into some form of visualization (Chen et al., 2012; Watson & Wixom, 2007; Turban et al., 2008). BI system is all about aggregating raw data from a variety of sources into concise actionable information. Business needs to pre-define the aggregation logic and desired output metrics (also called Key Performance Indicators or KPIs). By robustly and reliably presenting the KPIs, the BI tools help in providing uniform access across the organization to any information and reduce subjectivity in decision making. Thus, BI does an excellent job to provide value by way of reporting data that in turn helps answer high level business questions about what *has happened.* In this sense, a BI system is all about reporting the past.

The 2011 Gartner report (Sallam et al., 2011) suggests that the future of BI is to incorporate prediction framework, big data analytics and natural language processing. Currently, big data analytics is usually left to a data scientist who, in real world, will often bypass the BI tool altogether and directly access the raw "BIG" data (e.g., data stored in Hadoop) and apply one or several AI techniques to get the answer to a desired question.

However, various industry reports like McKinsey & Company (2016) have highlighted the extreme shortage of data scientists. Besides, assigning data scientists to every department within a company is an expensive task. A more fundamental issue that exists with existing BI tools is the issue of scalability to solve a diverse set of problems (Chaudhuri et al., 2011) along with dependence on a query-like language (e.g., SQL) to spin up dashboards for each ad-hoc request. As mentioned before, dashboards are good for reporting but fall short of providing the intelligence that stakeholders require for key decision making. Artificial Intelligence solves this problem. The advances in cloud computing (Larson & Chang, 2016; Marston et al., 2011; Zhang et al., 2010) have enabled cost effective ways of deployment and maintenance of these algorithms in the cloud, thereby offering flexibility and agility to the enterprise.

1.2 Artificial Intelligence

The human brain is an engineering marvel of nature - a system that has far more superior capabilities of cognition, pattern recognition, creativity and language/vision understanding than any other system (living or artificial) today in the world. However, our human brain is limited by how much information it can process at any given time for any given speed (Heyes, 2012; Russell & Norvig, 1995; Turing, 1950). As mentioned before, present day needs require a variety of ever increasing data sets at high speeds to be able to predict future events. If the prediction about future involves only learning from historical data sets (i.e. the future is fairly similar to the past), a machine can outperform human brain. Such a machine/system is loosely termed as an "Artificial Intelligent" system. Theoretically, the term Artificial Intelligence (AI) refers to science and technology aimed at building machines that try to mimic the human brain and help predict the future. It encompasses the field of Machine Learning, Optimization, Logical Reasoning and Control Theory (Jackson, 1985; Russell & Norvig, 1995).

Since this chapter is about the role that AI plays in BI systems, it is imperative to define the term "Intelligence" here. In humans, intelligence is defined as the mental power needed to perceive, reason, problem solve, abstract thinking, and to learn new ideas quickly and from experience (Colom et al., 2010, Gottfredson, 2004). It is a result of biological activation of neurons in the brain in response to the information acquired through interpretation of language and visual perception by our cortex. A system is said to be "Artificially Intelligent" if it is able to perform one or more of the tasks that make human intelligence. Intelligence in machines is acquired by making it learn from the logged data by way of constructing mathematical algorithms that can generalize enough a particular aspect it is trying to learn. While there is no agreed upon formal definition of intelligence in a BI system, it usually refers to the system's ability to distill down relevant information from vast amounts of logged data. In this sense, the term "intelligence" is not used in the same context in Artificial and Business Intelligence. An AI system exhibits intelligence and makes predictions, while a BI system enables humans to use their own intelligence to make inferences and predictions.

We conclude this section by summarizing AI and BI in Table 1.

Table 1. Comparison between business and artificial intelligence

	Business Intelligence	Artificial Intelligence
What is it?	Set of technologies & processes designed to provide reporting of pre-defined metrics.	Algorithms designed to provide predictions into the future.
Why is it required?	Transforms raw data into consumable relevant information.	By learning the non-linear dynamics from the data, machines are able to provide faster and reliable insights into the future thereby significantly improving decision making and outperforming humans in certain tasks.
How is it done?	Requires ETL servers, big data storage system, an aggregated data warehouse, data mart/model and user interface (dashboards, reports, etc.).	Requires access of raw data, data pre-processing, feature engineering, model running, model evaluation/ testing and user interface.
What does it achieve?	Provides consistency in reporting metrics and aggregated data across the organization for building customized reports.	Provides cutting edge insights about future learned from the data thereby providing competitive advantage

2. FUNDAMENTAL CONCEPTS IN ARTIFICIAL INTELLIGENCE

2.1 Machine Learning

The term "machine learning" refers to a paradigm where we use algorithms, that often use empirical models (as opposed to closed form analytical models) to detect patterns in the data and make a prediction about the future (Abu-Mostafa et al., 2012; Bishop, 2007; Hastie et al., 2009; Murphy 2012). For algorithms to be generic enough to explain the underlying mechanics, they need a large amount of data to "learn" from. Statistics, on the other hand, is about building analytical solutions by way of writing explicit mathematical equations. Statistics is about quantifying confidence intervals while machine learning is about quantifying performance on unseen data (also called as test or generalization error).

Mathematically, a machine learning model M learns from a data-set D for a given objective function O. The error E of model M is measured on another data-set D' that the model has not seen during the learning period. When $E < \varepsilon$ (ε is an acceptable threshold value), the model has completed learning and is ready to be used in the real-world.

There are three major buckets of machine learning (see figure 1):

Figure 1. Block diagram of three types of Machine Learning

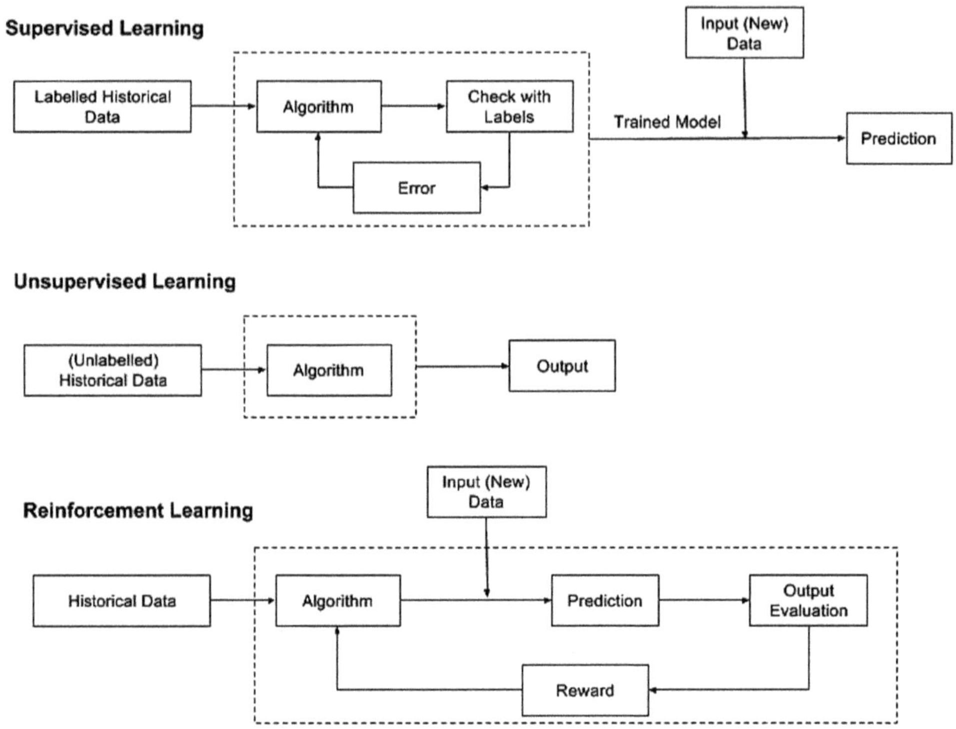

1. **Supervised Learning:** Here, the data-set D contains both input and output labels with the output labels having predefined classes. It is supervised because model learns about the output variable with help of predefined labels in data-set. If the output labels are discrete, then it's a classification problem. When the output labels are continuous, it is called regression problem. Model parameters are tuned iteratively by propagating the error backwards and is complete when error has reached acceptable threshold. It is called supervised because during model fitting we are able to estimate the error (due to presence of predefined labels in data) and tune the parameters such that error is reduced. Because learning is purely based on the availability of historical data, supervised learning works only if the real-world dynamics have been encountered sufficient number of times in the data set. Logistic regression, Decision/Boosting Trees and Random Forest are some of the classical supervised learning techniques that aim to learn from labelled data either by decreasing variance in the data or by decreasing bias.

2. **Unsupervised Learning:** Here, the data-set D does not contain any predefined output labels. There is just input, and the algorithm tries to make sense of the data without any external label. It does so by implicitly learning about the distribution from which the data is generated thereby implicitly learning non-linear complex relationships in the data-set (Raina et al., 2009). The other way to understand this is that unsupervised learning aims for a simpler (or low dimensional) representation of the data set, a representation that has less noise. Clustering is a classic example of unsupervised learning.
3. **Reinforcement Learning:** Here, learning happens by specifying the reward function when an expected goal is met. It is different from supervised and unsupervised learning because learning does not happen from the input data set, but via numerous outcomes of a particular task. Hence it is also sometimes called learning by experience. Learning by humans is a kind of reinforcement learning! When we learn to ride a bicycle, early on we will fall because of insufficient peddling or poor handle steering. Every time we fall, our brain learns not to repeat the same mistake. After sufficient practice, our brain masters how to ride the bicycle. This type of learning is beneficial where there is a reward function, for example, learning how to play a game, building a trading engine (reward = profit), learning to fly a helicopter or self-driving vehicle, and so on. Refer to (Dorigo et al., 2016; Kaelbling et al., 1996; Sutton & Barto, 1998) for in-depth understanding of Reinforcement Learning.

For integration into business intelligence tools, supervised and unsupervised learning paradigms are more relevant because of the manner in which they make prediction. Specifically, Clustering and Classification can be directly integrated into existing BI tools as described below:

1. **Clustering:** A type of unsupervised learning where the objective is to find clusters of similar data points. The learning happens by finding data with similar structure and grouping them together. Euclidean distance between two points in data sets is one way to measure similarity. If the points are correlated, then Mahalanobis distance might be the best. See (Cios et al., 2007; Murphy, 2012) for more details on similarity measures. K-means is one of the most effective clustering algorithms where we specify the number of clusters (or centroids) K and the algorithm uses Euclidean distance as a measure to cluster points together. For other clustering algorithms, refer to (Clarke et al., 2009; Hinton, 1999; Murphy, 2012). In the context of business intelligence, clustering can be used for:

a. Customer segmentation (e.g., cluster by browsing patterns, interests, number of clicks etc.)
b. Supply optimization and categorization (e.g., during winter, the sale of heaters, sweaters and jackets go up; hence they are one cluster)
c. Anomaly detection

2. **Classification:** A type of supervised learning where the objective is to classify the input to target output. Classification can be binary (yes or no, positive or negative) or multiclass. An example of binary classification problem is whether an individual will default a loan or not, while an example for multiclass classification would be whether an individual is likely to make a purchase and/or use promo code. Logistic Regression, Support Vector Machines (SVM), Random Forest, Boosting Trees, Neural Networks are some of the techniques for classification. See (Bishop, 2007; Hastie et al., 2009; Schölkopf & Smola, 2002) for more details.

Machine Learning techniques described above can be considered as a subset of broader Artificial Intelligence. Optimization, Control Theory, Logical Reasoning, etc. are various AI techniques. One of the earliest applications of machine learning was object recognition and image classification (Sebastiani, 2002). However, most of this work involved manually selecting the features from the data that the individual thought was the correct representation of the data. A major breakthrough came in early part of 2010 fueled by the invention of GPUs (Coates et al., 2009, Dean et al., 2012) that allowed these features to be automatically selected by machines and by applying the technique of breaking down a complex problem into numerous simpler problems, learn a specific thing about the data from these simpler problems and add them up to understand the original problem. This technique of automatic feature selection and using deep layers (aka breaking into simpler problems) is called Deep Learning. Deep Learning uses multiple layers of neural nets that pass the learning from one layer to another. There is one input layer, multiple (deep) hidden layers and one output layer. The mathematical foundation of neural nets is based on Universal Approximation Theorem that states that a feed-forward neural network can approximate any continuous function (aka it can capture non-linearity in the data). For more detailed analysis of neural nets, refer to (Goodfellow et al., 2016; Hastie et al., 2009).

2.2 Time Series

The term "time series" is often used to describe a specific discrete realization (or observation) of a stochastic process. It is called a "series" because the observations are indexed sequentially by time (which is assumed to be discrete). Most of the foundation of statistics and machine learning models is based on the assumption that the observations are independent and identically distributed aka i.i.d (e.g., rolling of a fair dice, fair coin flip). The unique thing about time series is that these observations have an internal structure due to the sequential arrangement of these observations. For instance, this sequential arrangement leads to correlation between the observations, also known as "autocorrelation" ("auto" because it measures correlation between the same variable) which renders Ordinary Least Squares (OLS) useless. For more on theoretical foundations of time series theory refer to (Box et al., 2015; Cryer & Chan, 2008; Hamilton, 1994; Kirchgässner & Wolters, 2007)

One of the main purposes of time series is to make a prediction about the future using the past (aka using the observations of the random variable). In order to do so, the past has to be stable enough or in equilibrium. Another way to think about this: if we look at the chunk of the time series at two distinct time periods, it should give us similar information about the variable we are observing. The analogous term for the same in time series is stationary. Because time series is observing time evolution of a single variable, the value of this variable might increase/decrease or become volatile etc. So stationarity can be defined with respect to the mean, variance and covariance of the variable as defined below:

1. **Mean Stationary:** The expected value of the variable at any instant of realization is constant (finite value) and does not change with time.
2. **Variance Stationary:** The variance of the variable at any instant of realization is constant (finite value) and does not change with time.
3. **Covariance Stationary:** The covariance between the two realizations is independent of time.

In almost all of time series analysis, we check for mean and covariance stationarity. If only mean and covariance stationarity is present, then the time series is called "weak stationary". If all moments of the stochastic process are constant with time, then the time series is called "strong stationary". See Brockwell and Davis (2013), Hamilton (1994), and Kendall (1990) for deep dive with rigorous mathematical foundations on the concepts of stationarity. There are two main approaches to analyze the time series data: in time domain and in frequency domain. In time domain, time series can be broken down into three main components (a) trend, (b) seasonality and (c) randomness. Decomposition helps us to understand the structure of the time series. We can build deterministic models for the trend and seasonality part, use some smoothing for the residuals and combine (additive or multiplicative) all the three together to build a model for the time series.

Another classical method that aims to explain time series by using trend and seasonality is exponential smoothing. In this method, the forecast is produced using

Figure 2. Demonstration of stationarity in time series

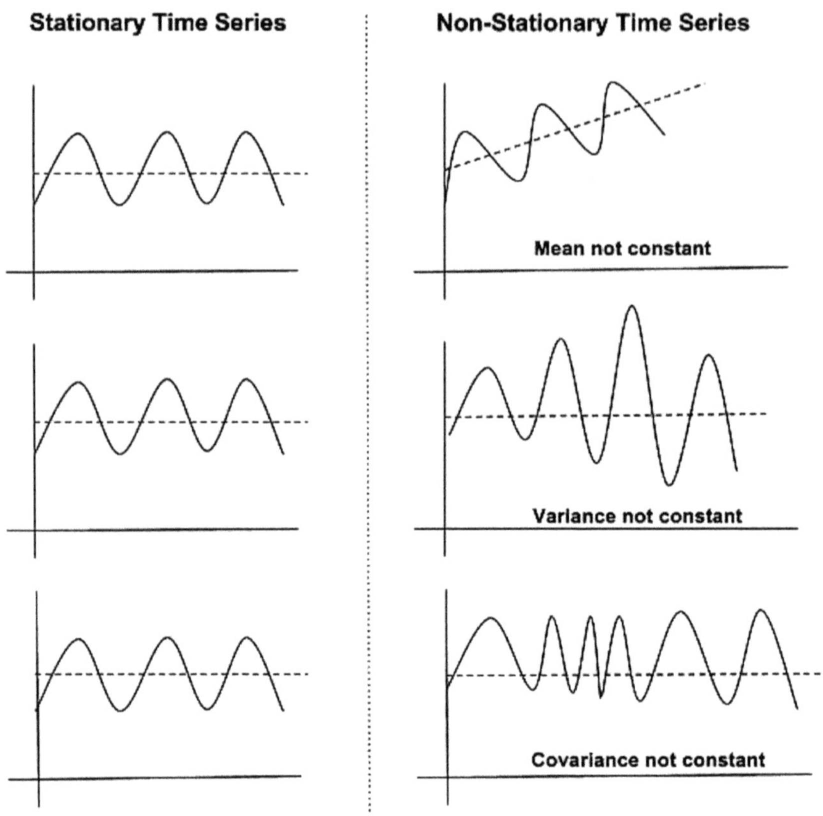

an exponentially weighted average of the past observations. If the time series data has significant dependence among each observations, exponential smoothing and decomposition may not work. In such situations, we make use of ARIMA (Auto Regressive Integrated Moving Average) models that aim to describe the time series by making use of autocorrelation and partial autocorrelation among the observations. One intuitive way to understand ARIMA model is to think of it as an equation that first makes time series stationary by differencing (I), then captures the linear trend and seasonality of the time series by linear combination of lagged observations (AR) and lagged errors (MA). If we want to incorporate exogenous variables to explain the time series, then additive nature of ARIMA models comes handy and we can simply add the covariates to ARIMA equation. ARIMA with covariates is called ARIMAX. If we have strong beliefs on the structure of time series components, we can also implement Bayesian Structural Time Series (BSTS) model. BSTS usually works when we have very little past data or when we want to control the structure of the individual components of the time series. ARIMA is restrictive in that sense. In BSTS, we can specify prior beliefs and can quantify the model's uncertainty (Scott, 2017).

3. INTEGRATING ARTIFICIAL INTELLIGENCE INTO BUSINESS INTELLIGENCE

Before we explore how to integrate AI into BI, it is essential to understand the baseline architecture of AI and BI. Figure 3 shows the detailed block architecture of modern day big data Business Intelligence systems that is capable of handling both real time streaming data and batch data. As mentioned earlier, the main objective of a BI system is to process all the incoming raw data into distilled consumable output. A BI system consists of the following components:

- Data sources and ETL pipelines,
- Data warehouse, marts, and
- Data reporting layer

Figure 3. Block diagram of a BI system that supports both streaming and batch data

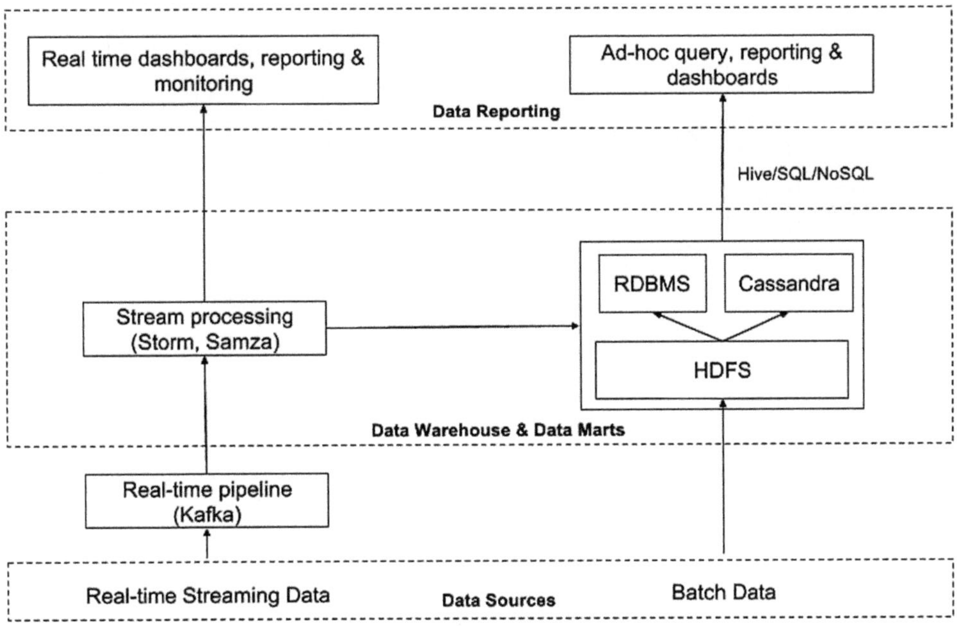

Figure 4 shows typical AI architecture. Usually, it involves two steps: (a) Model Learning, and (b) using trained model for prediction on new data. Model learning involves reading historical data either from HDFS (via Hive or similar language) or a relational database like Vertica via SQL, followed by data pre-processing (e.g., formatting, sampling, scaling the data) and doing feature engineering on processed data. Feature engineering is essential to the success of the algorithm (Domingos, 2012) and often involves generating large number of features that are iteratively selected during model learning. The next step after feature engineering is the model learning itself. Once the model errors have reached below the acceptable threshold, training is stopped and a trained model is produced. This trained model can be used in two ways: (a) in offline mode to deliver business insights and key learnings from the data; and (b) used in production (or in real time on new data) to make a prediction.

There are two ways AI can be integrated into a of BI system:

1. As an embedded unit, or
2. As stand-alone system

Figure 4. Block diagram of a AI system that is used to deliver business insights and used to make prediction in real time

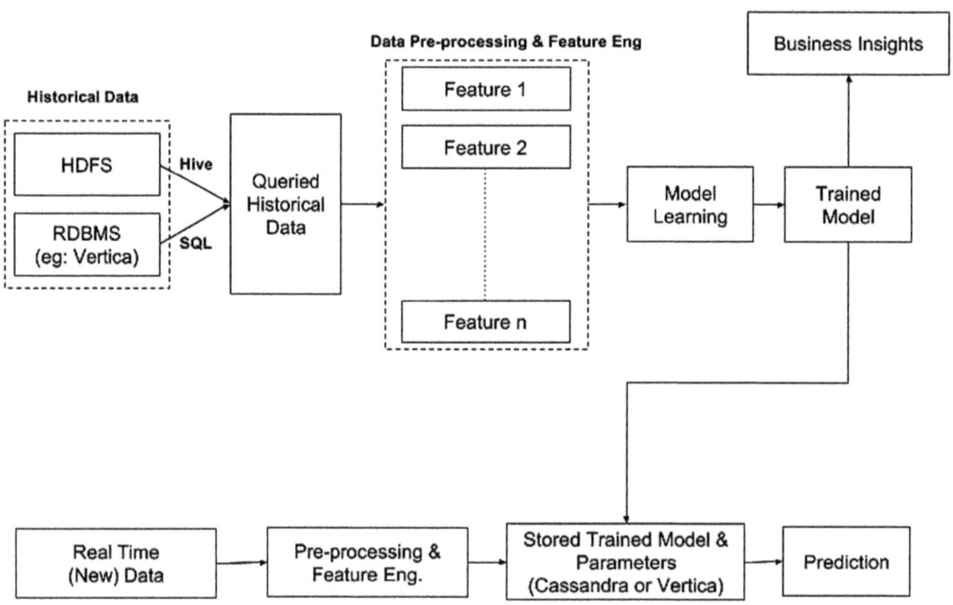

Embedding AI directly requires augmenting the existing BI system by implementing Apache Spark platform on top of HDFS and streaming data. Figure 5 shows one such implementation. Apache Spark is an open source distributed computing platform that can run on top of Hadoop as well as on streaming data and offers extensive machine learning library (MLlib or ML) for faster computation (Armbrust et al., 2015; Meng et al., 2016; Shanahan & Dai, 2015). The capability of MLlib to run on top of Hadoop makes Spark BI friendly and allows for easier integration. MLlib consists of numerous supervised and unsupervised learning algorithms, and utilities for data pre-processing and feature engineering. It can support online continuous learning by way of using streaming supervised (e.g: streaming linear regression) and unsupervised algorithms (e.g: streaming Kmeans). In batch mode, the historical data stored in HDFS can be queried as a dataframe either via classical MapReduce jobs or directly using Spark APIs. In streaming mode, Spark SQL is used to process the streaming data into desired dataframes to be used by MLlib. The BI system can still power real time dashboards/reporting and support for ad-hoc query and reporting as shown in Figure 5.

The key advantage of embedding Spark directly is access to faster, scalable and a unified platform for data management and machine learning. It also offers opportunity

Figure 5. Embedded AI architecture that uses Spark to stream and train the model

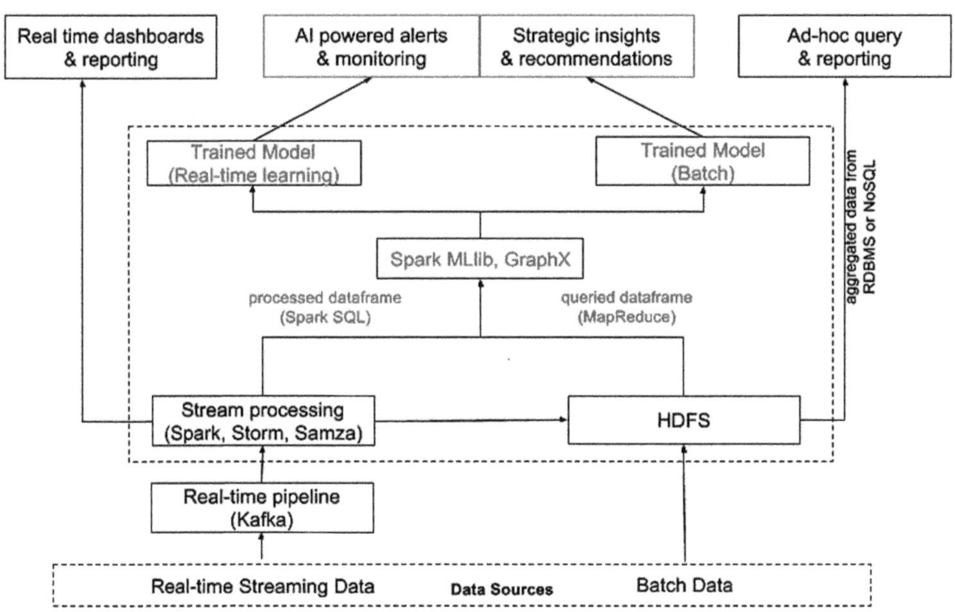

for online machine learning on streaming data. This approach also offers broader team alignment in terms of team structure and design. The data engineers can focus on systems engineering using Spark APIs, while data scientists can leverage speed and scale of Spark for faster learning. The main challenge for this to work is that organizations should have a large amount of historical data and have implementation of HDFS to store it. Although Spark can run on any other databases like Cassandra or Amazon S3, algorithm training requires a large amount of historical data.

AI could also be treated as a stand-alone system. It does so by making use of the functionality of data warehouse and data marts in the BI system as a way to access data required for training the model. Figure 6 shows the architecture for the same. The advantage of such a system is that it is relatively easy to set-up and operate. It is also good for ad-hoc scientific analysis aimed towards providing data driven insights. This also works relatively well when organizations do not have large amounts of historical data. The data scientist/analyst does not have to be coupled with the data engineer and could be self-serving. The disadvantage of this arrangement is that it becomes slow when the data becomes big as it is not leveraging in-memory computations that Spark etc. have to offer.

Figure 6. AI as stand-alone system

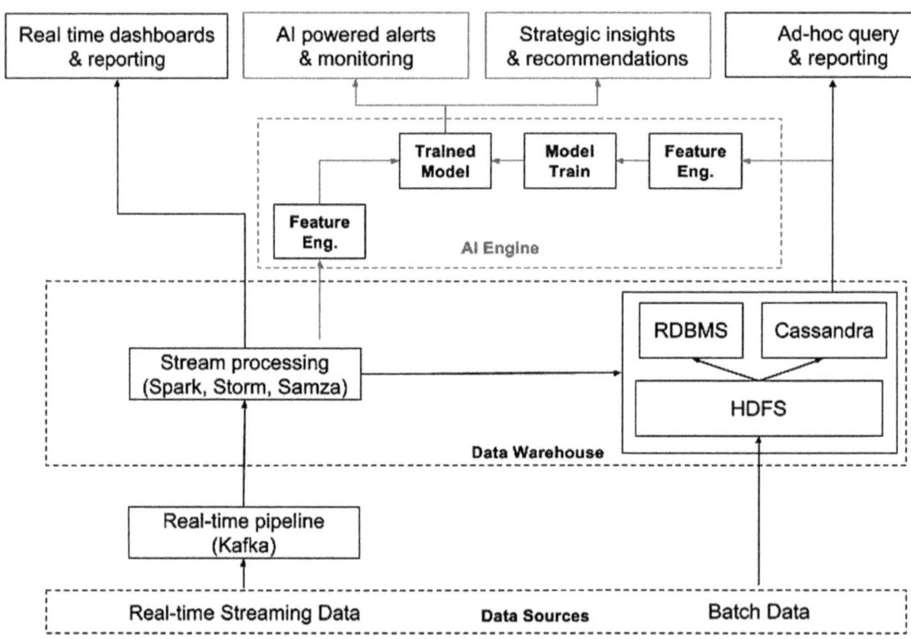

4. OPEN ISSUES AND CHALLENGES RELATED TO BIG DATA

The rationale for investments in big data is that it empowers an organization by providing deep insights, improving processes and providing competitive edge. To enable this, organizations need to:

1. Efficiently store the enormous amounts of heterogeneous data,
2. Provide a scalable way to access the data,
3. Invest in machine learning (e.g., self-serve machine learning platform) so as to derive insights from the data,
4. Build intuitive dashboards for business users to access the data, insights and predictions, and
5. Ensure that the security and privacy issues are taken into consideration.

In order to do the above effectively, it is imperative to understand the technical challenges and open issues related to the above tasks. We can put these challenges into the following categories of issues related to:

1. Learning from big data,
2. Philosophy and organizational structure for big data, and
3. Storage and processing issues for big data

4.1 Issues Related to Learning From Big Data

While there have been numerous successes of applying machine learning to wide array of problems, there are several challenges and open issues that need further consideration. For example,

1. Learning assumes that distribution of training data is same as the distribution of the future outcome. However, the future distribution can change either gradually or suddenly due to numerous reasons like non-stationarity, changing dynamics (e.g., demand shifting from retail shopping to e-commerce, increasing competition, etc.), and global events that may implicitly impact the features but are not part of the data itself (e.g., macro-economic changes, weather related events like cyclone, etc.). The main challenge is to identify *a priori* if the training data has the same distribution as the desired output. Bayesian techniques (Ghahramani, 2015) are useful in such scenarios as it relies on using a prior that can be iteratively updated with most recent data.

2. Interpretability of artificial intelligence techniques like machine learning is a major research area. At its core, a machine learning algorithm is trying to approximate a highly non-linear complex function that generalizes the training data well. Although results of this learning might produce accurate predictions for the future, it is very hard for the end user (or even data scientist) to decipher or interpret why the algorithm made the prediction it did, and what features were important in the data. Moreover, one can argue that most of machine learning success today is based on algorithms ability to capture correlations between features, as opposed to solid theoretical foundations (Pearl, 2018). A lack of rigorous theory may contribute towards lack of interpretability. At policy level, the so called "black box" modeling approach doesn't work because policymakers are interested more in understanding how the prediction was made in addition highly accurate predictions. For example, for autonomous driving there might be a legal requirement to explain and justify the autonomous decisions taken by the vehicle. Unless this issue is solved, it is hard for autonomous vehicles to gain adoption. Hence, to instill confidence not only in policymakers, but also in business stakeholders, there needs to for new class of algorithms that aim towards finding an optimal balance between accuracy and explainability.
3. The scale of big data adversely affects the performance of machine learning algorithms. The more the data volume and features, the larger is the training time. Almost all learning algorithms in use today are highly iterative that involve updating the model parameters in each iteration through use of gradient descent. Usually, the parameters in the model scale with the number of features. Models also require hyperparameter tuning. Both of these operations might require I/O operations to/from the memory that contribute to time complexity. For example, classical machine learning techniques like Random forest (Louppe, 2014) and Support Vector Machines (Bordes et al., 2005) have an average time complexity of $O(M*K*N*Log^2N)$ and $O(N^2)$, respectively (N = training size, M is number of trees, K is the number of features randomly drawn). A fully connected Neural Network will have computational complexity of $O(N*E*P)$ (N = training size, P = number of parameters (~ number of features), E = epochs). Learning by representations (e.g., deep learning, see section 2 for an overview) like CNNs and LSTMs also are computationally expensive with time complexity highly dependent on network architecture. For example, for a given architecture, LSTMs will have average time complexity of $O(T*N*E*P)$ where extra factor T is for number of periods in LSTM layer, while CNNs will have complexity of $O(X*N*E*P)$, with extra factor X representing the number of pixels. The recent advances in distributed training like Spark have

improved the training time by reducing I/O operations by having datasets cached in memory, and parallelizing matrix operations required during parameter update. However, it does not apply any model specific improvements to lower the time complexity. With increasing data volume, even storing data in cache will be challenging and hence there is a need for research into model specific improvements like training the model in parallel with aim of identifying weakly correlated features that could be learned in parallel.

4. Most of the deep learning methods like CNNs, LSTMs etc., require millions of labelled data for training. They also need big infrastructure of GPUs to save on training time, as described above. However, in case of paucity of labelled data, or when data sets are small, the deep learning techniques are not optimal choice. Smaller data sets are generally prone to overfitting (Forman & Cohen, 2004), and hence it is usually advised to either use Bayesian approach by defining a prior (Oniśko, 2001), or resort to high bias, low variance methods like linear regression. Learning from small data sets is an active topic of research and several approaches novel approaches like pre-training the using unsupervised learning (Wagner et al., 2013) have shown to improve the performance.
5. Next, there is an open issue of verification for intelligent algorithms. As described in section 2, a machine learning algorithm involves randomly splitting the available data set into training and test set (70/30 or 80/20), learning the model parameters using the training data, and then testing the learned parameters on the test data set. However, this very approach of testing the model on the available data set does not guarantee that model will perform well in all unforeseen circumstances or will be resistant to outliers in the future data upon which model will be used. Generative Adversarial Networks (Goodfellow et al., 2014; Radford et al., 2015) are an attempt towards verifying the machine learning algorithms by generating adverse data by arbitrary changing the input data so that it is representative of unknown future perturbations. Other approach to generate adversarial data is to use a transformation function to change the input data and placing a constrain (Pei et al., 2017). Another reason why we need verification for learning algorithms is the fact that, generally, machine learning algorithms are a part of a broader software system. While software quality testing ensures robustness of engineered software, it is due to the lack of verification of machine learning algorithms that the overall system cannot be guaranteed for satisfactory performance.
6. Most machine learning techniques learn as long as they have enough representation of learning instances in the training data. For a model to predict accurately, the scale of big data suggests that each class has enough

representation in the training data so as to generalize well. This assumption does not hold when predicting the so called "black swan" or long tail events. This issue is called as class imbalance and is an active topic of research. For example, class imbalance is especially a challenge in using machine learning to identify rare fraudulent transactions (Akbani et al., 2004), rare genetic disorders (Smedley et al., 2016) or cancer (Forbes et al., 2014) where the data used to train has number of negatives classes that are order of magnitude more than positive classes ($10^6 >> 10^3$). Various approaches to deal with this have been suggested in the research (Guo et al., 2008; Japkowicz, 2000; Nanni et al., 2015). With ever increasing adoption of machine learning algorithm, it is imperative to ensure that these systems perform well on long tail events.

7. Lastly, there is an open issue of whether machine learning can be used for causal inference. Causality is defined as a "cause & effect" relationship between two events (e.g., X causes Y). Most of the decisions in industry involve understanding the causality. For example: "what if we lowered the price?", or "what if we were to offer a product X instead of Y?" and so on. The classical method to attribute causality is to create counterfactuals via controlled randomized experimentation like A/B testing. However, there are practical challenges to implement these experiments (e.g., no price discrimination allowed for two sets of people due to regulations). State-space time series models (Brodersen et al., 2015) can be used to construct counterfactuals involving non-stationary data. Since almost all of learning algorithms foundations are based on finding correlations between the features, and hence it is very unlikely that machine learning can be used to attribute the cause-effect relationship with certainty (Pearl, 2003; Pearl, 2018; Spirtes, 2010), but it still remains a challenge whether modification of any of these techniques could be used to tease out causality.

4.2 Issues Related to Philosophy and Organizational Structure for Big Data

1. Before embarking on the big data mission, organizations need to ask the fundamental question of why they need big data? Alternatively, one can ask what can AI contribute to the bottom line of the company? Is AI and big data a means to automate the decision making of the tasks that are complex for human brain? In other words, is the objective to corroborate the *known knowns* (e.g., classification, regression), or to invest in finding the *known unknowns* (e.g., causal inference), or *unknown unknowns* (e.g., outlier detection, unsupervised learning). Aligning the objective is important because the choice(s) dictates what data to collect, storing solutions, and type of investments in algorithms

that need to be made. Philosophical alignment is important as it not only helps to create a data driven culture in the company, but also helps in deciding the organizational structure for the big data. Although a non-scientific issue, a sub-optimal organizational structure can contribute towards lower ROI on big data. For instance, should all the phases involved in big data (i.e., from data collection to prediction) be managed by the Chief Technology Officer (CTO)? Alternatively, should data infrastructure (i.e. data collection, storage and pre-processing) be managed by the office of CTO, while the other aspects such as deciding what data needs to be collected or what analysis needs to be done are managed by the Chief Data Officer (CDO)? In another plausible scenario, should all scientists working on AI be centralized i.e. reporting into a Chief Scientist, or maybe de-centralized i.e. reporting into business units? Should infrastructure required for big data be separated from data collection and processing? Is it even wise to separate out engineering tasks from scientific tasks? Will this create bottlenecks? There is no agreed upon organization structure for big data as it is still in its infancy. Industry is still learning by experimenting with various structures that help deliver most value.

2. Another philosophical debate is that of interaction of humans with machine. At organizational level, are we aiming for an AI solution that replaces humans (i.e.100% machine) or something that augments human decision making ability (man + machine). At implementation level, do these machine learning systems interact with humans in a different way? For example, do they provide recommendations or take actions that surprise humans as in the case of AlphaGo (Silver & Hassabis, 2016)? Is the organization prepared in case of any unintended consequence due to actions taken by these systems? For example, negative viral publicity due to chatbot learning racial words (Beres, 2016) or autonomous vehicle getting into accident due to unintended action by its algorithm, and so on. Do these unintended actions have long term effects on the image of the company? There is a need for guidelines and maybe a regulatory framework for using AI in our daily life.
3. Lastly, there is issue of ownership of the data. Do organizations own the data, or it is own by the humans whose actions result in generation of the data? Does using data to make personalized recommendation a violation of privacy? How can organizations ensure the general public that their data is stored securely and will not be shared? Most machine learning algorithms today require large amounts of data to learn from. Restricting access to data can negatively impact the performance of the algorithms. While some data like personalized medical records is and should be highly confidential, there is need to strike a balance between access to data and privacy.

4.2 Issues Related to Storage and Processing of Big Data

Recent advances in storage & data processing technology like Hadoop, MapReduce, Cloud Computing, NoSQL, Cassandra etc., have contributed towards addressing some of the challenges associated with big data. However, the ever increasing and insatiable demand for deeper insights has paved way for some key challenges. Below are some of the challenges associated with data storage, classified based on four Vs of big data:

Volume

1. Most of the data acquisition operations today will involve reducing the enormous volume of data so as to optimize for available network bandwidth, and for use by machine learning algorithms by way of removing duplicates, unreliable features etc. There are two ways to reduce/compress the data: (a) algorithmically, (b) using rule based filters. While the algorithmic data reduction techniques like network theory (Tsai et al., 2015), spatiotemporal (Yang et al., 2014), reference-based compression (Fritz et al., 2011) etc. are aimed towards preserving the main characteristics of data and lossless compression, they do add extra computational complexity. The rule based filters suffer from human judgement bias, and have higher probability to discard useful information (Jagadish et al., 2014). Research is needed to come up with reduction techniques that can work on the missing data (e.g., sensor failure), enable faster decompression, and do reduction/filtering at the time of acquisition itself. Machine learning techniques like unsupervised learning, anomaly detection could be helpful here.
2. A large volume of data also increases the probability of duplicates and correlated features. Not removing correlated features increases both space and time complexity of data storage algorithms, and may also increase model training time and reduce model interpretability. There is need for research to find the optimal data pipeline stage to check for duplicates and correlated features.
3. A large volume of data also has an impact on the querying time and hence the choice of database becomes important along with choice of efficient indexing techniques. Global query optimization is an active research area that aims to eliminate redundancies and do parallelization when simultaneous queries are to be executed by several users.

Variety

1. Heterogeneity of big data renders data integration task challenging and very expensive (Jagadish et al., 2014). Data integration is a process that enables integration of different types of data (e.g., structured, unstructured, different formats etc.) from different sources in order to provide a holistic view of the data. Data integration involves identifying common identifiers/labels in the data sets and merging them. If the common labels are not available, which is often the case, or if there are missing values or mislabeled labels, then integration requires data cleaning and entity extraction before merging the data sets. Generally, an entity extraction algorithms use hidden markov models to learn sequential data from unstructured data (Durbin et al., 1998). Existing state-of-art methods include learning sequence based on conditional probabilities (McCallum & Jensen, 2003) or using semi-Markov process (Cohen & Sarawagi, 2004). Improvement of entity extraction techniques with low latency from unstructured data is a key research area.
2. Deduplication is a challenging issue when heterogeneous data needs to be integrated (Halevy et al., 2006). The problem becomes even more challenging due to thousands of features that each data source might have. Most of deduplication techniques are rule based, though there has been some research using active learning (Sarawagi & Bhamidipaty, 2002). The advances in machine learning, especially unsupervised learning like clustering, Bayesian machine learning, and graph based probabilistic models can be used upstream to automate deduplication tasks for heterogeneous data. This is an active area of research (Chu et al., 2016, Stonebraker et al., 2013). The main challenge here is that machine learning needs to be applied upstream in data pipeline and hence time complexity dictates the algorithm choice.

Veracity

1. Since veracity refers to reliability in the data, it is imperative to figure out the inherent uncertainties in the big data we are collecting. Uncertainties can arise due to subjectivity of human judgement, or due to a faulty sensor, macro-events like weather, economic conditions etc. Currently, the algorithms that correct data from its uncertainty are infancy. If the uncertainty in the data is not acknowledged early on in the data pipeline, the machine learning algorithms learning from the data will yield imprecise results.

2. Moving large amounts of data (e.g., from logs to a structured database for analysis) requires a need for data provenance (Buneman et al., 2000) so as to ensure its reliability. Provenance is defined as storing all the information about any data movement and transformation during its journey through the pipeline. In case of big data, provenance can itself leads to storage issues (Wang et al., 2015). Hence there is need for technological solution for efficiently storing the data for the data provenance.
3. Lastly, there is issue of bias in the data. This is prevalent in data gathered from social media as humans share this data with their network thereby exaggerating the presence of bias in the collected data. Algorithms learning from this data will provide bias results thereby creating a negative feedback loop. There is need for research to develop protocols in identifying bias in the data and ensuring it does not reach the learning stage in the big data pipeline.

Velocity

1. Real-time access to data provides opportunity for incremental learning, thereby leading to real-time decision making. However, one of the main challenges related to velocity of the data is the lag between data generation, data pre-processing, and learning. Consider a scenario where one of the metrics used to make real-time decision is an outlier or missing. Does this imply real-time decision making to be halted? Thus, velocity of data warrants need for real-time monitoring/alerting systems that identify the reason for metric to be an outlier or impute missing values so as to have uninterrupted decision making.
2. Another challenge is that lag between velocity of heterogeneous data sources. The presence of this lag demands learning of correlation between various data sources so as to have as near quick decision making as possible. Learning this correlation itself on variety of data sources with low latency algorithms is an open research topic.

5. APPLICATIONS OF ARTIFICIAL INTELLIGENCE IN BUSINESS

Organizations are increasingly embracing the technological advancements and research in the field of Artificial Intelligence. We first discuss in detail the major application areas of AI that can have an immediate impact on business intelligence. Next we discuss some use currently being researched and potential applications of AI in the field of sharing economy, cyber security and finance.

5.1 Outlier Detection

A value (or an event) is considered an outlier if (a) it is far away from most of the other values observed in the past, or (b) if it is at a significant deviation from the expectation of the value. Some applications of outlier detection in industry are fraud detection, monitoring sensors' data, tracking flight path of aircraft, preventive maintenance, supply chain management and Internet of Things (IoT) data. Most of the data collected in these use cases is temporal in nature and is usually correlated with another event/value (Szmit & Szmit, 2012). Outlier detection can serve as revenue opportunity, quick connection with customers, and provide the ability to swiftly react to unseen events.

For batch data, most business intelligence tools use a rule of thumbs (e.g., 95th percentile or 2 standard deviations away) as a means to identify outliers. A more scientific approach to this will be to use time series techniques described in section 2.2 to identify outliers. Time series models like ARIMA will correctly account the internal structure (trend, seasonality, autocorrelation) in the data (Hyndman et al., 2015). The other approach to solve the outlier detection in time series data is using Neural Networks (Long Short Term Memory or LSTM) which also captures any non-linearity in time series (Hochreiter & Schmidhuber, 1997). For non-temporal data, one can use techniques like Principal Component Analysis to identify outliers. Unsupervised learning (e.g., clustering) can also be used to identify the same. For a deep dive into anomaly detection techniques using batch data, work by Chandola et al. (2009), and Hodge and Austin (2004) provides a comprehensive review.

Identifying outliers in streaming data is challenging (Gaber et al., 2005; Khalilian & Mustapha, 2010; Namiot, 2015) for few reasons: (a) dynamic nature of distribution of underlying data, (b) limited model performance measures (e.g., cross validation is not possible) and parameter tuning, and (c) challenges in handling missing values vs tagging them as outlier. Figure 7 represents example of streaming time series that demonstrates the same. For such cases, embedded architecture of using Spark streaming and MLlib in BI tool is optimal. As mentioned before, MLlib has support for continuous learning (e.g., streaming Kmeans, streaming regression). If one wants to develop proprietary packages, then Bayesian models (Adams & McKay, 2007), multivariate ARIMA (Tsay et al., 2000) or Hierarchical Temporal Models (Ahmad & Purdy, 2016; Li et al., 2015) are some good options.

5.2 Forecasting

Forecasting is a branch of statistics that deals with building classical and machine learning models to capture the structure of time series, and use the same to make

Figure 7. Outlier detection on non-stationary time series

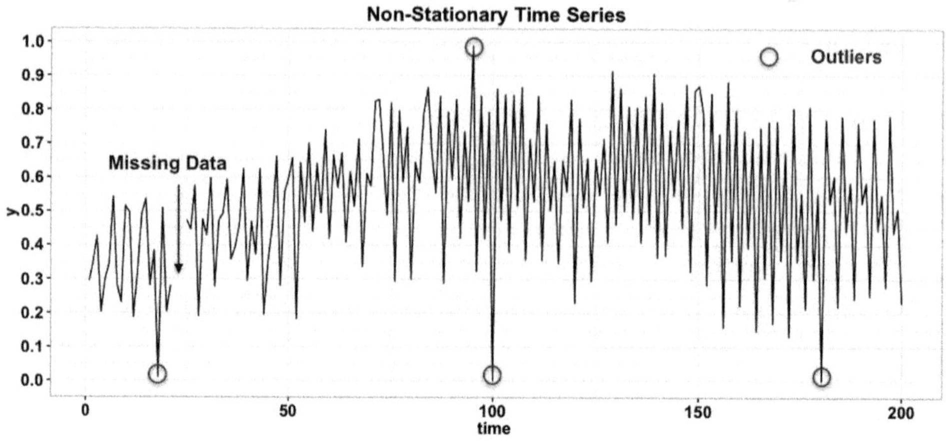

a prediction about the future. Forecasting is the logical next step once we have access to data. It is what helps bridge the gap between having data and making data driven decisions. However, forecasting has almost always been operated outside the traditional BI tools (Michalewicz et al., 2006) as BI tools have been focused on data collection, pre-processing, aggregation and reporting. One reason why forecasting may have been operated outside the business intelligence tools could be the performance of predictions itself. Even for univariate time series, multi-step forecasting is challenging because of errors accumulation and increased variance (Bhansali, 2002; Engle & Yo, 1987). This leads to increased error between the outcome from the models and the acceptable value from the business (or the actuals), thereby having business users rely more on gut feeling and intuition rather than investing in scientific forecasting. However, lack of a forecasting platform implies most business users will have to resort to simple rule-based forecasting or use tools provided in software like Microsoft Excel to build a model, and the cycle continues.

Forecasting has been an extensively studied problem in literature (Harvey, 1990, Hamilton, 1994; Box et al., 2015), however most of the academic and industry research has focused on linear time series models. Linearity assumption means that the stochastic process that governs the observed time series sequence has linearly interacting trend, seasonality and randomness components. However, time series observed in business settings demonstrate structural changes and thus are nonlinear. For a detailed review on nonlinear time series and forecasting, refer to work done by (De Gooijer & Hyndman, 2006; Judd & Mees, 1995; Kantz & Schreiber, 2004; Tong, 2011).

From the perspective of BI tools, an easy win would be to integrate a forecasting platform in it. In fact, it can be considered as an extension to Outlier Detection problem as both involve building time series models. As explained earlier, one can use either an embedded approach or stand-alone architecture for the same. Readily available packages in languages R, Python and Spark (Hyndman & Khandakar, 2007, Hyndman et al., 2015; McKinney et. Al., 2011) have democratized the access to forecasting techniques and made the underlying math a black box for business users. Recent advances in variance reduction techniques like ensemble averaging (Zhou, 2012) have shown to improve multistep model performance when compared to existing methods. Forecasting not only aids in daily decision making, but can help an organization in the following areas:

1. Using a more scientific approach to longer term financial planning,
2. Building counterfactuals to quantify the causality of market intervention (e.g., new product launch)
3. Forecast imbalance between supply and demand,
4. Sales and market share forecasts,
5. Forecasting server loads and engineering resource allocation

5.3 Natural Language Processing and Intelligent Search

Recent advancements in deep learning, specifically in the areas of Convolution Neural Networks (CNNs) and Recurrent Neural Networks (Bengio et al., 2003; Colbert et al., 2011), have unlocked an entire new application area of search-based analytics by applying Natural Language Processing (NLP) techniques (Lopez & Kalita, 2017). Today, business intelligence asks either need to be pre-defined or are bottlenecked by availability of analysts who have to write SQL like queries to pull data to answer the question. NLP has the potential to democratize Business Intelligence by allowing business users to have a search-like experience. For e.g., one can ask the following questions:

- What were the revenue numbers for the last holiday season?
- Which set of users or customer segments engaged with us on social media?
- What was the general market sentiment to recent product launch?
- Get me the demographics of our customer base in LATAM?
- Total T&E spend in last month?
- Shipments currently delayed by region?
- Give me a table of companies merged by industry type last year? so on...

NLP is a field in AI that deals with understanding the human language either through voice or through text. Human language is a complex mechanism which has a distinct quality of being compositional (Pagel, 2017) i.e. has infinite combinations to convey a message. We do so by creating sentences that have nouns, verbs to describe action, adjectives to describe quality and tense to convey time. NLP is an algorithmic attempt to understand this complex mechanism. Most NLP algorithms use a combination of semantics, rule based and deep learning techniques to extract context, sentiment, topic and theme discovery, and the ability to parse large amounts of structured and unstructured data in order to answer a given question. It does so by pre-processing the text (e.g., removal of punctuations, words normalization, spelling correction), identifying contextual features from the processed text, figuring out nouns (e.g., time, names, things) followed by classification of the text. An in depth review of how NLP works is beyond the scope of this chapter but there are many literatures on this subject (Bengio, Y. 2009; Bird et al., 2009; Collobert & Weston, 2008; Manning & Schütze, 1999). The optimal way to implement NLP-based search in BI would be using the embedded approach comprised of hybrid continuous learning and batch learning.

5.4 Unsupervised Learning

It is a widely accepted belief in Machine Learning and AI community that the future of AI hinges upon the success of Unsupervised Learning (LeCun et al., 2015, Radford et al., 2015). While supervised learning requires massive historical data sets with correct labels and involves human hand holding, unsupervised learning is at the opposite end of spectrum (i.e. no or less labeled data) and has shown promising results with less volume data (Fe-Fei, 2003, Yang et al., 2013). From the point of view of business intelligence applications, the most important application of unsupervised learning is clustering which can help identify patterns in the data without humans pre-defining the clusters. For example, the support industry (i.e., BPOs etc.) deals with vast amounts of data in the form of e-mails and app or web inputs. AI based clustering could provide insights on what type of tickets are raised by certain groups of customers or customers in certain regions, whether tickets get resolved faster under certain circumstances etc. Thus, the AI model determines the patterns hidden in the data as opposed to a human predefining labels i.e., hinting at possible patterns to the model.

5.5 Some Examples From Industry

Table 2 shows some examples of how various industries can use AI. In this section, we will discuss in detail few of them.

Table 2. Comparison of AI techniques for various data type/size and industry

Data Volume	Data Type	AI Task	AI Type	Industry
Big	Non-temporal, labelled	Classification, Regression	Supervised learning	social media, cyber security, default prediction, lifetime value
Big	Non-temporal, unlabeled	Clustering, Pattern recognition	Unsupervised learning	marketing analytics, political campaigns
Big	Temporal	Outlier detection, Forecasting	Unsupervised learning	fraud detection, cyber security, big financial institutions, ridesharing
Small	Non-temporal, labelled	OLS, Logistic Regression	Classical statistics	healthcare (clinical studies)
Small	Non-temporal, unlabeled	Clustering	Unsupervised learning	SMB
Small	Temporal	Outlier detection, Forecasting	Time Series, Regression	SMB

5.5.1 Cyber Security

Cyber security is a $200 billion industry that deals with building technologies that protect information stored on our personal computers, servers and in cloud. This means that every organization needs to have a dedicated business intelligence tool to continuously monitor, identify and alert data breaches, hacks and phishing attempts. The core problems in cyber security are anomaly detection on streaming data and identification of cyber-attack. Classical time series techniques like ARIMA can be used to identify anomalies on spikes in login attempts, Distributed Denial of Service (DDOS) attacks etc. by modeling seasonality, trend and randomness in historical data (Werner et al., 2017).

The key challenge in cyber security is that each attack has a slightly different profile from historical ones. This requires analyzing data from multiple sources to able to correctly and quickly classify the attack as malicious. This is where Apache Spark environment is very beneficial and an embedded AI architecture is suitable. Spark Streaming can help processes streaming data, GraphX can be used to build dynamic graphs from a variety of sources, and MLlib can be used to train model on historical data and use it in real time to make prediction.

5.5.2 Sharing Economy

Sharing economy offers a perfect example of how historical reporting, machine learning insights and human intuition work together to reach strategic decision.

This is because sharing economy is new (i.e. has relatively less data volume when compared to social media), and is growing rapidly. Rapid growth implies highly dynamic and non-stationary data that makes learning challenging. This implies man + machine model is optimal choice to make strategic decisions. A typical BI tool in sharing economy can report on pre-defined metrics like number of bookings, unique users, occupancy rates etc. Clustering methods could be used to cluster users together to offer personalized recommendations. Continuously evolving user behavior implies business user needs to look at historical data as well as real time data to decide on the next action.

For young and hyper growth industries like sharing economy, stand-alone model of integrating AI with BI is better as it offers engineers to first build a reliable reporting tool that can cater to ever increasing volume and variety of data. Data scientists can quickly deliver on ad-hoc requests by quickly doing analysis in R or Python using available data. As the company matures, it can invest in building dedicated AI platforms and can transition to embedded AI architecture.

5.5.3 Finance

Finance industry offers a unique challenge i.e. all 4 V's are present in the same data. The data is streaming (e.g., ticker data), is from various sources (structured and unstructured), needs authenticity (e.g., fake news, reliability of social media tweet, etc.) and is in massive quantities. The business model of financial institutions is based on deriving value from large volumes of unstructured data by distilling information from large volumes of historical documents, real time tweets, news sentiments etc. As such, Natural Language Processing can play a key role in the same. Proprietary nature of finance implies a steep learning curve for analysts to learn company specific language and build a logic to pull the data. Implementing NLP as a means to return results will enhance employee productivity and efficiency. Sentiment and contextual analysis on tweets, news and blogs can help identify the potential impact on financial markets. NLP can also help tag the news with relevant stock ticker and help rank the important news for the users. Bloomberg Terminal is currently using some NLP in its core product offering.

6. CONCLUSION

Integrating AI in BI along with automation is the future of BI tools. A futuristic platform for BI will harness the combined power of supervised/unsupervised learning, time series and natural language processing. This means a future where business users ask questions in language of choice and get detailed response that has reports along with strategic insights and recommendation at lightning speeds. This will not only lead to employee productivity but also increase in revenues with direct impact on bottom line.

ACKNOWLEDGMENT

The author is thankful to Divya Pari, Dr. Fan Yang, Ankit Gupta, Frank Xia, and Radhika Anand for scientific discussion on relevant topics related to artificial intelligence, machine learning and big data.

REFERENCES

Abu-Mustafa, Y., Magdon-Ismail, M., & Lin, H. T. (2012). *Learning from data: a short course.* AMLbooks.

Adams, R. P., & MacKay, D. J. (2007). *Bayesian online changepoint detection.* arXiv preprint arXiv:0710.3742

Ahmad, S., & Purdy, S. (2016). *Real-Time Anomaly Detection for Streaming Analytics.* arXiv preprint arXiv:1607.02480

Akbani, R., Kwek, S., & Japkowicz, N. (2004, September). Applying support vector machines to imbalanced datasets. In *European conference on machine learning* (pp. 39-50). Springer. 10.1007/978-3-540-30115-8_7

Armbrust, M., Xin, R. S., Lian, C., Huai, Y., Liu, D., Bradley, J. K., ... Zaharia, M. (2015, May). Spark sql: Relational data processing in spark. In *Proceedings of the 2015 ACM SIGMOD International Conference on Management of Data* (pp. 1383-1394). ACM. 10.1145/2723372.2742797

Bengio, Y. (2009). Learning deep architectures for AI. *Foundations and trends® in Machine Learning, 2*(1), 1-127.

Bengio, Y., Ducharme, R., Vincent, P., & Jauvin, C. (2003). A neural probabilistic language model. *Journal of Machine Learning Research, 3*(Feb), 1137–1155.

Beres, D. (2016). *Microsoft Chat Bot Goes On Racist, Genocidal Twitter Rampage.* Retrieved from https://www.huffingtonpost.com/entry/microsoft-tay-racist-tweets_us_56f3e678e4b04c4c37615502

Bhansali, R. J. (2002). Multi-Step Forecasting. *A Companion to Economic Forecasting*, 206-221.

Bird, S., Klein, E., & Loper, E. (2009). *Natural language processing with Python: analyzing text with the natural language toolkit*. O'Reilly Media, Inc.

Bishop, C. (2007). Pattern Recognition and Machine Learning (2nd ed.). Springer.

Bordes, A., Ertekin, S., Weston, J., & Bottou, L. (2005). Fast kernel classifiers with online and active learning. *Journal of Machine Learning Research*, *6*(Sep), 1579–1619.

Box, G. E., Jenkins, G. M., Reinsel, G. C., & Ljung, G. M. (2015). *Time series analysis: forecasting and control*. John Wiley & Sons.

Brockwell, P. J., & Davis, R. A. (2013). *Time series: theory and methods*. Springer Science & Business Media.

Brodersen, K. H., Gallusser, F., Koehler, J., Remy, N., & Scott, S. L. (2015). Inferring causal impact using Bayesian structural time-series models. *The Annals of Applied Statistics*, *9*(1), 247–274. doi:10.1214/14-AOAS788

Buneman, P., Khanna, S., & Tan, W. C. (2000, December). Data provenance: Some basic issues. In *International Conference on Foundations of Software Technology and Theoretical Computer Science* (pp. 87-93). Springer.

Chaudhuri, S., Dayal, U., & Narasayya, V. (2011). An overview of business intelligence technology. *Communications of the ACM*, *54*(8), 88–98. doi:10.1145/1978542.1978562

Chen, H., Chiang, R. H., & Storey, V. C. (2012). Business intelligence and analytics: From big data to big impact. *Management Information Systems Quarterly*, *36*(4).

Chu, X., Ilyas, I. F., & Koutris, P. (2016). Distributed data deduplication. *Proceedings of the VLDB Endowment International Conference on Very Large Data Bases*, *9*(11), 864–875. doi:10.14778/2983200.2983203

Cios, K. J., Swiniarski, R. W., Pedrycz, W., & Kurgan, L. A. (2007). Unsupervised learning: clustering. In Data Mining (pp. 257-288). Springer US. doi:10.1007/978-0-387-36795-8_9

Coates, A., Baumstarck, P., Le, Q., & Ng, A. Y. (2009, October). Scalable learning for object detection with GPU hardware. In *Intelligent Robots and Systems, 2009. IROS 2009. IEEE/RSJ International Conference on* (pp. 4287-4293). IEEE. 10.1109/IROS.2009.5354084

Cohen, W. W., & Sarawagi, S. (2004, August). Exploiting dictionaries in named entity extraction: combining semi-markov extraction processes and data integration methods. In *Proceedings of the tenth ACM SIGKDD international conference on Knowledge discovery and data mining* (pp. 89-98). ACM. 10.1145/1014052.1014065

Collobert, R., & Weston, J. (2008, July). A unified architecture for natural language processing: Deep neural networks with multitask learning. In *Proceedings of the 25th international conference on Machine learning* (pp. 160-167). ACM. 10.1145/1390156.1390177

Collobert, R., Weston, J., Bottou, L., Karlen, M., Kavukcuoglu, K., & Kuksa, P. (2011). Natural language processing (almost) from scratch. *Journal of Machine Learning Research, 12*(Aug), 2493–2537.

Colom, R., Karama, S., Jung, R. E., & Haier, R. J. (2010). Human intelligence and brain networks. *Dialogues in Clinical Neuroscience, 12*(4), 489. PMID:21319494

Cryer, J. D., & Chan, K. S. (2008). *Time series analysis: with applications in R*. Springer Science & Business Media. doi:10.1007/978-0-387-75959-3

De Gooijer, J. G., & Hyndman, R. J. (2006). 25 years of time series forecasting. *International Journal of Forecasting, 22*(3), 443–473. doi:10.1016/j.ijforecast.2006.01.001

Dean, J., Corrado, G., Monga, R., Chen, K., Devin, M., Mao, M., . . . Ng, A. Y. (2012). Large scale distributed deep networks. In Advances in neural information processing systems (pp. 1223-1231). Academic Press.

Devens, R. (1865). Cyclopædia of Commercial and Business Anecdotes, Volume 1. D. Appleton

Domingos, P. (2012). A few useful things to know about machine learning. *Communications of the ACM, 55*(10), 78–87. doi:10.1145/2347736.2347755

Dorigo, M., & Gambardella, L. M. (2016, January). Ant-Q: A reinforcement learning approach to the traveling salesman problem. *Proceedings of ML-95, Twelfth Intern. Conf. on Machine Learning*, 252-260.

Durbin, R., Eddy, S. R., Krogh, A., & Mitchison, G. (1998). *Biological sequence analysis: probabilistic models of proteins and nucleic acids*. Cambridge University Press. doi:10.1017/CBO9780511790492

Engle, R. F., & Yoo, B. S. (1987). Forecasting and testing in co-integrated systems. *Journal of Econometrics, 35*(1), 143–159. doi:10.1016/0304-4076(87)90085-6

Evelson, B., & Norman, N. (2008). *Topic overview: Business intelligence*. Forrester Research.

Fe-Fei, L. (2003, October). A Bayesian approach to unsupervised one-shot learning of object categories. In *Computer Vision, 2003. Proceedings. Ninth IEEE International Conference on* (pp. 1134-1141). IEEE. 10.1109/ICCV.2003.1238476

Forbes, S. A., Beare, D., Gunasekaran, P., Leung, K., Bindal, N., Boutselakis, H., ... Kok, C. Y. (2014). COSMIC: Exploring the world's knowledge of somatic mutations in human cancer. *Nucleic Acids Research, 43*(D1), D805–D811. doi:10.1093/nar/gku1075 PMID:25355519

Forman, G., & Cohen, I. (2004, September). Learning from little: Comparison of classifiers given little training. In *European Conference on Principles of Data Mining and Knowledge Discovery* (pp. 161-172). Springer. 10.1007/978-3-540-30116-5_17

Friedman, J., Hastie, T., & Tibshirani, R. (2001). The elements of statistical learning (Vol. 1). New York: Springer.

Fritz, M. H. Y., Leinonen, R., Cochrane, G., & Birney, E. (2011). Efficient storage of high throughput DNA sequencing data using reference-based compression. *Genome Research, 21*(5), 734–740. doi:10.1101/gr.114819.110 PMID:21245279

Gaber, M. M., Zaslavsky, A., & Krishnaswamy, S. (2005). Mining data streams: A review. *SIGMOD Record, 34*(2), 18–26. doi:10.1145/1083784.1083789

Ghahramani, Z. (2015). Probabilistic machine learning and artificial intelligence. *Nature, 521*(7553), 452–459. doi:10.1038/nature14541 PMID:26017444

Goodfellow, I., Bengio, Y., & Courville, A. (2016). *Deep learning*. MIT Press.

Goodfellow, I., Pouget-Abadie, J., Mirza, M., Xu, B., Warde-Farley, D., Ozair, S., . . . Bengio, Y. (2014). Generative adversarial nets. In Advances in neural information processing systems (pp. 2672-2680). Academic Press.

Gottfredson, L. S. (2004). Intelligence: Is it the epidemiologists' elusive" fundamental cause" of social class inequalities in health? *Journal of Personality and Social Psychology, 86*(1), 174–199. doi:10.1037/0022-3514.86.1.174 PMID:14717635

Guo, X., Yin, Y., Dong, C., Yang, G., & Zhou, G. (2008, October). On the class imbalance problem. In *Natural Computation, 2008. ICNC'08. Fourth International Conference on* (Vol. 4, pp. 192-201). IEEE 10.1109/ICNC.2008.871

Halevy, A., Rajaraman, A., & Ordille, J. (2006, September). Data integration: the teenage years. In *Proceedings of the 32nd international conference on Very large data bases* (pp. 9-16). VLDB Endowment.

Hamilton, J. D. (1994). *Time series analysis* (Vol. 2). Princeton, NJ: Princeton University Press.

Harvey, A. C. (1990). *Forecasting, structural time series models and the Kalman filter*. Cambridge University Press. doi:10.1017/CBO9781107049994

Hastie, T., Tibshirani, R., & Friedman, J. (2009). Overview of supervised learning. In *The elements of statistical learning* (pp. 9–41). Springer New York. doi:10.1007/978-0-387-84858-7_2

Heyes, C. (2012). New thinking: The evolution of human cognition. *Philosophical Transactions of the Royal Society of London. Series B, Biological Sciences, 367*(1599), 2091–2096. doi:10.1098/rstb.2012.0111 PMID:22734052

Hinton, G. E., & Sejnowski, T. J. (Eds.). (1999). *Unsupervised learning: foundations of neural computation*. MIT Press.

Hochreiter, S., & Schmidhuber, J. (1997). Long short-term memory. *Neural Computation, 9*(8), 1735–1780. doi:10.1162/neco.1997.9.8.1735 PMID:9377276

Hyndman, R. J., Athanasopoulos, G., Razbash, S., Schmidt, D., Zhou, Z., Khan, Y., ... Wang, E. (2015). Forecast: Forecasting functions for time series and linear models. *R Package Version, 6*(6), 7.

Hyndman, R. J., & Khandakar, Y. (2007). *Automatic time series for forecasting: the forecast package for R (No. 6/07)*. Monash University, Department of Econometrics and Business Statistics.

Jackson, P. C. (1985). *Introduction to artificial intelligence*. Courier Corporation.

Jagadish, H. V., Gehrke, J., Labrinidis, A., Papakonstantinou, Y., Patel, J. M., Ramakrishnan, R., & Shahabi, C. (2014). Big data and its technical challenges. *Communications of the ACM, 57*(7), 86–94. doi:10.1145/2611567

Japkowicz, N. (2000, July). Learning from imbalanced data sets: a comparison of various strategies. In AAAI workshop on learning from imbalanced data sets (Vol. 68, pp. 10-15). AAAI.

Judd, K., & Mees, A. (1995). On selecting models for nonlinear time series. *Physica D. Nonlinear Phenomena, 82*(4), 426–444. doi:10.1016/0167-2789(95)00050-E

Kaelbling, L. P., Littman, M. L., & Moore, A. W. (1996). Reinforcement learning: A survey. *Journal of Artificial Intelligence Research, 4*, 237–285.

Kantz, H., & Schreiber, T. (2004). *Nonlinear time series analysis* (Vol. 7). Cambridge university press.

Kendall, M. G., & Ord, J. K. (1990). *Time-series* (Vol. 296). London: Edward Arnold.

Khalilian, M., & Mustapha, N. (2010). *Data stream clustering: Challenges and issues.* arXiv preprint arXiv:1006.5261

Kirchgässner, G., & Wolters, J. (2007). *Introduction to modern time series analysis.* Springer Science & Business Media. doi:10.1007/978-3-540-73291-4

LeCun, Y., & Bengio, Y. (1995). Convolutional networks for images, speech, and time series. The handbook of brain theory and neural networks, 3361(10), 1995

LeCun, Y., Bengio, Y., & Hinton, G. (2015). Deep learning. *Nature, 521*(7553), 436–444. doi:10.1038/nature14539 PMID:26017442

LeCun, Y., Bottou, L., Bengio, Y., & Haffner, P. (1998). Gradient-based learning applied to document recognition. *Proceedings of the IEEE, 86*(11), 2278–2324. doi:10.1109/5.726791

Li, W., Mahadevan, V., & Vasconcelos, N. (2014). Anomaly detection and localization in crowded scenes. *IEEE Transactions on Pattern Analysis and Machine Intelligence, 36*(1), 18–32. doi:10.1109/TPAMI.2013.111 PMID:24231863

Lopez, M. M., & Kalita, J. (2017). *Deep Learning applied to NLP.* arXiv preprint arXiv:1703.03091

Louppe, G. (2014). *Understanding random forests: From theory to practice.* arXiv preprint arXiv:1407.7502

Luhn, H. P. (1958). A business intelligence system. *IBM Journal of Research and Development, 2*(4), 314–319. doi:10.1147/rd.24.0314

Manning, C. D., & Schütze, H. (1999). *Foundations of statistical natural language processing.* MIT Press.

McCallum, A., & Jensen, D. (2003). A note on the unification of information extraction and data mining using conditional-probability, relational models. *Computer Science Department Faculty Publication Series*, 42.

McKinney, W., Perktold, J., & Seabold, S. (2011). Time series analysis in Python with statsmodels. *Jarrodmillman. Com*, 96-102.

Meng, X., Bradley, J., Yavuz, B., Sparks, E., Venkataraman, S., Liu, D., ... Xin, D. (2016). Mllib: Machine learning in apache spark. *Journal of Machine Learning Research, 17*(1), 1235–1241.

Michalewicz, Z., Schmidt, M., Michalewicz, M., & Chiriac, C. (2006). *Adaptive business intelligence*. Springer Science & Business Media.

Murphy, K. P. (2012). *Machine Learning: A Probabilistic Perspective*. Cambridge, MA: The MIT Press.

Namiot, D. (2015). On big data stream processing. *International Journal of Open Information Technologies, 3*(8), 48–51.

Nanni, L., Fantozzi, C., & Lazzarini, N. (2015). Coupling different methods for overcoming the class imbalance problem. *Neurocomputing, 158*, 48–61. doi:10.1016/j.neucom.2015.01.068

Oniśko, A., Druzdzel, M. J., & Wasyluk, H. (2001). Learning Bayesian network parameters from small data sets: Application of Noisy-OR gates. *International Journal of Approximate Reasoning, 27*(2), 165–182. doi:10.1016/S0888-613X(01)00039-1

Pagel, M. (2017). Q&A: What is human language, when did it evolve and why should we care? *BMC Biology, 15*(1), 64. doi:10.118612915-017-0405-3 PMID:28738867

Pearl, J. (2003). Causality: Models, reasoning, and inference. *Econometric Theory, 19*(675-685), 46

Pearl, J. (2018). *Theoretical Impediments to Machine Learning With Seven Sparks from the Causal Revolution*. arXiv preprint arXiv:1801.04016

Pei, K., Cao, Y., Yang, J., & Jana, S. (2017). *Towards Practical Verification of Machine Learning: The Case of Computer Vision Systems*. arXiv preprint arXiv:1712.01785

Radford, A., Metz, L., & Chintala, S. (2015). *Unsupervised representation learning with deep convolutional generative adversarial networks*. arXiv preprint arXiv:1511.06434

Raina, R., Madhavan, A., & Ng, A. Y. (2009, June). Large-scale deep unsupervised learning using graphics processors. In *Proceedings of the 26th annual international conference on machine learning* (pp. 873-880). ACM. 10.1145/1553374.1553486

Russell, S., & Norvig, P. (1995). *Artificial Intelligence: A modern approach*. Englewood Cliffs, NJ: Prentice-Hall.

Sabherwal, R. (2007). Succeeding with business intelligence: Some insights and recommendations. *Cutter Benchmark Review*, *7*(9), 5–15.

Sallam, R. L., Richardson, J., Hagerty, J., & Hostmann, B. (2011). *Magic quadrant for business intelligence platforms*. Stamford, CT: Gartner Group.

Sarawagi, S., & Bhamidipaty, A. (2002, July). Interactive deduplication using active learning. In *Proceedings of the eighth ACM SIGKDD international conference on Knowledge discovery and data mining* (pp. 269-278). ACM. 10.1145/775047.775087

Schölkopf, B., & Smola, A. J. (2002). *Learning with kernels: support vector machines, regularization, optimization, and beyond*. MIT Press.

Scott, S. L. (2017). bsts: Bayesian Structural Time Series. *R package version 0.6. 2*.

Sebastiani, F. (2002). Machine learning in automated text categorization. *ACM Computing Surveys*, *34*(1), 1–47. doi:10.1145/505282.505283

Shanahan, J. G., & Dai, L. (2015). Large scale distributed data science using apache spark. In *Proceedings of the 21th ACM SIGKDD International Conference on Knowledge Discovery and Data Mining* (pp. 2323-2324). ACM. 10.1145/2783258.2789993

Shindler, M., Wong, A., & Meyerson, A. W. (2011). Fast and accurate k-means for large datasets. In Advances in neural information processing systems (pp. 2375-2383). Academic Press.

Silver, D., & Hassabis, D. (2016). *AlphaGo: Mastering the ancient game of Go with Machine Learning*. Research Blog.

Smedley, D., Schubach, M., Jacobsen, J. O., Köhler, S., Zemojtel, T., Spielmann, M., ... Haendel, M. A. (2016). A whole-genome analysis framework for effective identification of pathogenic regulatory variants in Mendelian disease. *American Journal of Human Genetics*, *99*(3), 595–606. doi:10.1016/j.ajhg.2016.07.005 PMID:27569544

Spark Packages. (2015). Retrieved from https://spark-packages.org

Spirtes, P. (2010). Introduction to causal inference. *Journal of Machine Learning Research*, *11*(May), 1643–1662.

Stonebraker, M., Bruckner, D., Ilyas, I. F., Beskales, G., Cherniack, M., Zdonik, S. B., . . . Xu, S. (2013, January). Data Curation at Scale: The Data Tamer System. CIDR.

Sutton, R. S., & Barto, A. G. (1998). Reinforcement learning: An introduction: Vol. 1. *No. 1*. Cambridge, MA: MIT press.

Szmit, M., & Szmit, A. (2012). Usage of modified Holt-Winters method in the anomaly detection of network traffic: Case studies. *Journal of Computer Networks and Communications*.

Tong, H. (2011). Nonlinear time series analysis. In *International Encyclopedia of Statistical Science* (pp. 955–958). Springer Berlin Heidelberg. doi:10.1007/978-3-642-04898-2_411

Tsai, C. W., Lai, C. F., Chao, H. C., & Vasilakos, A. V. (2015). Big data analytics: A survey. *Journal of Big Data*, *2*(1), 21. doi:10.118640537-015-0030-3 PMID:26191487

Tsay, R. S., Peña, D., & Pankratz, A. E. (2000). Outliers in multivariate time series. *Biometrika*, *87*(4), 789–804. doi:10.1093/biomet/87.4.789

Turban, E., Sharda, R., Aronson, J. E., & King, D. (2008). *Business Intelligence: A Managerial Approach*. Upper Saddle River, NJ: Prentice Hall Press.

Turing, A. M. (1950). Computing machinery and intelligence. *Mind*, *59*(236), 433–460. doi:10.1093/mind/LIX.236.433

Wagner, R., Thom, M., Schweiger, R., Palm, G., & Rothermel, A. (2013, August). Learning convolutional neural networks from few samples. In *Neural Networks (IJCNN), The 2013 International Joint Conference on* (pp. 1-7). IEEE 10.1109/IJCNN.2013.6706969

Wang, J., Crawl, D., Purawat, S., Nguyen, M., & Altintas, I. (2015, October). Big data provenance: Challenges, state of the art and opportunities. In *Big Data (Big Data), 2015 IEEE International Conference on* (pp. 2509-2516). IEEE.

Watson, H. J., & Wixom, B. H. (2007). The current state of business intelligence. *Computer*, *40*(9), 96–99. doi:10.1109/MC.2007.331

Werner, G., Yang, S., & McConky, K. (2017). Time series forecasting of cyber attack intensity. In *Proceedings of the 12th Annual Conference on Cyber and Information Security Research* (p. 18). ACM. 10.1145/3064814.3064831

Yang, C., Zhang, X., Zhong, C., Liu, C., Pei, J., Ramamohanarao, K., & Chen, J. (2014). A spatiotemporal compression based approach for efficient big data processing on cloud. *Journal of Computer and System Sciences*, *80*(8), 1563–1583. doi:10.1016/j.jcss.2014.04.022

Yang, Y., Saleemi, I., & Shah, M. (2013). Discovering motion primitives for unsupervised grouping and one-shot learning of human actions, gestures, and expressions. *IEEE Transactions on Pattern Analysis and Machine Intelligence*, *35*(7), 1635–1648. doi:10.1109/TPAMI.2012.253 PMID:23681992

Zhou, Z. H. (2012). *Ensemble methods: foundations and algorithms*. CRC Press.

Chapter 2
A Big Data Platform for Enhancing Life Imaging Activities

Leila Abidi
Université Paris 13, France

Tarn Duong
Université Paris 13, France

Hanene Azzag
Université Paris 13, France

Philippe Garteiser
Université Sorbonne Paris Cité, France

Salima Benbernou
Université Sorbonne Paris Cité, France

Mustapha Lebbah
Université Paris 13, France

Mehdi Bentounsi
Université Paris Descartes, France

Mourad Ouziri
Université Sorbonne Paris Cité, France

Christophe Cérin
Université Paris 13, France

Soror Sahri
Université Sorbonne Paris Cité, France

Michel Smadja
SISNCOM, France

ABSTRACT

The field of life imaging spans a large spectrum of scientific study from mathematics and computer science to medical, passing by physics, biology, etc. The challenge of IDV project is to enrich a multi-parametrized, quantitative, qualitative, integrative, and correlative life imaging in health. It deals with linking the current research developments and applications of life imaging in medicine and biology to develop computational models and methods for imaging and quantitative image analysis and validate the added diagnostic and therapeutic value of new imaging methods and biomarkers.

DOI: 10.4018/978-1-5225-4963-5.ch002

1. INTRODUCTION

The healthcare industry is a large generator of biomedical data. For instance, the U.S. healthcare system expected to reach the zettabyte (10^{21}) scale from electronic health records, scientific instruments, clinical decision support systems, or even research articles in medical journals (Raghupathi & Raghupathi, 2014).

In the last decade, we have witnessed the increasing resolution of imaging technologies which are considered as one of the most promising medical and health areas example and application of big data (e.g., NIH Brain initiative, n.d.) transforming case-based studies to large-scale, data-driven research (Luo, Wu, Gopukumar, & Zhao, 2016) and (Serrano, Blas, Carretero, & Desco,2017).

Interdisciplinary research in the field of imaging in the life sciences is essential. It requires the implication of different clinical and preclinical imaging departments yielding easy access to the state-of-the-art imaging equipment and patient data. Cooperative projects, including physicians, mathematicians, computer scientists, and physicists who are working closely together with bio scientists and clinicians are then launched in order to *(i)* develop computational models and methods for imaging and quantitative image analysis, and *(ii)* validate the added diagnostic and therapeutic value of new imaging methods and biomarkers.

Imaging is characterized by a large diversity in the types of data. Indeed, the data can originate from many different acquisition device, i.e., modalities, and the data format convention are quite loose with an important diversity in file formats and in completeness of annotation. The data themselves also strongly differ in their dimensionality, scale, size, and finality.

In such context, the life imaging project "IDV" (for Imageries Du Vivant) funded by University Sorbonne Paris Cité (USPC) launched the "Atlas IDV" initiative, which is a typical use case for data volume, variety and veracity in big data. The Atlas IDV initiative aims at *(i)* providing an integrated and agile environment supporting cooperation between scientists, and *(ii)* enabling to augment the research perimeter of imaging scientists and the extraction of new knowledge (data-driven research and images analytics) from the big multi-modal and multi-scale clinical and preclinical images available within the university.

A lot of studies in small animal imaging are hampered by small number of subjects, to the detriment of statistical quality of the findings. The junction of imaging data from a wide perimeter enables researchers to analyze a larger number of subjects, and hence to improve the statistical quality of their reports. Two use cases can be cited:

1. Many pathologies affect the normal physiology across many physical scales, and a complete understanding of these phenomena can only be obtained when examining images from a wide diversity of scales and contrasts. The "Atlas IDV" initiative, by virtue of its multidisciplinarity, will enable to put together datasets arising from a wide diversity of imaging techniques by the way of intelligent retrieval of heterogeneously stored data. As such, it will be a unique opportunity to make significant advances in the field of the life sciences.
2. The availability of such an infrastructure will also be helpful to facilitate standardization of the imaging methods. Indeed, an essential part of the validation process for imaging biomarkers is the possibility to share data obtained on a standardized object "phantom" across different vendors. The "Atlas IDV" initiative, by its distributed architecture, can allow to be carried out.

The "Atlas IDV" initiative brings together more than 200 scientists, affiliated with more than 20 research groups on 10 sites (Sts Pères Biomedical Center, HEGP, Necker Hosp., Bichat-Beaujon Hosp., Cochin Hosp., St Anne Hosp., Lariboisière Hosp., Cordeliers center, Chimie ParisTech, Villetaneuse Paris 13). The objective of the chapter is to give a global vision and feedbacks on an ambitious big data project for imaging research and what it brings to the IDV community.

Like organizations, one of the most important assets of any imaging research team is its image sets. Hence, the image sets are kept in two forms: using a set of dedicated cloud based operational systems of images records and processing supplying the "Atlas IDV" system (a.k.a data lake). The authors will show how the integrated imaging operational system promotes intra and inter-sites collaborative research work, while respecting data quality and privacy.

The Atlas IDV is based on the CIRRUS infrastructure available at USPC, more precisely the CUMULUS (n.d.) private cloud. Indeed, until recently USPC had no funding policy for platform development and sustainability, which has led to the need to disguise such development in call for proposals. With the CIRRUS platform, USPC has now made significant progress and the CIRRUS platform is used by projects in the 'deployment' phase. This implies requirements for stability through a deep control of the technical management to upgrade and to maintain the existing technology. In this chapter, a virtual datacenter inside CIRRUS is used to make concrete our ideas.

The business process as a service, i.e., BPaaS, implemented handles the imaging lifecycle of a variety of images' types (i.e., around 20 modalities acquired using heterogeneous imaging equipment's), with a large volume estimated at over 1 terabyte per day. For more information on BPaaS, see (Bentounsi, 2015).

To improve the images sets quality and indexing, native metadata (i.e., inserted by an imaging equipment) are enhanced using three main strategies:

1. A robust annotation scheme, which is the only way to ensure the scientific validity of the findings. Hence the availability of a web-based standardized annotation tools to enable researchers to associate datasets with accurate experimental information in a user-friendly manner, is of paramount importance (Kumar, Dyer, Kim, Li, Leong, Fulham, & Feng, 2016).
2. An enrichment of images sets via the crowdsourcing allows to harvest new annotations. Through an easy-to-use and intuitive interface, expert researchers (physicians, doctors, etc) submit their annotation tasks to non-expert contributors (students in medicine, biology, etc). Each task is a collection of one or more images. The contributors, categorized based on their experience, indicate their confidence for annotation. To collect high quality annotations, validation algorithm is used. It filters out annotations with low confidence and selects frequent and relevant annotations.
3. A semantic enrichment using linked open data and medical ontologies ("Radiology Lexicon", n.d.; "National Cancer Institute Thesaurus", n.d.; "Cell Ontology", n.d.).

Data enrichment strategies are helpful in big imaging data. This will improve images retrieval and analytics using innovative scalable algorithms based on MapReduce paradigm.

Privacy-enhancing technologies are used to preserve patient privacy by anonymizing images and metadata, and also by controlling the identification risk for the entire lifecycle of the "Atlas IDV" (Bentounsi & Benbernou, 2016) and (Bentounsi, Benbernou, & Atallah, 2016). In addition, a mechanism of images usage control in the Atlas is used leading to more transparency (Cao Huu, 2017).

E-Science has a better recognition of skills in software development as well as in large-scale infrastructure engineering in different disciplines. USPC should now recognize an interdisciplinary and complementary research on large scale systems and software in order to allow a sustainable development of the USPC platforms and to study a set of best (common) practices. The "Atlas IDV" initiative is a precursor project into that direction and their members are very excited by that idea.

The overall objective that we call for "interdisciplinary research" is preferably to apply well established methods inherited from e-Sciences for the building of systems for large scale computing and data management. The assumption is to check or to identify first what is common, in terms of Systems, between the disciplines versus the developments of new methods and technologies anchored in a unique discipline.

Finally, with such a System, USPC researchers can collectively be proactive in experimental science we obtain when using large scale platforms. We must not confuse the 'scientific problem' term and the 'System for scientific problem' term in order to serve the scientific community to solve scientific problems. We need scientists who develop software to support all the sciences we conduct at USPC. This cannot be the sole responsibility of computer scientists or engineers, but the informatics should rather percolate inside the disciplines, as we have shown in this chapter.

This Chapter is organized as follows. Section 2 introduces the Atlas IDV global architecture. Section 3 presents the project' private cloud and its architecture. Section 4 discusses how the crowdsourcing is used in the context of the project to annotate medical images. Semantic enrichment and Linked Open Data are presented in Section 5. Finally, Section 6 discusses images analytics in the context of the project and Section 7 concludes the chapter.

2. ATLAS IDV ARCHITECTURE

Like datasets for organizations, one of the most important assets of any imaging laboratory is its image sets, which represent the most visible part of a long (generally several years) and costly research process. First of all, like most areas of research, imaging researchers access to online research articles in medical journals and library reference collections to examine the state-of-art in a particular area. Based on their bibliographic studies, they develop research protocols specific to pathologies treated and results desired. The search protocol involves three key steps:

1. Develop new contrast agents or biomarkers.
2. Perform preclinical tests on cells and small animals to validate the efficiency and the non-harmfulness of the agents and/or biomarkers on living organisms.
3. If the first two steps have been conclusively established, clinical tests on humans are carried out before validating an agent or biomarker as a new medical diagnosis imaging.

During these stages, researchers need a set of data already available in several existing systems. In addition, the search process generates new information and knowledges to the community. Indeed, several operational systems and online databases are used to trace, index, and provide essential information to researchers and simplify the management of a research laboratory:

- Biobank databases which provide information on biological samples studied during the search protocol (Alfaro-Almagro, 2018).
- Animal facility management systems which provide information on small animals such as breed, weight, age, gender, model and lineage.
- Hospital Information Systems and Picture Archive and Communication System which provide patient data (Silva, Costa, & Oliveira, 2012).
- Materials for image acquisition which provide quantitative information on image acquisition process.

On the other hand, new knowledges and information are generated during the search protocol. They can be broken down into two categories. Experimental quantitative data and qualitative operational data on the functioning of the search protocol that assist the interpretation of quantitative finding (e.g., physical and biological properties of the contrast agent or the biomarker). This kind of data is at best saved in a Project Lifecycle Management system that keeps track of all the information generated during the search project (e.g., BenchSys, (2016) and Siemens Teamcenter (2018). Or at worst in a lab notebook or spreadsheet.

New knowledges take also the form of raw images acquired using a wide variety of medical imaging techniques (e.g, PET, CT, MRI, EPR), and also images processed using innovative image processing algorithms in order to detect the effect of studied contrast agents and biomarkers on organisms, and be able to diagnose pathologies as cancer, inflammation, etc.

Brutes and also processed images enrich the state-of-art in life imaging by providing online image bases allowing researchers to analyze a larger number of subjects, to test their image processing algorithms and hence to improve the statistical quality of their reports. This requires the implementation of image bases to index acquired images during research projects. We consider that a medical image may be indirectly identified by a combination of a set of metadata as for example a pathology, a contrast agent, and an organ. For that, we use all the metadata available to index medical images.

Implementing image bases can also reduce the costs and the duration of experimentations, and also proposing a new research paradigm in life imaging based on the statistical analysis of big image sets, i.e., data-driven research. However, the main obstacle to the implementation of image bases is the lack of storage resources at laboratories level. Often at the end of a project, the images are kept only for publications, then permanently deleted because of their volumes.

The "Atlas IDV" was implemented in the context of the project. Indeed, an integrated imaging operational system based on sis4web (n.d.) and connected to all systems and databases previously presented was developed. This leads to a base

Figure 1. Atlas IDV architecture

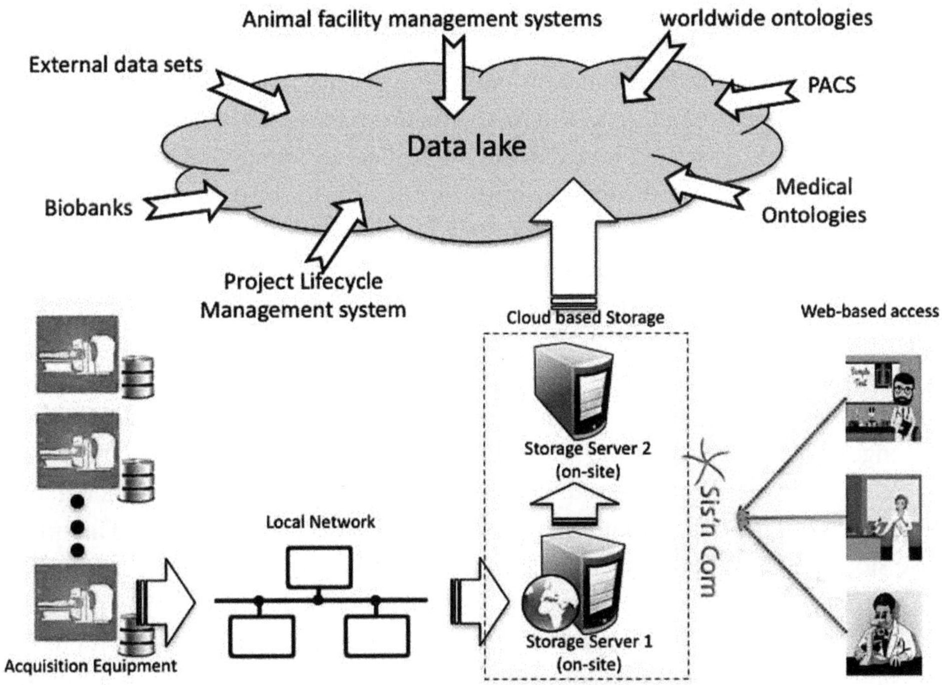

of indexed images using all operational and experimental information of the search protocol allowed the images' acquisition. The fact of having this mass of information related to the images makes feasible their re-use by researchers in future projects and feeds a large common base of images.

As depicted in Figure 1, at the end of the image acquisition process, a variety of raw images files are synchronized between acquisition servers and the storage server based on rsync (Mayhew, 2001).

Since health data are considered sensitive by the General Data Protection Reglement (Zerlang, 2017). Storing and processing health data requires a high level of security. Consequently, a dedicated private cloud based virtual servers have been used in the project (Krautheim, 2009).

The raw images have in their header a set of acquisition information (material, modality, date, time) and quantitative data (resolution, scale, etc.). These metadata are extracted from the DICOM and Bruker headers to be saved in the image base. In addition, the raw images are compressed using image compression algorithms in order to facilitate their transfer and visualization using web-based interfaces during collaborative work.

During the images storage process, researchers are asked to provide additional information such as: study objective, pathology studied, identifier of the object studied, the imaging agent characteristics, image processing algorithm, and physical measurements. These additional information enables the images base to query remote databases and operational systems via APIs in order to enrich images metadata. The proposed method based on internal and controlled enrichment allows researchers to index images through several attributes and be able to retrieve images via simple queries on a single attribute or via advanced filters on several attributes.

This architecture scheme is repeated on a multitude of laboratories and platforms within the project perimeter. However, slight modifications have been introduced in order to manage the volume and the velocity of acquired images and to face local network constraints. Indeed, in some cases, it was necessary to add an intermediate backup server on site which is synchronized in the night with the cloud so as not to congest the local network.

Periodically the compressed images and their metadata are extracted from distributed images bases, then integrated into a common images base. The images base stored in the cloud is accessible to all researchers on read only.

The export from private images bases is done in N3 format. The subject represents the image id, the predicate represents the attribute id, and the object represents the value. Records are stored in a csv file. Afterwards, the different csv files are imported into a single public NOSQL database accessible to researchers in order to make image analytics.

3. BUILDING THE DEDICATED CLOUD INFRASTRUCTURE

The current trend is to minimize the number of hosting datacenters while increasing the quality of data access. This principle is based essentially on the pooling of the resources of the various actors involved in the production and processing of health data. Another trend related to the previous one is to graft a scientific computing brick to the health data hosting part. This correlation will reduce the processing time of the data (reconciliation of the computing with the data) and minimize the security prerequisites for the transport of the health data between the hosting datacenters and those of processing. The adoption of the Cloud in the project is motivated, inter alia, by these two points.

Cloud computing technology potentially offers permanent access to data and services, from any device and anywhere at any time. Basically, it considers everything "as a service": computing, storage, network, and infrastructure. It pushes the user at the center of our concern by allowing him to deploy software on-demand, development platforms or even the infrastructure he needs. Currently, this is exactly what scientific project partners ask for.

The goal is to build a software ecosystem and offer a research support service to make the best use of large infrastructures. This allows partners to access a wide range of software tools and also a large amount of image sets. The aim is also to ensure maximum comfort for researchers and engineers, i.e. do not disrupt their current working methods.

3.1 Technical Architecture

In order to be able to carry out the project's private cloud, we had to work in collaboration with the IT directors of Université Paris Descartes since the Cloud infrastructure is physically located there. We began by reinforcing existing hardware so that it could support the needs and expectations of researchers. In 2015, there was an investment of 1 million euros to reach a total of 4500 cores and 3 PB of storage to setup a private cloud and renovate two clusters.

Conventionally, a virtualization-based solution has been chosen. This technique has the advantage of facilitating the cohabitation of several (operating) systems on the same physical support by providing complete isolation between systems and mutualized use of the resources of the system. The OpenNebula hypervisor, with a technical support, has been set up. OpenNebula operates as an orchestrator of the storage, network, supervision and security layers (Giovani, 2012).

Basically, a cloud-based solution consists in providing infrastructure, platform and software as services. Technically speaking, different templates of virtual machines (VM) are offered. These templates could be empty, i.e. containing only the OS, or predefined, i.e. containing a certain number of pre-installed tools. The selection of tools was not random; it was based on a survey carried out beforehand nearby the researchers involved in the project (Abidi, Cerin, Geldwerth-Feniger, & Lafaille, 2015).

Thus, we have set up VM templates and, for each of these templates, a virtual disk is defined, and an operating system is installed in this virtual disk. Different tools can be added to this system. Thereafter, one or many instances could be created from these templates. Each of these instances is associated with mandatory characteristics such as its name, memory size, the number of virtual processors.... One of the interests of the cloud is precisely to offer this type of mechanism which makes it possible to propose machines like a service i.e. "Infrastructure as a Service".

The Figure 2 summarizes the architecture adopted for the construction of the IDV cloud.

Figure 2. The different layers of the IDV cloud

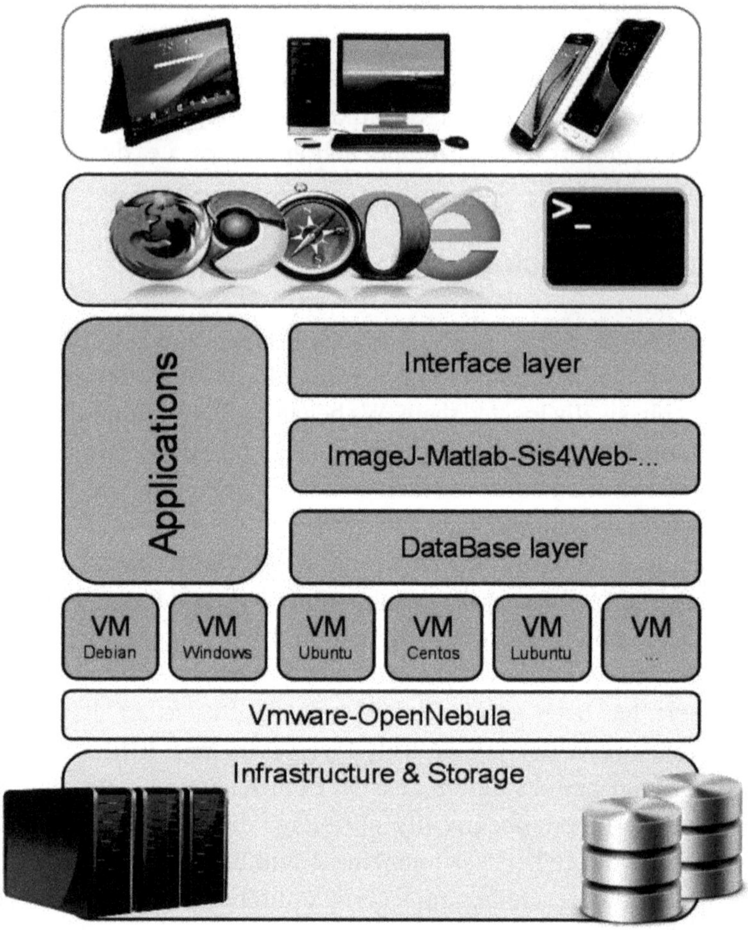

As shown in Figure 3, we have the possibility to use different virtual machines, simply through the browser. The researcher can deploy one or more virtual machines in one click and customize them with impressive characteristics (up to 64Go of memory, up to 20To of storage...).

Each researcher is the administrator of his own virtual machines. He have the possibility to customize his working environment, add/remove tools, add/remove users. There are also different ways to access the VM and work on it (VNC[1], SSH[2]…).

This first phase of the CUMULUS life allows to use the same tools as those used in laboratories but in a new operating context thanks to the deployment of virtual machines instead of machines isolated and disseminated in different physical places. The CUMULUS masks a lot of technical details. The centralization of data in the

Figure 3. Different operating systems are running in the browser's user

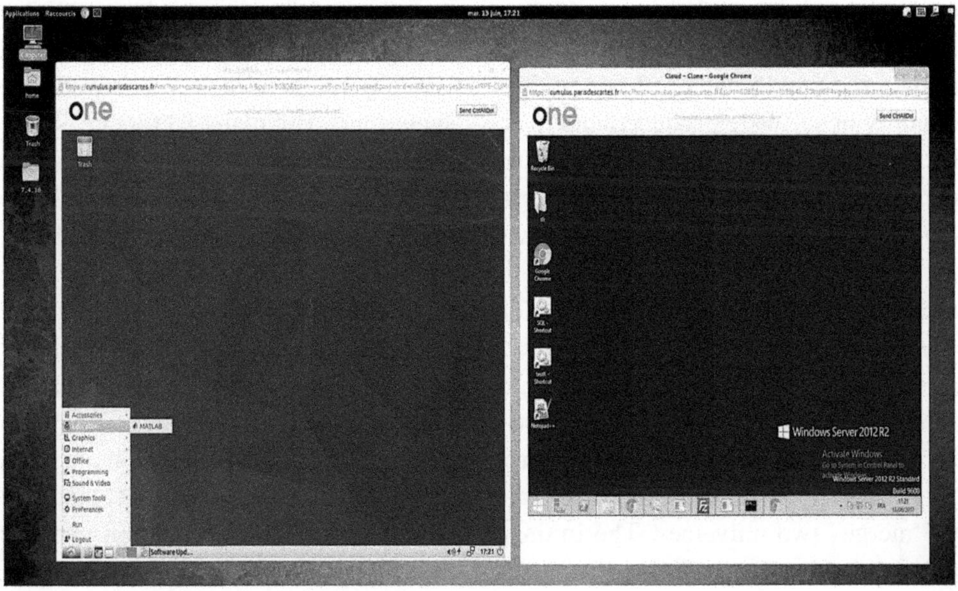

Cloud rationalizes the storage and avoid the multiplication of ad-hoc solutions to archive the data in the short term. This also facilitates access to data for the current atlas.

3.2 Discussion

3.2.1 High Performance Computing and Big-Data Convergence

Regarding the point of view of infrastructures for research in the academic sector, we still observe that large clusters, inherited from the HPC (High Performance Computing) community are still dominant. Large scale systems, such as clusters and clouds are systems with unprecedented amounts of hardware (>1M cores, >100 PB storage, > 100 Gbits/s interconnect). An ultra-large-scale system is an ecosystem with hardware, plus a large number of lines of source code, plus a large number of users, plus a large volume of data. In this context we have new issues, among them, how to build systems across multiple organizations; how to deal with conflicting purposes and needs; how to deal with heterogeneous parts with complex dependencies and emergent properties; how to deal with a continuous evolving; how to deal with software, hardware and human failures that are the norm, not the exception? Many answers can be found in the recent report from the Exascale (Asch & Moore, 2018) group of organizations, including academics and industrial partners.

Above all these considerations we still have issues regarding the problem of evaluating a large-scale system. If we evaluate clouds according to the metrics of the clusters, the comparison is not fair! We may evaluate both of them according to the productivity factor. Productivity traditionally refers to the ratio between the quantity of software produced and the cost spent for it. But many factors influence the decision, among them the programming language used, the program size, the experience of programmers and design personnel, the novelty of requirements, the complexity of the program and its data, the use of structured programming methods, the program class or the distribution method, the program type of the application area, the tools and environmental conditions, the maintaining of existing programs or systems, the reusing of existing modules and standard designs, etc

If we just make a focus on the programming language used, we may notice that the community of big-data do not use the same programming languages than the HPC community. However, the Harp project (Hadoop and Collective Communication for Iterative Computation) from the university of Indiana (n.d.) is a project that tries to "merge" two universes. The initial motivation is that communication patterns are not abstracted and defined in Hadoop, Pregel/Giraph, Spark. In contrary, MPI (Message Passing Interface) which is very used in HPC, has very fine grain based (collective) communication primitives (based on arrays and buffers).

Then Harp provides data abstractions and communication abstractions on top of them. It can be plugged into Hadoop runtime to enable efficient in-memory communication to avoid HDFS read/write. Harp works as a plugin in Hadoop. The goal is to make Hadoop cluster can schedule original MapReduce jobs and Map-Collective jobs at the same time. Collective communication is defined as movement of partitions within tables which are among the core data object. Collective communication requires synchronization. Hadoop scheduler is modified to schedule tasks in a bulk synchronous style (Wikipedia, n.d.) which allows predictions of the execution time (and in the theory). Harp also provides with fault tolerance with checkpointing. In other words, Harp attempts to realize a convergence between two layers in a system i.e. the programming layer (Hadoop like for the community of big-data) and efficient communication (MPI collective like communication for the community of HPC).

3.2.2 Cloud Computing

At this time the CUMULUS Cloud has been used to offer resources (CPU, RAM, disks...) to the project. But any project is faced to challenges such as communication and collaboration between product management, software development, integration, testing, deployment to cite a few. Our research group is currently focusing on the best methods and practices to put at the disposal of the IDV community, inside

CUMULUS, to deal with such issues that are not new issues. Indeed, we illustrate DevOps approaches that seems to be useful in this context because they are becoming increasingly widespread, especially in the community of practitioners.

DevOps (the contraction of Development and Operations) aims to establish a culture and environment where building, testing, and releasing software can happen rapidly, frequently, and more reliably (Samovskiy, 2010). There is no single "DevOps tool" but people consider "DevOps toolchains" consisting of multiple tools. Tools such as Docker (containerization), Jenkins (continuous integration), Puppet (Infrastructure as Code), Vagrant (virtualization platform) and Ansible (provisioning) -among many others- are often used and frequently referenced in DevOps discussions.

Let us comment two papers that exemplify the interest of DevOps approaches and DevOps toolchains to simplify the tasks of developers in large project. This part of the discussion is not addressed towards end-users but to developers in a broad sense. Final users do nothing, they just have to launch a script, in the worst case, if the job is not fully automated.

Stillwell & Coutinho (2015) deal with the problem to support the integration effort of HARNESS, an EU FP7 project. HARNESS is a multi-partner research project intended to bring the power of heterogeneous resources to the cloud. It consists of a number of different services and technologies that interact with the OpenStack cloud computing platform at various levels. Many of these components are being developed independently by different teams at different locations across Europe and keeping the work fully integrated is a challenge. Authors use a combination of Vagrant based virtual machines, Docker containers, and Ansible playbooks to provide a consistent and up-to-date environment to each developer. The same playbooks used to configure local virtual machines are also used to manage a static testbed with heterogeneous compute and storage devices, and to automate ephemeral larger-scale deployments to Grid'5000 (2017).

Indeed, authors present a development and operations (DevOps) workflow that allows: *(i)* teams of developers to work autonomously on specific parts of the software architecture; *(ii)* automated testing of individual projects as well as the integrated system deployments; and *(iii)* reproducible automated deployment on heterogeneous and large-scale testbeds. For that purpose, the authors introduce first a high-level view of the HARNESS DevOps workflow. Second, they describe how various deployment tools help to achieve reproducibility and why this is important for testing and quality assurance. The next topic covered in the article is to report the automated testing infrastructure and the novel methodology for testing full systems deployments. Finally, they describe two platforms where HARNESS is being deployed. To conclude, the paper demonstrates how to organize a research on DevOps approaches that serve multiple people, being working on the same project.

The second paper we would like to introduce is the very recent paper by Abidi, Saad, & Cérin (2017). In this paper, the authors are interested to deploying, in a multi-Cloud architecture, an infrastructure using the publish-subscribe paradigm for orchestrating the components of a framework that execute scientific workflows in highly heterogeneous and dynamic environments. More specifically they are in search of the adequate approaches to build deployment systems for heterogeneous and highly dynamic environments. The general objective is to offer « Workflow as a Service », as the concrete view, but we could imagine that the objective is to offer « X as a service », X being a utility function.

At least, we would like to mention the RosettaHub (n.d.) initiative that aims to facilitate the access to Amazon (AWS) computing and storage resources, from a basic user point of view. Services, now available free of charge to students and faculty members, include access to supercomputers, high-performance computing clusters, GPU and FPGA-accelerated machines, managed Hadoop and Spark clusters, storage services, databases and warehouses for big data, platforms for IoT and fog computing, machine learning services, etc.

The RosettaHUB platform creates, federates, manages and supervises the AWS accounts of some fifty higher education institutions around the world, totaling nearly 12,000 active AWS accounts of students and teachers. researchers. RosettaHUB also aims to establish a global, social and collaborative scientific meta-cloud. It simplifies and democratizes access to the infrastructures and tools needed for data science, big data and machine learning. Environments and tools such as Jupyter, RStudio, Zeppelin, TensorFlow, Spark, etc. are made instantly available as services to thousands of people. RosettaHUB enables real-time collaboration and sets up mechanisms for sharing all the scientific or educational artifacts produced on a cloud.

The platform exposes an API (Application Programming Interface) and federation model for clouds. Combined with the portability provided by the systematic use of container technologies (Docker), it makes possible and simple the transition from a 'classical' system (desktop like) to the cloud. The platform also exposes an API and federation model for compute engines and communicates R, Python, Scala, Mathematica, etc. in memory. through a common object model and deep integration of different virtual machines. RosettaHUB exposes above these federation models reactive programming frameworks for creating and publishing in multi-cloud and multi-language mode (R / Python / Scala) responsive microservices, collaborative interactive web interfaces, spreadsheets scientific and collaborative, data analysis workflows, etc. RosettaHUB's meta-formations capture all the dependencies of such data science / ML-oriented services and applications, allowing them to be reproduced and shared in one click. These meta-formations provide a foundation for reproducible research which is yet another issue that we need to address in the future.

3.2.3 Summary of the Work at the Infrastructure Level

The authors introduce a use case and they describe the different components of their DevOps architecture. They use the CUMULUS Cloud located at Université Sorbonne Paris Cité as the user's site. From CUMULUS the user starts a Vagrant script and this script automates all the deployment, installation, provisioning steps on multiple sites of the Grid'5000 tested for executing an application inside an infrastructure… that is also deploying. This is the key challenging point: how to automate the deployment of an infrastructure inside an infrastructure? DevOps approaches solve the problems in a convenient way.

4. CROWDSOURCING

Crowdsourcing is the process of outsourcing numerous tasks to an undefined, and generally large, network of people (the crowd). It is in widespread use in academic and industrial projects. Typical applications for the crowd include data collection, annotation or evaluation. For a wide array of tasks, the crowdsourcing paradigm has been shown to hold (Kittur, Chi & Suh, 2008).

In research domain, crowdsourcing platforms are a popular choice for researchers to replace expensive domain experts with crowd labour. It is particularly used to gather annotations quickly at scale. The most popular crowdsourcing scientific task is the categorization of galaxies (Raddick et al., 2013). In healthcare, great potential has been shown for various biomedical tasks, such as determination of protein folding (Eiben et al., 2012) and classification of malaria-infected red blood cells (Mavandadi et al., 2012). Crowdsourcing has also been used for clinical diagnosis (Nguyen et al., 2012) and for drug discovery (Lessl, Bryans, Richards & Asadullah, 2011).

Crowdsourcing was also recently used for image annotation in medical imaging. Many results showed that the annotation, via crowdsourcing, of a large amount of biomedical images can help at image classification. It has been shown in (Eickhoff, 2014), that the crowd can be much more effectively used to enhance the experts' performance and efficiency in detecting malignant breast cancer in medical images. In (Leifman, Swedish, Roesch, & Raskar, 2015), it has been demonstrated that crowdsourcing can be an effective, viable and inexpensive method for the preliminary analysis of retinal images. The work of (Herrera, Foncubierta-Rodríguez, Markonis, Schaer, & Müller, 2014) is based on the crowdsourcing for improving the quality of an automatic modality classification task based on the visual information of the images and the text of the figure captions. It particularly consists in verifying, by users familiar with medical images, the automatically detected modality of ImageCLEFmed images, and in reclassifying the images identified as wrongly classified.

In (Irshad, Montaser, Waltz, Bucur, Nowak, Dong, Knoblauch, & Beck, 2015), the crowdsourcing has been used for rapidly obtaining annotations by using the CrowdFlower platform for two core tasks in computational pathology: nucleus detection and nucleus segmentation. The results of this work show that the obtained annotations from crowdsourced non-expert-derived scores perform at a similar level to expert-derived scores and automated methods for nucleus detection and segmentation.

In our work and as part of the research project, we developed a crowdsourcing-based platform for the annotation of biomedical images. This platform referred as CrowdIDV, is an external module to the IDV atlas, that completes its semantic enrichment via the robust annotation scheme and the linked open data. A similar existing framework for the semantic enrichment of biomedical images, referred as SEBI, also includes a crowd-annotation module for biomedical images (Bukhari, Krauthammer, & Baker, 2014). Our CrowdIDV platform is a collaborative platform that is intended for students to annotate the biomedical images published by their expert researchers of the USPC community. It can also be considered as an educational platform.

The researchers or experts, referred as imagers, are the requesters of the collaborative platform; and the students, referred as the annotators, are the crowders or participants.

As depicted in Figure 4, the imagers submit their annotation tasks and the annotators contribute to the annotation of the published images. The imagers and annotators must be registered via this platform.

In order to have relevant annotations, each imager submits its tasks for only its students. For instance, a biologist researcher publishes its images for only biologist students. To do so, students have access to a given task with a specific code given by its imager.

CrowdIDV incorporates algorithmic part to ensure the good quality of the collected annotations by students. We specifically developed an approach to validate the annotation input from various annotators. Our approach, inspired by Apriori (Agrawal & Srikant, 1994), the classic algorithm to mine frequent itemsets, consists in extracting the most frequent annotations for each published image while considering the confidence of the annotators. Indeed, at the annotation process, the student associates its confidence with the annotation he proposes (confident, high confident or hesitant). To do so, we follow these steps: First, we collect the annotations entered by students (or users). We assume that the annotation task is defined by a query image. To apply the Apriori algorithm, we model each image as a transaction database, where each transaction corresponds to student' annotations

Figure 4. CrowdIDV architecture

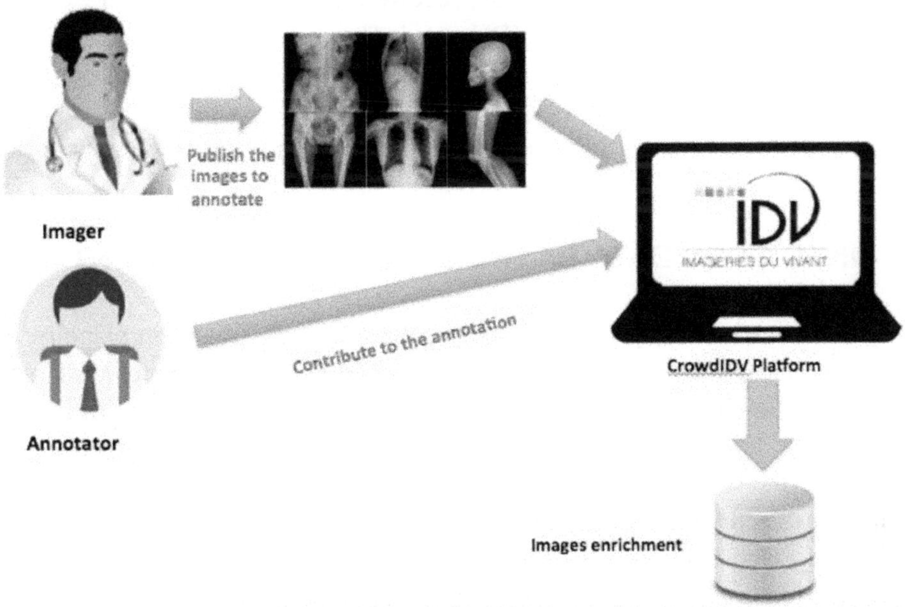

and then the annotations to the Apriori algorithm items. We recall that the Apriori algorithm have been proposed for generating association rules. The key idea of the algorithm is to begin by generating frequent itemsets with just one item (1-itemsets) and to recursively generate frequent itemsets with 2 items, then frequent 3-itemsets and so on until we have generated frequent itemsets of all sizes.

In our work, we use the Apriori algorithm to generate the frequent itemsets that represent the annotations. A wide variety of frequent itemsets mining algorithms exist in the literature such as Eclat, TreeProjection and FP-growth (Aggarwal, Bhuiyan, & Hasan, 2014). Apriori is the most commonly used algorithm and is a popular starting point for frequent itemset study (Heaton, 2016). Using Apriori, we consider the confidence of users at the generation of the frequent itemsets. The idea is to associate to each transaction (and then each user) a probability measure that corresponds to the user confidence. Consequently, only annotations resulting from this validation algorithm are considered and then proposed to the imager. This last can then lock the annotations if satisfied by the result or lets its images published for more annotations if not satisfied.

As future work, we will assess the accuracy of the annotations established by the crowd. Accordingly, we intend to consider the historical participation of each annotator to further estimate the error rate of annotations and also for rewarding students. The reward for students could receive credits (EU project for example). CrowdIDV is currently deployed in IDV cloud. The next step is testing the platform by the community and then validate our approach and prepare the eventual enhancing steps. Once done, the collected annotations from CrowdIDV will be integrated in the IDV Atlas as triplestore for further activities of enrichment with the linked open data.

5. LINKED OPEN DATA BASED SEMANTIC ENRICHMENT

Today, the clinicians deeply rely on images for diagnosis, treatment planning and follow up. In fact, they deal with complex and heterogeneous data including image annotations allowing retrieving those images. In the previous section, we discussed a way to provide the annotations and enrichment of medical images using crowdsourcing paradigm in the IDV platform.

In other side, there exist other kind of data related to multi-modal and multi-scale life imaging including text, pre-clinical data and images of cells etc. Therefore, the production of life imaging is exponential. However, different banks of images are stored in their acquisition place, and such spatial fragmentation leads to under exploitation of those available huge amount of data where doctors and biologists do not collaborate and operate on their respective type of images. Then, the aim of the project is to allow medical scientists of pre-clinical and clinical researchers talking each through the fusion of big images sets (Dong & Srivastava, 2015) by using semantic interlinking between different types of images (Howe, Franklin, Haas, Kraska, & Ullman, 2017). So, the challenge is to gather richer medical information by connecting clinical images with pre-clinical images.

For clinicians, the aim is to enrich their clinical medical data and images with pre-clinical data and images, and vise versa for biologist. To do so, we use the Linked Data concept (Auer, Berners-Lee, Bizer, Capadisli, Heath, & Lehmann, 2017) (i.e., using the Web to create typed links between data from different sources) is a first step towards semantic-based data retrieval for semantic enrichment in life imaging domain using ontology mapping (Arnold & Rahm, 2014). Linked Data has the potential to provide easier access to significantly growing, publicly available related data sets, such as those in the healthcare domain (Sonntag, Wennerberg & Zillner, 2010).

Furthermore, the image interlinking does not deal only with proprietary data and images but may use other publicly available data called *open data* sources such as published data sets (Données publiques, n.d.) and worldwide ontologies including

Foaf (n.d.), dbpedia (n.d.), or medical ontologies (Radiology Lexicon, n.d.; National Cancer Institute Thesaurus, n.d.; Cell Ontology, n.d., ... etc.). Consequently, the project aims to use Linked Open Data (LOD) for life imaging.

Linked Data is essentially based on the RDF representation format for data representation, where the data can be linked using RDF/OWL links developed by W3C's Semantic Web Consortium, that become available during an advanced medical engineering process. In this project, we investigate how medical images and linked data sets can be used to identify interrelations that are relevant for annotating and searching medical images using RDF/OWL (W3C, 2004) for image representation though image annotations and SPARQL language for querying different data sources that are heterogeneous (Chekol & Pirrò, 2016) in order to search adequate data, and using ontology mapping process to discover the link between data (Mao, Peng, Spring, 2010) and (Verhoosel, Bekkum & Evert, 2015). Consequently, it is helping to enhance the patient diagnostics. As the produced images are massive, we are using new technologies such as Apache Spark (Amplab, 2018) (Zaharia Xin, Wendell, Das, Armbrust, Dave, Meng, Rosen, Venkataraman,Franklin, Ghodsi, Gonzalez, Shenker & Stoica, 2016)(Engle, Lupher, Xin, Zaharia, Franklin, Shenker & Stoica, 2012) and provide innovative algorithms related to Linked Open Big Images (LOBI), we wish to introduce.

Moreover, with the widespread use of PACS in the hospitals, the amount of medical image data is rapidly increasing (Silva, Costa, & Oliveira, 2012). Thus, the more efficient and effective retrieval methods are required for better management of medical image information. So far, a variety of medical image retrieval systems have been developed using either method (text-based or content-based) or combining two methods (Qi & Snyder, 1999), (Müller, Michoux, Bandon & Geissbuhler, 2004), and (Kyung-Hoon, Haejun, & Duckjoo, 2012). Each method has its own advantages and disadvantages. Text-based method is widely used and fast, but it requires precise annotation. Content-based approach provides semantic retrieval, but effective and precise techniques still remains elusive. The existing method are not handling the huge amount of data, in the project we are handling the volume and the heterogeneous variety of data sources using new technologies for big data.

Next, we provide a motivation example related to life imaging in order to enchich semantically data owner by solving the problem of semantic heterogeneity of different data sources.

5.1. Motivating Example: Linking Life Imaging

In our work, we assume that linked data contributes to solving the problem of structural heterogeneity as well as identifying entities to improve the quality of big data fusion results (Benbernou & Ouziri, 2017). Nevertheless, RDF and its URI mechanism are not sufficient to solve the problem of semantic heterogeneity. For example, consider two data sources related to life imaging, clinical image representing the lung radiography of a patient namely Bob and a pre-clinical image representing an image of a cell extracted from human lung, as depicted in Figure 5 (All data sources are represented in RDF data). The challenge of our work is to connect clinical and pre-clinical images. For this aim, the images are annotated by doctors and biologists (or using a crowdsourcing system described previously). In the clinical source (at the top left side) is an IRM medical imaging on lung of a patient leaving in Paris area. A cancer is diagnosticated in the image. The second data source which is pre-clinical image represents a human cell infected with pollen of hazel. The annotation process generates databases containing descriptions of medical images.

Clinical and pre-clinical images are then linked through their respective databases. Linking can be made using direct connections between contents of databases or via intermediate other data sources namely open data sources dealing with air quality data.

In Figure 5, the concepts describing life imaging of data sources ds1 and ds2 are *Human* and *Cell*, respectively. The query over data sources is to retrieve all information related to the patient Bob.

Using an inference mechanism on clinical data source, we can infer only the knowledge *Bob has a cancer*. Such knowledge is *incomplete* because of the heterogeneity of the terminology used to describe the data from preclinical and

Figure 5. Example of linked data in life imaging

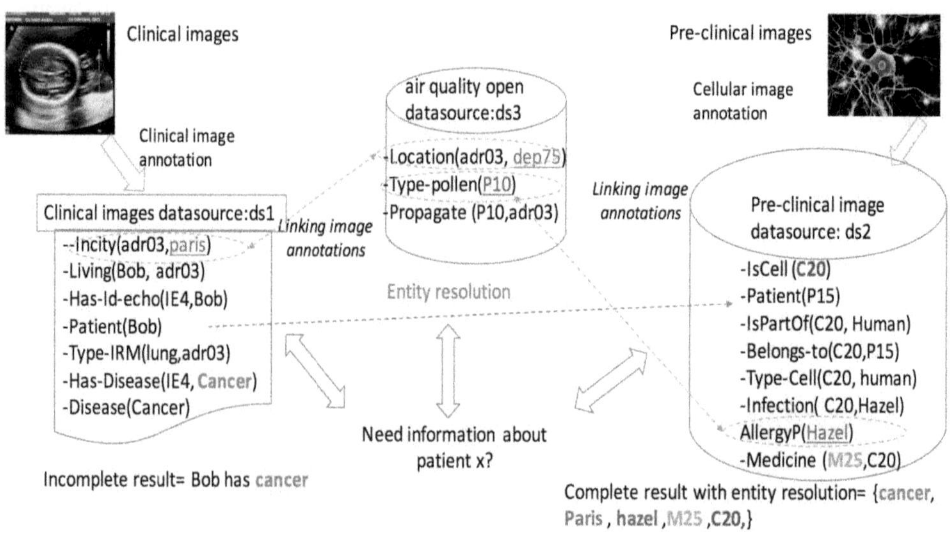

clinical sources and open data sources. Once a linking is processed between three data sources through *entity resolution* method between Paris and dept 75, Pollen P10 and Hazel related to the same entity, the query result becomes Complete result with entity resolution= {Bob has **cancer**, and is living in **Paris** having pollen **P10** and this type of pollen is **hazel** exists only in **Paris** and may can be applied on him a medicine **M25** to be cured because of its application on human cell **C20**}, Patient(P15) and Patient (Bob) are dealing with the same entity Bob. The entity resolution (ER) (Bhattacharya & Getoor, 2017), also known as record linkage or deduplication aims at *cleaning* a database by identifying tuples that represent the same external entity (Whang, Marmaros, & Garcia-Molina, 2013) and (Firmani, Saha, & Srivastava, 2016).

5.2. Open MEDICAL DATA and Semantics Representation (RDF and OWL)

RDF is a standard data model, proposed by W3C for representing semantic Web data. RDF data is usually stored as statements in terms of triples subject, predicate, object, representing a relationship, denoted by the predicate, between the subject and the object. Subjects and predicates in triples are URIs when objects can be either URIs or literal values. An RDF data set forms a directed graph, where subjects and objects are vertices and predicates are labels on the directed edges from subjects to objects. OWL is a Semantic Web language designed to represent rich and complex knowledge about things, groups of things, and relations between things. It is a language allowing to represent knowledge for authoring ontology. An ontology a formal way to describe taxonomies and classification networks, it is a structuration of knowledge for various domains. The OWL languages are characterized by formal semantics based on Description logic [Baader, Calvanese, McGuiness, Nardi, Patel-Schneider, 2003]. The logical approach is used to verify the consistency of the knowledge or to make implicit knowledge explicit. Consider the data sources displayed in Figure 5, in Figure 6 is depicted its RDF knowledge representation of clinical data sources ds1 as facts i.e., Bob i*s-type* of Patient, Bob *has-id-echo* IE4, Bob *is-living* adr03, adr3 *in-city* Paris etc.

5.3. Semantic Linking of Life Imaging Data for Semantic Enrichment

In this section we will show the reasoning mechanism we can apply on different data sources to discover new knowledge and therefore enrich semantically the owner data.

Life imaging data sources are linked at two levels: *data level* and *semantic level:*

Figure 6. An example of life imaging data in RDF graph

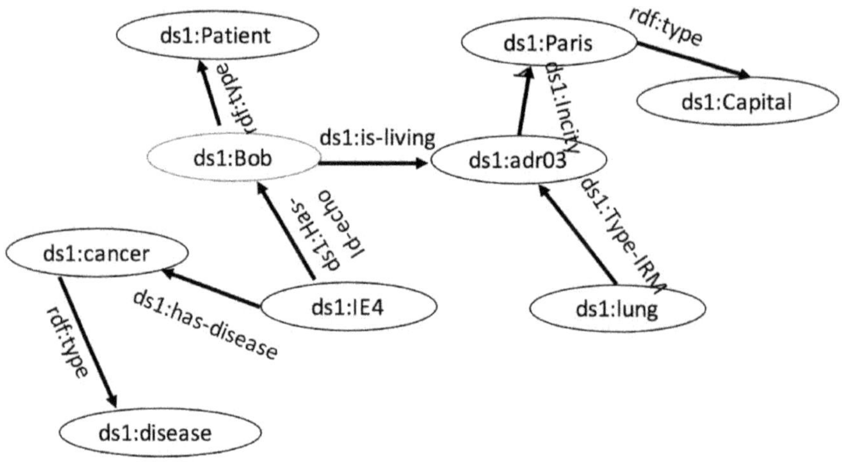

- At the data level, when querying data sources, the data sources linking process aims to identify the same real-life entities (such as patients, a human organ) and connect them using the owl relationship *sameAs*. This process is named *Entity Resolution* (ER). The ER is the task of disambiguating manifestations of real world entities in various resources by linking through inference across networks and semantic relationships in application (ontology alignment) (Nentwig, Hartung, Ngomo, & Rahm, 2017) and (Shvaiko & Euzenat, 2013) and (Cheatham, Cruz, Euzenat, Pesquita, 2017).
- At the semantic level, in the era of big data and life imaging, the need for high quality entity resolution is growing as we are overwhelming with more and more data that needs to be i*ntegrated* (data fusion), *aligned* and *matched* before further utility can be extracted. Therefore, achieving inferences across the networks using semantic relationships between entities for a better high quality entity resolution become a great challenge. The aim of the semantic linking is to *make explicit the implicit data* across the network, thereby enriching life imaging semantically. The semantic linking is achieved using appropriate inference mechanisms to deal with big data and at the same time cleaning the big data produced when processing data fusion (Benbernou & Ouziri 2017).

In order, to reconcile entities making entity resolution, we present in this section through an example, the inference mechanism that can be used to connect all heterogeneous RDF fragments of the same entity based on semantics and how the enrichment of life imaging is processed. At the semantic level, concepts that are used to describe data sources are linked using semantic relationships (Shvaiko & Euzenat, 2013).

For illustration, Figure 7 presents three RDF fragments of the use case depicted in Figure 5, where concepts, describing life imaging, of datasources ds1 and ds2 are *Human* and *Cell*, respectively, data source ds3 is describing open data related to AirQuality, as well as two ontologies foaf and dbpedia as open data. The figure shows how the semantic linking between all those five sources using RDF/OWL languages is established. Some knowledge are extracted following the semantic linking. Furthermore, the entity resolution is operating at the conceptual (semantic) and entity (data) level. The W3C has defined axioms to make the semantic connections between RDFS and OWL standards. The most common are rdfs:subClassOf, owl:subClassOf, owl:equivalentClass and owl:disjointWith as pointed out by red and blue lines in Figure 7. In what follow we explain the inference reasoning that can be applied to discover new knowledge:

The RDF data are represented i.e., serialized by *facts*, some of them are listed: (1) ds1:*Bob* is a ds1:*patient* and is living at ds1:*adr03* (2) ds1:*adr03 inCity* ds1:Paris (3) ds3:adr03 *location* ds3:dept75 (4) ds1:Paris *sameAs* ds3:dept75 (5) ds2:*C20 belongTo* ds2:*P15* (6)ds2:*C20 infection* ds2:*Hazel* (7) ds2:*Hazel* sameAs ds3:*p10*

Figure 7. An example of how the life imaging data sources and open data are linked together using RDF/OWL

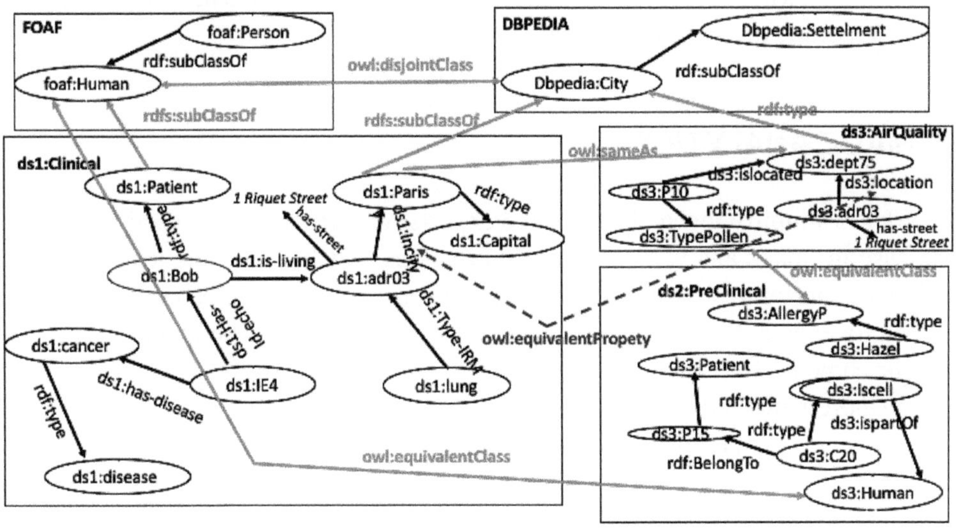

(8) ds3:p10 *propagate* ds3:adr03 (9) ds2:C20 *infection* ds2:Hazel. For instance the meaning of facts 7, the concept hazel is same as the concept p10, for fact 8, the concept p10 is propagated to adr03.

Besides, all those facts are along with *business rules* called also *domain rules* provided by the expert domain to make data compliant with them.

Therefore, the inference mechanism is processed as follow:The fact (4) when propagated (linked) to (2) and (3) infers that ds1:adr03 and ds3:adr03 are the same address and the given domain rule: *there can only one address street at a city*. The semantic linking in fact (7) when propagated to fact (8) infers that the adr03 is infected by hazel. By considering the fact (8) and given the domain rule: *there can only place infected by a Hazel*, the three resolutions can propagate to fact (1) and infer the place Bob is living is infected by Hazel. This resolution when propagate to fact (9) and (5) infers ds1:Bob and ds3:p15 is the same patient. And then the medicine can be applied to the patient to be cured.

The entity resolution is operating at the conceptual (semantic) and entity (data) level. The W3C has defined axioms to make the semantic connections between RDFS and OWL standards. The most common are rdfs:subClassOf, owl:subClassOf, owl:equivalentClass and owl:disjointWith as depicted in Figure 7. The inference mechanism is using such basic semantic connections to infer connections as well as operators of description logics to infer other knowledge for instance (1) dbpedia: City ⊑ ¬foaf: Human (2) ds1: Capital ⊑ dbpedia: City (3) ds2: Hazel ⊑ ds2: p10. For more details of different propagation that can be applied in the context of big data can be found in (Benbernou, Huang, Ouziri, 2017).

Once the owner data is enriched, it is ready to be translated to the image analytics process module discussed in the next section.

6. IMAGE ANALYTICS

In order to simplify the analysis for the experts, we present in this section through use case in image analytics our contributions in scalable machine learning. This task is important to simplify the inference mechanism that can be used to connect all heterogeneous RDF fragments presented in section 5.3. The global purpose is the enrichment of the expert knowledge.

In fluorescent medical imaging, a biological structure (e.g. gene, chromosome, cell, tissue or organ) is visualised by the expression levels of so-called marker proteins which attach specifically to this structure. A fundamental question in cellular biology is the identification of the regions of homogenous pixels delimited by these marker proteins via image segmentation by unsupervised learning. A segmented image is the partition of these pixels into the clusters induced by a learning method. We focus on the class of modal clustering methods where clusters are defined in terms of the local modes of the probability density function which generates the data. The most well-known model clustering method is the k-means clustering (Lloyd, 1982). A segmentation based on solely on the fluorescence level is inadequate as the fluorescence level of marker proteins varies according to multiple factors, including most importantly the unavoidable natural, biological variation. A more adaptive segmentation would take into account other important data variables derived from the image other than the fluorescence levels, e.g. spatial localisation, topology etc. The *k*-means clustering currently used is capable of partitioning multi-dimensional variables but the resulting clusters are constrained to be ellipsoidal. These constraints imply that the *k*-means clustering is not well-suited to complex medical images. In our work, we decided to focus on density based algorithm, the most famous in that category is the DBScan (He, Tan, Luo, Feng & Fan, 2014) algorithm which is a density based algorithm which takes two parameters, ” which defines the radius of the hypersphere and minPts, which is the required number of points to consider the hypervolume as dense enough. Each times the density threshold is reached, dots are considered in the same clusters, the process is extended to catching points until the density is under the threshold. Rest of the points are considered as noise. One notable benefit of this algorithm is to detect automatically number of clusters with random shape but it remains hard to tuned efficiently.

On the other hand, Mean-Shift clusters are defined in a more flexible manner as the regions where these multi-dimensional variables are the densest. This leaves the clusters to evolve according to the local characteristics, which is well-suited to the task of delimiting pixels for complex biological structures. Mathematically these clusters are the basins of attraction to the local modes of the probability density function. For an image, each pixel is associated with a local mode by following the gradient ascent of the density function, and all the pixels associated with the same mode form a segmented region. The gradient ascent is estimated by the sequences of the nearest neighbour local means (Fukunaga & Hostetler, 1975).

On the other hand, Mean-Shift clusters are defined in a more flexible manner as the regions where these multi-dimensional variables are the densest. This leaves the clusters to evolve according to the local characteristics, which is well-suited to the task of delimiting pixels for complex biological structures. Mathematically these clusters are the basins of attraction to the local modes of the probability density function. For an image, each pixel is associated with a local mode by following the gradient ascent of the density function, and all the pixels associated with the same mode form a segmented region. The gradient ascent is estimated by the sequences of the nearest neighbour local means (Fukunaga & Hostetler, 1975).

In our recent work, we demonstrated that the nearest neighbour Mean-Shift is effective for 2-dimensional non-medical images of a modest resolution. The factor which hinders a more widespread use of the Mean-Shift is that the sequential calculation of the nearest neighbours (via the dissimilarity matrix) quickly becomes computationally too onerous. To respond to the challenge, we have implemented a massively distributed version of it in the Spark-Scala Big Data ecosystem (Duong, Beck, Azzag, & Lebbah, 2016) and (Beck, Duong, Azzag & Lebbah, 2016).

We implement our algorithm in Scala because it is the native language in which Spark was implemented and so allows for optimal performance. Apache Spark is a fast-general purpose cluster computing system based on a master-slaves' architecture. The primary abstraction of Spark is a distributed collection of items called a Resilient Distributed Dataset (RDD) on which we apply the map and $reduce$ functions. Calculation times have been reduced by 10- to 100-fold, due notably to a rapid choice of the number of nearest neighbours and the calculation of approximate nearest neighbours via the random scalar projections of the "locality sensitive hashing" method (Indyk & Motwani, 1998) and (Slaney & Casey, 2008).

A part of experiments were realized on the Grid'5000 testbed which is the French national testbed for computer science research. It allows the deployment of a user's own operating system within the Grid'5000 hardware. We use a dedicated Spark Linux image1 optimized for Grid'5000 where Apache Spark is deployed on top of Hadoop YARN. Only the deployment of the image is automatized: we manually reserved the nodes as well as manually providing the Spark cluster with our executable code. For production purposes with CUMULUS we hide the configuration, deployment, provision of the services starting with a pool of dynamically allocated resources.

As mentioned previously, image segmentation can be made more precise by taking to account other available information. The Mean-Shift, as we have implemented it, uses the spatial localisation of dense data regions. Spatial coordinates are a continuous variable and could be utilised as the Mean-Shift clustering has been developed to treat continuous variables. On the other hand, incorporating categorical variables (e.g. yes/no, A/B/C) whenever intermediate values which have no intuitive interpretation is not yet feasible.

As future work, we propose to translate the successful technique for processing categorical data in other clustering methods via the recoding of categorical variables as a series of binary variables and replacing the mean with a median. Thus, we aim to develop a Median-Shift clustering method that is capable of handling composite data, consisting of a mixture of continuous and categorical variables, in the medical imaging and Big Data contexts.

7. CONCLUSION

We presented in this chapter a big data platform for enhancing life imaging activities in the setting of a multidisciplinary project IDV. We developed an ecosystem to the bio scientists and clinicians helping them to cooperate at the different levels for enabling to augment the research perimeter of imaging scientists and the extraction of new knowledge from the big multi-modal and multi-scale clinical and preclinical images available within the university. The platform is offering different services including sharing images in the same space, annotating their images using crowdscourcing system, linking their images through linked data technology, analysing their images, adding diagnostic and therapeutic value of new imaging methods and biomarkers. Several perspectives and enhancements raised regarding our experiences since the projects started three years ago, one can site enforcing the ethical and privacy aspects when sharing images and results, enhancing the multidisciplinary understanding through the platform still not mature and finally enlarge the platform to the international collaborations.

REFERENCES

Abidi, L., Cérin, C., Geldwerth-Feniger, D., & Lafaille, M. (2015). *Cloud Computing for e-Sciences at Université Sorbonne Paris Cité*. Taormina, Italy: Advances in Service-Oriented and Cloud Computing - Workshops of ESOCC.

Abidi, L., Saad, W., & Cérin, C. (2017). A Deployment System for highly Heterogeneous and Dynamic Environments. *International Conference on High Performance Computing & Simulation*, Genoa, Italy. 10.1109/HPCS.2017.98

Aggarwal, C., Bhuiyan, M., & Hasan, M. (2014). Frequent Pattern Mining Algorithms: A Survey. In C. Aggarwal & J. Han (Eds.), *Frequent Pattern Mining*. Cham: Springer. doi:10.1007/978-3-319-07821-2_2

Agrawal, R., & Srikant, R. (2014). *Fast algorithms for mining association rules*. VLDB.

Alfaro-Almagro, F., Jenkinson, M., Bangerter, N. K., Andersson, J. L. R., Griffanti, L., Douaud, G., ... Smith, S. M. (2018). Image processing and Quality Control for the first 10, 000 brain imaging datasets from UK Biobank. *NeuroImage, 166*, 400–424. doi:10.1016/j.neuroimage.2017.10.034 PMID:29079522

Amplab. (2018). *Amplap UC Berkeley*. Retrieved from https://amplab.cs.berkeley.edu/tag/spark/

Arnold, P., & Rahm, E. (2014). Enriching ontology mappings with semantic relations. *Data & Knowledge Engineering*, *93*, 1–18. doi:10.1016/j.datak.2014.07.001

Asch, M., & Moore, T. (2018). *Big Data and Extreme-Scale Computing: Pathways to Convergence*. Retrieved from http://www.exascale.org/bdec/sites/www.exascale.org.bdec/files/whitepapers/bdec2017pathways.pdf

Auer, S., Berners-Lee, T., Bizer, C., Capadisli, S., Heath, K., & Lehmann, J. (2017). *Workshop on Linked Data on the Web co-located with 26th International World Wide Web Conference (WWW 2017). CEUR Workshop Proceedings*. CEUR-WS.org.

Baader, F., Calvanese, D., McGuinness, D., Nardi, D., & Patel-Schneider, P. (2003). *The Description Logic Handbook: Theory, Implementation, and Applications*. Cambridge University Press.

Beck, G., Duong, T., Azzag, H., & Lebbah, M. (2016). Distributed mean shift clustering with approximate nearest neighbours. *International Joint Conference on Neural Networks*. 10.1109/IJCNN.2016.7727595

Benbernou, S., Huang, X., Ouziri, M. (2017). Semantic-based and Entity-Resolution Fusion to Enhance Quality of Big RDF Data. *IEEE Transaction on Big Data*.

Benbernou, S., & Ouziri, M. (2017). Enhancing Data Quality by Cleaning Inconsistent Big RDF Data. IEEE Big Data conference, Boston, MA. doi:10.1109/BigData.2017.8257913

BenchSys. (2016). Retrieved from https://www.benchsys.com/

Bentounsi, M. (2015). *Business Process as a Service - BPaaS: Securing Data and Services* (PhD Thesis). Sorbonne Paris Cité - Université Paris Descartes, France.

Bentounsi, M., & Benbernou, S. (2016). Secure complex monitoring event processing. *NCA*, *2016*, 392–395.

Bentounsi, M., Benbernou, S., & Atallah, M. J. (2016). Security-aware Business Process as a Service by hiding provenance. *Computer Standards & Interfaces*, *44*, 220–233. doi:10.1016/j.csi.2015.08.011

Bhattacharya, I., & Getoor, L. (2017). Entity Resolution. Encyclopedia of Machine Learning and Data Mining, 402-408.

Brain Initiative. (n.d.). *What is the Brain Initiative?* Retrieved from https://www.braininitiative.nih.gov/

Bukhari, A. C., Krauthammer, M., & Baker, C. J. O. (2014). Sebi: An architecture for biomedical image discovery, interoperability and reusability based on semantic enrichment. *Proceedings of the 7th International Workshop on Semantic Web Applications and Tools for Life Sciences.*

Cao Huu, Q. (2017). *Policy-based usage control for trustworthy data sharing in smart cities* (PhD Thesis). Telecom & Management Sud, Paris, France.

Cell Ontology. (n.d.). Retrieved from https://bioportal.bioontology.org/ontologies/CL

Cheatham, M., Cruz, I. F., Euzenat, J., & Pesquita, C. (2017). Special issue on ontology and linked data matching. *Semantic Web*, *8*(2), 183–184. doi:10.3233/SW-160251

Chekol, M. W., & Pirrò, G. (2016). Containment of Expressive SPARQL Navigational Queries. *International Semantic Web Conference.*

CUMULUS. (n.d.). Retrieved from https://cumulus.parisdescartes.fr/

DBPedia. (n.d.). Retrieved from http://wiki.dbpedia.org/

Dong, X. L., & Srivastava, D. (2015). *Big Data Integration. Synthesis Lectures on Data Management.* Morgan & Claypool Publishers.

Données publiques. (n.d.). Retrieved from https://donneespubliques.meteofrance.fr/

Duong, T., Beck, G., Azzag, H., & Lebbah, M. (2016). Nearest neighbour estimators of density derivatives, with application to mean shift clustering. *Pattern Recognition Letters*, *80*, 224–230. doi:10.1016/j.patrec.2016.06.021

Eiben, C. B., Siegel, J. B., Bale, J. B., Cooper, S., Khatib, F., Shen, B. W., ... Baker, D. (2012). Increased Diels-Alderase activity through backbone remodeling guided by Foldit players. *Nature Biotechnology*, *30*(2), 190–192. doi:10.1038/nbt.2109 PMID:22267011

Eickhoff, C. (2014). Crowd-Powered Experts: Helping Surgeons Interpret Breast Cancer Images. *ECIR Workshop on Gamification for Information Retrieval.* 10.1145/2594776.2594788

Engle, C., Lupher, A., Xin, R., Zaharia, M., Franklin, M. J., Shenker, S., & Stoica, I. (2012): Shark: fast data analysis using coarse-grained distributed memory. *SIGMOD Conference*, 689-692. 10.1145/2213836.2213934

Firmani, D., Saha, B., & Srivastava, D. (2016). *Online Entity Resolution Using an Oracle.* PVLDB.

Foaf. (n.d.). Retrieved from http://www.foaf-project.org/

Fukunaga, K., & Hostetler, L. (1975). The estimation of the gradient of a density function, with applications in pattern recognition. *IEEE Transactions on Information Theory*, *21*(1), 32–40. doi:10.1109/TIT.1975.1055330

Garcia Seco de Herrera, A., Foncubierta-Rodriguez, A., Markonis, D., Schaer, R., & Müller, H. (2014). Crowdsourcing for medical image classification. *Annual congress SGMI.*

Giovanni, T. (2012). *OpenNebula 3 Cloud Computing*. Packt Publishing Limited.

Grid5000: Home. (2017). Retrieved from https://www.grid5000.fr/mediawiki/index.php/Grid5000:Home

He, Y., Tan, H., Luo, W., Feng, S., & Fan, J. (2014). Mr-dbscan: A scalable mapreduce-based dbscan algorithm for heavily skewed data. *Frontiers of Computer Science*, *8*(1), 83–99. doi:10.100711704-013-3158-3

Heaton, J. (2016). Comparing Dataset Characteristics that Favor the Apriori, Eclat or FP-Growth Frequent Itemset Mining Algorithms. *Proceeding of the IEEE SoutheastCon*, 1-7. 10.1109/SECON.2016.7506659

Howe, B., Franklin, M. J., Haas, L. M., Kraska, T., & Ullman, J. D. (2017). *Data Science Education: We're Missing the Boat, Again*. ICDE.

Indyk, P., & Motwani, R. (1998). Approximate nearest neighbors: Towards removing the curse of dimensionality. *Annual ACM Symposium on Theory of Computing*. 10.1145/276698.276876

Irshad, H., Montaser-Kouhsari, L., Waltz, G., Bucur, O., Nowak, J. A., Dong, F., ... Beck, A. H. (2015). Crowdsourcing image annotation for nucleus detection and segmentation in computational pathology: Evaluating experts, automated methods, and the crowd. *Pacific Symposium on Biocomputing*, 294. PMID:25592590

Kittur, A., Chi, E. H., & Suh, B. (2008). Crowdsourcing user studies with mechanical turk. SIGCHI conference on human factors in computing systems, Florence, Italy. doi:10.1145/1357054.1357127

Krautheim, F. J. (2009). Private Virtual Infrastructure for Cloud Computing. *Proceedings of the 2009 conference on Hot topics in cloud computing HotCloud'09*, Article No. 5.

Kumar, A., Dyer, S., Kim, J., Li, C., Leong, P. H. W., Fulham, M. J., & Feng, D. (2016). Adapting content-based image retrieval techniques for the semantic annotation of medical images. *Computerized Medical Imaging and Graphics*, *49*, 37–45. doi:10.1016/j.compmedimag.2016.01.001 PMID:26890880

Kyung-Hoon, H., Haejun, L., & Duckjoo, C. (2012). *Medical Image Retrieval: Past and Present*. Healthc Inform Research.

Leifman, G., Swedish, T., Roesch, K., & Raskar, R. (2015). *Leveraging the Crowd for Annotation of Retinal Images*. EMBC. doi:10.1109/EMBC.2015.7320185

Lessl, M., Bryans, J. S., Richards, D., & Asadullah, K. (2011). Crowd sourcing in drug discovery. *Nature Reviews. Drug Discovery*, *10*(4), 241–242. doi:10.1038/nrd3412 PMID:21455221

Lloyd, S. P. (1982). Least squares quantization in PCM. *IEEE Transactions on Information Theory*, *28*(2), 129–137. doi:10.1109/TIT.1982.1056489

Luo, J., Wu, M., Gopukumar, D., & Zhao, Y. (2016). Big Data Application in Biomedical Research and Health Care: A Literature Review. *Biomedical Informatics Insights*, *8*, BII.S31559. doi:10.4137/BII.S31559 PMID:26843812

Mao, M., Peng, Y., & Spring, M. (2010). *An adaptive ontology mapping approach with neural network based constraint satisfaction*. J. Web Sem.

Mavandadi, S., Dimitrov, S., Feng, S., Yu, F., Sikora, U., Yaglidere, O., ... Ozcan, A. (2012). Distributed Medical Image Analysis and Diagnosis through Crowd-Sourced Games: A Malaria Case Study. *PLoS One*, *7*(5), e37245. doi:10.1371/journal.pone.0037245 PMID:22606353

Mayhew, A. (2001). File Distribution Efficiencies: cfengine Versus rsync. *Proceedings of the 15th Conference on Systems Administration LISA*, 273-276.

Müller, H., Michoux, N., Bandon, D., & Geissbuhler, A. (2004). A review of content-based image retrieval systems in medical applications. Clinical benefits and future directions. *International Journal of Medical Informatics*, *73*(1), 1–23. doi:10.1016/j.ijmedinf.2003.11.024 PMID:15036075

National Cancer Institute Thesaurus. (n.d.). Retrieved from https://bioportal.bioontology.org/ontologies/NCIT

Nentwig, M., Hartung, M., Ngomo, A. N., & Rahm, E. (2017). A survey of current Link Discovery frameworks. *Semantic Web*.

Nguyen, T. B., Wang, S., Anugu, V., Rose, N., McKenna, M., Petrick, N., ... Summers, R. M. (2012). Distributed human intelligence for colonic polyp classification in computer-aided detection for CT colonography. *Radiology*, *262*(3), 824–833. doi:10.1148/radiol.11110938 PMID:22274839

Qi, H., & Snyder, W. E. (1999). Content-based image retrieval in picture archiving and communications systems. *Journal of Digital Imaging*, *12*(S1), 81–83. doi:10.1007/BF03168763 PMID:10342174

Raddick, M. J., Bracey, G., Gay, L. G., Lintott, C. J., Cardamone, C., Murray, P., Schawinski, K., Szalay, A. S., & Vandenberq, J. (2013). *Galaxy Zoo: Motivations of Citizen Scientists*. Academic Press.

Radiology Lexicon. (n.d.). Retrieved from https://bioportal.bioontology.org/ontologies/RADLEX

Raghupathi, W., & Raghupathi, V. (2014). *Big data analytics in healthcare: promise and potential*. Health Information Science and Systems.

RosettaHub. (n.d.). Retrieved from http://www.rosettahub.com

Samovskiy, D. (2010). *The Rise of DevOps*. Retrieved from http://www.somic.org/2010/03/02/the-rise-of-devops/

Serrano, E., Blas, F.J.G., Carretero, J., & Desco, M. (2017). Medical Imaging Processing on a Big Data platform using Python: Experiences with Heterogeneous and Homogeneous Architectures. *IEEE/ACM CCGRID*, 830-837.

Shvaiko, P., & Euzenat, J. (2013). Ontology Matching: State of the Art and Future Challenges. *IEEE Trans. Knowl. Data Eng*.

Sis4web. (n.d.). Retrieved from http://www.sisncom.com/IMG/pdf/sis4web.pdf

Siemens. (2018). Retrieved from https://www.plm.automation.siemens.com/fr/products/teamcenter/

Silva, L. A., Costa, C., & Oliveira, J. L. (2012). A PACS archive architecture supported on cloud services. *International Journal of Computer Assisted Radiology and Surgery*, *7*(3), 349–358. doi:10.100711548-011-0625-x PMID:21678039

Slaney, M., & Casey, M. (2008). Locality-sensitive hashing for finding nearest neighbors. *IEEE Signal Processing Magazine*, *25*(2), 128–131. doi:10.1109/MSP.2007.914237

Sonntag, D., Wennerberg, P., & Zillner, S. (2010). Applications of an Ontology Engineering Methodology. *AAAI Spring Symposium: Linked Data Meets Artificial Intelligence*.

Stillwell, M., & Coutinho, J. G. F. (2015). A DevOps approach to integration of software components in an EU research project. *Proceedings of the 1st International Workshop on Quality-Aware DevOps*. 10.1145/2804371.2804372

University of Indiana. (n.d.). *Harp Project*. Retrieved from http://salsaproj.indiana.edu/harp/

Verhoosel, J. P. C., Bekkum, M. V., & Evert, F. V. (2015). Ontology matching for big data applications in the smart dairy farming domain. *International Semantic Web Conference*.

W3C. (2004). *World Wide Web Consortium Issues RDF and OWL Recommendations*. Retrieved from https://www.w3.org/2004/01/sws-pressrelease.html.en

Whang, S. E., Marmaros, D., & Garcia-Molina, H. (2013). Pay-as-you-go entity resolution. *IEEE Trans. Knowl. Data Eng*.

Wikipedia. (n.d.). *Bulk synchronous parallel*. Retrieved from https://en.wikipedia.org/wiki/Bulk_synchronous_parallel

Zaharia, M., Xin, R. S., Wendell, P., Das, T., Armbrust, M., Dave, A., ... Stoica, I. (2016). Apache Spark: A unified engine for big data processing. *Communications of the ACM*, *59*(11), 56–65. doi:10.1145/2934664

Zerlang, J. (2017). GDPR: A milestone in convergence for cyber-security and compliance. *Network Security*, *6*(6), 8–11. doi:10.1016/S1353-4858(17)30060-0

ENDNOTES

1 Virtual Network Computing.

2 Secure file transfer protocol.

Chapter 3
A Survey of Parallel Indexing Techniques for Large-Scale Moving Object Databases

Eleazar Leal
University of Minnesota – Duluth, USA

Le Gruenwald
University of Oklahoma, USA

Jianting Zhang
City College of New York, USA

ABSTRACT

A moving object database is a database that tracks the movements of objects. As such, these databases have business intelligence applications in areas like trajectory-based advertising, disease control and prediction, hurricane path prediction, and drunk-driver detection. However, in order to extract knowledge from these objects, it is necessary to efficiently query these databases. To this end, databases incorporate special data structures called indexes. Multiple indexing techniques for moving object databases have been proposed. Nonetheless, indexing large sets of objects poses significant computational challenges. To cope with these challenges, some moving object indexes are designed to work with parallel architectures, such as multicore CPUs and GPUs (graphics processing units), which can execute multiple instructions simultaneously. This chapter discusses business intelligence applications of parallel moving object indexes, identifies issues and features of these techniques, surveys existing parallel indexes, and concludes with possible future research directions.

DOI: 10.4018/978-1-5225-4963-5.ch003

INTRODUCTION

Through the use of location-sensing devices, very large moving object datasets can be collected. These datasets make it possible to issue spatio-temporal queries with which users can gather real-time information about the characteristics of the movements of objects involved in these datasets, derive patterns from that information, and then make decisions based on these patterns. Examples of these large datasets are Geolife (Zheng, Xie, & Ma, 2010) and T-drive (Yuan et al., 2010).

Geolife consists of trajectories (i.e., the time-ordered sequence of positions that an object occupies in time) collected with the use of GPS phones by researchers of Microsoft Research Asia as they went through their daily lives. T-drive contains the GPS logs of the positions occupied by taxis in Beijing. Both datasets are large: Geolife contains 17,000+ trajectories whose lengths add up to 1,200,000+ kilometers, and span an interval of 48,000+ hours. T-drive, on the other hand, contains the trajectories of 10,000+ taxis, whose lengths span 9,000,000 Km. Datasets like these can be used to support decisions in the transportation domain, such as: helping taxis find the fastest routes by mining taxi trajectories (Yuan et al., 2010), finding driving directions, and for urban planning (Wang, Zheng, & Xue, 2014).

Other uses of moving object datasets are the following: in epidemiology, to help centers for disease control and prevention make decisions on how to avoid the spread of the avian influenza, by tracking and studying the movements of mallards (Hill et al., 2017); in meteorology, to help predict the path of a developing hurricane, which can be done by exploiting the tendency of hurricanes to follow similar trajectories, thereby aiding meteorologists issue more accurate recommendations on which areas must be evacuated (Li et al., 2010); in law enforcement, to automatically detect drunk drivers, and then help police departments make decisions on how to better allocate their police force by area (Ge et al., 2010); in trajectory-based mobile advertising (Ammar, Elsayed, Sabri, & Terry, 2015), where shopping malls, by tracking the positions of shoppers using the mall's WiFi, can increase their revenue by sending online advertising that has been tailored to the shoppers based on their movement patterns around the mall (Ghose, 2017); for city planning in places like Shanghai, to help planners decide where to build new bike lanes, while taking into account Shanghai's budget limitations, and the way existing bike lanes are utilized (Bao, He, Ruan, Li, & Zheng, 2017); in online trajectory-sharing applications, to suggest attractive travel destinations based on the trajectories that others have enjoyed (Zheng et al., 2010); and in sports, to deduce the common plays of a given sports team (Buchin, Dodge, & Speckmann, 2014) from video footage, and then help coaches make decisions about their team's next play.

However, in order to obtain these spatio-temporal patterns used for decision making, data must be retrieved from the datasets. The problem is that moving object data have a large volume, come at a high velocity from different sources, and are uncertain. Faced with these challenges, moving object databases use *indexes* that guide the execution of the query by reducing the number of data entries that need to be accessed, thus providing better query performance. Indexes are also in charge of accurately retrieving the moving objects that satisfy the query predicate. Nonetheless, in order to have scalable moving object index algorithms that are able to cope with Big Data, indexes should be designed to be parallel, thereby allowing simultaneous execution of multiple instructions. In this chapter, these indexes that are designed to exploit the characteristics of parallel computer architectures (multicore CPUs, GPUs and MapReduce) are called *parallel moving object indexes*. We now formalize the context in which these indexes work.

The context of parallel moving object indexes is the following: there is a set of moving objects whose physical states (i.e., identifiers and positions, possibly along with other data like their velocities, accelerations, etc.) are continuously updated, but these reports have an associated noise that arises from the sensor devices used to measure the physical states of the objects. At the same time, there may be many users that could be continually submitting queries about the past, present, and future states of these objects. The constraints on the expected execution times for these queries are application dependent. In applications like disease prevention or hurricane path prediction, since the process to collect the data takes a significant time, there are no hard constraints on the execution time. On the other hand, in applications like drunk-driver detection, queries have harder time constraints because there are lives at risk, so these queries should not take more than a few seconds. Faced with such a scenario, indexing techniques should be able to accelerate the processing of these queries, while processing the new movement updates in parallel, and doing so in a scalable and consistent manner.

Most of the work on moving object indexes has focused on serial, instead of parallel, algorithms. For example: (Chakka, Everspaugh, & Patel, 2003), (Ni, & Ravishankar, 2005), (Šaltenis, Jensen, Leutenegger, & Lopez, 2000), (Tao, Papadias, & Sun, 2003), (Jensen, Li, & Ooi, 2004), (Yiu, Tao, Mamoulis, 2008), (Chen, Ooi, Tan, & Nascimiento, 2008), (Pelanis, Šaltenis, & Jensen, 2006), (Fang, Cao, Wang, Peng, & Song, 2012), (Emrich, Kriegel, Mamoulis, Renz, & Züfle, 2012), and (Ranu et al., 2015). There are also some works dedicated to the study of distributed moving object indexes, like (Gedik, & Liu, 2004), (Wang, Zimmermann, & Ku, 2006) and (Yu, Liu, Yu, & Pu, 2015). These distributed moving object indexes, compared with parallel moving object indexes, as we have defined them above, have additional issues like communication costs, partition tolerance, etc. and, despite doing distributed processing of queries on moving objects, do not assume that each individual computing node is running a parallel architecture.

This chapter studies the design dimensions (i.e., characteristics) and research issues (i.e., challenges) associated with parallel indexes for moving object databases. There are other works dedicated to the discussion of research issues of moving object data indexes. Among them we find (Wolfson, Xu, Chamberlain, & Jiang, 1998), which is one of the earliest works that identified some of the issues related to the design of serial indexes for moving objects. Another work in the area is (Güting, & Schneider, 2005), which describes many of the early serial techniques for indexing. The survey work (Hendawi, & Mokbel, 2012) discusses the challenges related to the evaluation of predictive spatio-temporal queries, and presents a succinct survey of indexes to support these queries. We also find the works (Mokbel, Ghanem, & Aref, 2003) and (Nguyen-Dinh, Aref, & Mokbel, 2010), which are short surveys for general moving object indexes up to the year of 2010, a time when still not many parallel spatio-temporal indexes were available. Hence, to the best of our knowledge, there is no survey that focuses on the design dimensions, and the research issues that need to be addressed in order to design moving object indexes that work on parallel architectures such as multicore chips and GPUs; nor is there a survey that presents a more up-to-date discussion of issues for the design of moving object indexes than (Wolfson, Xu, Chamberlain, & Jiang, 1998), that reflects the research done in the area in the last decade. The aim of this chapter is to fill this gap by presenting a discussion of such issues and design dimensions, a taxonomy based on these design dimensions, along with a survey of the known parallel indexes for moving object data and identification of possible future research directions.

The remainder of this chapter is organized as follows. The first section introduces moving object indexes and their applications to business intelligence. Then follows a section containing a discussion of the main issues that arise when designing parallel moving object indexes. Next comes a section that discusses the design dimensions of this type of indexes, and introduces a taxonomy to classify the existing work. The following four sections present the different design dimensions of parallel moving object indexes, and discuss existing techniques in each design dimension. Finally, the last section provides concluding remarks and future research directions.

BACKGROUND

This section discusses moving objects indexes and presents a discussion about their business intelligence applications.

Moving Object Indexes

Location-sensing devices have made it possible to collect large datasets, like Geolife and T-drive, of locations of moving objects. Then, thanks to data analytics techniques, it is possible to extract knowledge from these datasets, and then use this knowledge when making business decisions (Ghose, 2017). Nonetheless, the techniques to extract knowledge from moving object datasets can be expensive both in terms of time and space, and this, added to the fact that location-sensing data will continue to grow, makes this problem of knowledge extraction from moving object datasets quite challenging. Therefore, there is a need for efficiently retrieving data from moving object datasets in order to support the expensive algorithms used in business intelligence.

In database systems, and in particular in moving object databases, it is often the case that queries have result sets that are much smaller than the tables in the database; therefore, these queries do not require a scan through all the data in order to be answered. For example, the query "find all delivery trucks that were within 200m of the shopping mall at 1 p.m." does not concern vehicles that were not close enough to the mall at that time, which we assume were the majority of the trucks. In this query it would be advantageous, from a performance perspective, to only consider as initial candidate set the one composed by those trucks that were within 200m of the mall, instead of just testing that spatio-temporal predicate on every single truck in the dataset. Moving Object Databases take advantage of this fact through the use of special data structures, called *moving object indexes*, that help guide the execution of the query by reducing the number of data entries that need to be explored. By doing this, indexes reduce the number of memory accesses, whose times dominate the total query execution time; thereby providing better query performance.

Now follows an example that makes use of a spatial index called the R-tree, and that illustrates how moving object indexes work. The right-hand side of Figure 1 presents trajectories that are contained within rectangles, while the left-hand side shows an R-tree that indexes the trajectories in the right. To find the closest trajectory to the query trajectory Q, the tree is traversed from top to bottom, starting at the node Rec_1. Since Q intersects only Rec_2, there is no need to check if the trajectories in Rec_3 and Rec_4 are closest to Q, because these rectangles do not intersect Q. This is one example of how spatial indexes can speed up queries: by eliminating from the candidate result set those elements in the dataset that for sure cannot form part of the result set.

Figure 1. Example of a spatial index

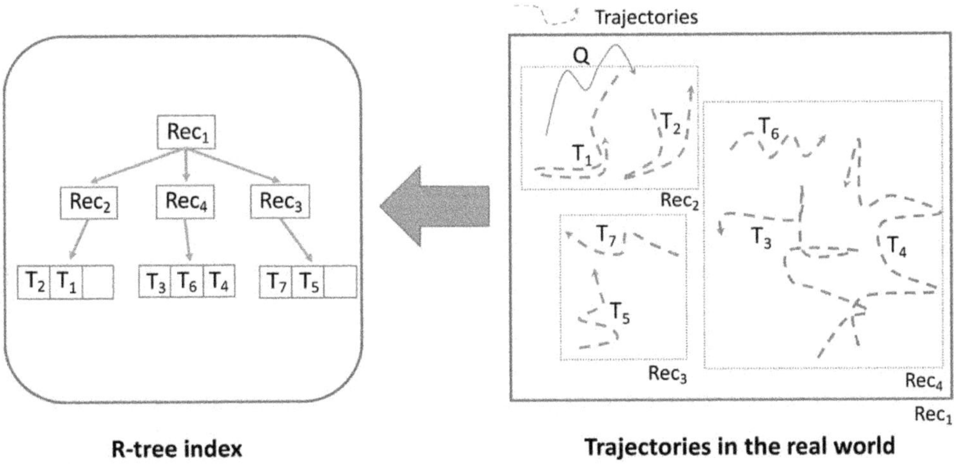

Using Moving Object Indexes for Business Intelligence

This section provides additional details on two applications of moving object indexes and datasets, and highlights the role that these indexes play in supporting business intelligence.

Moving object indexes and datasets can be used for *trajectory-based mobile advertising* where, by using the WiFi services provided to shoppers, malls can keep track of the trajectories (i.e., the sequence of positions that a moving object occupies as time goes by) of consumers as they wander between stores. These trajectories can be used to identify, in real-time, groups of shoppers that move similarly within the mall, and then to instantly send to these people, through their phones' WiFi, targeted advertising that takes into account the stores that consumers have visited, how much time they spent in each shop, the crowdedness in the mall, etc. One way to solve the problem of grouping consumer paths is by doing trajectory clustering (Lee, Han, & Whang, 2007), which consists in forming clusters or groups such that trajectories in each cluster are very similar to each other, but very different from those in other groups. Once these trajectory clusters have been found, malls can deduce that individuals whose trajectories belong to any given group are candidates for being sent similar advertising material. Figure 2 illustrates this application. In this figure it is possible to see that several trajectories, shown with dashed lines, have been grouped into trajectory clusters. These clusters capture the movement patterns of shoppers in a mall.

A second problem that can be tackled with this strategy of trajectory clustering is *real time drunk-driver detection* (Ge et al., 2010). By using traffic cameras, streams of trajectory points can be collected. Then, by finding outliers in these streams, it is possible to find trajectories that deviate from the normal driving behavior, which could correspond to drunk drivers, speeding drivers, or drivers whose cars have malfunctions. This knowledge can then be used by police departments to identify efficient ways of allocating their police forces in a city.

In both these problems there are potentially large amounts of data involved. This is because, in the case of mobile advertising, large malls receive tens of millions of visitors each year, visitors whose movements need to be tracked at a relatively high frequency. In the case of drunk-driver detection, there are also large volumes of data involved because police departments need to install many cameras on the streets, each tracking the movement of every vehicle on those roads. Added to this challenge of the large data volume are two others: first, applications like these require that a decision be made as quickly as possible using the latest data sensed, and second, the moving object mining algorithms on which the solutions to these applications rest can have high computational costs.

In this panorama, there is a need for efficient moving object mining algorithms, which implies that there is also a need for moving object indexes that can efficiently feed data into these algorithms. Moreover, it has been proved that moving object indexes can greatly reduce the time complexity of trajectory clustering algorithms like TRACLUS, where the use of a spatial index brings down the worst-case time complexity from $O(n^2)$ to $O(n\log n)$, where n is approximately the number of points recorded in the dataset (Lee, Han, & Whang, 2007).

Therein lies the importance of moving object indexes: they are an essential algorithmic tool to help moving object mining algorithms, and business intelligence, quickly access the data they need in order to generate knowledge and make decisions.

ISSUES OF PARALLEL MOVING OBJECT INDEXES

The following are the issues that a parallel indexing technique designed to support spatio-temporal queries on moving objects should address:

Measurement Uncertainty

As a consequence of the limitations of the devices (GPS, RFID, Bluetooth, etc.) used to retrieve and communicate the positions and velocities, there is uncertainty about the physical states of the moving objects (Chen, & Lian, 2012). If a moving object index is oblivious to measurement uncertainty, then the moving objects could be indexed with incorrect data, thus leading to incorrect query results. For example, it can be the case that because of a failing battery, the location sensor of an object

Figure 2. Finding trajectory patterns in mall shoppers

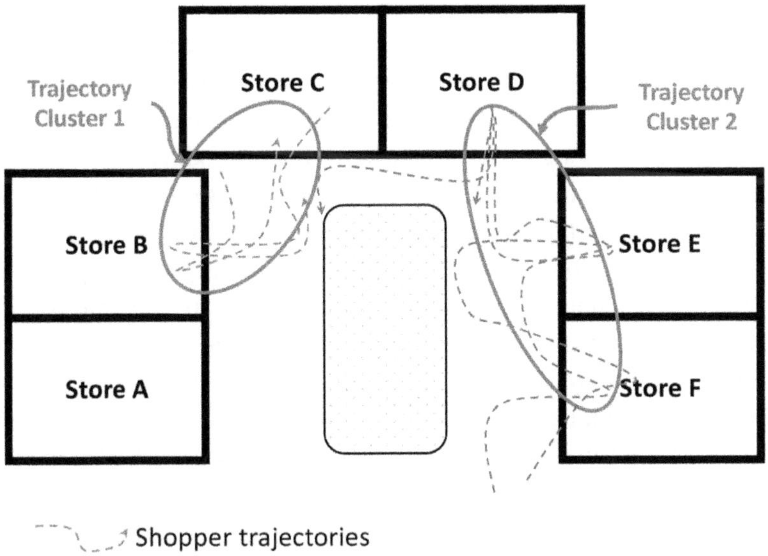

reports incorrect positional data that get stored in an index that is oblivious to data uncertainty. Then, a query such as "find the average speed of taxi number 3," will use the distorted data to produce an incorrect answer.

Works like (Ma, & Lu, 2013), (Emrich, Kriegel, Mamoulis, Renz, & Züfle, 2012a) and (Emrich, Kriegel, Mamoulis, Renz, & Züfle, 2012b) proposed serial algorithms that address the issue of measurement uncertainty in moving object indexes. However, to the extent of our knowledge there does not exist any parallel technique that addresses this issue.

Missing and/or Inconsistent Movement Updates

As objects move through space, they report their physical states to the database. However, it is not possible to guarantee that the position and velocity of a moving object will be known at every instant, nor is it realistic to assume that the updates of a given object will always be emitted at regular intervals. A moving object may, for example, enter a geographical area where it cannot keep emitting periodic updates, or it may temporarily exit the activation range of a Bluetooth base station. Hence, a moving object indexing technique should be able to handle the case when movement updates of any given object are missing, and make adequate position estimates in such cases.

Consistency in a Scenario of Parallel Updates and Queries

Parallel moving object indexes need to concurrently process several updates and queries. Nonetheless, this poses a consistency issue because of two reasons: the first is that multiple updates to the same set of objects *S* may lead to missed writes, and the second is that even though all objects in *S* may have produced updates at the same time, the results of any query may only reflect the updates of a subset of *S*. This is because updates usually take longer to process than queries, so some queries may have seen some updates but not others. This problem has greater significance with parallel indexing techniques since these seek to expose all available parallelism in order to maximize the utilization of the computational resources; therefore, concurrent updates and queries are more likely in these techniques. Faced with such scenario, parallel indexing techniques should address this issue of guaranteeing consistency with multiple parallel updates and queries, while at the same time exploiting all available parallelism.

Load Balancing

Load balancing refers to evenly dividing the computational tasks among computing units in a way that each processor performs a similar amount of work. This issue impacts the performance of indexing because the time spent by the computational unit that receives the most time-consuming subtask dominates the overall cost of the algorithm. This issue has special significance in the context of moving object indexes because the movements of objects tend to be skewed. For example, during the day in New York City, more cars will move around downtown than anywhere else (Ma, Yang, Qian, & Zhou, 2009). To achieve adequate load balancing, the indexing techniques should take advantage of the characteristics of the data to achieve good load balancing (Trajcevski, Yaagoub, & Scheuermann, 2011). Therefore, a parallel indexing technique for moving object indexes should address the load balancing issue.

Computer Architecture and Data Access Pattern

The data access pattern refers to the manner and timing of the accesses to data on memory. For example, a processor can access data elements located consecutively in memory or it can perform random access to memory by following pointer structures; it may also be the case that two separate processors access consecutive elements in a round-robin fashion. Modern computer architectures are equipped with a variety of mechanisms to reduce memory access time, such as caches. The efficiency of these mechanisms relies on the way that data are accessed. So, if data access does not respect temporal and spatial locality, and if data access works against cache coherence mechanisms, then the benefit of caches is mostly discarded. With regard to moving object indexes, ensuring the preservation of temporal and spatial locality of the data accesses depends on the queries that they are designed to support. In the case of indexes designed for efficiently querying trajectories, it is desirable that consecutive segments of the same trajectory are stored in nearby memory addresses. In the case of an index designed to efficiently support range queries, it is desirable that the data concerning moving objects that are close together in space be kept in adjacent memory addresses. Hence, a parallel indexing technique should be aware of the underlying computer architecture and adopt data access patterns that exploit the benefits of such architecture.

Indoor or Outdoor Movement

Indexing indoor trajectories poses different challenges than indexing outdoor trajectories. This is because in an indoor environment, the movement is constrained by furniture, walls, doors, etc., so the moving object may consecutively report two positions such that the line that connects them intersects with a wall, which will be an incorrect approximation to the movement of the object. Therefore, the linear interpolation model, which lies at the very essence of a trajectory, may either fail in indoor spaces (Jensen, Lu, & Yang, 2009) or force the objects to report their movement updates very frequently. Additionally, indoor trajectories are not sampled through GPS but through Bluetooth, RFID, or WIFI devices (Gu, Lo, & Niemegeers, 2009) that do not report the velocity or an exact position of the object. Instead, these devices generate records containing the identifier of the moving object and the period during which the object stayed within the activation range (Jensen et al., 2009) (Yang, Lu, & Jensen, 2010). Therefore, a technique oblivious to the fact that its objects describe indoor trajectories may not be able to work correctly if it requires data that is not readily available, or if it makes the assumption that the movement of the object is not constrained by elements in the environment.

Number of Manually-Tuned Index Parameters

Database indexes sometimes have an associated set of parameters that govern its behavior. For example, most database indexes, such as the B-tree (Bayer, & McCreight, 1970), have as parameter the number of entries that fit within a node.

In general, the index parameters pose a difficulty for the incorporation of the index into a database system because the database administrator may need to periodically and manually tune those parameters to ensure the best performance. This tuning job becomes increasingly difficult as the number of index parameters increases, and even more so if the parameters influence one another.

TAXONOMY OF PARALLEL MOVING OBJECT INDEXES

In the following sections we discuss the design dimensions (i.e., characteristics) concerning the design of parallel moving object indexes, and then use these design dimensions to categorize existing work. These design dimensions are the targeted computer architecture, the types of queries supported, the temporal nature of the queries, the assumptions for load balancing, and the possibility of stale query results. Figure 3 depicts this chapter's proposed taxonomy.

Targeted Computer Architecture

The targeted computer architecture refers to the programming models for which the index is specifically designed. We classify existing parallel moving object indexes based on the targeted computer architectures as follows:

Figure 3. Classification of parallel moving object indexes

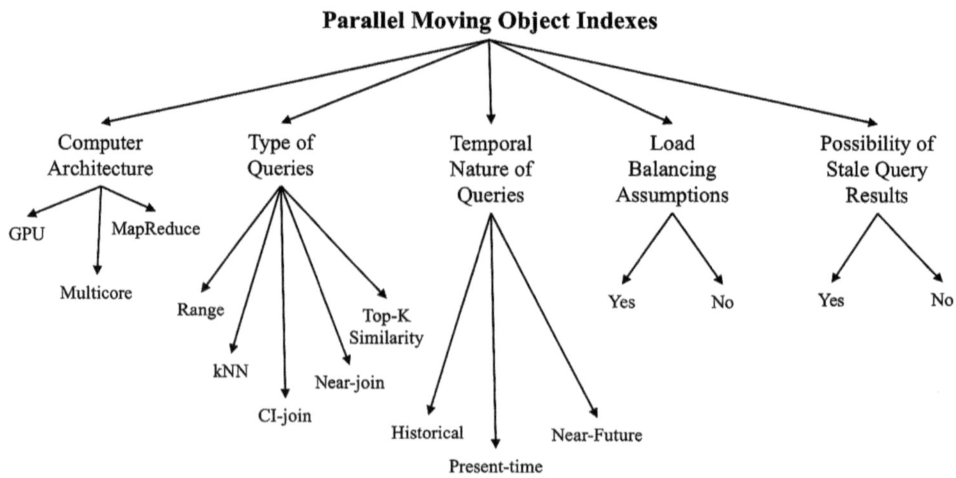

- **Multicore:** This model assumes that there is a given number of latency-oriented processors that have shared access to main memory and collaborate to accomplish a common task. Examples of techniques designed for multicore processors are MPB-tree (He, Kraak, Huisman, Ma, & Xiao, 2013), Sim-tree (Xu, & Tan, 2014), TwinGrid (Šidlauskas, Ross, Jensen, & Šaltenis, 2011), PGrid (Šidlauskas, Šaltenis, & Jensen, 2012), Toss-it (Akdogan, Shahabi, & Demiryurek, 2014), and MOVIES (Dittrich, Blunschi, & Vaz Salles, 2009).
- **GPU:** This model assumes that there is a GPU composed of a given number of throughput-oriented streaming processors designed to exploit hardware multithreading and vector-like instructions (Garland, & Kirk, 2010). GPU devices have several advantages: they are relatively inexpensive; on tasks that offer sufficient parallelism, they perform up to an order of magnitude better than a multicore chip (Lee et al., 2010); and they are already available in many desktops and workstations. These benefits, combined with the fact that moving object indexing offers ample parallelism opportunities, make GPUs another important architectural target for the design of these indexes. There are, however several issues concerning GPUs. First, GPUs have a relatively small global memory, so algorithms should be space efficient. Second, global memory access should be coalesced by having threads with consecutive indexes access adjacent memory locations. Third, due to the low throughput of the PCIe bus, indexes should avoid unnecessary communications from the host computer to the GPU. Examples of techniques designed for GPUs are U^2STRA (Zhang, You, & Gruenwald, 2012), GPUTemporal (Gowanlock, & Casanova, 2014), R2GridGPU (Silvestri, Lettich, Orlando, & Jensen, 2014) and MLG-join index (Ward, He, Zhang, & Qi, 2014).
- **MapReduce:** This model assumes that there is a cluster of machines with a shared and redundant file system. Data are partitioned in different files that can be processed in parallel by applying a mapping function. Later these results are sorted and reduced into a single value (Dean, & Ghemawat, 2004). Examples of techniques designed for MapReduce are CloST (Tan, Luo, & Ni, 2012) and Pradase (Ma, Yang, Qian, & Zhou, 2009).

Types of Queries

In this section we present several spatio-temporal queries following the work of (Pfoser, Jensen, & Theodoridis, 2000), which classifies these into coordinate-based and trajectory-based queries. The main difference between these two kinds of query categories is that coordinate-based queries do not require the full knowledge of the path that a moving object has taken in order to be answered, while trajectory-based queries do.

Coordinate-Based Queries

Among the most common coordinate-based queries are the following:

- *Range or Window query*. Given the spatial region defined by the rectangle R with the bottom-left corner $[l_x, r_x]$ and upper-right corner $[b_y, t_y]$, and a time interval $[t_1, t_2]$, find all objects in the database that are located within the region R during the period $[t_1, t_2]$. An example of this type of query is "find all the New York taxis located in the region between 5th and 7th avenues, and between 29th and 34th streets from 3pm to 4pm."
- *K-nearest-neighbor query*. Given a moving object o and a time interval $[t_1, t_2]$ find the K other objects that are located closest to o during the interval $[t_1, t_2]$. An example of this query is "find four of my friends that are located closest to me between 2pm and 5pm."
- *Spatio-temporal join* (Sun, Tao, Papadias, & Kollios, 2006). Given two sets of moving objects A and B, a tolerance distance $d > 0$, and a time interval $[t_1, t_2]$, find all the object pairs (o_A, o_B) in $A \times B$ such that the distance between o_A and o_B is less than d during the interval $[t_1, t_2]$. An example of this type of query is "find all the container ships in Newark Bay that will be within 100 meters of a whale in the next 5 minutes."
- *Continuous-intersection join* (CI-join) (Zhang, Lin, Ramamohanarao, & Bertino, 2008). Given two sets of moving objects A and B, find the pairs (o_A, o_B) in $A \times B$ such that the extents of o_A and o_B intersect at some point in $[t_q, \infty)$, where t_q is the time where the query is issued. An example of this type of query is "find all whale pods feeding on krill swarms in the next 30 minutes."

Trajectory-Based Queries

Trajectory-based queries are those that in order to be processed require the whole trajectory. Among the most common types of similarity queries there are:

- **Near-Join Similarity Query (Gowanlock, & Casanova, 2014):** Given two sets P and Q of trajectories, a real number $\varepsilon > 0$, find for every trajectory $p \in P$ a trajectory $q \in Q$ that is most similar to p, such that the similarity between p and q is not smaller than ε. For example "find the bird species whose migration patterns have a similarity not greater than 1.25 with that of the ruby-throated hummingbird."
- **Top-K Similarity Query (Ding, Trajcevski, & Sheuermann, 2008):** Given a set S of moving object trajectories, a similarity measure $\sigma : S \times S \rightarrow \mathbb{R}$, a set of query trajectories $P \subseteq S$ (the query set), a set of trajectories $Q \subseteq S$

(the database), and a positive integer K, retrieve for every trajectory $p \in P$ the set $S_p \subseteq Q$ such that $|S_p|=K$, and for every $q \in S_p$ and $q_{other} \in Q-S_p$ it is the case that $\sigma(q_{other},p) \leq \sigma(q,p)$. For example, "find two other bird species whose migration patterns are the most similar to that of the ruby-throated hummingbird."

Temporal Nature of the Supported Queries

The temporal nature of a query refers to whether we wish to obtain the status of a moving object in the past, present, or future. Therefore, we classify the existing parallel moving object indexes based on the temporal nature of the queries they support as follows:

- *Historical query.* A moving object query is historical if it finds out where the objects were in the past. This class of queries has applications in finding out patterns in the movement of animals (Güting, Behr, & Xu, 2010), vehicles, etc. Because of this query's nature, techniques supporting this type of query must store all the previous locations of each object. In the case where the queries are historical and concern trajectories, the past locations of an object may need to be stored consecutively in memory to maximize the performance of the caches. If the historical queries supported do not involve trajectories, then techniques could choose to place the objects in memory in such a way so as to respect the spatial proximity of their locations. Pradase, MOIST, CloST, U^2STRA, MPB-tree and GPUTemporal are examples of techniques supporting historical queries.
- *Present-time query.* A moving object query is present-time if it seeks to find out where the objects are at the time of the query. This class of queries is essential in applications such as airplane surveillance, emergency services, car tracking (Jensen, & Pakalnis, 2007), etc. Since this type of query requires only one location for each object, then indexes should store objects in memory such that spatially close objects are close in memory. MOVIES, Pradase, TwinGrid, PGrid, MOIST, CloST, MPB-tree, ToSS-it, R2GridGPU and SimTree are examples of techniques that support present-time queries.
- *Predictive query.* A moving object query is predictive if it seeks to find out where the moving objects will be in the near future. This class of queries is essential in applications such as airplane surveillance, emergency services, car tracking, etc.

Assumptions for Load Balancing

Load balancing refers to whether every processor is assigned the same amount of work. Some techniques, like R2GridGPU, only ensure load balancing if the input data is uniformly distributed. Other techniques, like Toss-it, ensure load balancing without making any assumptions on the distribution of the data.

Possibility of Stale Query Results

A query result is *stale* if it does not reflect the last-known location of every object. Some techniques, like PGrid, do not allow stale query results, but need expensive serialization steps to ensure that the indexes used to report the query results are always up-to-date. On the other hand, indexes like MOVIES allow stale query results to maximize the availability of the index.

Impact of the Design Dimensions on Parallel Moving Object Indexing Techniques

Table 1 presents a comparison of the surveyed moving object indexing techniques in terms of their features (i.e., the challenges they address and their design dimensions). This table marks for each technique its respective design dimensions along with the issues it addresses. For example, R2GridGPU (Silvestri et al., 2014) is a GPU technique that supports both range and kNN present-time queries, makes assumptions in order to ensure load balancing, may produce stale query results, is for outdoor moving objects, does not address the issue of uncertainty, and does not support compression. Regarding the issue of stale query results, the techniques U^{2}STRA, GPUTemporal, and TKSimGPU are checkmarked to denote that they address this isssue. However, these are techniques designed for processing historical queries and they assume that all the data is already available in memory. Therefore, queries results cannot be stale, not by explicitly making provisions to address the issue, but by the very definition of historical queries.

In Table 1 we observe that none of the parallel techniques surveyed addresses any of the issues of uncertainty, or support for indoor movement. We have left the columns corresponding to these features/issues empty in order to stress this point, and to also emphasize that these are avenues for possible future research.

We now justify our taxonomy by giving examples of how the design dimensions can impact parallel moving object indexing techniques:

- **Impact of the Targeted Computer Architecture:** The targeted computer architecture/model greatly impacts the underlying technique. For example, a GPU moving object index must efficiently use the very limited global memory of the device, as opposed to a multicore or a MapReduce index, where this issue is of a slightly lesser concern because of the larger memory space of these models. Another example is that MapReduce indexes, by their own nature, are structured in terms of a map and a reduce stages, which is not necessarily the case of GPU or multicore indexes. Programming models like MapReduce are primarily designed for batch processing instead of real-time processing. This means that MapReduce indexes receive as input a set of spatial queries, and then process these queries with no hard time constraints. However, in some applications, like real-time drunk-driver detection, there are stricter time constraints because lives are at stake. In these cases, indexes that can handle real-time queries are preferred, which usually implies that the index must be for a model other than MapReduce.
- **Impact of the Type of Queries Supported:** This impacts the design of parallel moving object indexes because it determines the nature of the query processing algorithm and the type of data that needs to be stored and retrieved. For example, near-join similarity queries require finding trajectories with a similarity at least greater than a certain value, and the algorithm to process this query is completely different than that to process a CI-join algorithm.
- **Impact of the Temporal Nature of the Queries:** The temporal nature of the queries has an impact on how much data the index must store. This is because, for example, historical queries need to store a large portion of the past states of the moving objects, while present-time queries need to store only the most recent positions.
- **Impact of the Assumptions for Load Balancing:** By making additional assumptions about the distribution of the objects, the algorithm can be made simpler while at the same time ensuring load balancing. For example, a technique that assumes that objects are uniformly distributed in space may, for example, assign a processor to process the objects contained in each cell in a grid (e.g. R2GridGPU). However, if the distribution is not uniform, the computational load will be unbalanced.
- **Impact of the Possibility of Stale Query Results:** This impacts parallel moving object indexes because in order to avoid stale query results, indexes must answer queries using the last-known information about the moving objects, and for this, parallel indexes may need to ensure correct synchronization between different processors.

Table 1. Feature comparison of the surveyed parallel moving object indexing techniques

	Architect.			Query Type					Temp. Dim. Query			Assumptions for Load Balancing		No Stale Query Results	Indoor/ Outdoor		Uncertainty	Compression Support
	GPU	Multicore	MapReduce	Range	kNN	CI-join	Near-join	Top-K	Historical	Present-time	Near-future	No	Yes		Indoor	Outdoor		
MOVIES		✓		✓	✓					✓			✓			✓		✓
PRADASE			✓	✓	✓					✓			✓			✓		
TwinGrid		✓		✓	✓					✓			✓			✓		
PGrid		✓		✓	✓					✓			✓	✓		✓		
CloST			✓	✓	✓					✓			✓			✓		✓
U²STRA	✓						✓		✓				✓	✓		✓		
MPB-tree		✓		✓	✓					✓			✓			✓		
ToSS-it			✓	✓	✓					✓		✓				✓		
R2GridGPU	✓			✓	✓					✓			✓			✓		
MLG-join	✓					✓				✓			✓			✓		
Sim-tree		✓		✓	✓					✓			✓			✓		
GPUTemporal	✓						✓		✓				✓	✓		✓		
TKSimGPU	✓							✓	✓				✓	✓		✓		

TARGETED COMPUTER ARCHITECTURE DIMENSION

In this section we discuss techniques based on the computer architecture that they target. These architectures can be GPUs, multicore CPUs and MapReduce.

Multicore

This section presents moving object indexes designed for multicore architectures. Examples of techniques in this category are the MPB-tree (He et al., 2013) and the Sim-tree (Xu, & Tan, 2014).

The key idea of MPB-tree consists in decomposing the moving object data, which lives in d-dimensional time-space, into its projections over each of the d dimensions of the time-space. Each dimension is indexed separately using special binary trees. These d dimensions can then be searched independently and in parallel using different CPU threads. For example, to process a two-dimensional query window with the bottom-left corner having coordinates (l,b), and the top-right corner with coordinates (r,t), the window is split into 2 intervals: the one in the x axis is $[l,r]$, and the one in the y axis is $[b,t]$. These two intervals are then searched independently and in parallel, producing two separate candidate sets. Then the algorithm proceeds to intersect these two sets, so that it can find the objects that were located exactly inside the window during time t_q.

Another example of a moving object index for multicore architectures is Sim-tree, which is designed to support traffic simulations on road networks. Its key idea consists in using the average number of objects per unit of area to build a nearly-balanced binary tree whose leaves contain the moving objects. Each step of the simulation consists of an initial stage where the range queries of all objects are processed, and a second stage that cannot start until all objects have finished their initial stage for that simulation step; during this second stage all objects send their movement updates. This means that Sim-tree has the disadvantage that updates and queries are not processed concurrently. Moreover, Sim-tree only parallelizes range queries by assigning separate threads to separate queries.

Both the MPB-tree and the Sim-tree make special assumptions about the distribution of moving objects in order to guarantee load balancing. MPB-tree assumes that the objects follow a uniform distribution, while Sim-tree assumes that the density of objects is constant at each step.

GPU

In this section we will discuss techniques for indexing moving objects on GPUs. R2GridGPU (Silvestri et al., 2014) and MLG-join index (Ward et al., 2014) are examples of techniques in this category.

R2GridGPU's fundamental idea consists in dividing the time domain into equal-length periods, called ticks, and then batch processing all the queries and movement updates that take place within each of these ticks. The purpose of this is to accumulate the tasks that need to be performed, and then submit this set of tasks to the GPU. By doing this, the GPU can better utilize its simultaneous multi-threading-focused design. To help ensure that the computational load can be distributed among the processing units, this technique relies on a uniform grid of cells that is rebuilt at the start of the processing stage of each tick. Each object is then assigned to the unique grid cell that contains them, and every window query is assigned to the grid cell that contains its lower left corner.

To process a set U of updates and a set Q of queries, both corresponding to the same tick, R2GridGPU does as follows. A regular grid is placed over the MBRs of all objects and updates. After this, it builds for each cell c a corresponding two-dimensional array B^c (called a bitmap) that satisfies $B^c[o][q]=1$ if and only if object o's last location belongs to c, query q's primary cell is c, and o belongs to the query result set of q. To calculate these bitmaps B^c, a single GPU thread block is assigned to every c. Each GPU thread T_i within a GPU thread block B_i is in charge of a query q that has c_i as primary cell. T_i tests for all objects o in c_i whether o belongs to q or not.

The MLG-join index computes CI-joins between two sets of objects A and B on GPUs. Its key idea consists in placing the objects in A in an array, and then partitioning that array into multiple consecutive chunks of objects (partitions). Then each of these partitions is independently indexed by a uniform grid, called *layer*. This allows threads with consecutive thread indexes to access objects located in adjacent memory locations, which is an efficient memory access pattern for GPUs.

To build the index, this technique takes as inputs two arrays of objects A and B, and such that every entry of the arrays contains the state of an object. Then the array corresponding to A is partitioned into n consecutive equi-sized subarrays (partitions) $A_1, A_2 \ldots, A_n$. Each thread block is assigned a partition A_i to work on, so that cell c of the layer corresponding to A_i has value 1 if there exists an object in A_i whose extent intersects with c. To this end, threads with consecutive indexes access consecutive object data.

To process a CI-join, this technique first builds the index. After this, the algorithm constructs a matrix M with $|B|$ rows and n columns satisfying that $M[b][i]=1$ if the extent of object b intersects with the extent of some object in partition i during the interval $[t,t+\Delta]$, where $\Delta>0$ is a user-defined parameter. To construct this matrix, a thread is assigned to each $b\in B$ and these threads read the data associated with the movement of b. Again, threads with consecutive indexes access consecutive elements of B in the array. Finally, during the intersection step every thread block tests, for every object a in its corresponding partition A_i, whether the extent of a intersects with the extents of those objects $b\in B$ such that $M[b][i]=1$ at some point during the interval $[t,t+\Delta]$.

TKSimGPU (Leal, Gruenwald, Zhang, & You, 2015) is a top-K trajectory similarity query processing algorithm for GPUs. Its key idea consists in estimating a parameter ε of a near-join similarity query, and then performing successive near-join similarity queries with increasingly larger ε until every trajectory has at least K most similar trajectories. All this is done, while ensuring efficient memory accesses by storing the points of trajectories consecutively in memory.

R2GridGPU, MLG-join index and TKSimGPU exploit the issue of global memory coalescing on GPUs by having threads with consecutive indexes access consecutive memory locations. However, the issue of the limited size of GPUs is not addressed by either technique because if the input datasets are larger than the limited memory space, then they cannot be processed on the GPU.

MapReduce

An example of a technique designed for MapReduce (Dean, & Ghemawat, 2004) is PRADASE (Ma et al., 2009), designed to answer trajectory and range queries. This technique keeps two data structures: the partition-based multilevel index (PMI), to answer range queries, and the object inverted index (OII), to answer trajectory queries.

To create the PMI, during the map phase, the space is recursively partitioned just like with quadtrees (Samet, 1984). Then, each trajectory segment s is split into multiple trajectory segments $s_1,s_2,\ldots$ to ensure that each of the s_i is wholly contained inside a single grid cell (Chakka, Everspaugh, & Patel, 2003). The computing nodes then generate pairs of the form (*pid,seg*), where *pid* is the grid cell identifier, and *seg* is the segment. During the reduce phase, each reduce node receives a pair $(pid,\{s\})$, where $\{s\}$ denotes the set of all indexed trajectory segments that are wholly contained inside the grid cell with identifier *pid*. The set of pairs $\{(pid,\{s\})\}$ constitutes the PMI index. PRADASE creates the OII as follows. During the map phase, the compute nodes generate pairs of the form (*oid,seg*), with the same meaning as above. Then, during the reduce phase, each object with identifier *oid* has a single pair of the form $(oid, \{s\})$. After this, PRADASE builds a hash index that maps *oid* to its corresponding trajectory segments.

To answer range queries, during the map phase, each computing node *n* is assigned a grid cell *c* of the PMI. Then, node *n* checks if the grid cell c_i intersects with the window *W*, and if it does, it uses the PMI to generate a set of pairs of the form $(oid, segments(oid, c_i))$, where *oid* is the object identifier and $segments(oid, c_i)$ denotes the trajectory segments described by the object with identifier *oid* that lie completely inside the grid cell c_i. During the reduce phase, each reduce node receives tuples of the form $(oid, \cup_{c_i \in grid} segments(oid, c_i))$, where $\cup_{c_i \in grid} segments(oid, c_i)$ denotes the set of all segments corresponding to the object with identifier *oid* that lie inside the query window.

Another example of a moving object index for MapReduce is CloST (Tan, Luo, & Ni, 2012), which is a technique to answer spatio-temporal range queries. Its key idea consists in using a mixed hierarchical partitioning that combines temporal and spatial criteria to divide the data into chunks that can later be exploited to process queries in parallel.

TEMPORAL NATURE OF SUPPORTED QUERIES DIMENSION

In this section we discuss different parallel moving object indexes based on the temporal nature of the queries that they support. The temporal nature of the supported queries can be either historical queries, present-time queries, or predictive queries, depending on whether they seek to find the location of a moving object in the past, in the present or in the future, respectively. We categorize parallel moving object indexes, according to the temporal nature of the queries supported, into three groups described in the following sections.

Historical Queries

This section presents techniques designed to support historical queries, i.e., queries that retrieve the past locations of objects. U^2STRA (Zhang, You, & Gruenwald, 2012) and GPUTemporal (Gowanlock, & Casanova, 2014) are two examples of techniques in this category.

The U²STRA index was proposed to process trajectory similarity queries on GPUs. Its key ideas consist in adapting the filter-and-refine strategy (Jacox, & Samet, 2007) for the case of trajectory data, and then arranging trajectory data in contiguous locations in memory, so that accesses to the GPU's global memory can be easily coalesced.

To store trajectories, U²STRA uses two arrays: the trajectory index array (TRI) and the array of points. Points in a trajectory are stored consecutively in memory such that the ith entry in TRI is the index of the first point (in the array of points) of the ith trajectory.

To process a near-join trajectory similarity query, U²STRA places a uniform grid on the space of the trajectories. Then, this technique associates with every trajectory p in P its ε-expanded minimum bounding rectangle (eMBR), where ε is the range parameter of the near-join similarity query. An ε-expanded eMBR is an MBR that has been expanded by ε in all directions. The idea behind this is that if the eMBR of a trajectory p does not intersect with the MBR of another trajectory q, then the distance between p and q is greater than ε. U²STRA then generates candidate trajectory pairs (p,q) if the eMBR of p and the MBR of q both intersect the same grid cell. During the refine phase, every thread block b is in charge of finding the Hausdorff distance between a pair (p,q) of trajectories.

GPUTemporal (Gowanlock, & Casanova, 2014) is another historical query index for answering near-join similarity queries. This index works using CPUs and GPUs. Its key idea consists in partitioning trajectories into disjoint sub-trajectories, then dividing the temporal dimension into uniformly-sized bins, and then placing the segments that make up the trajectories of the database into these bins. Every segment will belong to exactly one bin. The advantage of this index is that, to answer near-join similarity queries, if a trajectory segment s does not intersect with bin b, then there is no need to compare trajectory segment s against the trajectory segments in b, thus pruning away all segments in b.

GPUTemporal has the disadvantage that it uses a single CPU thread to perform certain critical tasks within the construction of the index and the processing of queries, and this, according to Amdahl's law, can limit the speedup attained by this GPU algorithm when compared against a serial algorithm.

Present-Time Queries

This section discusses techniques that support present-time queries, i.e., queries that find the current positions of objects. MOVIES (Dittrich et al., 2009) (Dittrich et al., 2011) is an example of an algorithm in this category.

MOVIES uses the *snapshot idea*, consisting in servicing updates and queries at time i with two separate indexes. Both indexes consist of two elements: an update buffer U_i and an index I_i, to serve queries. Then, to ensure consistency, it periodically suspends updates and copies the update buffer onto the index. The update buffer contains for each object a tuple with the object identifier, the position and velocity of its last update. The index, on the other hand, consists of entries with the structure (*zCode*,*v*,*oid*), where *zCode* is the location code that indicates in which cell the object is located, *v* is the velocity vector and *oid* is the object identifier.

To process range queries, MOVIES receives the window and the time parameter. Then it finds the corresponding z-order values (following the Z-curve that was imposed over the space domain) for the cells that contain *A* and *B*, which we call z_{low} and z_{high}, respectively. Then it performs a search with z_{low} over the *zCode* field of the index to locate the first object *o* such that $o.zCode \geq z_{low}$. Once *o* is found, the algorithm linearly scans forward over the index table testing if each object it finds belongs to the window range defined by *A* and *B*, until it finds the first object *o'* such that $o'.zCode > z_{high}$.

MOVIES takes advantage of shared-memory processing by dedicating some threads to query processing, one to update processing, and others to prepare the indexes at each time frame *i*. Since query processing is done on the update buffers, and update processing is done on the indexes, no contention arises for the same data, so there are no locks necessary for parallel update and query processing. Regarding parallel preparation of the indexes, this is done by partitioning both the indexes and the update buffers into equally-sized domains or partitions (to ensure load balancing) such that, at time frame T_i, multiple threads can work on separate data by copying the updates of its own partition from U_i to I_{i+1}.

Two disadvantages of MOVIES are: first, that during the periods when the update buffer is copied to the index, it is not available to process any other queries, and second, that it its query results can be stale, i.e., they may not reflect the true location of the object at the time of the query.

Predictive Queries

To the extent of our knowledge, there do not exist parallel moving object indexes for predicting the future locations of objects.

ASSUMPTIONS TO ENSURE LOAD BALANCING

This section presents techniques based on the assumptions that they make in order to ensure load balancing. To this end, some techniques assume that the spatial distribution of the objects is uniform, while others do not assume anything about the distribution of the objects.

Make Assumptions to Ensure Load Balancing

R2GridGPU (Silvestri et al., 2014) achieves load balancing when answering range queries by placing a uniform grid in the space where objects move, and then assigning a processing unit (GPU thread block in this case) to process each cell *c*. Then, each processing unit checks if the objects intersecting cell *c* are contained in each of the range queries intersecting *c*. The disadvantage of this approach is that it only works if the moving objects are distributed uniformly in space, an assumption that may not always hold (Ma et al., 2009).

No Assumptions to Ensure Load Balancing

Parallel moving object indexes in this category guarantee load balancing under all kinds of distributions. An example technique in this category is ToSS-it (Akdogan et al., 2014), which is a multicore index that to answer present-time queries. Its key idea consists in periodically re-building from scratch an index structure composed of a hierarchy of Voronoi diagrams, and combining this with strategies to ensure load balancing under all distributions, and to minimize the communication overhead between different processors.

The key idea behind ToSS-it is to first select a set of objects, called *pivots*, such that $pivots = \arg\max_{P_i}\left(\sum_{o,o' \in P_i} dist(o,o')\right)$. Then, it partitions, in parallel, the set of objects O into equally-sized subsets (partitions), O_i, by different subsets to different processors. Each O_i has a pivot object p_i, and all objects in O_i satisfy that they are closest to O_i's pivot than to other pivots.

To answer a range query q, one of the computational nodes of ToSS-it, called N_{init}, receives the query parameters. This node then finds the node N_q whose associated partition contains p, and then N_{init} forwards the query to N_q.

STALE QUERY RESULTS DIMENSION

In this section we discuss techniques based on whether their query results could have stale data. We classify techniques into those that allow stale query results, and those that do not.

Stale Query Results Allowed

This section presents techniques that may return stale query results. An example of these techniques is TwinGrid (Šidlauskas et al., 2009) (Šidlauskas et al., 2011).

TwinGrid is a moving object index for present-time queries. This technique uses multiple threads of execution to process movement updates and queries in parallel. TwinGrid follows the *snapshot idea* (Dittrich et al., 2009) consisting in servicing updates with the writer-store, and queries with the reader-store.

TwinGrid statically partitions the space into uniform cells. Each cell has an associated list of buckets. Each bucket is composed of adjacent entries, which ensures data locality when processing range queries because objects that are near each other in space are more likely to be loaded into the same cache line. Each entry has the format (oid,x,y) where oid is the identifier of the object and x and y are its coordinates. Additionally, TwinGrid has a dictionary (secondary index) that, given the identifier of an object, returns the bucket and the grid cell where the object is located. The reason for this is to efficiently support updates: once an object reports an update it can be determined in constant time whether the new update is located in the same cell, and then, the entry of the object is found to make modifications.

To deal with concurrent updates to the writer-store, each time a worker thread updates an object o to position A_{new} it first needs to fetch the old position A_{old} of o using the secondary index. Then it checks whether A_{new} belongs to the same cell as A_{old}. If it does (i.e, the update is *local*), the thread acquires a lock on o in the secondary index to avoid other conflicting updates to o from other threads. Then the thread updates the bucket entry for o. If the update is not local, the thread needs to try to acquire a lock on the cells $cell(A_{old})$ and $cell(A_{new})$ (the order of lock acquisition is fixed among all threads to avoid deadlock). The purpose of this is to avoid missing writes to the lists of buckets associated to both cells in the case when two threads perform non-local updates to the same cells. Once the thread locks $cell(A_{old})$ and $cell(A_{new})$, it tries to acquire the lock on o in order to remove the old entry for o from the buckets of $cell(A_{old})$ and insert the new entry in the list of buckets for $cell(A_{new})$.

To process range queries, the reader-store is used. First, it finds all the cells that are completely contained within the window, and then adds all the entries associated with the bucket lists of these cells to the result set. After doing this, it finds all the cells that partially overlap (but are not wholly contained) with the window and explores all the object entries associated with these cells one by one, testing them against the query predicate to decide whether they will form part of the result set or not.

Stale Query Results Not Allowed

This section presents techniques that do not allow stale query results. An example of such techniques is PGrid (Šidlauskas et al., 2012), which is designed to answer present queries. Just like TwinGrid, it processes movement updates and queries on multicore CPUs. Unlike TwinGrid, PGrid keeps only a single version of the spatial grid and avoids the need to copy from the writer-store to the read-store, which impacts database availability and is responsible for wasted CPU cycles when copying objects that did not change their positions. Now, since queries and updates are performed concurrently over the same reader/writer-store, it can be the case that while a query is in the process of execution there are objects within the query region that are being updated. Hence, to ensure a well-defined behavior, PGrid introduces *freshness semantics* which guarantees that all the updates to moving objects that occurred before the time at which the query began processing will be reflected in the query result, and that for those objects whose last updates occurred during the execution of the query either their last updates or their second-to-last updates will be reflected in the result.

This technique uses almost identical structures as those of TwinGrid. The grid is also uniform and statically partitioned, and each cell points to a list of buckets containing the objects located within that cell, such that the first bucket of each cell is not full, just as it does in TwinGrid in order to ensure that updates do not need to scan through the whole list of buckets of a cell. Each entry in the bucket has the structure *(oid,x,y,tu)*, where *oid* is the identifier of the object, *x* and *y* are its coordinates and *tu* is the update timestamp. The secondary index consists of a dictionary indexed by object identifiers. Each entry in the secondary index has the structure *(oid,cell,bckt,idx,ldCell,ldBckt,ldIdx,lock)*, where *oid* corresponds to the identifier of the object, *cell* is a pointer to the cell within the grid, *bckt* is the pointer to the bucket, *idx* is the offset within the bucket of the entry that corresponds to the object, *ldCell* is the logically deleted cell, *ldBckt* is the logically deleted pointer to the bucket and offsets, and *lock* is the associated lock. The purpose of these logically deleted entries is to store the second-to-last updates, which are necessary in order to guarantee freshness semantics.

To perform an update to a moving object *o*, PGrid (just like TwinGrid) acquires a lock for the object to avoid missing writes with other updater threads. After this it uses the secondary index to find the cell and bucket entries associated with *o*. Once this is done, it verifies whether there are any logical deletions performed on *o*. Then it verifies if the update to *o* is local (the new position falls in the same cell as the previous one); if it is, it just modifies the entry for *o* with the new data; otherwise, it inserts the new position of *o* into the new cell and then performs a logical deletion of the old entry. To perform this insertion, the updater thread needs to acquire a lock on the new cell to avoid that other threads modify the list of buckets and leave it in an inconsistent state. Then it writes the object in the first block and frees the cell lock. PGrid processes range queries like TwinGrid.

CONCLUSION AND FUTURE RESEARCH DIRECTIONS

This work identified design dimensions and research issues concerning parallel moving object indexes, and surveyed existing techniques in this area. As shown in Table 1, none of the surveyed parallel techniques addresses all the issues. In particular, none of them is a parallel indexing technique that supports queries with uncertain data, and none of them is a parallel indexing technique supporting indoor movement. Hence, developing an indexing technique that addresses these issues would be another important research avenue. The idea of such technique would be to cope with volume and velocity of Big Data by exploiting parallelism, and to cope with veracity by considering probabilistic models to quantify uncertainty.

From Table 1 we can see that among the surveyed techniques, only MoVIES (Dittrich et al., 2009) and CloST (Tan et al., 2012) are designed to support data compression. We believe that this issue deserves to be addressed by future techniques because of two reasons. The first one is that in the context of Big Data there is a very high volume of data that needs to be shared. In this scenario, compression algorithms can help reduce communication costs. The second reason is that the memory space is usually much smaller than the data; this in turn may lead to wasting time performing I/O. By using compression algorithms, it is possible to increase the size of the working set of the algorithm, thereby decreasing the I/O cost.

After examining Table 1, we observe that a substantial number of the surveyed techniques do not explicitly address the issue of ensuring computational load balancing for arbitrarily distributed sets of moving objects. On the other hand, techniques such as R2GridGPU make the explicit assumption that the objects distribute themselves uniformly in time and space, and then distribute the loads to the computational resources accordingly. However, the movement of many objects, such as people walking at noon around the downtown area of any major city in the USA, tends to exhibit a non-uniform behavior in time and space, which may cause a situation in which some processing units stay idle while others are working. Ideally, one would like a technique that achieves adequate load balancing with diverse spatio-temporal distributions of moving objects. Addressing this issue may, of course, lead to higher complexity in the maintenance of the index, which may negatively impact other performance measures. In this regard, it would be an interesting topic for future research to find indexes that achieve acceptable load balancing without sacrificing altogether simplicity and performance.

From Table 1 we can conclude that, with the exception of Sim-tree, almost all non-MapReduce-based multicore indexes focus exclusively on addressing only present-time queries, and do not strive to provide support for historical and trajectory queries. We consider that, given the importance of these types of queries and the prevalence of multicore machines, another future research topic could be to design non MapReduce-based multicore indexes that support these queries.

ACKNOWLEDGMENT

This work was supported in part by National Science Foundation No. 1302429; and National Science Foundation No. 1302423.

REFERENCES

Akdogan, A., Shahabi, S., & Demiryurek, U. (2014). ToSS-it: A Cloud-based Throwaway Spatial Index Structure for Dynamic Location Data. *International Conference on Mobile Data Management*. 10.1109/MDM.2014.37

Ammar, K., Elsayed, A., Sabri, M., & Terry, M. (2015). BusMate: Understanding Mobility Behavior for Trajectory-based Advertising. *International Conference on Mobile Data Management*. 10.1109/MDM.2015.71

Bao, J., He, T., Ruan, S., Li, Y., & Zheng, Y. (2017). *Planning Bike Lanes based on Sharing-Bike's Trajectories*. SIGKDD. doi:10.1145/3097983.3098056

Bayer, R., & McCreight, E. (1970). Organization and Maintenance of Large Ordered Indices. *ACM SIGFIDET Workshop on Data Description, Access and Control*. 10.21236/AD0712079

Boehm, C., & Krebs, F. (2004). The k-Nearest Neighbour Join: Turbo Charging the KDD Process. *Knowledge and Information Systems*, *6*(6), 728–749. doi:10.100710115-003-0122-9

Buchin, M., Dodge, S., & Speckmann, B. (2014). Similarity of Trajectories taking into account geographic context. *Journal of Spatial Information Science*.

Chakka, P., Everspaugh, A., & Patel, J. (2003). *Indexing Large Trajectory Datasets With SETI*. CIDR.

Chen, L., & Lian, X. (2012). *Query Processing over Uncertain Databases*. Morgan & Claypool Publishers.

Chen, S., Ooi, B., Tan, K., & Nascimento, M. (2008). *ST2B-tree: A Self-tunable Spatio-temporal B+-tree Index for Moving Objects*. SIGMOD. doi:10.1145/1376616.1376622

Dean, J., & Ghemawat, S. (2004). Mapreduce: Simplified data processing on large clusters. *Conference on Symposium on Operating Systems Design & Implementation*.

Ding, H., Trajcevski, G., & Scheuermann, P. (2008). Efficient Similarity Join of Large Sets of Moving Object Trajectories. *International Symposium on Temporal Representation and Reasoning*. 10.1109/TIME.2008.25

Dittrich, J., Blunschi, L., & Vaz Salles, M. A. (2009). Indexing Moving Objects Using Short-Lived Throwaway Indexes. *International Symposium on Advances in Spatial and Temporal Databases*. 10.1007/978-3-642-02982-0_14

Dittrich, J., Blunschi, L., & Vaz Salles, M. A. (2011). Movies: Indexing moving objects by shooting index images. *GeoInformatica*, *15*(4), 727–767. doi:10.100710707-011-0122-y

Emrich, T., Kriegel, H., Mamoulis, N., Renz, & Züfle, M. (2012a). Querying Uncertain Spatio-Temporal Data. *IEEE International Conference on Data Engineering*.

Emrich, T., Kriegel, H., Mamoulis, N., Renz, & Züfle, M. (2012b). Indexing Uncertain Spatio-Temporal Data. *CIKM*.

Fang, Y., Cao, J., Wang, J., Peng, Y., & Song, W. (2012). Htpr*-tree: An efficient index for moving objects to support predictive query and partial history query. *International Conference on Web-Age Information Management*. 10.1007/978-3-642-28635-3_3

Garland, M., & Kirk, D. (2010). Understanding Throughput-oriented Architectures. *Communications of the ACM*, *53*(11), 58–66. doi:10.1145/1839676.1839694

Ge, Y., Xiong, H., Zhou, Z., Ozdemir, H., Yu, J., & Lee, K. (2010). Top-Eye: top-k evolving trajectory outlier detection. *International Conference on Information and Knowledge Management*.

Gedik, B., & Liu, L. (2004). MobiEyes: Distributed Processing of Continuously Moving Queries on Moving Objects in a Mobile System. *EDBT*, 67–87.

Ghose, A. (2017). *Tap: Unlocking the Mobile Economy*. Cambridge, MA: MIT Press.

Gowanlock, M., Casanova, H. (2014). Distance Threshold Similarity Searches on Spatiotemporal Trajectories using GPGPU. *HiPC*.

Gowanlock, M., & Casanova, H. (2016). Distance threshold similarity searches: Efficient Trajectory Indexing on the GPU. *IEEE Transactions on Parallel and Distributed Systems, 27*(9), 2533–2545. doi:10.1109/TPDS.2015.2500896

Gu, Y., Lo, A., & Niemegeers, I. (2009). A survey of indoor positioning systems for wireless personal networks. *IEEE Communications Surveys and Tutorials, 11*(1), 13–32. doi:10.1109/SURV.2009.090103

Güting, R., Behr, T., & Xu, J. (2010). Efficient K-nearest Neighbor Search on Moving Object Trajectories. *The VLDB Journal, 19*(5), 687–714. doi:10.100700778-010-0185-7

Güting, R., & Schneider, M. (2005). *Moving Objects Databases*. Morgan Kaufmann Publishers.

He, Z., Kraak, M., Huisman, O., Ma, X., & Xiao, J. (2013). Parallel indexing technique for spatio-temporal data. *ISPRS Journal of Photogrammetry and Remote Sensing, 78*(0), 116–128. doi:10.1016/j.isprsjprs.2013.01.014

Hendawi, A., & Mokbel, M. (2012). Predictive Spatio-temporal Queries: A Comprehensive Survey and Future Directions. *ACM International Workshop on Mobile Geographic Information Systems*. 10.1145/2442810.2442828

Hill, N., Hussein, I., Davis, K., Ma, E., Spivey, T., Ramey, A., ... Runstadler, J. (2017). Reassortment of Influenza A Viruses in Wild Birds in Alaska before H5 Clade 2.3.4.4 Outbreaks. *Emerging Infectious Diseases, 23*(4), 654–657. doi:10.3201/eid2304.161668 PMID:28322698

Jacox, E. H., & Samet, H. (2007). Spatial join techniques. *ACM Transactions on Database Systems, 32*(1), 7, es. doi:10.1145/1206049.1206056

Jensen, C., Lin, D., & Ooi, B. (2004). *Query and Update Efficient B+-tree Based Indexing of Moving Objects*. VLDB. doi:10.1016/B978-012088469-8.50068-1

Jensen, C., Lu, H., & Yang, B. (2009). Indexing the Trajectories of Moving Objects in Symbolic Indoor Space. *International Symposium on Advances in Spatial and Temporal Databases*. 10.1007/978-3-642-02982-0_15

Jensen, C., & Pakalnis, S. (2007). *TRAX: Real-world Tracking of Moving Objects*. VLDB.

Leal, E., Gruenwald, L., Zhang, J., & You, S. (2015). TKSimGPU: A Parallel Top-K Trajectory Similarity Query Processing Algorithm for GPGPUs. *IEEE International Conference on Big Data*. 10.1109/BigData.2015.7363787

Lee, J., Han, J., & Whang, K. (2007). Trajectory Clustering: A Partition-and Group Framework. *SIGMOD Conference*.

Lee, V., Kim, C., Chhugani, J., Deisher, M., Kim, D., Nguyen, A., ... Dubey, P. (2010). Debunking the 100x gpu vs. cpu myth: An evaluation of throughput computing on cpu and gpu. *SIGARCH Computer Architecture News*, *38*(3), 451–460. doi:10.1145/1816038.1816021

Li, Z., Ji, M., Lee, J., Tang, L., Yu, Y., Han, J., & Kays, R. (2010). *MoveMine: Mining Moving Object Databases*. SIGMOD. doi:10.1145/1807167.1807319

Ma, C., & Lu, H. (2013). KSQ: Top-K Similarity Query on Uncertain Trajectories. *IEEE Transactions on Knowledge and Data Engineering*.

Ma, Q., Yang, B., Qian, W., & Zhou, A. (2009). Query Processing of Massive Trajectory Data Based on MapReduce. *International Workshop on Cloud Data Management*. 10.1145/1651263.1651266

Mokbel, M., Ghanem, T., & Aref, W. (2003). Spatio-temporal access methods. *A Quarterly Bulletin of the Computer Society of the IEEE Technical Committee on Data Engineering*, *26*(2), 40–49.

Nguyen-Dinh, L., Aref, W., & Mokbel, M. (2010). Spatio-Temporal Access Methods: Part 2 (2003 - 2010). *A Quarterly Bulletin of the Computer Society of the IEEE Technical Committee on Data Engineering*, *33*(2), 46–55.

Ni, J., & Ravishankar, C. (2005). PA-tree: A Parametric Indexing Scheme for Spatio-temporal Trajectories. *International Conference on Advances in Spatial and Temporal Databases*, 254–272. 10.1007/11535331_15

Pelanis, M., Šaltenis, S., & Jensen, C. (2006). Indexing the past, present, and anticipated future positions of moving objects. *ACM Transactions on Database Systems*, *31*(1), 255–298. doi:10.1145/1132863.1132870

Ranu, S., Deepak, P., Telang, A., Deshpande, P., & Raghavan, S. (2015). Indexing and Matching Trajectories under Inconsistent Sampling Rates. *IEEE International Conference on Data Engineering*. 10.1109/ICDE.2015.7113351

Šaltenis, S., Jensen, C., Leutenegger, S., & Lopez, M. (2000). *Indexing the Positions of Continuously Moving Objects*. SIGMOD. doi:10.1145/342009.335427

Samet, H. (1984). The quadtree and related hierarchical data structures. *ACM Computing Surveys*, *16*(2), 187–260. doi:10.1145/356924.356930

Šidlauskas, D., Ross, K., Jensen, C., & Šaltenis, S. (2011). Thread-level Parallel Indexing of Update Intensive Moving-object Workloads. *International Conference on Advances in Spatial and Temporal Databases*. 10.1007/978-3-642-22922-0_12

Šidlauskas, D., Šaltenis, S., & Jensen, C. (2012). *Parallel Main-memory Indexing for Moving-object Query and Update Workloads*. SIGMOD. doi:10.1145/2213836.2213842

Silvestri, C., Lettich, F., Orlando, S., & Jensen, C. S. (2014). GPU-Based Computing of Repeated Range Queries over Moving Objects. *International Conference on Parallel, Distributed and Network-Based Processing*. 10.1109/PDP.2014.27

Sun, J., Tao, Y., Papadias, D., & Kollios, G. (2006). Spatio-temporal join selectivity. *Information Systems*, *31*(8), 793–813. doi:10.1016/j.is.2005.02.002

Tan, H., Luo, W., & Ni, L. (2012). Clost: A hadoop-based storage system for big spatio-temporal data analytics. *ACM International Conference on Information and Knowledge Management*. 10.1145/2396761.2398589

Tao, Y., Papadias, D., & Sun, J. (2003). *The TPR*-tree: An Optimized Spatio-temporal Access Method for Predictive Queries*. VLDB. doi:10.1016/B978-012722442-8/50075-6

Trajcevski, G., Yaagoub, A., & Scheuermann, P. (2011). Processing (Multiple) Spatio-temporal Range Queries in Multicore Settings. *International Conference on Advances in Databases and Information Systems*. 10.1007/978-3-642-23737-9_16

Wang, H., Zimmermann, R., & Ku, W. (2006). Distributed Continuous Range Query Processing on Moving Objects. *International Conference on Database and Expert Systems Applications*. 10.1007/11827405_64

Wang, Y., Zheng, Y., & Xue, Y. (2014). Travel Time Estimation of a Path using Sparse Trajectories. *KDD: Proceedings / International Conference on Knowledge Discovery & Data Mining. International Conference on Knowledge Discovery & Data Mining*.

Ward, P., He, Z., Zhang, R., & Qi, J. (2014). Real-time continuous intersection joins over large sets of moving objects using graphic processing units. *The VLDB Journal*, *23*(6), 1–21. doi:10.100700778-014-0358-x

Wolfson, O., Xu, B., Chamberlain, S., & Jiang, L. (1998). Moving objects databases: Issues and solutions. *International Conference on Scientific and Statistical Database Management*.

Xu, Y., & Tan, G. (2014). Sim-tree: Indexing moving objects in large-scale parallel microscopic traffic simulation. *ACM Conference on Principles of Advanced Discrete Simulation*. 10.1145/2601381.2601388

Yang, B., Lu, H., & Jensen, C. (2010). Probabilistic Threshold K-Nearest Neighbor Queries over Moving Objects in Symbolic Indoor Space. *International Conference on Extending Database Technology*. 10.1145/1739041.1739083

Yiu, M., Tao, Y., & Mamoulis, N. (2008). The B^{dual}-Tree: Indexing Moving Objects by Space Filling Curves in the Dual Space. *The VLDB Journal*, *17*(3), 379–400. doi:10.100700778-006-0013-2

Yu, Z., Liu, Y., Yu, X., & Pu, K. (2015). Scalable Distributed Processing of K-Nearest Neighbor Queries over Moving Objects. *IEEE Transactions on Knowledge and Data Engineering*, *27*(5), 1383–1396. doi:10.1109/TKDE.2014.2364046

Yuan, J., Zheng, Y., Zhang, C., Xie, W., Xie, X., Sun, G., & Huang, Y. (2010). T-drive: Driving Directions Based on Taxi Trajectories. *SIGSPATIAL International Conference on Advances in Geographic Information Systems*. 10.1145/1869790.1869807

Zhang, J., You, S., & Gruenwald, L. (2012). U2STRA: High-Performance Data Management of Ubiquitous Urban Sensing Trajectories on GPGPUs. *City Data Management Workshop*. 10.1145/2390226.2390229

Zhang, R., Lin, D., Ramamohanarao, K., & Bertino, E. (2008). Continuous intersection joins over moving objects. *IEEE International Conference on Data Engineering*.

Zheng, Y., Xie, X., & Ma, W. (2010). GeoLife: A Collaborative Social Networking Service among User, Location and Trajectory. *A Quarterly Bulletin of the Computer Society of the IEEE Technical Committee on Data Engineering*, *33*(2), 32–39.

KEY TERMS AND DEFINITIONS

GPU: Graphics processing unit; a parallel co-processor that is designed to render the graphics in a computer, but that can also be used for general purpose programming.

Moving-Object Index: A database index that stores a set of moving objects and that allows the efficient retrieval of their spatio-temporal properties.

Parallel Index: A database index that is designed to exploit the characteristics of parallel architectures (multicore CPUs, GPUs, MapReduce, etc.) by allowing the simultaneous execution of several queries.

Spatio-Temporal Query: A type of query that involves a spatio-temporal predicate. For example, "retrieve all the cars located in a 2 miles radius from Times Square".

Stale Query Result: A query result set such that it does not reflect the current spatio-temporal state in the real world.

Trajectory: The time-ordered sequence of positions that a moving object occupies in space as time goes by.

Trajectory Clustering: A data mining task that consists in dividing a set of trajectories into groups or clusters, such that the trajectories contained in any cluster are very similar to each other, and very dissimilar from trajectories in different clusters.

Chapter 4
Privacy and Security in Data-Driven Urban Mobility

Rajendra Akerkar
Western Norway Research Institute, Norway

ABSTRACT

A wide range of smart mobility technologies are being deployed within urban environment. These technologies generate huge quantities of data, much of them in real-time and at a highly granular scale. Such data about mobility, transport, and citizens can be put to many beneficial uses and, if shared, for uses beyond the system and purposes for which they were generated. Jointly, these data create the evidence base to run mobility services more efficiently, effectively, and sustainably. However, generating, processing, analyzing, sharing, and storing vast amounts of actionable data also raises several concerns and challenges. For example, data privacy, data protection, and data security issues arise from the creation of smart mobility. This chapter highlights the various privacy and security concerns and harms related to the deployment and use of smart mobility technologies and initiatives, and makes suggestions for addressing apprehensions about and harms arising from data privacy, protection, and security issues.

INTRODUCTION

The concept of a data-driven mobility involves an intensive use of information technologies for collecting and processing the information that the city generates using the sensors deployed or other data sources, such as traffic cameras or any other source of unstructured information. At their very core, data-driven mobility utilizes the power of data and connectivity to enable a better functioning environment. Like

DOI: 10.4018/978-1-5225-4963-5.ch004

managing traffic lights in line with the street's flow, or introducing a smart parking system. Nevertheless, city-managing mobility is a tough one. The larger the city, the bigger the problem. Though restricting access, such as introducing traffic fees, could have its merits, a future solution may want to focus less on private cars and more on other players in the traffic system. The road, the buildings, the busses and taxi fleets are all part of the same city, the same problem, and could potentially be part of the solution. Thousands of sensors are constantly recording massive amounts of data which can help not only in predicting traffic trends, but also with making emergency events more seamless. Having better functioning public transport can contribute to decreasing congestion and better traffic management on its own. Using big data applications could potentially improve the public transport system with minimal investment. It could help with balancing supply and demand such as by tracking passenger flow and managing the fleet accordingly or provide customized solutions to users, and incentivize or penalize the use of a specific route choice as opposed to another. In this regard, first need to gather, validate, link, and store the data, which is an ongoing challenge for many cities.

Urban mobility technologies generate huge quantities of data, much of them in real-time and at a highly granular scale. These data about cities and their citizens can be put to many beneficial uses and, if shared, for uses beyond the system and purposes for which they were generated. Collectively, these data create the evidence base to run cities more efficiently, productively, sustainably, transparently and fairly. However, generating, processing, analyzing, sharing and storing enormous amounts of actionable data also raise many concerns and challenges.

Key amongst these are the data privacy, data protection, and data security issues that arise from the creation of smart mobility. Many smart mobility technologies capture personally identifiable information (PII) and household level data about citizens – their characteristics, their location and movements, and their activities – link these data together to produce new derived data, and use them to create profiles of people and places and to make decisions about them. As such, there are concerns about what a smart mobility means for people's privacy and what privacy harms might arise from the sharing, analysis and misuse of urban big data. In addition, there are questions as to how secure smart mobility technologies and the data they generate are from hacking and theft and what the implications of a data breach are for citizens. While successful cyberattacks on cities are still relatively rare, smart mobility technologies raise many cybersecurity concerns that require attention.

To date, the approach to these issues has been uncoordinated due to the ad-hoc way they were developed. However, given the potential harms to citizens and the associated costs that can arise, and the potential benefits at stake, this approach should not be allowed to continue. The challenge is to devise smart mobility solutions and gain the benefits of their deployment while maintaining infrastructure and system security and systematically minimizing any pernicious effects and harms.

This chapter presents the development of smart mobility and urban big data, highlights the various privacy and security concerns and harms related to the deployment and use of smart mobility technologies and initiatives, and makes several suggestions for addressing fears about and troubles arising from data privacy, protection and security issues. The chapter concludes that a core requirement for creating smart mobility is the adoption of an ethical, principle-led approach designed to best serve the interests of citizens.

URBAN MOBILITY

Mobility has significantly evolved in the past, under the influence of industrial evolutions. Following the first industrial revolution enabled by the invention of steam powered technology, the railway industry emerged. The second industrial revolution with mass production enabled the emergence of the automobile industry and, closer to us, the third industrial revolution with digitalization enabled the emergence of computer-aided travelling (for example GPS in a car). Today we are entering what could be called a fourth industrial revolution, represented by industry and technology convergence, leading to the emergence of for example clean energy vehicles or connected mobility solutions. This evolution is particularly noticeable over past years in network industries (such as telecommunication and media, utilities and the mobility industry) as well as in B2C industries (such as retail and healthcare) where, driven by evolving customer needs and enabled by rapidly evolving technology, business models are continuously evolving.

Urban mobility is one of the toughest challenges that cities face today as existing mobility systems are close to breakdown. In addition to the increasing demand for urban mobility, mobility needs are evolving. Shifting travel habits, demand for services to increase convenience, speed and predictability, as well as growing customer expectations toward individualization and sustainability will require mobility services portfolio extension as well as business model transformation, while expert players from other sectors are assessing prospects to play a role in the extended mobility ecosystem.

Data-Driven Urban Mobility

The promises of data-driven mobility are appealing and there is no doubt that data-driven mobility technologies help to create smart cities. The drive to create data-driven mobility also raises several concerns and risks, which can be classified into eight broad types (Kitchin 2014a):

1. It typically treats the city as a coherent, rational machine, rather than a complex system full of wicked problems and competing interests;
2. It promotes a strong emphasis on creating technical solutions and overly promotes top-down technocratic forms of governance, rather than political/ social solutions and citizen-centered deliberative democracy;
3. The technological solutions forwarded often treat cities as a historical and as generic markets, promoting one-size fits all technical fixes rather than recognizing the need for bespoke solutions tailored to city characteristics and needs;
4. The technologies deployed are portrayed as being objective, commonsensical, pragmatic and politically benign, rather than thoroughly political, reflecting the views and values of their developers and stakeholders;
5. It promotes the corporatization and privatization of city services, with the developers of smart mobility technologies capturing city functions as market opportunities which are run for profit rather than the public good, and potentially create propriety technological lock-ins;
6. It prioritizes the values and investments of vested interests, reinforces inequalities, and deepens levels of control and regulation, rather than creating a more socially just and equal society;
7. The technologies deployed have profound social, political and ethical effects: introducing new forms of social regulation, control and governance; extending surveillance and eroding privacy; and enabling predictive profiling, social sorting and behavioral nudging;
8. The technologies deployed potentially produce buggy, brittle and hackable urban systems which create systemic vulnerabilities across critical infrastructure and compromise data security, rather than producing stable, reliable, resilient, secure systems.

These concerns and risks, and associated debates, are generally little known within wider society. As such, we are still very much at the stage of trying to understand and grapple with the consequences of producing smart mobility and data-driven urbanism, and to create new policies, standards, regulations and laws that enable their benefits to be realized whilst minimizing any pernicious effects.

URBAN DATA

Central to the creation of smart mobility is the generating, processing, analyzing and sharing of vast quantities of data about city infrastructure, services, and citizens. Indeed, smart mobility technologies are precisely about making cities data-driven: enabling city systems and services to be responsive to and act upon data, preferably real-time data. It is thus no coincidence that the drive to create smart mobility dovetails with the unfolding data revolution. This revolution consists of five main elements (Kitchin 2014a, 2014b, 2015):

1. The wide scale production of big data: data that are continuously produced, exhaustive to a system, fine-scaled, relational, and flexible;
2. The scaling of traditional small data into data infrastructures (digital repositories), enabling datasets to be shared, conjoined and analyzed in innovative ways;
3. The creation of linked data that seeks to transform the internet into a 'web of data', enabling all documents to be rendered as data and to be harvested and linked together;
4. The publishing of open data, making data publicly available and free to use that was previously locked inside institutions;
5. The development of new data analytics that often rely on machine learning techniques which can cope with and draw insight from very large datasets (e.g., data mining and pattern recognition; data visualization and visual analytics; statistical analysis; and prediction, simulation, and optimization modelling).

Most technologies are producing urban big data of varying kinds. Four are explicitly open data infrastructures (CorkOpenData, Dublinked, Fingal Open Data, Dublin Dashboard). Many of them have accompanying apps (that further leverage the data, and which can themselves produce further data) and APIs (that enable the data to be accessed and repurposed).

In addition to the big data generated by the initiatives, a deluge of other big open data is being produced around the world by a range of public and private organizations:

- Transport providers (location/movement, traffic flow)
- Mobile phone operators (location/movement, app use, behavior)
- Travel and accommodation websites (reviews, location/movement, consumption)
- Social media sites (opinions, photos, personal info, location/movement)
- Crowdsourcing and citizen science (maps (e.g., OpenStreetMap), local knowledge (e.g., Wikipedia), weather (e.g., wunderground.com))

- Government bodies and public administration (services, performance, surveys)
- Emergency services (security, crime, policing, response)

While much of these data are closed and considered a private asset, some of them are shared with third party vendors and some are open (through data infrastructures or APIs). The wealth of data and new analytics are also helping to create new analytical fields such as urban informatics (an informational and human-computer interaction approach to examining and communicating urban processes) and urban science (a computational modelling and simulation approach to understanding, explaining and predicting city processes).

DATA PRIVACY AND PROTECTION ISSUES

Privacy and Privacy Harms

Data privacy is an important field in every smart technology. When you look at transport it seems apparent to look at navigation or speed, but it's not limited to what the car provides on its own – it's also data transmitted via your smartphone, your online posts, your tweets, etc. There's been an unresolved debate for a long time on ownership of data shared online, and regulation has a key role in defining how to deal with privacy in the first place. Even defining who owns the data (i.e. whose privacy needs to be protected) is not as straightforward as it may seem.

At the same time, getting access to sufficient amounts of data for the big data effect to kick in is important and restricting access, in some cases, does more harm than good. In that sense, the type of data benefiting the society can be looked upon as an enabler for a greater public good.

Privacy is a condition that many people value and it is considered a basic human right in most jurisdictions, enshrined in national and supra-national laws in many ways. How privacy is understood both as an everyday and legal concept, however, varies between cultures and contexts. In general terms, privacy debates concern acceptable practices with regards to accessing and disclosing personal and sensitive information about a person (Elwood & Leszczynski, 2011). Such sensitive information can relate to several personal facets and domains creating several inter-related privacy forms including:

- Identity privacy (to protect personal and confidential data);
- Bodily privacy (to protect the integrity of the physical person);
- Territorial privacy (to protect personal space, objects and property);

- Locational and movement privacy (to protect against the tracking of spatial behavior);
- Communications privacy (to protect against the surveillance of conversations and correspondence); and
- Transactions privacy (to protect against monitoring of queries/searches, purchases, and other exchanges).

Approach to Privacy Breaches

From a legal perspective, privacy breaches and harms are mostly covered under the rubric of privacy laws in the United States, whereas in the European Union it falls within the realm of data protection. In both cases, the legal frameworks draw on fair information practice principles (FIPPs) that are largely constructed around personal rights regarding the generation, use, and disclosure of personal data and the obligations of data controllers with respect to these rights. However, different emphasis is placed on these FIPPs. Moreover, while there is common ground on how to address privacy harms, such as advocating privacy by design, enhanced data security, and access rights to check and correct data, there are differences in approach and how to implement them (in terms of obtaining consent, notification of data breaches, cross-border data flows). Other jurisdictions have their own approaches.

The varying legal framings and policies across jurisdictions create a fractured regulatory and compliance landscape, with different obligations existing for smart mobility technologies deployed within different nations.

Nonetheless, across all jurisdictions smart mobility technologies are challenging existing legal and regulatory provisions, as well as societal norms and expectations, with respect to privacy.

Big Data Encryption

Cryptography can be defined as a study of communication over an "insecure" channel. The fundamental aims of cryptography are privacy and authenticity. Depending on the structure of the keys, encryption schemes could be of two types: symmetric (or private key) and asymmetric (or public key).

Symmetric encryption takes readable data, scramble it to make it unreadable, and then unscramble it again when it's needed. Various symmetric encryption algorithms include Triple DES, Blowfish and Twofish (Bradford, 2014). Asymmetric encryption takes readable data, scrambles it, and unscrambles it again at the other end, but a different key is used for each end. This method is easier since only the party that needs to decrypt needs access to the private key (Behrens, 2014). RSA is considered an asymmetric algorithm (Bradford, 2014). Examples of other methods are Hashing, Advanced Encryption Standard (AES), Honey Encryption and Quantum key distribution (Bradford, 2014).

Anonymization and Pseudo Anonymization

Data anonymization is a type of information sanitization whose intent is personal privacy protection. It is the process of either encrypting or removing personally identifiable information from data sets, so that the individuals whom the data describe remain anonymous. Data anonymization enables the transfer of information while reducing the risk of unintended disclosure (Raghunathan, 2013).

In general term anonymized data refers to data from which the individual cannot be identified by the recipient of the information. Attributes within the data set which immediately identify an individual (e.g. name, address, postal code, etc.) must be suppressed or pseudo-anonymized (i.e. substituted with random data). Other attributes which, in conjunction with other data held by or disclosed to the recipient, could identify the patient must be generalized (e.g. birthdate changed from yyyymmdd to yyyymm or yyyy). These attributes are called quasi-identifiers. De-anonymization is the reverse process in which anonymous data is cross-referenced with other data sources to re-identify the anonymous data source.

There are many ways to address this use case but two popular techniques, which are more relevant into two high-level methods of data anonymization: K-Anonymity and Differential Privacy (Weber, 2012).

K-Anonymity is the technique "to release person-specific data such that the ability to link to other information using the quasi-identifier is limited" (Sweeney, 2002). K-Anonymity realizes this through suppression of identifiers and output perturbation. A release of data is said to have the k-anonymity property if the information for each person contained in the release cannot be distinguished from at least k-1 individuals whose information also appear in the release. Precisely, the data set has k-anonymity if all records within the data have at least k-1 records with the same grouping of quasi-identifier values (an equivalence class) (Babu et al., 2013). A data holder can frequently recognize attributes in their data that also appear in outside sources, and these attributes are candidates for linking. They are called quasi-identifiers, and it is essentially the combinations of these quasi-identifiers that must be protected (Samarai & Sweeney, 1998).

Differential privacy promises to protect individuals from any additional harm that they might face due to their data being in the private database. The risk of harm is not significantly greater when compared to not being in the private database. Though individuals may certainly face harm once the results of a differentially private mechanism have been released, differential privacy promises that the probability of harm was not significantly increased by their choice to participate. To satisfy the differential privacy constraint, a query-releasing mechanism needs to send a randomized query output to the analyst in a way such that the probability distribution of the query output does not differ too much, whether any individual record is in the database. In application, it attempts to do "two important things at once. First, it defines a measure of privacy, or rather, a measure of disclosure—the opposite of privacy. And second, it allows data producers to set the bounds of how much disclosure they will allow" in a given set of database queries (Sherer et al., 2015).

CHALLENGES TO CURRENT REGULATORY APPROACHES

Smart mobility technologies create many potential privacy harms for inter-related reasons, each of which also raises significant challenges to existing approaches to protecting privacy. As a few studies have highlighted, these issues are of significant concern to the public, civil liberties organizations, legislators and regulators, and have been the focus of public campaigns against smart mobility technologies in some cases.

Intensifies Datafication

Smart mobility technologies capture data relating to all forms of privacy and radically expand the volume, range and granularity of the data being generated about people and places. Notably, the capture and circulation of these data are:

1. Indiscriminate and exhaustive (involve all individuals, objects, transactions, etc.);
2. Distributed (occur across multiple devices, services and places);
3. Platform independent (data flows easily across platforms, services, and devices);
4. Continuous (data are generated on a routine and automated basis).

Such datafication has four effects with respect to privacy. First, people are now subject to much greater levels of intensified scrutiny and modes of surveillance and dataveillance than ever before, with smart mobility technologies providing deeply personal pictures of individual lives, especially when datasets are combined. Second, the pervasiveness of digitally-mediated transactions and surveillance, plus the increasing use of unique identifiers and PII to access services (e.g., names, usernames, passwords, account numbers, addresses, emails, phone details, credit card numbers, smart card ID, license plates, faces), means that it is all but impossible to live everyday lives without leaving digital footprints (traces we leave ourselves) and shadows (traces captured about us). Third, the mass recording, organizing, storing and sharing of big data about a phenomenon changes the uses to which such data can be put, both for good and for ill. Fourth, such data enables a lot of inference beyond the data generated to reveal insights that have never been disclosed (Lyon, 2014; Murphy, 2015).

Predictive Privacy Harms

Predictive modelling using urban big data can generate inferences about an individual that are not directly encoded in a database but constitute what many would consider to be PII and which produce 'predictive privacy harms. For example, co-proximity and co- movement with others can be used to infer political, social, and/or religious affiliation, potentially revealing membership of groups. Likewise, the volunteered information of a few people on social media can unlock the same undisclosed information about the many through social network analysis and pattern recognition. It has been calculated that knowing the sexual orientation of just twenty percent of social media users will enable the orientation of all other users to be inferred with a high degree of accuracy (Crawford & Schultz, 2014).

Moreover, the inferences can generate inaccurate characterization that then stick to and precede an individual. This is an issue in predictive policing and anticipatory governance, where the profiling of both people and places can reinforce or create stigma and harm, particularly when the underlying data or models are poor.

Anonymization and Re-Identification

One of the key strategies for ensuring individual privacy is anonymization, either using pseudonyms, aggregation or other strategies. The generation of big data and new computational techniques, however, can make the re-identification of data relatively straightforward in many cases. Pseudonyms simply mean that a unique tag is used to identify a person in place of a name. As such, the tag is anonymous in so far that code is used to identify an individual. However, the code is persistent and distinguishable from others and recognizable on an on-going basis, meaning it can be tracked over time and space and used to create detailed individual profiles. As such, it is no different from other persistent pseudonym identifiers such as social security numbers and in effect constitutes PII. The term 'anonymous identifier', as used by some companies, is thus somewhat of an oxymoron, especially when the identifier is directly linked to an account with known personal details (e.g., name, address, credit card number). Even if the person is not immediately identifiable, the persistence of the pseudonym enables data controllers to act on that data and shape how they interact with individuals. As such, pseudonyms 'enable holders of large datasets to act on individuals, under the cover of anonymity, in precisely the ways anonymity has long promised to defend against' and they place no inherent limits on an institution's ability to track and trace the same person in subsequent encounters.

Further, inference and the linking of a pseudonym to other accounts and transactions means it can potentially be re-identified. Certainly, it is possible to reverse engineer anonymization strategies by combing and combining datasets unless the data are fully de-identified. De-identification requires both direct identifiers and quasi-identifiers (those highly correlated with unique identifiers) to be carefully removed. The extent to which this is happening before data are shared with third parties is highly doubtful. Moreover, there are some companies that specialize in re-identification of data across big data datasets.

The emerging big data landscape is complex and fragmented. Various smart mobility technologies are composed of multiple interacting systems run by several corporate and state actors. For example, the app ecosystem (including app developers, app owners, app stores, operating systems, mobile carriers, devices) is conjoined to the data source ecosystem (e.g., an API of real-time bus data), which similarly consists of a range of hardware, software and organizations. Data are thus passed between synergistic and interoperable 'devices, platforms, services, applications, and analytics engines' and shared with third parties. Moreover, across this maze-like assemblage they can be 'leaked, intercepted, transmitted, disclosed, dis/assembled across data streams, and repurposed' in ways that are difficult to track and untangle.

DATA SECURITY CONCERNS

There are two key security concerns with respect to smart mobility. The first is the security of smart mobility technologies and infrastructures and the extent to which they are vulnerable to being hacked via a cyberattack. The second is the security of the data generated, stored and shared across such technologies and infrastructures. The latter is directly related to the former as improper access to data is often achieved via security weaknesses in a system's components, architecture and operation. In this sense, information security (data protection) has converged with operational security (making sure things work reliably and with integrity) (Brenner, 2014).

Operational Security and Cyberattack

Smart mobility solutions utilize complex, networked assemblages of digital technologies and ICT infrastructure to manage various city systems and services. Any device that relies on software to function is vulnerable to being hacked. If a device is networked, then the number of potential entry points multiples across the network, and the hack can be performed remotely. Once a single device is compromised, then the whole assemblage becomes vulnerable to cyberattacks that seek to 'alter, disrupt, deceive, degrade or destroy computer systems and networks or the information and/ or programs resident in or transiting these systems or networks. There are three forms of cyberattack: availability attacks that seek to close a system down or deny service use; confidentiality attacks that seek to extract information and monitor activity; and integrity attacks that seek to enter a system to alter information and settings (such as changing settings so that components exceed normal performance, erasing critical software, planting malware and viruses). The vulnerability of systems is exacerbated by many issues including weak security and encryption; the use of insecure legacy systems and poor maintenance; large and complex attack surfaces and interdependencies; cascade effects; and human error and disgruntled (ex) employees. The result is that the process of making city systems and infrastructures 'smart' has also made them vulnerable to a suite of cyber-threats (Peters, 2015).

Cyberattacks can be performed by hostile nations, terrorist groups, cyber-criminals, hacker collectives, and individual hackers. Most of attacks are presently being repulsed using cybersecurity tools, or their effects have been disruptive or damaging but not critical for the long-term delivery of services. Indeed, it needs to be recognized that to date, successful cyberattacks on cities are still relatively rare and when they have occurred their effects generally last no more than a few hours or involve the theft of data rather than creating life threatening situations. There is a cybersecurity arms race underway between attackers and defenders, and that more severe disruption of critical infrastructure has been avoided through the threat of mutually assured destruction between nations. This is not to suggest that smart mobility initiatives should be avoided, but rather that the cybersecurity challenges of creating secure smart mobility are taken seriously.

Security of Data

Data-driven urban mobility produces, processes, stores, and shares vast quantities of data and derived data and information. Much of these data are sensitive in nature. While some data can be made open and shared freely, as with data released through urban dashboards, most is considered private and needs to be held securely and kept protected. Given the value of data to cybercriminals for identity theft and blackmail, to companies for gaining industrial secrets, and nation states for security and cyberwar, they are much sought after.

News concerning major data breaches or national surveillance programmes is, at present, an almost weekly occurrence, and data security has become a significant weak point of networked endeavors.

Data breaches occur for several reasons and have become more common because the lines of attack have grown as more and more systems and infrastructures become networked. And yet, it is apparent that in too many cases, security is an afterthought, applied after a system has been developed and prototyped, and that companies are often more interested in convenience, minimization of downtime, and marginal efficiency than security and compliance.

TACKLING DATA PRIVACY AND SECURITY CONCERNS

It is clear from the discussion so far that there are many data privacy, protection and security concerns and challenges created through the rollout of smart mobility technologies.

Addressing these issues is no simple task, both politically and pragmatically. Indeed, there are two distinct levels to the debate. The first examines more general normative questions concerning the ethics and politics of mass surveillance enabled by smart mobility technologies and the use of urban big data in predictive profiling, social sorting, anticipatory governance and the management of city populations, infrastructures and services. The second level is more concerned with how to best implement data privacy, protection and security given present legislation and expected norms.

These two levels are strongly related given that a position held with respect to the first directly influences the position taken with respect to the second. For example, a position that accepts the need for mass surveillance and the erosion of privacy will advocate for different interventions than a position that is much more committed to individual privacy and personal autonomy. At present, the debate over the mass surveillance of society largely hinges on two inherent trade-offs: between privacy and national security; and between privacy and economic growth (Santucci, 2013).

Firstly, surveillance is cast as a choice between creating safer societies or defending personal autonomy. On the one side, trust is traded for control, and all citizens are treated as potential threats without warranted suspicion for the greater good of national security. Whereas, privacy is an indispensable structural feature of liberal political systems and is foundational to informed and reflective citizenship and to freedom of expression. The danger of mass surveillance for the latter is the loss of core societal values of freedom and liberty to be replaced by highly controlled and authoritarian societies.

Secondly, the mass generation of data about customers is cast as a choice between creating new products, markets, jobs and wealth or individual and collective rights. On the other hand, it is said that data privacy and security should not hinder innovation and the extraction of economic value of individual data, or impede customer experience. On the other side, it is contended that it is possible to extract value from big data and create new products without infringing on privacy and aggressively micro-targeting and profiling individuals.

The privacy is often situated as mutually exclusive from national security and economic development. Privacy, the argument goes, is dead or dying, even if there are those who do not fully realize it yet; it has been sacrificed for the supposed greater good. Further, those in favor of the mass generation of data resort to arguments such as 'if you have nothing to hide, you have nothing to fear', or 'if you do not like how we operate, do not use our service.' As critics note, the first assertion conflates privacy with the concealment of suspicious behavior, as opposed to personal autonomy, freedom of expression, and the selective choice to reveal oneself. The second is entirely impractical and unreasonable given that email, online banking and shopping, credit cards, smartphones, social media, and so on, are the tools of modern life, necessary for a career and social life. Opting out is not a viable choice. Indeed, with respect to many smart mobility technologies, opting out is not even an option.

The following practical and pragmatic solutions to data privacy, protection and security concerns and harms related to smart mobility are framed within a position that does not see privacy and security/development as mutually exclusive. Rather a suite of solutions is needed, some of which are market driven, some more technical in nature, others more governance and management orientated, and some more policy, regulatory and legally focused. Together these will enact what has been termed 'smart privacy' – a broad arsenal of protections including: 'privacy by design; law, regulation and independent oversight; accountability and transparency; market forces; education and awareness; audit and control; data security; and fair information practices. Importantly, the approaches advocated are not heavy handed in nature, seeking mutual consensus, collaboration and to be enabling rather than restrictive. Moreover, they should be relatively inexpensive to implement as they are principally about changing practices and redeploying existing resources and staff more effectively.

Market Solutions

Market solutions to privacy and security issues generally fall into two parts. The first is a contention that the market will adapt to self-regulate privacy and data security in line with societal demand for fear of losing customers and market share. The main problem with this argument is that it assumes that companies will actively self-regulate as opposed to resist and block change, that individuals have the freedom and choice to move their custom, and that any abuses of privacy will be enough to enact such behavior. Some companies are effectively quasi-monopolies in particular domains, with consumers having few other choices. Further, while some companies will be ethical and conscientious in seeking to ensure data privacy and security, market regulation does not solve the issue of vendors who willfully abuse privacy rights or are negligent in their data security practices. Moreover, individuals often do not understand the implications of terms and conditions associated with assorted products and systems, nor their privacy rights, and often do not act in their own self-interest.

The second market solution is for companies to see consumer privacy and data security as a competitive advantage, developing privacy and security protocols and tools that will attract consumers away from other vendors. For example, companies developing products that have limited tracking or profiling, or end-to-end encryption. While welcome, the concern is that privacy and security might become a two-tiered system, available for a fee rather than as a right. In addition, as data breaches and privacy scandals continue to tarnish the development of inter-networked products and services, the cybersecurity industry itself will continue to grow to provide enhanced privacy and security tools and technologies. Such technical solutions will be aimed at individuals so that they can more effectively manage their privacy, and companies and public authorities so that they can better protect their operational security, data resources, and the privacy of their customers and clients.

Technology Solutions

As noted, too many smart mobility technologies have large attack surfaces that have a number of vulnerabilities, especially in systems that contain legacy components using old software which has not been regularly patched. Technology solutions to data privacy and security seek to use technical fixes and products to effectively manage systems and tackle risks. At one level, this consists of implementing best practice solutions in building and maintaining secure smart mobility infrastructures and systems.

This includes:

- Strong, end-to-end encryption;
- Strong passwords and access controls;
- Firewalls;
- Up-to-date virus and malware checkers;

- Security certificates;
- Audit trails;
- Isolating trusted resources from non-trusted;
- Disabling unnecessary functionality;
- Ensuring that there are no weak links between components;
- Isolating components where possible from a network;
- Implementing fail safe and manual overrides on all systems;
- Ensuring full backup of data and recovery mechanisms; and
- Automatically installing security patch updates on all components, including firmware, software, communications, and interfaces.

The aim is to reduce the attack surface as much as possible and to make the surface that is visible as robust and resilient as possible.

At balancing level, the approach has been to develop a suite of Privacy Enhancing Technologies (PETs) that seek to provide individuals with tools to protect their PII and dictate how PII should be handled by different services. PETs have been defined by the European Commission as ‘a coherent system of information and communication technology measures that protect privacy by eliminating or reducing personal data or by preventing redundant and/or undesired processing of personal data without losing the functionality of the information system. In effect, PETs seek to minimize data generation, rise individual control of PII, choose the degree of online anonymity and linkability of data, track the use of their data, gain meaningful consent, and facilitate legal rights of data inspection, correction and deletion. PETs include relatively simple tools such as ad blockers, cookie blockers and removers, malware detection and interception, site blocking, encryption tools, and services to opt-out of databases held by data brokers. In general, these kinds of PETs are aimed at protecting PII on websites and smartphones and managing how data are handled by data brokers and have limited application with respect to many smart mobility technologies which generate data about people in a sole way (through cameras, smart card readers, sensors, etc.). Other approaches such as statistical disclosure control (SDC), privacy information retrieval (PIR), and privacy-preserving data mining (PPDM) are aimed at protecting confidentiality in data analysis and the release of public datasets, database retrieval, and data mining.

Policy, Regulatory, and Legal Solutions

While market-driven and technological solutions will have many positive effects, how they are administered is framed by the wider policy, regulatory and legal landscape.

The present regulatory and legal tools with respect to privacy and security are not fit for purpose in the age of urban big data and algorithmic governance and need revision. It is not the intention of this report to prescribe new legal and regulatory provisions for smart mobility and privacy and security more broadly. Indeed, this is the focus of several initiatives already at the EU and national level. Instead, it advocates the use of four pragmatic policy approaches which seek to address privacy and security harms and concerns.

Fair Information Practice Principles (FIPPs)

FIPPs are the fundamental principles underlying the generation, use and disclosure of personal data and the obligations of data controllers. The fact that FIPPs are now difficult to apply in practice and are routinely being circumvented has highlighted the need to revisit and revise them.

- **Individual Control:** Consumers have a right to exercise control over what personal data companies collect from them and how they use it.
- **Transparency:** Consumers have a right to easily understandable and accessible information about privacy and security practices.
- **Respect for Context:** Consumers have a right to expect that companies will collect, use, and disclose personal data in ways that are consistent with the context in which consumers provide the data.
- **Security:** Consumers have a right to secure and responsible handling of personal data.
- **Access and Accuracy:** Consumers have a right to access and correct personal data in usable formats, in a manner that is appropriate to the sensitivity of the data and the risk of adverse consequences to consumers if the data is inaccurate.
- **Focused Collection:** Consumers have a right to reasonable limits on the personal data that companies collect and retain.
- **Accountability:** Consumers have a right to have personal data handled by companies with appropriate measures in place to assure they adhere to the Consumer Privacy Bill of Rights.

The updated FIPPs extend those officially advocated by the FTC, and widen the scope of shared principles, expanding consumer control over information at issue and how the data are used.

Privacy by Design

One means by which FIPPs can become much more central to the development of smart mobility technologies is through the adoption of privacy by design. Privacy by Design is an approach that promotes technology design and engineering to incorporate privacy into the design process from the start. The concept includes seven guiding principles on privacy and security. While regulatory and legislative compliance seeks to ensure that vendors and cities fulfil their obligations with respect to privacy by correctly and fairly handling the data they generate and manage, privacy by design proposes that privacy is the default mode of operation. Rather than collecting data, assuming they are all available for use (unless the individual does not consent, which effectively means they are denied the service), all data remain private unless the consumer explicitly says otherwise. In other words, privacy is hardwired into the design specifications and usage of information technology, business practices, physical environments, and infrastructure of systems and apps through the adoption of seven foundational principles (see Table 1). Because these are principles and not a set of prescribed methods, they provide latitude for different modes of implementation. The approach is positioned as a 'positive-sum' (rather than zero-sum) solution that does not rely on trade-offs between privacy rights and other issues such as security or economic development, but rather seeks to maximize both. The use of privacy by design has been advocated by the EU, FTC and a few national information/data protection commissioners.

Table 1. The principles of privacy by design

Principle	Description
Proactive not reactive; preventative not remedial	IT systems should seek to anticipate privacy concerns rather than seeking to resolve privacy infractions once they have incurred
Privacy as the default setting	Privacy is automatically protected and does not require action on behalf of an individual
Privacy embedded into design	Privacy protections are core features of the design and architecture of IT systems and is not a bolt-on feature
Full functionality - positive-sum, not zero-sum	All legitimate interests and objectives are accommodated, rather than there being trade-offs between privacy and other considerations such as security
End-to-end security - full lifecycle protection	Privacy is embedded into the system from ingestion to disposal
Visibility and transparency - keep it open	Component parts and operations are visible and transparent to users and providers alike and are subject to independent verification
Respect for user privacy - keep it user-centric	A system should be built around, protect the interests, and empower individuals

Cavoukian 2009.

Security by Design

Complementary to privacy by design is security by design. Likewise, a proactive and preventative rather than reactive and remedial approach is taken to security, seeking to build it into systems from the outset rather than layering it on afterwards. This requires security risk assessment to be a fundamental part of the design process and security measures to be rigorously tested before the product is launched, including a test pilot phase within a living lab environment that includes testing the security of a product when deployed as part of a wider network of technologies (to ensure end-to-end security). It also means having in place an on-going commitment to cybersecurity, including a mechanism to monitor products throughout their life cycle, a process of supporting and patching them over time, and a procedure for notifying customers when security risks are identified. A key commitment of security by design is for end-to-end encryption and strong access controls, including forcing adopters to change default passwords, and to only keep data essential for the task being performed and transferring data in aggregated form where possible.

Governance Solutions

An important constituent of efficient mobility systems and infrastructures is their governance and management structures and processes. Governance provides the framework through which strategic direction is deliberated and set, and regulation and oversight administered. Management consists of leading and driving forward initiatives and stewarding the day-to- day running of services. Together they frame the rollout and maintenance of city systems and infrastructures and ensure they work as intended, fulfil their ambitions and strategic intent, and stay within legal and regulatory parameters.

Putting in place robust principle-led governance and management is therefore a prerequisite for creating a smart mobility that seeks to maximize benefits while minimizing harms. And yet, to date, there are very few documented cases of such governance and management structures being constituted. Instead, smart mobility initiatives have been procured and developed with little coordinated consideration of privacy and security harms and slotted into existing city management in an ad hoc manner with nominal strategic oversight.

Given the potential harms and the associated costs that can arise, and the potential benefits at stake, this piecemeal approach needs to be discontinued to be replaced with a more strategic, coordinated approach that consists of interventions at three levels: vision and strategy (smart mobility advisory board); oversight of delivery and compliance (smart mobility governance, ethics and security oversight committee);

and routine delivery (core privacy/security team and computer emergency response team). This approach identifies that there is a need for collaboration between experts in different domains to ensure sharing of knowledge and shared learning.

CONCLUSION

Overlooking or deliberately avoiding smart mobility technologies is not a practicable approach; nor is developing smart mobility that create a range of harms and reinforce power imbalances. Rather we need to create a kind of smart mobility that has a set of ethical principles and values at its heart. Such a balanced approach is not straightforward to conceive or implement given the diverse set of stakeholders and vested interests at work in the smart mobility space.

This chapter provides one vision of a composed strategy to data privacy, data protection and data security in the context of smart mobility and suggests a multi-pronged approach that merges together market, technical, governance and management, and policy, and legal solutions. This will promote equality and protect citizens and cities from harms, and aid the benefits of smart mobility and urban big data to be realized.

ACKNOWLEDGMENT

The research has received funding from a grant of the from the Research Council of Norway (RCN) and the Norwegian Centre for International Cooperation in Education (SiU) through INTPART programme.

REFERENCES

Babu, K., Ranabothu, N., & Kumar, N. (2013). Achieving k-anonymity Using Improved Greedy Heuristics for Very Large Relational Databases. *Trans. Data Priv.*, *6*(1), 1–17.

Behrens, M. (2014). Understanding Encryption – Symmetric, Asymmetric, & Hashing. *Atomic Spin*. Retrieved from https://spin.atomicobject.com/2014/11/20/encryption-symmetric-asymmetric-hashing/

Bradford, C. (2014). *5 Common Encryption Algorithms and the Unbreakables of the Future – StorageCraft*. StorageCraft Technology Corporation. Available: http://www.storagecraft.com/blog/5-common-encryption-algorithms/

Brenner, J. (2014). Nations everywhere are exploiting the lack of cybersecurity. *Washington Post*. Retrieved from www.washingtonpost.com/opinions/joel-brenner-nations-everywhere- are-exploiting-the-lack-of-cybersecurity/2014/10/24/1e6e 4b70-5b85-11e4-b812- 38518ae74c67_story.html

Cavoukian, A. (2009). *Privacy by Design: A Primer*. Retrieved from www.privacybydesign.ca/content/uploads/2013/10/pbd-primer.pdf

Crawford, K., & Schultz, J. (2014). Big Data and Due Process: Toward a Framework to Redress Predictive Privacy Harms. *Boston College Law Review. Boston College. Law School*, *55*(1), 93–128.

Elwood, S., & Leszczynski, A. (2011). Privacy reconsidered: New representations, data practices, and the geoweb. *Geoforum*, *42*(1), 6–15. doi:10.1016/j.geoforum.2010.08.003

European Data Protection Supervisor. (2014). *Privacy and competitiveness in the age of big data: The interplay between data protection, competition law and consumer protection in the Digital Economy*. Retrieved from secure.edps.europa.eu/EDPSWEB/webdav/shared/Documents/Consultation/Opinions/2014/14-03-26_competitition_law_big_data_EN.pdf

Fung. (2010). *Introduction to privacy-preserving data publishing: concepts and techniques*. Chapman & Hall/CRC.

Fuster, G. G., & Scherrer, A. (2015). *Big Data and smart devices and their impact on privacy*. Committee on Civil Liberties, Justice and Home Affairs (LIBE), Directorate-General for Internal Policies, European Parliament. Retrieved from http://www.europarl.europa.eu/RegData/etudes/STUD/2015/536455/IPOL_STU(2015)536455_EN.pdf (last accessed 4 November 2015)

Kitchin, R. (2014a). The real-time city? Big data and smart urbanism. *GeoJournal*, *79*(1), 1–14. doi:10.100710708-013-9516-8

Kitchin, R. (2014b). *The Data Revolution: Big Data, Open Data, Data Infrastructures and Their Consequences*. London: Sage.

Kitchin, R. (2015). Data-driven, networked urbanism. *Programmable City Working Paper 14*. Retrieved from http://ssrn.com/abstract=2641802

Lyon, D. (2014). Surveillance, Snowden, and Big Data: Capacities, consequences, critique. *Big Data and Society*, *1*(2), 1–13. doi:10.1177/2053951714541861

Murphy, M. H. (2015). The introduction of smart meters in Ireland: Privacy implications and the role of privacy by design. *Dublin University Law Journal*, *38*(1).

Peters, S. (2015). Smart Cities' 4 Biggest Security Challenges. *InformationWeek: Dark Reading*. Retrieved from http://www.darkreading.com/vulnerabilities---threats/smart-cities-4-biggest- security-challenges/d/d-id/1321121

Raghunathan, B. (2013). *The Complete Book of Data Anonymization: From Planning to Implementation*. CRC Press.

Samarati, P., & Sweeney, L. (1998). Generalizing data to provide anonymity when disclosing information (abstract). In *Proceedings of the seventeenth ACM SIGACT-SIGMOD-SIGART symposium on Principles of database systems (PODS '98)*. ACM. 10.1145/275487.275508

Santucci, G. (2013). Privacy in the Digital Economy: Requiem or Renaissance? *Privacy Surgeon*. Retrieved from www.privacysurgeon.org/blog/wp-content/uploads/2013/09/Privacy-in-the- Digital-Economy-final.pdf

Sherer, J. A., Le, J., & Taal, A. (2015, July). Big Data Discovery, Privacy, and the Application of Differential Privacy Mechanisms. *Comput. Internet Lawyer*, *32*(7), 10–16.

Sweeney, L. (2002). *K-anonymity: A model for protecting privacy*. Retrieved from https://epic.org/privacy/reidentification/Sweeney_Article.pdf

Weber, R. H., & Heinrich, U. I. (2012). *Anonymization: SpringerBriefs in Cybersecurity*. Springer. doi:10.1007/978-1-4471-4066-5

KEY TERMS AND DEFINITIONS

Big Data: Big data is nothing more than recognizing patterns in the billions and billions of data points created every day worldwide. Powerful computer algorithms analyze any data generated by the intelligent infrastructure of a smart city, or evaluate data from millions of navigation systems.

Data Protection: Making sure personal information gathered by public or private organizations in the delivery of a service is not used for other purposes or shared without the permission of the individual involved.

Data Security: It refers to the protection of data with a view to the respective security requirement. Sensitive data should be protected during processing against forgery, destruction and unauthorized disclosure.

Personal Data: Details that refer to a specific person. According to the Data Protection Act, the term includes information, such as name, address, e-mail address and account number, as well as previous convictions, customer, patient and personnel data.

Smart Cities: Think of a city as a nervous system. Everything that moves within it – be it people or vehicles – generates data. In a smart city these bits of information are assessed by sensors via an intelligent, invisible infrastructure hidden behind traffic lights, street lamps and waste containers.

Smart Mobility: Smart mobility moves people and freight while enhancing economic, environmental, and human resources by emphasizing convenient and accessible multimodal travel (ensuring safety and operating at suitable speeds).

Chapter 5
C-Idea:
A Fast Algorithm for Computing Emerging Closed Datacubes

Mickaël Martin-Nevot
Aix-Marseille Université, France

Sébastien Nedjar
Aix-Marseille Université, France

Lotfi Lakhal
Aix-Marseille Université, France

Rosine Cicchetti
Aix-Marseille Université, France

ABSTRACT

Discovering trend reversals between two data cubes provides users with novel and interesting knowledge when the real-world context fluctuates: What is new? Which trends appear or emerge? With the concept of emerging cube, the authors capture such trend reversals by enforcing an emergence constraint. In a big data context, trend reversal predictions promote a just-in-time reaction to these strategic phenomena. In addition to prediction, a business intelligence approach aids to understand observed phenomena origins. In order to exhibit them, the proposal must be as fast as possible, without redundancy but with ideally an incremental computation. Moreover, the authors propose an algorithm called C-Idea to compute reduced and lossless representations of the emerging cube by using the concept of cube closure. This approach aims to improve efficiency and scalability while preserving integration capability. The C-Idea algorithm works à la Buc and takes the specific features of emerging cubes into account. The proposals are validated by various experiments for which we measure the size of representations.

DOI: 10.4018/978-1-5225-4963-5.ch005

1. INTRODUCTION AND MOTIVATIONS

Decision makers are generally interested in discovering relevant trends by using a data warehouse to analyze data collected from a "population". The data warehouse contains data concerning various measures which are observed with respect to different attributes called dimensions. More precisely, all the possible combinations of dimensions can be relevant and considered at all possible granularity levels. In order to meet this need, the concept of data cube was introduced (Gray et al., 1997). It groups the tuples according to all the dimension combinations along with their associated measures. The main interest of this structure is to support an interactive analysis of data because all the possible trends are yet computed. Of course, due to its very nature (the very great volume of original data and the exponential number of dimension combinations), a data cube is especially voluminous.

Let us assume that we have a data cube costly computed from a set of data accumulated until now in a data warehouse. Let us imagine that a refreshment operation has to be performed in order to insert new collected data. A particularly interesting knowledge can be exhibited from the comparison between the cubes of these two data sets: which novelties does the refreshment bring? which trends, unknown until now, appear? or in contrast, which existing trends disappear? Similar knowledge can be exhibited every time that two semantically comparable data cubes have to be compared. For instance, if two data sets are collected in two different geographical areas or for two population samples, it is possible to highlight the behavior modifications, the contrast between their characteristics or the deviations with respect to a witness sample.

In order to capture trend reversals in data warehouses, we have proposed the concept of Emerg- ing Cube (Nedjar et al., 2013). It results from coupling two interesting structures: the data cube (Gray et al., 1997) and the emerging patterns (Dong & Li, 2005, 1999). From the cube of two database relations, the Emerging Cube gathers all the tuples satisfying a twofold emergence constraint: the value of their measure is weak in a relation (C_1 constraint) and significant in the other relation (C_2 constraint). Computing an Emerging Cube is a difficult problem because two data cubes have to be computed and then compared. As above-mentioned, the computation of the cubes is costly and their comparison has likely a significant cost because their size is really tremen- dous. Then, to really take advantage of the new knowledge captured by the Emerging Cube, it is critical to avoid the computation of the two data cubes.

Although the Emerging Cube limits the results to the ones potentially relevant, its size remains enormous in part because it encompasses a lot of redundancies. In order to discard such superfluous information, we propose the Emerging Closed

Cube which is originated by the concept lattice and adapted to the data cube features. The Emerging Closed Cube is one of the smallest representations from which any Olap query can be answered.

Providing decision makers with the novelties emerging from vast amounts of data is particulary relevant but the underlying computation has to be especially efficient. In such a context of big data, providing a nearly incremental algorithm means for decision makers a thin monotoring of enormous volumes of data and result trace in real-time. With this approach, users can anticipate and detect trend reversals and quickly be informed of what changes. This feature brings an answer to certain big data issues.

Column-oriented database systems have attracted a lot of attention in the last years. Column-database, in a nutshell, store each database table column separately, with attribute values belonging to the same column stored contiguously, compressed, and densely packed, as opposed to traditional database systems that store entire records (rows) one after the other. Reading a subset of a table's columns becomes faster, at the potential expense of excessive disk-head seeking from column to column for scattered reads or updates. In the datawarehousing domain, the more efficient algorithms use subsquently an approach which aggregate column by column. In this context, our contribution will be implemented with Apache HBase in order to take the maximal benefits of the column-oriented nature of the IDEA platform (Abouzeid et al., 2009). The IDEA platform is a data analytics tool able to carry out big data problems (Pavlo et al., 2009).

In this paper, we place emphasis on computing the Emerging Closed Cube. We propose an algorithm called C-Idea which uses the good properties of E-Idea (Nedjar et al., 2011). Its un- derlying objective is to preserve the nice capability of integration within Dbmss because it does not make use of sophisticated data structures not available in a relational database context. C-Idea browses the search space from the most aggregated tuple to the more detailed ones and takes ad- vantage of the emergence constraint combination to prune irrelevant tuples. Our algorithm differs from the classical closed cubing algorithms like Star-Cubing and CCubing because of its inte- grability. Furthermore, all the previous algorithms are dedicated to compute only Iceberg Closed Cubes (Beyer & Ramakrishnan, 1999; Xin et al., 2007) whereas the C-Idea algorithm can yield several variants of data cubes such as Window Cube (Casali et al., 2007) or Emerging Cube (Ned- jar et al., 2013, 2011, 2009, 2010). In order to validate our approach, we perform comparative experiments on various data sets used by classical cubing algorithms. The experimental results focus on the size of the Emerging Cube and the Emerging Closed Cube.

The remainder of the article is organized as follows. Section 2.1 describes the constrained cube lattice framework. In section 2.2, we summarize the structure of the Emerging Closed Cube.

2. RELATED WORK

The approaches addressing the issue of Datacube computation and storage attempt to reduce at least one of the quoted drawbacks. The algorithms Buc (Beyer & Ramakrishnan, 1999) and Hcubing (Han et al., 2001) enforce anti-monotone constraints and partially compute Datacubes (iceberg cubes) to reduce both execution time and disk storage requirements. The underlying argument is that Olap users are only interested in general trends (and not in atypical behaviors). With a similar argumentation, other methods use the statistic structure of data to compute density distributions and give approximate answers to Olap queries (see for details (Morfonios et al., 2007)).

The above mentioned approaches are efficient and meet their twofold objective (reduction of execution time and space storage). However, they are not able to answer whatever query (although Olap queries are, by their very nature, ad hoc queries).

Another category of approaches is the so-called \information lossless". They aim to find the best compromise between Olap query efficiency and storage requirements without discarding any possible query (even unfrequent). Their main idea is to pre-compute and store frequently used aggregates while preserving all the data (possibly at various aggregation levels) needed to compute on line the result of a not foreseen query. They are mostly found in view materialization research.

The following five methods also _t in the information lossless trend:

- The Dwarf Cube (Sismanis et al., 2002),
- The Condensed Cube (Wei et al., 2002),
- The CURE for Cubes (Morfonios and Ioannidis, 2006),
- The Quotient Cube (Lakshmanan et al., 2002),
- The Closed Cube (Casali et al., 2009a, 2003b; Xin et al., 2007).

They favor the optimization of storage space while preserving the capability to answer whatever query. The two latter compute the two smallest representations of a Datacube and thus are the most efficient for both saving storage space and answering queries like \Is this behavior frequent or not?". From these two representations, the exact data of a whole Datacube can be retrieved by performing a computation on line, because all the results of queries are not precomputed and preserved.

The two following sections are the core of our contribution. The former one presents the C-Idea algorithm and the latter details the experimental results. Finally, through a discussion, we compare our approach with related work.

3. EMERGING CUBES

3.1. Constrained Cube Lattice Framework

When computing data cubes, the cuboid lattice is frequently considered. By organizing all the possible dimension combinations within a lattice, it can be used for choosing navigation and computation strategies. However, it is not the search space for cube computation.

In this section, we recall the concept of the cube lattice (Casali et al., 2003) proposed as a general and soundly founded framework to state and solve several Olap mining problems, including the Emerging Cube characterization.

Let us consider a database relation *r* with a set of attributes dimensions D (denoted by $D_1, \ldots, D_n$) and a set of measures (noted M). The Constrained Datacube characterization fits in the more general framework of the cube lattice of the relation *r*: *CL*(*r*) (Casali et al., 2003). The latter is a suitable search space which is to be considered when computing the data cube of *r*. It organizes the multidimensional tuples, possible solutions of the problem, according to a specializa- tion / generalization order, denoted by *s* (Lakshmanan et al., 2002). These tuples are structured according to the attributes dimensions of *r* which can be provided with the value ALL (Gray et al., 1997). Moreover, we append to these tuples a virtual tuple which only encompasses empty values in order to close the structure. Any tuple of the cube lattice generalizes the tuple of empty values.

For handling the tuples of *CL*(*r*), the operator + is defined. This operator is a specification of the meet operator (Greatest Lower Bound) applied to the cube lattice framework (Casali et al., 2003): provided with a couple of tuples, it yields the most specific tuple in *CL*(*r*) which generalizes the two operands. Dually, the Product operator, noted •, is a specification of the join operator (Lowest Upper Bound) in our framework. The Product of two tuples yields the most general tuple which specializes the two operands.

3.1.1. Mathematical Foundation: The Cube Lattice Framework

The multidimensional space of the categorical database relation *r* groups all the valid combina- tions built up by considering the value sets of attributes in D, which are enriched with the symbolic value ALL or $*$. The latter, introduced in (Gray et al., 1997) when defining the operator Cube-By, is a generalization of all the possible values for any dimension.

The multidimensional space of r is noted and defined as follows: $space(r) = \{\times A \in D\ (r(A) \cup \text{ALL})\} \cup \{(\emptyset, \ldots, \emptyset)\}$ where $\times$ symbolizes the Cartesian product, $r(A)$ is the projection of r on the attribute A and the tuple $(\emptyset, \ldots, \emptyset)$ stands for the combination of empty values. Any combination belonging to the multidimensional space is a tuple and represents a multidimensional pattern.

The multidimensional space of r is structured by the generalization / specialization order be- tween tuples, denoted by <s

Definition 1 (Generalization / Specialization Order): Let u, v be two tuples of the multidi- mensional space of r:

$u\ s\ v \Leftrightarrow \forall A \in \text{D}$ such that $u[A]$ 6= ALL, $u[A] = v[A]$ or $v = (\emptyset, \ldots, \emptyset)$

The ordered set ($space(r)$, <s) is a complete lattice called Cube Lattice denoted by $CL(r)$ (Casali et al., 2003).

If u <s v, we say that u is less specific (more general) than v in $CL(r)$. In other words, u captures a similar information than v but at a rougher granularity level.

Example 1: A website sells various products to customers and accumulates data about sales in a data warehouse. Table 1 exemplifies such data. The various dimensions are the following: the customer's city, the sale month and day, the product category and the year.

Table 1. Relation example sales

City	Month	Category	Year	Quantity
Paris	11/06	Clothes	2016	100
Paris	11/06	Video Game	2016	100
London	11/09	Video Game	2016	100
Berlin	11/09	Video Game	2016	600
London	11/06	Video Game	2016	100
London	11/06	Clothes	2017	300
London	11/09	Video Game	2017	300
London	11/06	Video Game	2017	300
Paris	11/06	Clothes	2017	300
Berlin	11/09	Video Game	2017	200
Berlin	11/09	Clothes	2017	200
Berlin	11/06	Video Game	2017	100

Let us consider the June's sales in Paris, *i.e.* the multidimensional tuple (Paris, 11/06, ALL, ALL). This tuple is specialized by the following two tuples of the relation: (Paris, 11/06, Clothes, 2016) and (Paris, 11/06, Video Game, 2016). Furthermore, (Paris, 11/06, ALL, ALL) *s* (Paris, 11/06, Clothes, 2016) exemplifies the specialization order between tuples.

The two basic operators provided for tuple construction are: Sum (denoted by +) and Product (noted •). The Sum of two tuples yields the most specific tuple which generalizes the two operands.

Definition 2 (Sum Operator): Let u and v be two tuples in $CL(r)$,

$t = u + v \Leftrightarrow \forall A \in \mathrm{D}, t[A] = u[A]$ if $u[A] = v[A]$ ALL otherwise.

We say that t is the Sum of the tuples u and v.

Example 2: In our example, we have (Paris, 11/06, Clothes, 2016) + (Paris, 11/06, Clothes, 2017) = (Paris, 11/06, Clothes, ALL). This means that the tuple (Paris, 11/06, Clothes, ALL) is built up from the tuples (Paris, 11/06, Clothes, 2016) and (Paris, 11/06, Clothes, 2017).

The Product of two tuples yields the most general tuple which specializes the two operands. If it exists, for these two tuples, a dimension A having distinct and real-world values (i.e. existing in the original relation), then the only tuple specializing them is the tuple (∅, . . ., ∅) (apart from it, the tuple sets which can be used to retrieve them are disjoined).

Definition 3 (Product Operator): Let u and v be two tuples in $CL(r)$, then:

$t = (\varnothing, \ldots, \varnothing)$ if $\exists A \in \mathrm{D}$ such that $u[A]$ 6= $v[A]$ 6= ALL,

$t = u \bullet v \Leftrightarrow$

otherwise $\forall A \in \mathrm{D}$

$t[A] = u[A]$ if $v[A] =$ ALL

$t[A] = v[A]$ if $u[A] =$ ALL.

We say that t is the Product of the tuples u and v.

Example 3: In our example, we have (ALL, 11/06, ALL, ALL) • (Paris, ALL, Clothes, ALL) = (Paris, 11/06, Clothes, ALL). This means that (ALL, 11/06, ALL, ALL) and (Paris, ALL, Clothes, ALL) are less specific than (Paris, 11/06, Clothes, ALL) and this latter tuple participates to the construction of (ALL, 11/06, ALL, ALL) and (Paris, ALL, Clothes, ALL) (directly or not). The tuples (London, ALL, ALL, ALL) and (Paris, ALL, ALL, ALL) have no common specific tuple apart from the tuple of empty values (∅, . . ., ∅).

By providing the multidimensional space of r with the Generalization / Specialization order between tuples and using the above-defined operators Sum and Product, we define an algebraic structure which is called cube lattice. Such a structure provides a sound foundation for several multidimensional data mining issues.

Theorem 1: *Let r be a categorical database relation over* D ∪ M. *The ordered set CL(r) = (space(r), <s) is a complete, graded, atomic and co-atomic lattice, called cube lattice in which Meet* (∧) *and Join* (∨) *elements are given by:*

$\forall\, T \subseteq CL(r), \wedge T = +t \in T\, t$

$\forall\, T \subseteq CL(r), \vee T = \bullet t \in T\, t$

3.1.2. Constrained Datacube

In the remainder of this section, we study the cube lattice structure faced with conjunctions of monotone and anti-monotone constraints according to the specialization / generalization order. We show that this structure is a convex space which is called Constrained Datacube. We propose condensed representations (with borders) of the Constrained Datacube with a twofold objective: defining the solution space in a compact way and deciding whether a tuple t belongs or not to this space.

We consider the monotone and anti-monotone constraints the most used in database mining (Pei et al., 2004). They are applied on:

- Measures of interest like pattern frequency, confidence, correlation. In these cases, only the dimensions of D are necessary;
- Aggregates computed from measures of M and using statistic additive functions (Sum, Count, ...) or algebraic ones (Avg, ...).

We recall the definitions of convex space, monotone and/or anti-monotone constraints according to the specialization / generalization order <s.

Definition 4 (Convex Space): Let (P, $\leq$) be a partial ordered set, C $\subseteq$ P is a convex space *if and only if* $\forall x,y,z \in$ P, $(x \leq y \leq z \wedge x,z \in$ C$) \Rightarrow y \in$ C. Thus, C is bordered by two sets:

1. An *"Upper set"*, noted U, defined by $U = \max_{\leq}(C)$, and
2. A *"Lower set"*, noted L and defined by $L = \min_{\leq}(C)$.

Definition 5 (Monotone/anti-monotone constraints):

1. A constraint *Const* is monotone according to the specialization order if and only if $\forall t,u \in$

$CL(r)$, $(t <_s u \wedge Const(t)) \Rightarrow Const(u)$.

2. A constraint *Const* is anti-monotone according to the specialization order if and only if

$\forall t,u \in CL(r)$, $(t <_s u \wedge Const(u)) \Rightarrow Const(t)$.

Notations: We note *cmc* (*camc* respectively) a conjunction of monotone constraints (anti-monotone respectively) and *chc* a hybrid conjunction of constraints.

Theorem 2: *The cube lattice with monotone and/or anti-monotone constraints const = cmc* $\wedge$ camc is a convex space which is called Constrained Datacube. It is defined:

$CD(r) = \{t \in CL(r)$ *such that* $const(t)\}$

Any tuple belonging to the Constrained Datacube is called a constrained tuple.

The characterization of the Constrained Datacube as a convex space makes it possible to know whether a tuple satisfies or not the constraint conjunction by only knowing the classical *L*ower and *U* pper borders [L; U] (Casali et al., 2007) of the Constrained Datacube. Actually, if a conjunction of anti-monotone constraints holds for a tuple of $CL(r)$, then any tuple generalizing it also respects the constraints. Dually if a tuple fulfills a monotone constraint conjunction, then all the tuples specializing it also satisfy the constraints.

Now we present another couple of borders for the Constrained Datacube: the borders]$U^{\sharp}$; U] (Ned- jar et al., 2013, 2009). This representation is based on the maximal tuples satisfying the anti- monotone constraint without verifying the monotone one.

Definition 6 (Borders]U$^\sharp$;U]): The Constrained Datacube can be represented through two bor- ders: U and $U^\sharp$ encompassing all the maximal tuples not satisfying the monotone constraint but satisfying the anti-monotone constraint. Thus, we have:

$$U^\sharp = \max_{\leq_s} (\{t \in CL(r) \mid \neg cmc(t) \wedge camc(t)\})$$

$$U = \max_{\leq_s} (\{t \in CL(r) \mid cmc(t) \wedge camc(t)\})$$

Proposition 3: *The borders* $]U^\sharp; U]$ *are a condensed representation for the Constrained Datacube:* $\forall\, t \in CL(r)$, *t is a constrained tuple if and only if* $\forall\, l \in U^\sharp$, l s t *and* $\exists u \in U$ *such that* t s u. *Thus t is a constrained tuple if and only if it belongs to the "range"* $]U^\sharp; U]$.

3.2. Structure of Datacubes

The idea behind our representation is to remove redundancies existing within Constrained Datacubes. In fact, certain multidimensional tuples are built up by aggregating the very same tuples of the original relation but at different granularity levels. Thus, a single tuple, the most specific of them, can stand for the whole set. The Cube Closure operator is intended for computing these representative tuples, called closed tuples.

In contrast with the frequent closed patterns as well as the Iceberg Closed Cube which provide reduced representations only encompassing closed elements, such a type of representation is not possible in the context of constrained Datacubes. We propose the information to be appended to the set of closed constrained tuples in order to achieve lossless representations.

3.2.1. Cube Closure

The cube connection (Casali et al., 2009) is a couple of functions $rc = (\lambda,\sigma)$, such that λ is defined from the cube lattice of r to the power set lattice of $Tid(r)$ (defined above) and σ is the dual function of λ. We show that rc is a special case of Galois connection between two lattices (Ganter & Wille, 1999). Hence, we obtain a closure operator over $CL(r)$ under r.

Definition 7 (Cube Connection): Let $Rowid$: $r \rightarrow N^*$ be a mapping which associates each tuple with a single positive integer and $Tid(r) = \{Rowid(t) \mid t \in r\}$ (*i.e.* the set of the tuple identifiers of the relation r). Let λ and σ be two functions defined as follows:

λ: $CL(r) \longrightarrow$ P($Tid(r)$), $\subseteq$

$t \longrightarrow \cup \{Rowid(t') \mid t <s\, t' \wedge t' \in r\}$

σ: P($Tid(r)$), $\subseteq \longrightarrow CL(r)$

$P \longrightarrow +\{t \in r \mid Rowid(t) \in P\ \}$

P($Tid(r)$) stands for the power set of the tuple identifiers of the relation r.

Proposition 4: *The cube connection rc = (λ,σ) is a Galois connection between the cube lattice of r and the power set lattice of Tid(r).*

Definition 8 (Cube Closure): Let $T \subseteq CL(r)$ be a set of tuples, the Cube Closure operator C: $CL(r) \rightarrow CL(r)$ according to T can be defined as follows:

$\mathrm{C}(t,T) = \sigma \circ \lambda(t) = (\varnothing, \ldots, \varnothing) + \sum t'$

$t' \in$T,t st'

Let us consider all the tuples t' in T. Let us aggregate them together by using the operator $\sum$. We obtain a new tuple which generalizes all the tuples t' and which is the most specific one. This new tuple is the closure of t.

Definition 9 (Measure function compatible with the cube closure): A measure function f from $CL(r) \rightarrow$ R is compatible with the closure operator C over $T \subseteq CL(r)$ if and only if $\forall t, u \in T$, it satisfies the three following properties:

1. $t \leq_s u \Rightarrow f(t,T) \geq f(u,T) \vee f(t,T) \leq f(u,T)$,
2. $\mathrm{C}(t,T) = \mathrm{C}(u,T) \Rightarrow f(t,T) = f(u,T)$,
3. $t \leq_s u \wedge f(t,T) = f(u,T) \Rightarrow \mathrm{C}(t,T) = \mathrm{C}(u,T)$.

This function is an adaptation of the weight function introduced in (Stumme et al., 2002) for any closure system of the power set. For example, the measure functions Count and Sum are compatible with the Cube Closure operator.

Definition 10 (Cover): Let $t \in CL(r)$, the cover of t is the set of tuples of r that are generalized by t (*i.e.* $cov(t,r) = \{t' \in CL(r)$ such that $t \leq_s t'\}$).

The cover relation is strongly related to the cube closure. Actually, two tuples $t,t \in CL(r)$ share the same closure on r, $\mathrm{C}(t,r) = \mathrm{C}(t,r)$, if and only if $cov(t,r) = cov(t,r)$.

By using the closure operator, we can yield the closed constrained tuples which are representa- tive of the other ones. By this way, redundancies can be discarded.

Definition 11 (Constrained Closed Tuple): Let $t \in CL(r)$ be a tuple, t is a constrained closed tuple if and only if:

1. t is a constrained tuple;
2. $C(t, r) = t$.

Of course, the closure of any constrained tuple is a constrained closed tuple because, by its very definition, it is the most specific among all the tuples which generalize it. Thus, it is necessarily equal to its own closure.

Unfortunately, the set of constrained closed tuples is not a lossless representation of the Con- strained Datacube because for certain tuples it is not possible to decide whether they are con- strained or not. They are all the tuples more general than the most general constrained closed tuples.

In order to achieve a lossless representation, we combine on the one hand the set of constrained closed tuples from which the measure values can be retrieved and on the other hand the borders which form the boundaries of the solution space. However, the border U is already included in the closed tuple set, because the elements of U are the most detailed (specific) constrained tuples. Thus, they are necessarily closed tuples.

3.2.2. Constrained Closed Datacubes

In this section, we introduce a new structure: the Constrained Closed Datacubes. It includes both the set of constrained closed tuples and the border $U^{\sharp}$. From definition 9, we can provide another characterization of the tuples of the border $U^{\sharp}$: they are closed tuples satisfying the anti- monotone constraint, but not the monotone constraint.

Definition 12 (Constrained Closed Datacube): The Constrained Closed Datacube is defined as follows: $CCD(r) = \{t \in CL(r)$ such that t is a constrained closed tuple$\} \cup U^{\sharp}$

In order to prove that the Constrained Closed Datacube is a lossless representation for the Constrained Datacube we introduce two propositions. The first one shows that for any constrained tuple, we can compute its cube closure from either r or the Constrained Closed Datacube, and of course obtain the same result. The second one shows that two tuples having a same cube closure have a same measure.

Proposition 5: *For all constrained closed tuples t,* C(t, CCD) = C(t, r)

Proof.
Let t be a constrained closed tuple

$\Rightarrow C(t,r) = (\varnothing, \ldots, \varnothing) + \sum t' = t$ such that $t' \in r$ and $t \, s \, t'$

$\Rightarrow C(t, CCD(r)) = (\varnothing, \ldots, \varnothing) + \sum t'$ such that $t' = (\varnothing, \ldots, \varnothing) + \sum v$, $t' <s\, v$ and $t <s\, t'$

$\Rightarrow C(t, CCD(r)) = (\varnothing, \ldots, \varnothing) + \sum\sum v$ such that $v \in r$ and $t <s\, v$

According to the properties of $\sum$, we have:

$C(t, CCD(r)) = (\varnothing, \ldots, \varnothing) + \sum v = C(t, r)$ with $v \in r$ and $t <s\, v$

Proposition 6: *The Constrained Closed Datacube is a lossless representation for the Constrained Datacube:* $\forall\, t \in CL(r)$, *t is a constrained tuple if and only if:* $C(t, CCD(r)) \in CCD(r) \backslash U^{\sharp}$.

Proof. If t is constrained, we know that $t' = C(t,r)$ has a measure equal to the one of t. Since t is constrained, t' is also constrained. Thus t' is a constrained closed tuple, according to proposition 5:

$C(t', r) = C(t', CCD(r)) = C(t, CCD(r))$

Thus we have $C(t, CCD(r)) \in CCD(r)$.
If t is not constrained then $\exists u \in U^{\sharp}$ such that $t <s\, u$ and thus for all the constrained closed tuples t', $t s t'$. Since the closure of a tuple is the sum of all the tuples specializing it and t is only specialized by tuples of $U^{\sharp}$ then $C(t, CCD(r) \backslash U^{\sharp}) \notin CCD(r) \backslash U^{\sharp}$.

3.2.3. Reduced Constrained Closed Datacubes

In the previous section, we have shown that the border $U^{\sharp}$ must be appended to the constrained closed tuples in order to achieve an information-lossless representation of the Constrained Datacube. By making use of the cube closure, we simplify the border $U^{\sharp}$ by discarding all the redundancies that it can encompass. By this way, we obtain a new lossless representation: the Reduced Constrained Closed Datacube.

Definition 13 (Redundant Closed Tuple): For all tuple $t \in U^{\sharp}$, t is a redundant closed tuple if and only if:

$$C(t, CCD(r) \setminus \{t\}) = t$$

Let us notice that the above definition is proposed in the same spirit as the elimination of redundant attributes when computing minimal covers for functional dependencies.

Definition 14 (*Reduced U*$^{\sharp}$ Border): The *Reduced U*$^{\sharp}$Border is defined as follows:

$$U^{\sharp\sharp} = \{t \in U^{\sharp} \mid t \text{ is not a redundant closed tuple}\}$$

Let us recall that, like all the tuples of $U^{\sharp}$, all the tuples of $U^{\sharp\sharp}$ satisfy the anti-monotone constraint. If we consider the lattice L which encompasses all the constrained closed tuples satisfying the anti- monotone constraint, the tuples of $U^{\sharp\sharp}$ are$_k$ the meet-irreducible elements of L which do not verify the monotone constraint.

Table 2. Relation example sales 2016

City	Month	Category	Quantity
Paris	11/06	Clothes	100
Paris	11/06	Video Game	100
London	11/09	Video Game	100
Berlin	11/09	Video Game	600
London	11/06	Video Game	100

Table 3. Relation example sales 2017

City	Month	Category	Quantity
London	11/06	Clothes	300
London	11/09	Video Game	300
London	11/06	Video Game	300
Paris	11/06	Clothes	300
Berlin	11/09	Video Game	200
Berlin	11/09	Clothes	200
Berlin	11/06	Video Game	100

2.3. Emerging Cubes Characterization

In this section, we resume and summarize the issue addressed when proposing the concept of Emerging Cube which is an instance of the Constrained Cube.

Definition 15 (Measure Function): Let *f* be an aggregate function, *r* a database relation and *t* a multidimensional tuple. We denote by $f_{val}(t,r)$ the value of the aggregate function *f* for the tuple *t* in the relation *r*.

Example 4: In the $Sales_{2016}$ relation (*cf.* Table 2), the total sale in Paris for the month 11/06 and any product category can be given by Sum_{val}((Paris, 11/06, ALL), $Sales_{2016}$) = 200.

In the remainder of the chapter, we only consider additive aggregate functions (Pei et al., 2004):

Count, Sum, Min, Max.

Definition 16 (Emerging Tuple): Let r_1 and r_2 be two compatible relations (same set of di- mensions and measures). A tuple $t \in CL(r_1 \cup r_2)$ is said emerging from r_1 to r_2 if and only if it satisfies the following two constraints C_1 and C_2:

$f_{val}(t,r_1) \leq MinThreshold_1$ (C_1)

$f_{val}(t,r_2) > MinThreshold_2$ (C_2)

Example 5: Let us consider the $Sales_{2016}$ and $Sales_{2017}$ (*cf.* Table 3) relations. We suppose that they correspond to the dataset of a website for two different years. Let $MinThreshold_1 = 200$ be the threshold for the relation $Sales_{2016}$ and $MinThreshold_2 = 200$ the threshold for $Sales_{2017}$. Then the tuple t_1 = (London, 11/06, ALL) is emerging from $Sales_{2016}$ to $Sales_{2017}$ because $Sum_{val}(t_1, Sales_{2016}) = 100$ ($\leq MinThreshold_1$) and $Sum_{val}(t_1, Sales_{2017}) = 600$ (> *Min- Threshold*$_2$). In contrast, the tuple t_2 = (Berlin, 11/06, ALL) is not emerging because $Sum_{val}(t_2, Sales_{2017}) = 100$ (< $MinThreshold_2$).

Definition 17 (Emergence Rate): Let r_1 and r_2 be two compatible relations, $t \in CL(r_1 \cup r_2)$ a tuple and *f* an additive function. The emergence rate of *t* from r_1 to r_2, denoted by *ER*(*t*), is defined by:

0 if $f_{val}(t,r_1) = 0$ and $f_{val}(t,r_2) = 0$

$ER(t) = \infty$ if $f_{val}(t,r_1) = 0$ and $f_{val}(t,r_2)$ 6= 0

$f_{val}(t,r_2)$

$f_{val}(t,r_1)$

otherwise.

We observe that when the emergence rate is greater than 1, it characterizes trends significant in r_2 and not so clear-cut in r_1. In contrast, when the rate is lower than 1, it highlights disappearing trends, relevant in r_1 and not in r_2.

Example 6: From the two relations, Sales_{2016} and Sales_{2017}, we compute *ER*((London, 11/06, ALL)) = 600/100. Of course, the higher the emergence rate is, the more distinctive the trend is. Therefore, the quoted tuple means a jump of the sales in London for the month 11/06 between Sales_{2016} and Sales_{2017}.

Definition 18 (Emerging Cube): Let $C_1(t)$ and $C_2(t)$ be given emerging constraints (*cf.* Defi- nition 16). The set of all the tuples of $CL(r_1 \cup r_2)$ emerging from r_1 to r_2 is called the Emerging Cube and we denote it by $\text{Ec}(r_1, r_2)$:

$$\text{Ec}(r_1, r_2) = \{t \in CL(r_1 \cup r_2) \mid C_1(t) \wedge C_2(t)\}$$

Example 7: Table 4 provides the Cube emerging from the relations Sales_{2016} to Sales_{2017} with the thresholds $MinThreshold_1 = 200$ and $MinThreshold_2 = 200$.

This Emerging Cube is also depicted in Figure 1 (the emerging tuples are the ones appearing in a rectangle). For the sake of readability, the dimension values are coded as follows:

City | Month | Category

Paris = P | 11/06 = 1 | Video Game = V

London = L | 11/09 = 2 | Clothes = C

Berlin = B |

Moreover, ∗' stands for the ALL value.

2.4. Emerging Closed Cubes

In this section, we introduce a new structure: the Emerging Closed Cube. It includes both (i) the set of emerging closed tuples and (*ii*) the border $U^\sharp$. This new approach

Figure 1. Representation of the emerging cube and its borders over the cube lattice of sales 2017

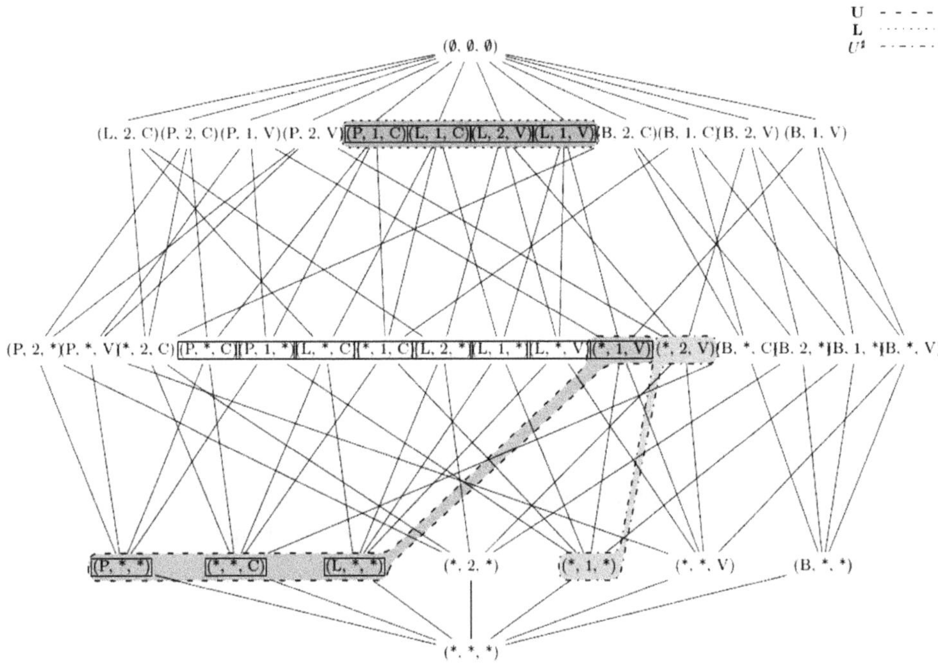

is different from the one proposed in (Bonchi & Lucchese, 2004) in the context of transaction databases and which encompasses the constrained closed patterns and the *Lower* border (*L*).

For reason of simplicity we use, from now on, *t* instead of $(t, f_{val}(t))$ to handle a complete tuple with its dimension values and its measure. In a similar way, we use $U^\sharp$ instead of $(U^\sharp, -)$.

Definition 19 (Emerging Closed Tuple): Let $t \in CL(r)$ be a tuple, *t* is an emerging closed tuple if and only if:

1. *t* is an emerging tuple;
2. $C(t, r_1 \cup r_2) = t$.

Of course, the closure of any emerging tuple is an emerging closed tuple because, by its very definition, it is the most specific among all the tuples which generalize it. Thus, it is necessarily equal to its own closure.

Example 8: The tuple (Paris, 11/06, Clothes) is an emerging closed tuple because:

1. (Paris, 11/06, Clothes) is an emerging tuple (*cf.* Figure 1)
2. C((Paris, 11/06, Clothes), $Sale_1 \cup Sale_2$) = (Paris, 11/06, Clothes)

The set of emerging closed tuples is not a cover of the Emerging Cube because for certain tuples it is not possible to decide whether they are emerging or not.

Example 9: Let us consider the set of all emerging tuples (T) in Table 6. The tuple (London, ALL, Video Game) is not emerging whereas its closure on T (London, 11/06, Video Game) is emerging.

Definition 20 (Emerging Closed Cube): The Emerging Closed Cube is defined as follows: $Ecc(r_1, r_2) = \{t \in CL(r_2)$ such that t is an emerging closed tuple$\} \cup U^\sharp$.

Example 10: The Emerging Closed Cube is represented through table 6 giving the set of emerging closed tuples and table 5 which proposes the upper border $U^\sharp$.

In order to prove that the Emerging Closed Cube is a cover for the Emerging Cube we introduce two propositions. The former shows that for any emerging tuple, we can compute its cube closure from either $r_1 \cup r_2$ or the Emerging Closed Cube, and of course obtain the same result. The latter shows that two tuples having a same cube closure have a same emergence rate.

Table 4. Cube emerging from $Sales_{2016}$ to $Sales_{2017}$

City	Month	Category	ER
London	11/06	Clothes	∞
London	11/06	Video Game	3
London	11/06	ALL	6
London	11/09	Video Game	3
London	11/09	ALL	3
London	ALL	ALL	4
Paris	11/06	Clothes	3
Paris	11/06	ALL	1
Paris	ALL	ALL	1
London	ALL	Clothes	∞
Paris	ALL	Clothes	3
NULL	ALL	Clothes	8
London	ALL	Video Game	3
NULL	11/06	Clothes	6
NULL	11/06	Video Game	2

Table 5. Border $U^\sharp$

(ALL, 11/09, Video Game)	-
(ALL, 11/06, ALL)	-

Table 6. Set of emerging closed tuples

Emerging Closed Tuple	ER
(London, 11/06, Clothes)	∞
(London, 11/06, Video Game)	3
(London, 11/06, ALL)	6
(London, ALL, ALL)	4
(Paris, 11/06, Clothes)	3
(Paris, 11/06, ALL)	1
(Paris, ALL, Clothes)	3
(ALL, ALL, Clothes)	8
(London, ALL, Video Game)	3
(ALL, 11/06, Clothes)	6
(ALL, 11/06, Video Game)	2

Proposition 7: *For all emerging closed tuples t,* $C(t, Ecc(r_1, r_2)) = C(t, r_1 \cup r_2)$
Proposition 8: *Let t and u be two emerging tuples, if t and u have a same cube closure over* $r_1 \cup r_2$*, thus their emergence rate is the same.* $\forall t, u \in EC(r_1, r_2)$ *such that* $C(t, r_1 \cup r_2) = C(u, r_1 \cup r_2)$*, we have* $ER(t) = ER(u)$.

3. COMPUTING EMERGING CLOSED CUBES

Providing the Emerging datacube with representations reduced as much as possible is critical because of the tremendous volume of managed data. But such representations without computing tools have a poor interest. In this section, we propose an algorithm for computing Emerging Closed Cubes. It is devised as an operator offered to OLAP users and which can be fully integrated within DBMSS. We take benefit of the cube closure properties because by discarding data redundancies, we also discard superfluous computations. The strong reduction of our representation originates an especially efficient algorithm.

Due to the heterogeneous nature of our representation, we need to develop two algorithmic approaches; one devoted to the borders and the other dedicated to the closed emerging tuples. Even if the two parts of the representation are different, they are based on similar concepts associated to the Emerging Cube. We rely on the E-Idea (Nedjar et al., 2011, 2013) algorithm in order to develop a generic framework which can be instantiated for the efficient computation of, on the one hand, the borders and on the other hand the closed tuples. With the choice of E-Idea as a work basis, the instantiations of our framework inherit of its interesting properties: integrability within Dbmss, modularity, low memory consumption and execution efficiency.

3.1. The Idea Framework

In this section, we present our general algorithmic schema. It makes use of the enforced con- straints in order to explore the search space in an adaptive way. In order to provide the user with an operator which can be directly applied, the algorithm that we propose must be integrated within DBMSS. By devising an integrated relational approach, it is possible to take advantage of existing ROLAP analysis tools. Then, the Closed Emerging Cube will be a particular data cube and like for the original one it will be possible to express queries, explore and navigate within it.

A feature of the Idea algorithm is to efficiently take into account any conjunction of mono- tone/antimonotone constraints. This conjunction is divided in two parts: *cmc* which is monotone and *camc* which is antimonotone. The way used to explore the cube lattice favors the antimonotone constraint. Indeed, the more aggregate tuples are dealt before the less aggregate ones. The former will likely satisfy the *camc* constraint while the latter have a smaller probability to have a measure above the threshold. When the other constraint no longer holds, the algorithm stops.

At the beginning of the processing, the considered tuples do not satisfy the *cmc* constraint but verify *camc*: these tuples are not emerging, they must be ignored. Once these tuples are discarded, Idea deals with the emerging tuples which will be written on disk. Then, the algorithm leaves the solution space when *camc* no longer holds and the encountered tuples as well as all their successors are no longer emerging and the algorithm stops. Figure 2 illustrates within a cube lattice the different steps of the algorithm while navigating through the search space.

In order to consider all the possible cases, the algorithm encloses several steps and for each one it has a specific behavior. As shown in Figure 2, three steps are distinguished (P_1, P_2 and P_3) and each one corresponds to the state (verified or not verified) of the constraints *cmc* and *camc*. The following schema gives the correspondence between the constraint state and the step of the algorithm.

| *camc* | ¬*camc*

cmc | P2 |P3

Figure 2. Illustration of the different steps encountered by idea

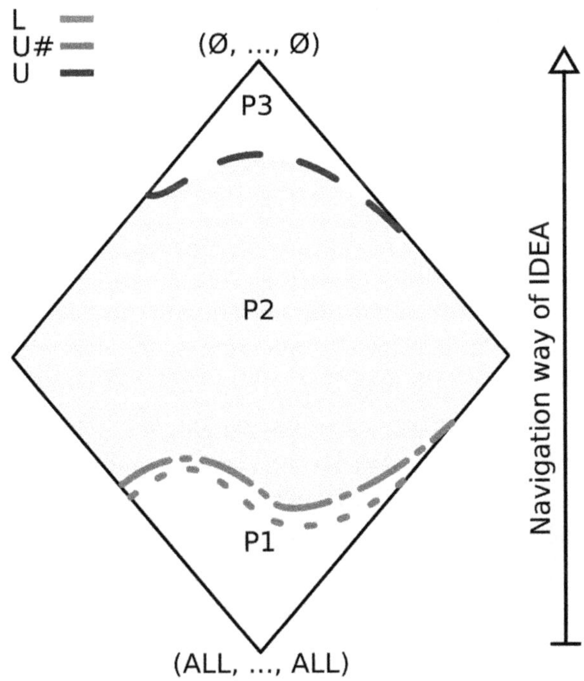

**For a more accurate representation see the electronic version.*

¬*cmc* | *P1* |

As underlined above, *cmc* and *camc* have a particular nature. The depth first exploration of Idea means that the monotone constraint is likely not satisfied at the beginning of the algorithm and it will hold further. In contrast, the antimonotone constraint is verified at the beginning whereas it does not hold later. All the transitions between steps cannot happen. For instance, if the algorithm is in the P_3 step (the *camc* constraint is no longer verified), it cannot enter any other step.

The automaton given in Figure 3 describes the various possible transitions.

Let us describe the behavior of the algorithm in each of these steps.

- **Initial Step $\mathbf{P_1}$:** This step corresponds to the starting up of the algorithm and the processing of the first tuples which are likely not relevant because the *cmc* constraint is not satisfied yet. The algorithm makes a partition of the relation without writing any result. A step transition is performed by Idea as soon as one of the two constraints is in a new state.
- **Main Step $\mathbf{P_2}$:** During this step, all the encountered tuples are emerging. Idea must write them on disk. These Input/output operations are very costly, this

step is the most time consuming. It ends when a tuple not satisfying the *camc* constraint is encountered. Then, the algorithm enters the third step.

- **Final Step P_3:** When the algorithm reaches this step, the *camc* constraint does not hold for the current tuple *t*. Since the constraint is monotone, it cannot be verified for all the tuples more specific than *t*. It is no longer necessary to scan the search space and the algorithm ends.

3.1.1. Detailed Description of the Idea Algorithm

Idea is an adaptation of the Buc's algorithmic schema to compute the Emerging Cube. The algorithm scans the search space from bottom to top. It begins with the cuboid according to ∅ and goes up through the cuboid lattice by using the lexicographic order. For the sake of simplicity, we assume that the order between attributes (≤D) is the alphabetical order. Hence, the lexicographical order for scanning the nodes is the very same as the dictionary order. The order relation ≤D does not affect the algorithm correctness but can have serious consequences on its efficiency. From a practical point of view, several heuristics to find the best order between attributes have been proposed in Beyer & Ramakrishnan (1999) and experimented by Nasr & Badr (2003).

Idea is a recursive algorithm based on the horizontal partitioning. In a rather rough way, Idea can be seen as a version of Partitioned-Cube which never calls

Figure 3. Automaton of the idea algorithm

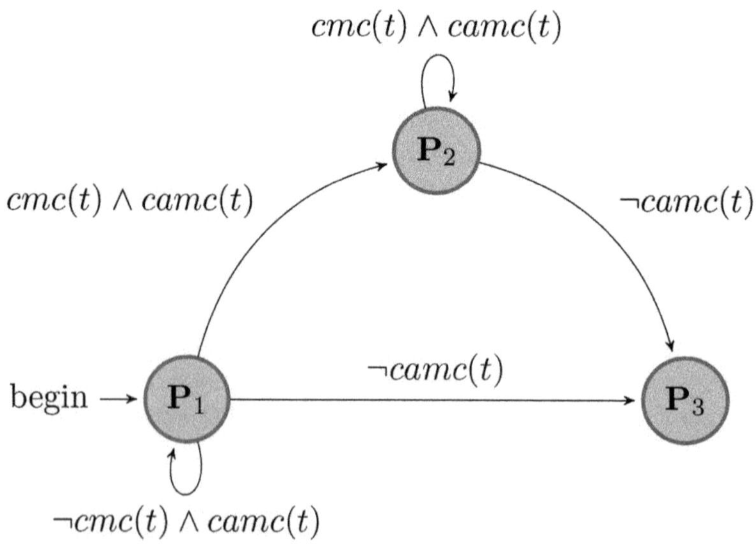

Memory-Cube (Ross & Srivastava, 1997). Therefore, it takes advantage of the good I/O efficiency of Partitioned-Cube and the pruning *`a la* APRIORI (Agrawal et al., 1996).

Our algorithm is cut up in the following sub-algorithms:

- Idea (*cf.* Algorithm 4)
- WriteSuccessors (*cf.* Algorithm 3) which writes the results directly on disk when the aggregate value of the current partition is obvious to compute.
- Partition (*cf.* Algorithm 1) which efficiently cuts up the relation in fragments according to the values of the current attribute. The operation is performed by a counting sort with linear complexity.
- Aggregate (*cf.* Algorithm 2) which computes the measure value for the current partition.

For a sake of efficiency, we do not work on the two relations r_1 and r_2 but instead on a merged relation being provided with two measures attributes, the aggregate function must apply on each attribute. From these two aggregate values, the emergence rate can be achieved for the current multidimensional tuple.

The feature of the Idea algorithm (*cf.* Algorithm 4) is to adapt its behavior according to its current step. For the first call, the current cell given in parameter is ('ALL', . . ., 'ALL'). The first aggregate operation performs a pass over r in order to compute the measure value (*cf.* Algorithm 2). Once this operation is achieved, the algorithm verifies if r contains a single tuple. In such a case, the aggregate tuple is already computed. WriteSuccessors is called (*cf.* Algorithm 3) and the algorithm ends. WriteSuccessors replaces, attribute after attribute, each ALL value of the current cell by the value of the single tuple of the partition. This operation is particularly important when data are very sparse. In this case, numerous and very reduced partitions are likely to be generated. Therefore, the algorithm saves both numerous recursive calls and much execution time. If the input relation is not reduced to a single tuple, the current cell is written. Let us explain now the core of the algorithm. For each d_j dimension given in parameter, the current relation is partitioned according to its values. Two tuples t and t' will belong to the same partition if and only if $t[d_j] = t'[d_j]$. This step requires a sorting operation hence it is costly. In order to reach an optimal efficiency, we choose to use a counting sort having a linear time complexity. Partition is described in algorithm 1. Once the operation is achieved, Idea is recursively called for each partition verifying the *camc* constraint. Once all the partitions have been dealt for the d_j dimension, all the cuboids containing d_j have also been dealt. The ALL value is then affected to the d_j dimension for the current cell.

Example 11: Figure 4 illustrates how the Idea algorithm navigates within the cuboid lattice to compute the Emerging Cube of Sales_{2016} and Sales_{2017}. Each dimension is denoted by its initial. Figures 5 give the details of all the fragments computed by Idea when traversing the search space. Within each node, the tuples (t_i stands for the tuple provided with the Id i) in the fragment of $\text{Sales}_{F\,us}$ (*cf.* Table 7) appear as well as the partition attributes. The dotted edges correspond to the nodes obtained without any aggregation operation. The dotted nodes correspond to the moment when Idea backtracks and reuses a similar input in order to pursue the computation.

Table 7. Fusionated relation example sales f us

RowId	City	Month	Category	Quantity_1	Quantity_2
1	Paris	11/06	Clothes	100	300
2	Paris	11/06	Video Game	100	0
3	London	11/06	Video Game	100	300
4	Berlin	11/09	Video Game	600	200
5	London	11/09	Video Game	100	300
6	London	11/06	Clothes	0	300
7	Berlin	11/09	Clothes	0	200
8	Berlin	11/06	Video Game	0	100

Figure 4. Tree followed by the Idea algorithm to navigate within cuboids for the sales f us relation

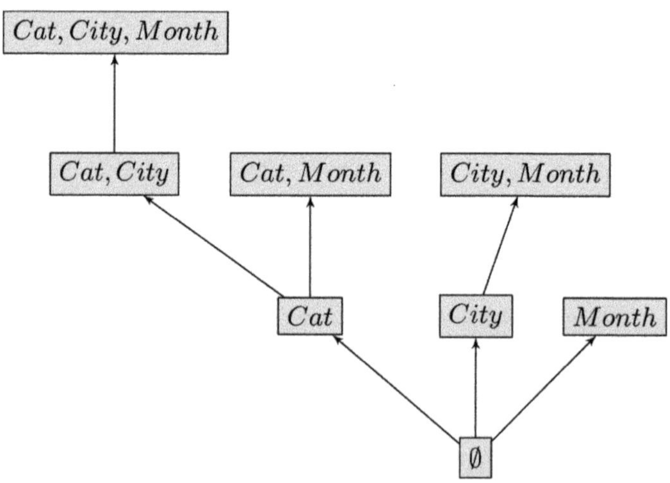

3.2. Border Computation

In this section we present, the first instantiation of our framework for the computation of the $U^{\sharp}$ border. The borders encompass particular tuples which are the boundaries of the solution space. They are encountered when step transitions are performed. Before giving the algorithm, we give some propositions which ensure the correctness of our approach.

The borders have been widely studied in the context of binary data mining. Efficient algorithms have been proposed for computing maximal borders (Burdick et al., 2005; Gouda & Zaki, 2005; Jr., 1998). However, solutions do not exist for yielding this kind of representation in a multidimensional context.

In figure 2, let us notice that the borders mark the boundaries of the algorithm steps. In other words, the border tuples correspond to ones for which the algorithm performs a step transition. We give several propositions for showing the link between the step transitions and the borders.

Definition 21 (Agreeing tuple set): Let $P \subseteq r$ be a subset of the r relation tuples and $D \subseteq \mathrm{D}$ a set of dimensions, we say that P agrees on D if and only if $\forall t, t' \in P$ we have $t[D] = t'[D]$.

Definition 22 (Idea-Successor): Let $D = \{d_1, \ldots, d_j\}$ be an ordered subset of dimensions ($D \subseteq \mathrm{D}$) and $P \subseteq r$ a subset of the r relation tuples agreeing on D. A set of tuples P' is called Idea- Successor of P with respect to D if and only if $P' \subseteq P$ and $\exists d_k \in \mathrm{D} \backslash D$ (with $k > j$) such that

$$\forall t,t' \in P', t.d_k = t'.d_k .$$

In other words, p' is an Idea-Successor of P according to D if P' is a subset of P which agrees on a direct superset of D having an additional dimension d_k greater (according to $\geq$D) than the greatest dimension of D (d_j in the above definition).

Example 12: By resuming our relation example $\mathrm{Sales}_{F\,us}$ (*cf.* Table 7), let $P = \mathrm{Sales}_{F\,us} = \{t_1, t_2, t_3, t_4, t_5, t_6, t_7, t_8\}$ be a set of tuples agreeing on $D = \emptyset$, the set of tuples $P' = \{t_1, t_2, t_3, t_6, t_8\}$ agrees on $D' = \{Mounth\}$ a direct superset of D. Hence, P' is an Idea-Successor of P according to D.

Definition 23 (Maximal Idea-Successor): Let $D = \{d_1, \ldots, d_j\}$ be an ordered subset of di- mensions ($D \subseteq \mathrm{D}$) and P be a a subset of the r relation tuples such that $\forall t, t' \in P$ we have $t[D] = t'[D]$. A fragment P' is said a maximal Idea-Successor of P according to D if and only if P' is an Idea-Successor of P according to D and $\nexists t \in P \backslash P'$ such that $t \cup P'$ is an Idea-Successor of P according D.

The notion of maximal Idea-Successor clearly formalizes the order according to which the Idea framework navigates through the partition of the input relation (*cf.* Figure 5). Hence, when a *P '* fragment is maximal Idea-Successor of *P* according to *D* then we are sure that if we call Idea with the parameters *P* and *D* then the one of the direct recursive calls will be provided with the arguments *P'* and $D \cup d_k$. In the recursive call tree, an edge links the two calls with the parameters (*P*, *D*) and (P', $D \cup d_k$).

Example 13: According the previous example, $P' = \{t_1, t_2, t_3, t_4, t_5\}$ is an Idea-Successor of $P = \{t_1, t_2, t_3, t_4, t_5, t_6, t_7, t_8, t_9, t_{10}\}$ with respect to $D = \emptyset$. *P'* is not a maximal Idea-Successor because t_8 shares the same values as the tuples of *P'* on *D'*. $P' \cup t_8$ is a maximal Idea-Successor of *P* according to *D* because there is no tuple sharing the same values for the attributes of *D'*. The multidimensional tuple associated to *P* is (ALL, ALL, ALL, ALL). The one associated to $P' \cup t_8$ is the tuple (ALL, Marseille, ALL, ALL).

When Idea is running, step transitions are performed just after a recursive call to the algorithm. If, for a call to Idea, with the parameters *P* and *D*, the step of the algorithm is P_i and if during the processing of one of the maximal Idea-successors *P'*, the algorithm step is P_j then *P'* is originated by a transition $P_i \rightarrow P_j$ and *P* is the origin of the transition $P_i \rightarrow P_j$.

Proposition 9: *Let* $t \in L$ *be a multidimensional tuple. The set of tuples P' used for computing t comes from a transition* $P_1 \rightarrow P_2$.

Proof.

$t \in L$

$\Leftrightarrow t \in \min_{\leq_s} (\{t \in CL(r_1 \cup r_2) \mid cmc(t) \wedge camc(t)\})$

$\Leftrightarrow \forall t'$ such that $t' <s\ t$ we have $\neg cmc(t') \wedge camc(t')$

Figure 5. Tree used by the Idea algorithm to navigate within cuboids for the sales f us relation

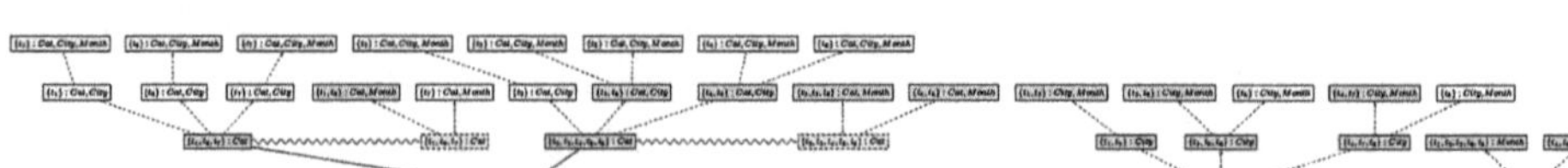

$\Rightarrow \forall t'$ such that $t' <s\ t$, Idea algorithm generates t' during P_1 step (1)

Similarly

$t \in L$

$\Leftrightarrow t \in \min\leq_s (\{t \in CL(r_1 \cup r_2) \mid cmc(t) \wedge camc(t)\})$

$\Rightarrow t$ is an emerging tuple

$\Rightarrow$Idea algorithm generates t during P_2 step (2)

According to (1) and (2) the transition passing from the tuple t' to t is of type $P_1 \rightarrow P_2$

Proposition 10: *Let $t \in U$ be a multidimensional tuple. The set of tuples P ' used for computing t comes from a transition $P_2 \rightarrow P_3$.*

Proof.

$t \in U$

$\Leftrightarrow t \in \max\leq_s (\{t \in CL(r_1 \cup r_2) \mid cmc(t) \wedge camc(t)\})$

$\Rightarrow t$ is an emerging tuple

$\Rightarrow$Once t is generated, the Idea algorithm is in the P_2 step (3)

Let us assume that a transition exists which is not $P_2 \rightarrow P_3$. In such a case, according to the state machine (*cf.* Figure 3), this transition is necessarily $P_2 \rightarrow P_2$. This means that the tuple t' generated during this transition is an emerging tuple more general than t. This contradicts $t \in U$.

Proposition 11: *Let $t \in U^\sharp$ be a multidimensional tuple. The set of tuples P ' used for computing t does not generate any transition $P_1 \rightarrow P_1$.*

Proof.

$t \in U^\sharp$

$\Leftrightarrow t \in \max\leq_s (\{t \in CL(r_1 \cup r_2) \mid \neg cmc(t) \wedge camc(t)\})$

$\Leftrightarrow \forall t'$ such that $t <s\ t'$ we have $cmc(t') \wedge camc(t')$ or $\neg\neg cmc(t) \wedge \neg camc(t)$

$\Rightarrow \forall t'$ such that $t <s\ t'$, the Idea algorithm generates t' during the P_2 or P_3 step (4)

Similarly

$t \in U^\sharp$

$\Leftrightarrow t \in \max\leq_s (\{t \in CL(r_1 \cup r_2) \mid \neg cmc(t) \wedge camc(t)\})$

$\Rightarrow$Once t is generated, the Idea algorithm is in the P_1 step (5)

According to (4) and (5) all the transitions passing from a tuple t to t' is of type $P_1 \rightarrow P_2$ or $P_1 \rightarrow P_3$. If it exists one transition which is not of these types then t is not maximal.

These two propositions are the foundation for the additions to the Idea framework in order to instantiate it for the border computing.

The first modification is to avoid all the operations concerning the tuples generated during the P_2 step. Because all the tuples of $U^\sharp$ are achieved during the P_1 step. The second addition concerns the management of *Base Single Tuples*. The partition of such tuples is made of a single element for which it is not necessary to examine all its successors but just the maximal one. The projection of the tuple on the dimensions which remain to be dealt is then appended to the border. The last modification to be performed is the verification of the condition given in proposition 11.

After each recursive call, we verify that the transition is not $P_1 \rightarrow P_1$. If such a transition is not encountered, the current tuple is tested and appended to the $U^\sharp$ border. The AppendToBorder procedure just verifies the maximal feature of the tuple and appends it to the result.

3.3. Constrained Closed Tuple Computation

The second instantiation of our framework is devoted to the constrained closed tuples. These tuples satisfy the constraints and thus they are encountered during the P_2 step. In this section, we give the propositions which justify the elimination of non-closed tuples during the computation.

Providing the Emerging Cube with representations as much reduced as possible is critical, but having a reduced representation without means of efficiently computing it has poor interest. In this section, our objective is to add to the Idea generic software platform the possibility to compute the different loss-less information representations. According to the propositions given above, all our representations of the Constrained Closed Cube Family make use of at least one of the borders and the set of emerging closed tuples. This is why we choose F-Idea as a basis to build a new algorithm devoted to the computation of our representations: C-Idea (for Closed Integrable DatabasE Algorithm). This algorithm uses certain properties of F-Idea in order to efficiently compute the emerging closed tuple set. Before the presentation of the algorithm C-Idea, we give some propositions which prove the robustness of our approach.

Proposition 12 (Not Closed Constrained Tuples): *Let P be a set of tuples of r which agree for the dimension set D ⊆* D *generated by a* F-Idea *partitioning and P ' one of its maximal* Idea- *Successors according to D (P' is an agree set on* $D \cup d_k$*). If* $|P| = |P'|$ *then the tuple t associated to P is a not closed constrained tuple.*

Proof. Let *P* be a set of constrained tuples which agree on dimension set *D* ⊆ D and *P '* one of its maximal Idea-Successors according to *D*. *t* and *t'* are the tuples associated to *P* and *P '*. Since *P '* is one of the maximal Idea-Successors of *P*, we know that *t <s t'*. Due to the definition of the cover relation, *cov*(*t*) = *P* and *cov*(*t'*) = *P '*. *t s t'* ⇒ *cov*(*t'*) ⊆ *cov*(*t*). If $|P| = |P'|$ then *cov*(*t*) = *cov*(*t'*) ⇔ *t* ≡cov *t'* ⇔ *t* ≡C *t'*. According to the extensivity property of the closure operator:

(*t <s t'*) ∧ (*t'* <s C(*t'*,*r*)) ∧ (C(*t'*,*r*) = C(*t*,*r*)) ⇒ C(*t*,*r*) 6= *t*

Hence the tuple *t* is not closed.

With this proposition, most of the not closed tuples are discarded. This is why it is critical to enforce it as soon as possible within F-Idea. The remaining tuples are called closed candidates. For avoiding generating erroneous solutions, we add a second test which proves that the considered tuple is really a closed tuple.

Proposition 13 (Idea fragment closure): Let P be one of the nonempty fragments generated by an F-Idea partitioning. The closure of the tuple t associated to P is defined as follows:

$C(t, r_1 \cup r_2) = + t'$

$t \in P$

Algorithm 1. Partition Algorithm

```
Input:
A relation r
The dimCur dimension according to which r has to be partitioned
Output:
The r relation partitioned according to the values of the dimCur attribute in C fragments:
r1, . . ., rC
let C: an integer containing the number of distinct values in r for the dimCur attribute
let hist: an array of |Dom(dimCur)| integers initialized to 0
let nbTuples: an integer initialized to the number of tuples in r
for i = 1, . . ., nbTuples do
        hist[ti.dimCur]:= hist[ti.dimCur] + 1; //The number of occurrences for each value of the dimCur attribute
end for
//We make use of the histogram
let indTab: an array of integers initialized to 0;
let first: an integer initialized to 0;
let last: an integer initialized to 0;
for i = 1, . . ., |Dom(dimCur)| do
        if hist[i] 6= 0 then
        C:= C + 1;
        end if
        last:= hist[i];
        indTab[i]:= first;
        first:= first + last;
end for
let indTab2: a local copy of indTab;
for i = 1, . . ., nbTuples do
        let v: the value of the tuple ti for the dimension dimCur;
        rTmp[indTab2[v]]:= ti;
        indTab2[v]:= indTab2[v] + 1;
end for
let j: an integer initialized to 1;
for i = 1, . . ., |Dom(dimCur)| do
        if hist[i] 6= 0 then
        rj:= rTmp[indTab[i]..indTab[i] + hist[i]];
        j:= j + 1;
        end if
end for
return r1, . . ., rC ;
```

Algorithm 2. Aggregate Algorithm

Input:
A merged relation r
The current cell *CurrentCell*
An aggregation and additive function f
1: let r_1 the projection of r on D ∪ M_1 2: let r_2 the projection of r on D ∪ M_2 3: for all $t \in r$ do
4: *CurrentCell*.M_1 = *CurrentCell*.M_1 + f (t, r_1); 5: *CurrentCell*. M_2 = *CurrentCell*.M_2 + f (t, r_2); 6: end for

Algorithm 3. Algorithm WriteSuccessors(t, D, CurrentCell)

Input:
A tuple t
The set of dimensions which still need to be processed D = $\{d_i, \ldots, d_n\}$
The current cell *CurrentCell*
1: if D is empty then
2: return;
3: end if
4: for all $d_j \in$ D do
5: *CurrentCell*.d_j:= t.d_j ;
6: Write(*CurrentCell*);
7: end for
8: for all $d_j \in$ D do
9: *CurrentCell*.d_j:= ALL;
10: end for
11: WriteSuccessors(t, $\{d_{i+1}, \ldots, d_n\}$, *CurrentCell*)

Proof. Let P be one of the nonempty fragments generated by an F-Idea partitioning. Hence P is the maximal Idea-Successor of a sequence of maximal Idea-Successors originated by $r_1 \cup r_2$. This property proves that $P = cov(t)$ with $cov(t) = \{t' \in r \mid t <s\, t'\}$. According to the definition of the cubic closure operator:

$$C(t, r_1 \cup r_2) = + t'$$

$$t' \in r \mid t <st' = + t'$$

Algorithm 4. C-Idea algorithm

```
Input:
A merged relation r
The set of dimensions D = {d_1, . . ., d_n} which remain to be
processed The current cell CurrentCell
The current step of the algorithm P_Cur Output:
The Emerging Cube of r.
The output step of the algorithm
DimCour:= d_1;
Aggregate(r, CurrentCell, f); //Computes the values of the
function and writes them in the current cell
let P_Succ:= FindNextStep(P_Cur, CurrentCell); //cf. Figure 3
  if P_Succ = P_3 then
        return P_Succ;
  else if P_Succ = P_2 then
        if |r| = 1 then
        Write(r[0]);
        return P_3;
         end if
   end if
for all d_j ∈ D do
         C:= |r(d_j )|;
         Partition(r, d_j); //r is partitioned, according to
the values of the d_j  attribute, into C
fragments:  r_1, . . ., r_C
         for i = 1, . . ., C do
         if (P_Succ = P_2) ∧ (|r_i|≠|r|) then
         t:= Sum(r); //Closure computation
         if t = CurrentCell then
         Write(CurrentCell); //t satisfies the proposition
14

         end if
         end if
         CurrentCell.d_j:= r_i[0].d_j ; //The current cell is
provided with the value of the d_j dimen- sion for r_i
         C-Idea (r_i, {d_j+1, . . ., d_n}, CurrentCell, P_Succ);
         end for
         CurrentCell.d_j:= ALL; //The d_j dimension is entirely
processed
end for
 return P_Succ;
```

$t' \in cov(t) = + t'$

$t' \in P$

The proposition main interest is that the closure computation cost is minimized. This compu- tation is performed on a minimal fragment of the original relation, we avoid to uselessly scan the whole dataset. Moreover, due to proposition 13, the computation number is itself reduced.

Proposition 14 (Closure test): *Let t be a closed candidate tuple and P the corresponding frag- ment of r. t is a closed tuple if and only if* $+t \in P\ t = t$.

The C-Idea algorithm is a variant of F-Idea which, during the step P_2, makes use of the above propositions in order to efficiently compute the constrained closed tuples and thus achieves the Constrained Cube reduced representations. Our approach takes benefit of the successive par- titioning performed by the algorithm for optimizing as much as possible the computation of the Constrained Closed Cube. Furthermore, the approach preserves the Idea property of integration within Dbmss. The algorithm 4 gives the pseudo-code of C-Idea.

4. EXPERIMENTAL EVALUATIONS

In this section, we present the results of various evaluations. However, there is no comparable algorithm to compute Emerging Cubes. This is why we have developped an adaptation of the Buc algorithm. However, this adaptation performs poorly when compared to C-Idea, simply because it was not originally intended for this goal. This is the reason why we do not present the obtained results for execution times. Instead we focus on the size of the Emerging Cube and the Closed Emerging Cube.

In order to assess performances of Idea, the algorithm was implemented using the language C++. The executable file is generated with GNU g++ compiler version 4.4.3. Experiments were performed on an Intel Core 2 Duo CPU E6550 with 2 GB of main memory, running on Linux 2.6.32.

To perform the presented evaluations, we use the same database relations as in (Xin et al., 2007). Experiments are conducted on data issued from a large and various scope of domains.

For synthetic data[1], we use the following notations to describe the relations: D the number of dimensions, C the cardinality of each dimension, T the number of tuples in the relation, M_1 (M_2, respectively) the threshold corresponding to the C_1 constraint (C_2, respectively), and S the skewness of data according to the Zipf's law[2]. When

S is equal to 0, data are uniform. As S increases, data become more synthetic, data sets are called J1, J2, J3, J4. For real data, we use the weather relations SEP82L. DAT and SEP85L.DAT used by Xin et al. (2006), which have 1,002,752 tuples with 8 selected dimensions. The attributes (with their cardinalities) are as follows: year month day hour (238), latitude (5260), longitude (6187), station number (6515), present weather (100), change code (110), solar altitude (1535) and relative lunar luminance (155). We also make use of the synthetic generator belonging to the Olap benchmark APB-1[3], which is a standard in data warehousing (Morfonios & Ioannidis, 2006). The generated fact table has two measures (Unit Sales and Dollar Sales) and the four following dimensions (with their cardinalities): Product (6,500), Customer (640), Time (17), and Channel (10). The size of the fact table is tuned by a density factor varying from 0.1% to 40%. The lowest density factor generates a fact table consisting of 1.2×10^6 tuples occupying approximately 30 MB. The similar features for the highest density are 400 times larger (4.9×10^9 tuples and 12 GB). The two datasets used for this experiment are generated with the density set to 1%. All the characteristics of the used datasets are reported in table 8, and summary of the experiments Table.

Table 8. Characteristics of datasets

Dataset	Type T	C	S	D	M_1	M_2
J1	Synthetic [10^5; 10^6]	100	2	10	5	150
J2	Synthetic 10^6	[100; 1000]	2	10	5	150
J3	Synthetic 10^6	100	[0; 4]	10	5	150
Weather data	Real 2,013,207	6,515		8	[50; 200]	200

Table 9. Summary of the experiments

Dataset	$\|DC(r_1 \cup r_2)\|$	$\|EC(r_1,r_2)\|$	TeBuc	TIdea	TSql
J1	[7.9×10^8; 6.2×10^9]	[2.0×10^6; 4.0×10^8]	[2,274; 18,265]	[25; 427]	[3,610; 33,022]
J2	[1.1×10^9; 1.2×10^9]	[3.5×10^6; 4.0×10^6]	[3,114; 3,213]	[21; 29]	[4,747; 6,293]
J3	[1.9×10^8; 1.3×10^9]	[4.5×10^5; 7.4×10^6]	[565; 3,706]	[27; 52]	[1,045; 6,685]
J4	[1.2×10^7; 2.5×10^{10}]	[2.1×10^5; 3.2×10^7]	[29; 80,573]	[2; 211]	[43; 149,013]
Weather data	2.9×10^8	[1.3×10^5; 2.1×10^6]	[931; 976]	[8; 26]	[1,446; 1,857]
APB-1 benchmark	2.6×10^7	[1.0×10^6; 2.7×10^6]	[79; 81]	[18; 30]	[113; 146]

In Figures 6a and 6b, we give results obtained when comparing the size of the Emerging Cube with the Emerging Closed Cube for synthetic data. Whatever the size of the relation r_2 (*cf.* Figure 6a) or the cardinality of its dimensions (*cf.* Figure 6b), the size of the Emerging Closed Cube is comparable on slightly reduced when compared to the size of the Emerging Cube. The reason behind this weak reduction of space is the following: synthetic data are very weakly correlated and thus they encompass very few redundancies. Moreover, we set the data skew to 0 and thus we do not impact the original emergence rate. As expected by varying the data skew, we observe that, compared to the Emerging Cube, the Emerging Closed Cube has a size more and more reduced while the data skew increases. The reduction rate varies from 1 to 7. The phenomenon is illustrated in Figure 6c. Furthermore, we use real data, known as being strongly correlated, for comparing the Emerging Cube with the Emerging Closed Cube. The parameter which varies is the minimal threshold applied to the relation r_2. We observe, in Figure 6d, that the more the threshold increases, the more the size of the Emerging Cube and the Emerging Cube Closed Cube decreases. Actually, when the minimal threshold is high, obviously the number of emerging tuples is weak. Nevertheless, the Emerging Closed Cube

Figure 6.

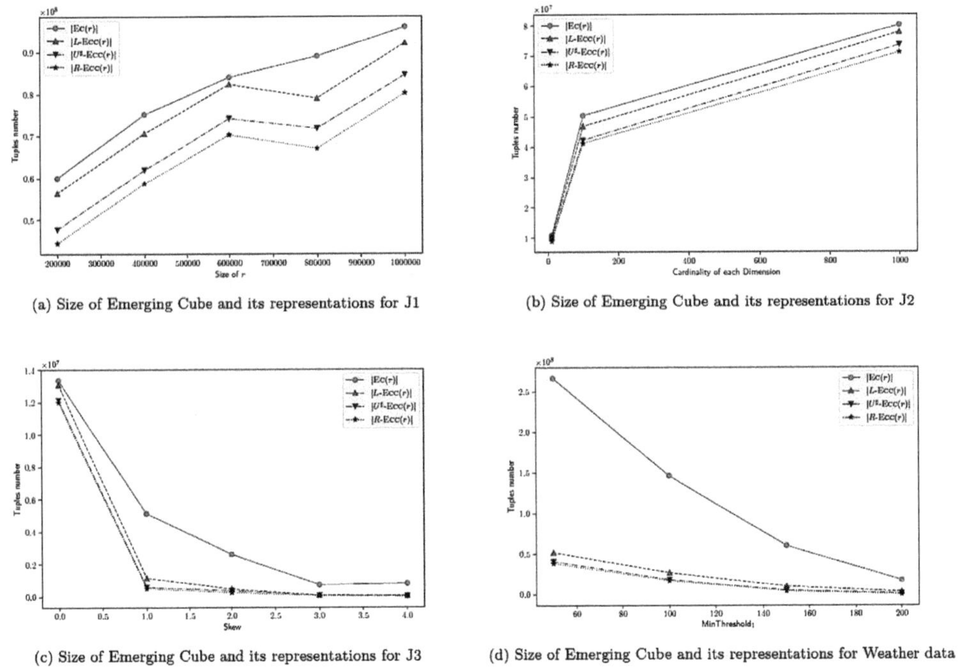

(a) Size of Emerging Cube and its representations for J1

(b) Size of Emerging Cube and its representations for J2

(c) Size of Emerging Cube and its representations for J3

(d) Size of Emerging Cube and its representations for Weather data

is always more reduced than the Emerging Cube with a relevant reduction. This feature is highlighted by Figure 7a, Figure 7b, Figure 7c and Figure 7d which give the reduction ratios between the different representations.

5. DISCUSSION

The storage explosion is a well-known problem related to the tremendous volume of computed data cubes. In order to reduce this drawback, a first solution is to partially materialize data cubes by focusing on the most relevant tuples. The Iceberg Cube (Beyer & Ramakrishnan, 1999) exemplifies such a solution and it is generalized by the constrained cube which enforces any combination of monotone and/or antimonotone constraints. Despite discarding less interesting tuples, the resulting data cube remains voluminous. Hence, approaches attempt to reduce its size but without eliminating more knowledge. The idea under these approaches is the following: certain tuples share an equivalent semantics. They can be gathered in equivalence classes for which it is sufficient to keep only a representative tuple. Hence these approaches bring semantical reduced representations. Among them, let

Figure 7.

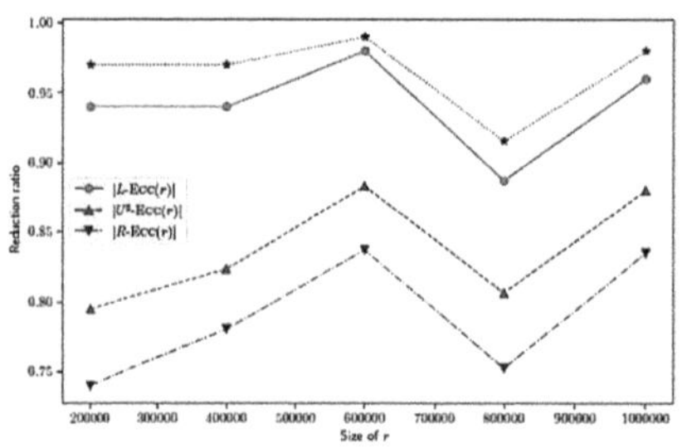

(a) Reduction ratio of Emerging Cube and its representations for J1

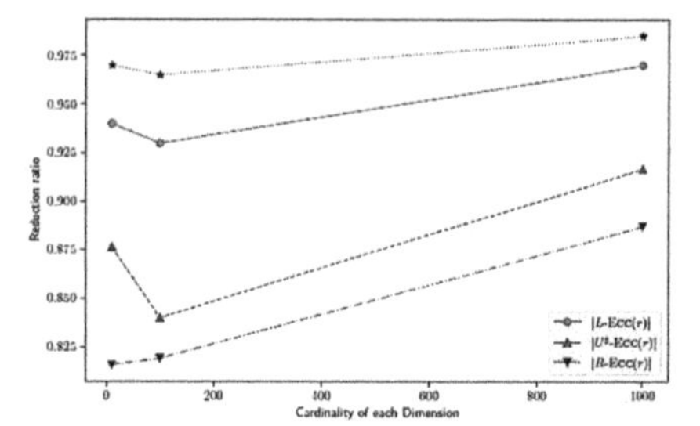

(b) Reduction ratio of Emerging Cube and its representations for J2

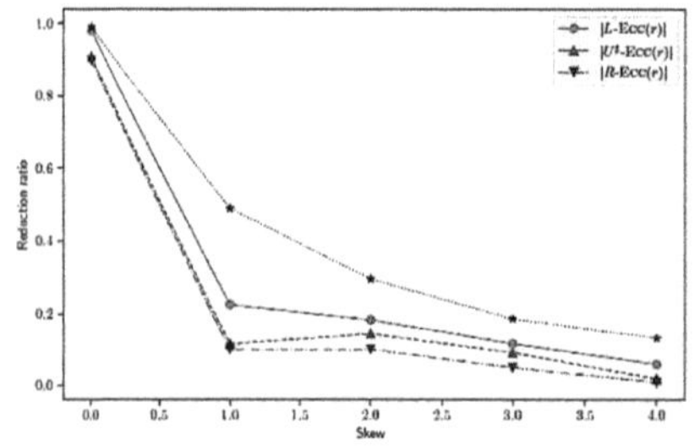

(c) Reduction ratio of Emerging Cube and its representations for J3

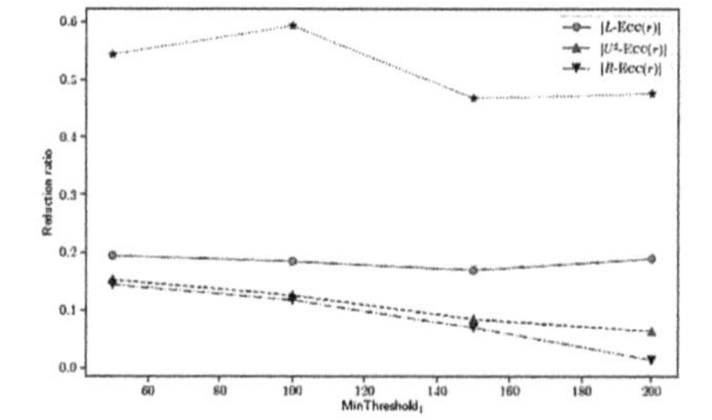

(d) Reduction ratio of Emerging Cube and its representations for weather data

us quote the Quotient Cube (Lakshmanan et al., 2002) and the Closed Cube (Xin et al., 2006). Let us underline that the Constrained Closed Cube is the most generic solution which results from the non-trivial combination of the Constrained Cube, the borders and the Closed Cube.

Based on Constrained Close Cube, the Emerging Cube highlights the trend reversals and gives the decision makers the relevant information as quickly as possible.

Along with these representations, cubing algorithms are devised. No one can be compared directly with our algorithmic solution because of its genericity, nevertheless links can be stated between them. We briefly review such links and place emphasis on the features and advantages of the different algorithms. Buc (Beyer & Ramakrishnan, 1999) is the first algorithm intended for computing Iceberg Cubes. Its bottom-up and depth first computation order facilitates the enforce- ment of the antimonotone constraint `*a la* APRIORI. It is mainly based on sort and partitioning. Because it does not make use of complex data structure, it can be directly integrated within a BDMS. When designing C-Idea, one of our main objectives is the integrability. This is why we adopt the Buc strategy of sorting and partitioning.

The common points between P-Cube (Cicchetti et al., 2011) and Buc are to compute Iceberg Cubes by performing partitioning and to navigate through the search space in a bottom-up and depth first way. However, P-Cube does not use a sort method but instead enforces partition products. Another difference is that P-Cube enumerates the aggregates to be computed according to the lectic order. P-Cube also proposes a syntactic reduction. Instead of the classical relational representation, P-Cube takes advantage of partitions in order to propose a syntactic reduction and a more compact relational representation.

Cure-for-Cube (Morfonios & Ioannidis, 2006) also computes Iceberg Cubes. Like P-Cube, it proposes a syntactic reduction of cubes. Like Buc, its computation is based on sorting and partition- ing but it takes advantage of semantical redundancies to improve its efficiency. Cure-for-Cube and P-Cube share with C-Idea the same concern and they preserve the integrability property.

6. CONCLUSION

We have proposed the concept of Emerging Cube in order to capture trend reversals between the data cubes of two comparable relations. Emerging Cubes can be represented through the classical borders $[L; U]$. Such a representation is especially reduced when compared to the size of the Emerging Cube, and useful to know whether an aggregated tuple captures a trend reversal or not. Thus, if the Emerging Cube is intended for the quoted use, its representation through borders is the best candidate because of the small amount of storage which is required. However, provided with borders, the measure values cannot be retrieved and it is not possible to answer whatever Olap query. To meet this goal, we propose the Emerging Closed Cube which is the most reduced and lossless representation of Emerging Cubes. It is of course more voluminous than the borders but the counterpart is that it makes it possible to answer any query on the Emerging Cube while storing minimal information. Thus, if the use of the Emerging Cube is querying then the Emerging Closed Cube is the best representation for optimizing storage space.

We propose a computation approach devoted to Emerging Closed Cubes: the C-Idea algorithm.

It is provided with two interesting properties: its efficiency which is validated through various experiments and its integrability within Dbmss then existing Rolap tools remain relevant for Emerging Closed Cubes.

We perform experimental evaluations by using various data sets. In the most disadvantageous cases when data encompasses very few redundancies, the Emerging Closed Cube which discards redundancies in order to reduce the size of the representation is not favoured while the representation through borders is incomparably smaller than the Emerging Cube. Fortunately, the quoted cases concern synthetic data. In the most common situations, when real data is managed, the Emerg- ing Closed Cube is actually a reduced representation of the Emerging Cube with an appreciable reduction of space.

REFERENCES

Abouzeid, A., Bajda-Pawlikowski, K., Abadi, D., Rasin, A., & Silberschatz, A. (n.d.). *HadoopDB: An Architectural Hybrid of MapReduce and DBMS Technologies for Analytical Workloads*. Retrieved from http://www.vldb.org/pvldb/2/vldb09-861.pdf

Agrawal, R., Mannila, H., Srikant, R., Toivonen, H., & Verkamo, A. I. (1996). Fast discovery of association rules. In *Advances in Knowledge Discovery and Data Mining* (pp. 307–328). AAAI/MIT Press.

Beyer, K. S., & Ramakrishnan, R. (1999). Bottom-up computation of sparse and iceberg cubes. In A. Delis, C. Faloutsos, & S. Ghandeharizadeh (Eds.), *Special Interest Group on Management of Data (SIGMOD) Conference* (pp. 359–370). ACM Press. doi:10.1145/304182.304214

Bonchi, F., & Lucchese, C. (2004). On closed constrained frequent pattern mining. In K. Morik & R. Rastogi (Eds.), *ICDM* (pp. 35–42). IEEE Computer Society.

Burdick, D., Calimlim, M., Flannick, J., Gehrke, J., & Yiu, T. (2005). *Mafia: A maximal frequent itemset algorithm*. Academic Press.

Burdick, D., Calimlim, M., Flannick, J., Gehrke, J., & Yiu, T. (2005, November). MAFIA: A maximal frequent itemset algorithm. *IEEE Transactions on Knowledge and Data Engineering*, *17*(11), 1490–1504. doi:10.1109/TKDE.2005.183

Casali, A., Cicchetti, R., & Lakhal, L. (2003). Cube lattices: A framework for multidimensional data mining. *Proceedings of the 2003 Society for Industrial and Applied Methods (SIAM) International Conference on Data Mining*. Retrieved from https://epubs.siam.org/doi/pdf/10.1137/1.9781611972733.35

Casali, A., Nedjar, S., Cicchetti, R., & Lakhal, L. (2007). Convex Cube: Towards a Unified Structure for Multidimensional Databases. In R. Wagner, N. Revell, & G. Pernul (Eds.), Lecture Notes in Computer Science: Vol. 4653. *Database and Expert Systems Applications. DEXA 2007*. Berlin: Springer. doi:10.1007/978-3-540-74469-6_56

Casali, A., Nedjar, S., Cicchetti, R., & Lakhal, L. (2009). Closed cube lattices. *Annals of Information Systems*, *3*, 145–164.

Cicchetti, R., Lakhal, L., Nedjar, S., Novelli, N., & Casali, A. (2011). Summarizing datacubes: Semantic and syntactic approaches. In D. Taniar & L. Chen (Eds.), *Integrations of Data Warehousing, Data Mining and Database Technologies - Innovative Approaches* (pp. 19–39). Information Science Reference. doi:10.4018/978-1-60960-537-7.ch002

Dong, G., & Li, J. (1999). Efficient mining of emerging patterns: Discovering trends and differences. In Knowledge Discovery and Data Mining (pp. 43–52). Academic Press.

Dong, G., & Li, J. (2005). Mining border descriptions of emerging patterns from dataset pairs. *Knowledge and Information Systems*, *8*(2), 178–202. doi:10.100710115-004-0178-1

Ganter, B., & Wille, R. (1999). *Formal Concept Analysis: Mathematical Foundations*. Berlin: Springer-Verlag Berlin Heidelberg. doi:10.1007/978-3-642-59830-2

Gouda, K., & Zaki, M. J. (2005). Genmax: An efficient algorithm for mining maximal frequent itemsets. *Data Mining and Knowledge Discovery*, *11*(3), 223–242. doi:10.100710618-005-0002-x

Gray, J., Chaudhuri, S., Bosworth, A., Layman, A., Reichart, D., Venkatrao, M., ... Pirahesh, H. (1997). Data cube: A relational aggregation operator generalizing group-by, cross-tab, and sub totals. *Data Mining and Knowledge Discovery*, *1*(1), 29–53. doi:10.1023/A:1009726021843

Han, J., Pei, J., Dong, G., & Wang, K. (2001). *Efficient computation of iceberg cubes with complex measures. In Proceedings of Special Interest Group on Management of Data (SIGMOD)* (pp. 1–12). ACM.

Jr, R. J. B. (1998). Efficiently mining long patterns from databases. In L. M. Haas & A. Tiwary (Eds.), *Proceedings of Special Interest Group on Management of Data (SIGMOD) Conference* (pp. 85–93). ACM Press.

Lakshmanan, L. V. S., Pei, J., & Han, J. (2002). Quotient cube: How to summarize the semantics of a data cube. *Proceedings of VLDB '02 the 28th international conference on Very Large Data Bases,* 778-789.

Morfonios, K., & Ioannidis, Y. E. (2006). Cure for cubes: Cubing using a rolap engine. In *Proceedings of 32nd International Conference on Very Large Data Bases* (pp. 379–390). ACM Digital Library.

Morfonios, K., Konakas, S., Ioannidis, Y. E., & Kotsis, N. (2007). Rolap implementations of the data cube. *ACM Computing Surveys*, *39*(4), 12, es. doi:10.1145/1287620.1287623

Nasr, G. E., & Badr, C. (2003). Buc algorithm for iceberg cubes: Implementation and sensitivity analysis. In I. Russell, & S. M. Haller (Eds.), *FLAIRS Conference* (pp. 255–260). AAAI Press.

Nedjar, S., Casali, A., Cicchetti, R., & Lakhal, L. (2009). Emerging cubes: Borders, size estimations and lossless reductions. *Information Systems*, *34*(6), 536–550. doi:10.1016/j.is.2009.03.001

Nedjar, S., Casali, A., Cicchetti, R., & Lakhal, L. (2010). Reduced representations of emerging cubes for olap database mining. *International Journal of Business Intelligence and Data Mining*, *4*(3-4), 267–300.

Nedjar, S., Cicchetti, R., & Lakhal, L. (2011). Extracting semantics in olap databases using emerging cubes. *Information Sciences*, *181*(10), 2036–2059. doi:10.1016/j.ins.2010.12.022

Nedjar, S., Lakhal, L., & Cicchetti, R. (2013). Emerging data cube representations for olap database mining. In G. Dong & J. Bailey (Eds.), *Contrast Data Mining* (pp. 109–128). CRC Press.

Pavlo, A., Paulson, E., Rasin, A., Abadi, D., DeWitt, D., Madden, S., & Stonebraker, M. (2009). *A comparison of approaches to large-scale data analysis. In Special Interest Group on Management of Data (SIGMOD)* (pp. 165–178). ACM.

Pei, J., Han, J., & Lakshmanan, L. V. S. (2004). Pushing convertible constraints in frequent itemset mining. *Data Mining and Knowledge Discovery*, *8*(3), 227–252. doi:10.1023/B:DAMI.0000023674.74932.4c

Ross, K. A., & Srivastava, D. (1997). Fast computation of sparse datacubes. *Proceedings of the 23rd International Conference on Very Large Data Bases*, 116–125.

Sismanis, Y., Deligiannakis, A., Roussopoulos, N., & Kotidis, Y. (2002). Dwarf: shrinking the petacube. Special Interest Group on Management of Data (SIGMOD) Conference, 464–475. doi:10.1145/564691.564745

Stumme, G., Taouil, R., Bastide, Y., Pasquier, N., & Lakhal, L. (2002). Computing iceberg concept lattices with titanic. *Data & Knowledge Engineering*, *42*(2), 189–222. doi:10.1016/S0169-023X(02)00057-5

Wei, W., Lu, H., Feng, J., & Yu, J. X. (2002). Condensed cube: An efficient approach to reducing data cube size. *Proceedings of the 18th International Conference on Data Engineering*, 155–165.

Xin, D., Han, J., Li, X., Shao, Z., & Wah, B. W. (2007). Computing iceberg cubes by top-down and bottom-up integration: The starcubing approach. *IEEE Transactions on Knowledge and Data Engineering*, *19*(1), 111–126. doi:10.1109/TKDE.2007.250589

Xin, D., Shao, Z., Han, J., & Liu, H. (2006). C-cubing: Efficient computation of closed cubes by aggregation-based checking. *Proceedings of the 22nd International Conference on Data Engineering (ICDE)*.

ENDNOTES

1 The synthetic data generator is given at http://illimine.cs.uiuc.edu/.

2 Zipf's law models the occurrence of distinct objects in particular sorts of collections. This law predicts that out.

3 Olap Council. APB-1 Olap Benchmark: http://www.olapcouncil.org.

Chapter 6
Large Multivariate Time Series Forecasting:
Survey on Methods and Scalability

Youssef Hmamouche
Aix-Marseille Université, France

Hana Alouaoui
Aix-Marseille Université, France

Piotr Marian Przymus
Aix-Marseille Université, France

Alain Casali
Aix-Marseille Université, France

Lotfi Lakhal
Aix-Marseille Université, France

ABSTRACT

Research on the analysis of time series has gained momentum in recent years, as knowledge derived from time series analysis can improve the decision-making process for industrial and scientific fields. Furthermore, time series analysis is often an essential part of business intelligence systems. With the growing interest in this topic, a novel set of challenges emerges. Utilizing forecasting models that can handle a large number of predictors is a popular approach that can improve results compared to univariate models. However, issues arise for high dimensional data. Not all variables will have direct impact on the target variable and adding unrelated variables may make the forecasts less accurate. Thus, the authors explore methods that can effectively deal with time series with many predictors. The authors discuss state-of-the-art methods for optimizing the selection, dimension reduction, and shrinkage of predictors. While similar research exists, it exclusively targets small and medium datasets, and thus, the research aims to fill the knowledge gap in the context of big data applications.

DOI: 10.4018/978-1-5225-4963-5.ch006

INTRODUCTION

Time series analysis and time series data mining aim to describe patterns and evolutions occurring in data over the time. Among the many useful applications of time series data mining and analysis, time series forecasting is especially salient as it contributes crucial information to corporate and/or institutional decision-making. Thus, to no surprise, is often an important part of business intelligence (BI) systems, which allow a company to gather, store, access, and analyze corporate data to aid in decision-making.

In today's information-driven world, countless numbers of numerical time series are generated by industry and researchers on any given day. For many applications -- biology, medicine, finance, industry, among others -- high dimensional time series are required. Modern time series analysis systems are expected to process and store millions of such high dimensional data points per minute, twenty-four hours a day, seven days a week, generating terabytes of logs. Needless to say, dealing with such voluminous datasets raises various new and interesting challenges.

The first models developed for time series forecasting were univariate models based on auto-regression principle. In such models, historic observations are used to make future forecasts. The most popular of these univariate models include the Auto-Regressive (AR), Auto-Regressive Moving Average (ARMA), and the Auto-Regressive Integrated Moving Average (ARIMA) models (Box, 2013). Let us detail the ARIMA model, which takes three integer parameters (p, d, q).

Where p is the lag parameter of the auto-regressive part, d is the non-stationarity order of the time series, and q is lag parameter of the moving average part.

The non-stationarity of time series is allowed with this model. Consider a time series that is non-stationary of order d.

The ARIMA (p, d, q) model consists in applying the ARMA (p, d) model after transforming the time series to stationary by differencing it d times, where d is the order of integration or non-stationarity. The ARMA (p, q) model expresses a stationary times series y(t) according to the q last error terms and the p past observations. It can be expressed as follows:

$$y(t) = \alpha_0 + \sum_{i=1}^{p} \alpha_i y(t-i) + \sum_{i=1}^{q} \beta_i \in (t-i) + \in (t)$$

where $\in (t)$ are the error terms, α_i and β_i are the parameters of the model.

Despite their advantages, univariate forecasting approaches have some drawbacks: for one, they do not take into account potentially exploitable data of other time series in the same dataset.

Therefore, multivariate forecasting models, which incorporate such data into their analysis, were developed, including the extended version of the AR model; the Vector Auto-Regressive (VAR) and the co-integrated VAR model; the Vector Error Correction model (VECM) (Johansen, 1991). The principle underlying multivariate forecasting models is that the value of a given variable often depends on past values of itself and of other related variables. Such models are still popular today and are used independently or in combination with other new techniques, for instance, artificial neural network non-linear modeling (Thielbar & Dickey, 2011).

Despite significant developments in multivariate forecast modeling, two main issues still appear when dealing with highly dimensional data: (i) how to select predictors for a target variable; (ii) how to assess whether the quantity of variables used has affected the accuracy of predictions. Both problems have been examined by researchers in recent years, yielding original findings and novel approaches. Namely, recent literature (J. H. Stock & Watson, 2012), (Jiang, Athanasopoulos, Hyndman, Panagiotelis, & Vahid, 2017), suggests that for econometric data specifically, methods performance depends on the dataset and the target variable. Thus, it is advisable to evaluate wide variety of methods before making the final decision on used model.

An upper limit exists on the number of variables that can be used to improve the forecasting quality of existing multivariate models.

The organization of this paper proceeds as follows: In the next section, we provide preliminaries and formulate the problem. Next, we formulate the state of the art divided into three subsections, were we discuss existing approaches grouped by their underlying mathematical principle: we examine methods based on Dynamic Factor Models (DFMs), shrinkage, and regression methods, and two-step approaches based on feature selection and dimension reduction. In the second to last section, we discuss eligibility of state of art methods when facing massive datasets. Finally, we conclude.

PRELIMINARIES AND THE PROBLEM STATEMENT

In this section, we discuss basics of multivariate forecasting and state the problem at study. Let us start by discussing the notation used throughout this paper.

Notations

Let Y be a numerical matrix, we adopt the classical notations, i.e., $Y_{i,j}$ refers to the element of Y where i is the row number and j is the column number. Consider a k-dimensional time series $Y = (Y_1, \cdots, Y_k)$, where each element of Y is a univariate time series containing n observations, i.e., a series of observations indexed in time order.

- Each univariate time series from Y can be considered as variable.
- Y can be considered also as numerical matrix, thus $Y_{i,j} = Y_j(i)$. In the following, we prefer the notation $Y_j(i)$ instead of $Y_{i,j}$ for time series, where i indicates to time and j indicates the index of variable.
- The set of target variables $T \subset Y$, is the set variables to forecast.
- The set of predictors, is a subset $P \subset Y$ containing variables that can be used in a multivariate model in order to predict target variables. Note that $P \cap T \neq \varnothing$, which means that the target variables can be also considered as predictors for other target variables.
- Time series differencing refers to computing the difference between consecutive points:

$$\Delta Y_i(t) = Y_i(t) - Y_i(t-1) \forall t \in [2, n].$$

Multivariate Time Series in the Context of Big Data

As with all neologisms, the term 'Big Data' is ambiguous and deserves some clarification (Ward & Barker, 2013). We arrange our discussion around the "Five V's" of Big Data as it offers a manner for explaining the objectives of Big Data challenges, in a way that is widely adopted by researchers and industry professionals (Beyer & Laney, 2012), (Ward & Barker, 2013). The 5V's of Big Data are: data volume, variety, velocity, variability, and veracity.

Although all five of these components are in some way relevant to analyzing multivariate time series data, the current study focuses on the volume of multivariate time series, for the reason that it poses a particular conundrum for scientists. On one hand, the modern information age has brought to hand an explosion in the volume of available data, which, for both the public and private sectors, represents a potential gold mine of information that can be exploited to maximize profits and increase competitiveness. On the other hand, scientists are required to keep the pace with industry needs, that is to say by providing the tools allowing this data to be readily transformed into accurate and actionable information.

Data's volume may refer to either the number of observations over time, the number of observed variables, or both. Usually the number of observations over time will be the inferior problem as typically, time series are processed in 'rolling windows' because otherwise they may be affected by large number of external factors over a long history. We assume that the data may be subject to trends, seasonality, mood swings, sentiments, or events that potentially change the dynamics, thus making it hard for one model to accommodate efficiently very long history. This is basic assumption when forecasting econometric indexes, prices, cash flows, marketing data or other time series desired in business analytics. Assuming usage of the 'rolling windows' with reasonable size we have a natural way of dividing the problem into independent sub problems that can be easily computed in distributed environment.

The more challenging problem is when the number of observed variables is large. Recall, that not all the predictors will impact the forecasted variable, and unrelated variables will add unnecessary noise to data. Thus, a proper subset of variables has to be used when building a model. Unfortunately, this leads to exponential growth of number of possible subsets of the predictor variables that should be taken into account, thus, making the problem more challenging. This fall into other common way of specifying Big Data in terms of complexity o the problem, see (Ward & Barker, 2013) and references therein. In this work, we mainly focus on business analytics cases, and more specifically on those with a large number of observed variables when the relationships between the variables are not necessarily known.

The two components of data's volume-- the frequency of the observations and the number of observed variables-- are also related to the data's velocity, which is a measure of how fast data is coming in. However, even in the presence of massive datasets, variety of solutions exists to support high data velocity. Many NoSQL databases support time series data natively, in other cases, specialized variants or extensions exist to provide such support (Wlodarczyk, 2012). While the scalable acquisition of large amounts of high frequency data is already being thoroughly investigated in ongoing research, there is a wide demand for more advanced data mining and machine learning techniques capable of high frequency modeling of time series. Scalability of the models are some of the ways to achieve this.

Time series are sequences of observed values associated with an observed time period. The type of values may include numbers, vectors, images or a variety of different value types. In general, it is perfectly feasible to discuss heterogeneous multivariate time series data that can fit the variety characteristic of Big Data. However, in this chapter we will concentrate only on multivariate numerical data.

The variability and veracity of data are also an issue. Often time series will suffer from missing values, outliers, varying frequency, among other problems to accuracy. Research that focuses on correcting the aforementioned problems is an ongoing effort, but is outside the limits of the current chapter. For more details, please refer to (García, Ramírez-Gallego, Luengo, Benítez, & Herrera, 2016) for an overview of scalable approaches to cleaning data.

Practical Application of Time Series Prediction in the Context of Big Data

We show here how Big Data can influence the standard way of predicting time series. For instance, this work is a part of the eBob (e-Business Optimization with Big data) project, under Future Investments Development of the Digital Economy in France. It aims to revolutionize consumer goods business management by taking advantage from multiple sources of information, and then provide decision support for the users by guiding them in their choices.

Our work focuses on the study and the development of prediction models, and building a prototype for large time series forecasting (in terms of the number of attributes). The data consist of 11.000 international indexes and 350 articles, and in average, 350.000 values are extracted per month.

The goal is to predict the 350 articles based on their historical values and also using the 11.000 indexes. It is clear that using one prediction model that takes into account all these attributes is not the appropriate way to handle this problem. Instead of making a global and scalable model, the idea is to simplify the data as much as possible and to provide optimized models for each target attribute, and finally make the whole process scalable. Thus, time series prediction in Big Data context must be handled with a particular way depending on the current problematic.

In the next subsection, we review the basics of multivariate forecasting models.

The Vector Autoregressive Models

Let us consider a k-dimensional time series Y_t. The VAR (p) process expresses each variable from Y_t as a linear function of the p previous values of itself and the p previous values all of the other variables (Whittle, 1953):

$$Y(t) = \mu_0 + \sum_{i=1}^{p} A_i Y(t-i) + \in (t).$$

The VAR(p) process may be non-stationary, i.e., non-stable, if the matrix $\Pi = (I_k - A_1 - \cdots - A_k)$ is singular. In this case, non-stationary time series can be made stationary by, for example, computing the difference between two consecutive observations. To test the stationarity Augmented Dickey Fuller statistical test (Mushtaq, 2011) can be used.

A time series has an order of integration d or $I(d)$, if $\Delta(d)Y(t)$ is stationary while $\Delta(d-1)Y(t)$ is not. For instance, in the case when $Y(t)$ is non-stationary of order 1, then $\Delta Y(t)$ is stationary and the model can be re-written as follows:

$$\Delta Y(t) = \mu_0 + \sum_{i=1}^{p-1} A_i \Delta Y(t-i) + \in(t).$$

The Vector Error Correction Model (VECM) introduced in (Johansen, 1991) transforms the VAR model by adding cointegration equations. To simplify its formulation, let us consider a multivariate time series $Y(t)$ integrated of order one, which means all the variables of Y_t are $I(0)$ or $I(1)$. The VECM Model can be written as follows:

$$\Delta Y(t) = \Pi Y(t-1) + \sum_{i=1}^{p-1} \Gamma_i \Delta Y(t-i) + \in(t),$$

where Π is the matrix representing co-integration equations, that can be obtained by VAR model, and Γ_i are the parameters of the model. If Π is not singular, then there are no cointegration equations and the VECM model is reduced to the VAR model on the transformed time series.

Proper fitting of Π and Γ_i coefficients becomes more difficult with the increase of the dimension of a time series. Intuitively, not all predictors in the multivariate time series will have the same impact on the predicted variable and, in some cases, adding more noise will decrease the accuracy of the model, as the model has to accommodate some unnecessary noise.

Artificial Neural Networks Models

Using Artificial Neural networks (ANNs) for time series can be made using the following steps. First, normalize the data, then transform the time series data into supervised learning problem depending on the lag parameter p, which can be seen as the memory of the network, next, construct and train the neural network using a network function f_{nn}:

$$Y(t) = f_{nn}(Y(t-1), \cdots, Y(t-p)) + \in(t),$$

finally, denormalize the predictions.

Thus, this follows the traditional feedforward model with back-propagation through time using for example gradient or stochastic gradient descent algorithms in order to update the weights of network, while minimizing the error function after each training experiment. All classical models seen in the previous subsection can be extended to non-linear version via ANNs. For instance, in (G. P. Zhang, 2003), a comparison between ARIMA model and univariate ANNs model is performed. The authors propose a combination of these two models, since they outperform depending on the datasets. In (Kaastra & Boyd, 1996), the authors use a multilayer perceptron network to forecast financial time series. In (Wutsqa, 2008), a Vector Autoregressive Neural Network (VAR-NN) model is proposed as non-linear extension of the classical VAR model, based on a fully connected multilayer perceptron network.

Several research works highlighted also the use of deep learning models in time series forecasting. Deep learning has been developed to compensate for the shortcomings of shallow neural networks.

The method proposed in (Yanjie et al., 2016), explores the application of the Long Short-Term Memory (LSTM) deep learning model in travel time prediction. LSTM neural network can be defined as a specific Recurrent Neural Network and it has a complex structure named LSTM cell in its hidden layer. The proposed model considers the sequence relation in data. 66 series prediction were constructed for the 66 links in the data set provided by Highways England. Experiments show that deep learning models considering sequence relation are promising in traffic series data prediction.

In (Takashi and Kuniaki, 2016), the proposed approach predicts financial time series by regression from both textual and numerical information. The proposed approach is based on deep learning models like (LSTM). Experiments were conducted on market simulation and results showed that LSTM outperforms other models in capturing time series influence of input data.

The aim of the method described in (Mladen, 2015) is to explore the use of deep neural networks in wind time series forecasting. Experiments have shown that the use of an algorithm for input variable selection simplifies the training of the deep neural networks. Results demonstrate that deep networks outperform classic neural networks.

In (Shen et al., 2015), a Deep Belief Network (DBN) was used to predict exchange rate movements.

In the training process, continuous restricted Boltzmann machines (CRBM) and a conjugated gradient method were applied.

To evaluate the prediction performance, several criteria were taken into account namely; prediction error, direction accuracy, correlation between actual exchange rate series and predictive ones, and the prediction stability.

The results showed that the proposed model outperforms a feed forward neural network-based model.

In (Ghaderi et al., 2017), the proposed approach is based on deep learning, particularly Recurrent Neural Network to forecast wind speed. Compared to a widely-used benchmarks model, experimental results showed that the proposed DL algorithm improves short term forecasts.

Another deep learning time series forecasting approach was proposed in (Takaomi et al., 2017) and compared to the conventional back-propagation method. The proposed method uses DBN with Restricted Boltzmann machines (RBMs) to capture the feature of input space of time series data. Evaluation was done on three time series based on natural phenomena.

According to the above cited works, using a deep neural network shows high predicting performance. However, it takes much longer to train than do shallow models.

Additionally, the higher the number of observed variables, the more complicated the problem will be. Thus, this raises the question of how to diminish the significance of non-related variables.

Building Forecasting Models in the Presence of Many Predictors

While this paper is devoted to automatic approaches, using the domain knowledge should always be the first step taken when pre-grouping variables. For example, given macroeconomic data in which time series are observations (indexes) of different aspects of the economy, one may group the variables cohesively using domain knowledge. Similarly, since the price of a product may heavily depend on the price of the subcomponents used to construct said product, it may be a good choice to limit the number of predictors in use to only those related to the prices of subcomponents.

While it is hard to overstate its importance, domain knowledge alone may be insufficient for pre-grouping variables, especially in cases of multivariate time series with many predictors. Data might be highly dimensional even after grouping, or pre-grouping is simply impossible given the complexity of observed stochastic processes. Hence, the need of automatic approaches.

For the purpose of clarity, we treat existing models as three-step processes, consisting of pre-forecasting, forecasting, and post-forecasting, where pre- and post- forecasting steps are optional.

The minimal setup of the process will entail only the forecasting step, which we refer to later in the paper as the 'one-step approach'. The idea here is to minimize the impact of various unrelated variables and fit the forecasting model at once. Usually, this will mean that the model will force the coefficients of unrelated variables close to 0 or set them explicitly to 0. Examples of such approaches include shrinkage approaches and neural networks.

In cases, when a pre-forecasting step is required, the number of predictors will be reduced either through features selection or dimension reduction. In the former case, a subset of predictors is selected and, in the latter case, new predictors are created. In both cases, the forecasting step will be processed on a space of predictors with a lower dimension than the original. Any multivariate forecasting model may be used in this step, which implies that the aforementioned one-step approaches are suitable as well.

The post-forecasting step is used to construct a forecast for a variable based on forecasts of other predictors. Consider an example where there are n different forecasting models possible for different variables: the target forecast may be constructed using the Bayesian averaging model. Some models will use both pre- and post- forecasting steps. The family of dynamic factor models serve as examples of this; in the pre-forecasting step, we search for common factors that drive all of the observed time series. We then forecast the common factors and use them in post-forecasting to reconstruct the target variables.

Problem Statement

Let us consider a multivariate time series with a large number of variables for which it is assumed that all predictors are sampled with the same frequency and no values are missing. Accordingly, in practice, the observed time series will have to be pre-processed, cleaned and all data gaps filled. If necessary, domain knowledge may be used to pre-group the data, then each group can be processed separately.

The main goal of multivariate time series forecasting is to improve the predictive quality of forecasting models through proper utilization of the predictors available in the dataset. The complexity of this task rises with the number of predictors. The second goal is to extract knowledge that is both novel and interesting. In some cases, this can be achieved as a byproduct of the original model. For example, if we can obtain a subset of predictors that improve the forecast of the target variable, this may imply that there is some kind of relationship between this subset and the target variable.

While those are subjects of many ongoing studies, we are mostly interested in methods that are scalable. Those aspects are either treated too simplistically or not at all in current literature.

Thus, in this chapter we give a synopsis of state of the art methods and discuss their eligibility in scalable environments in a compact way. Our target audience is both researchers and professionals interested in this topic.

STATE OF THE ART

In short, in multiview forecasting, a considerable number of factors (e.g., economic, political, environmental factors) are to be considered during the forecasting process. Data of this kind may be noisy, non-stationary, and subject to moods swings or various unfolding events, which suggests that its distribution may change over time. In order to minimize noise, extract the most relevant information, and improve the forecasting process, different techniques can be used, namely: dimensionality reduction techniques (e.g., independent component analysis, principal component analysis, kernel principal component analysis, and factor analysis), feature selection techniques, and shrinkage techniques.

The next section is devoted to discussion of the methods above. In the follow section, we outline several works and their contribution to multivariate time series analysis.

Dynamic Factor Models

Dynamic factor models (DFMs) have received considerable attention for the past two decades due to their ability to model time series in which the number of series is large or exceeds the number of observations (J. H. Stock & Watson, 2011).

Let us consider a n-dimensional multivariate stationary time series $Y(t)$. The classical factor model expresses each variable of $Y(t)$ linearly using a small number of factors r < n, and error terms:

$$Y(t) = A_1 f_1 + \cdots + A_r f_r + U(t),$$

where $[A_1, \cdots, A_r]$ are the parameters of the model, $[f_1, \cdots, f_r]$ is a vector of the r-factors, and $U(t)$ are idiosyncratic error terms.

The first DFM was introduced as an extension of the classical factor model (Geweke, 1977) with the aim of adapting the factor model for forecasting purposes, such that the n-dimensional time series $Y(t)$ can be represented dynamically based on the lagged factors, following for instance a VAR process. Formally, the DFM (p) can be expressed in a compact way as follows:

$$Y(t) = Af(t) + U(t),$$

$$f(t) = B_1 f(t-1) + \cdots + B_p f(t-p) + \in(t),$$

where $A = [A_1, \cdots, A_r], \in_t$ are independent error terms, and $[B_1, \cdots, B_p]$ are the matrix parameters of the VAR model.

The DFM can be seen as a three-step forecasting process. First, the latent factors are determined using, for example, factor analysis or principal component analysis. A forecasting model, most commonly the VAR or Bayesian VAR process, is then applied on those factors. Finally, the target variable is reconstructed from latent factors. This approach is slightly different from methods that are based on dimension reduction techniques, for which, first we determine the reduced predictors variables and then put them in the multivariate model alongside the target variable. In (PEÑA, 2009), a comparison study shows the similarities between those two approaches under certain conditions.

In (J. Stock & Watson, 2002), Principal Components Analysis (PCA) was used to forecast time series using a large number of predictor variables. A two-step forecasting model was adopted: PCA was first applied to reduce the number of predictors, a forecasting VAR model was then used to predict the discovered latent variables, and finally, the forecast for target variable was constructed using the forecasts of the latent predictors. Like the previous approach, this is also a three-step approach.

Later, in (J. H. Stock & Watson, 2012), an extended analysis was completed, forecasting US macroeconomic time series datasets with large numbers of predictors. Various shrinkage methods were compared to the Dynamic Factor Model (DFM). The results illustrate that those approaches outperform the DFM for considerable number of variables (See Shrinkage Methods subsection).

Approaches Based on Feature Selection and Dimension Reduction Techniques

This section is devoted to the feature selection and dimension reduction approaches to forecasting time series with a large number of variables. Handling high dimensionality time series makes traditional statistical forecasting models inappropriate (Fan, Han, & Liu, 2014). In the context of big time series prediction, the goal is to extract hidden relationships between time series, then construct a multivariate optimized model on the reduced subset of the predictors variables for each target variable. Thus, such approaches could be categorized as two step approaches with pre-forecasting and forecasting steps.

Feature selection methods extract the relevant features from a multidimensional data, whereas dimension reduction methods expose some hidden (or generate new, depending on point of view) variables, generally by finding the minimal number of uncorrelated factors that represent as much as possible the original variables. Both techniques can be used in forecasting large time series, as they will reduce the number of predictors used to forecast each of the target variables.

The PCA based dimension reduction method was also used in (Zhong & Enke, 2017), and was evaluated using financial data. The authors proposed a data mining forecasting process, in which, they tested three versions of PCA. Finally, they have used a fully connected layer of Artificial Neural Network (ANN) for forecasting.

In (Abraham, Nath, & Mahanti, 2001), the authors propose an hybrid process for stock market forecasting and trends analysis. A pre-forecasting step is performed using the PCA technique to reduce the dimension of the input variables. Similarly, a fully connected neural network layer is used for forecasting the stock outputs. Finally, a neuro-fuzzy system is used in order to analyze the forecasts trends.

A feature selection algorithm for time series based on PCA, recursive feature elimination and support vector machines was proposed in (Yoon & Shahabi, 2006). The experimentation was on human brain datasets with a number of features that was larger than the number of observations.

In (Koprinska, Rana, & Agelidis, 2015), a two-step forecasting approach was introduced to forecast two years of Australian electricity time series. First, correlation, mutual information and instance-based feature selection methods are applied in order to extract the relevant lagged variables. Then, a fully connected neural network layer combined with statistical models was used to forecast the variables.

The models utilising the Granger causality ((Granger, 1980)) have been also investigated in the context of prediction (Y. Sun et al., 2014). Variables were selected if they had a significant causality on the target. The authors reported good performance, compared to a selection dimension reduction methods, for regression and classification tasks.

A different approach based on Granger causality was proposed in (Hmamouche, Casali, & Lakhal, 2017).

First, a Granger causality graph was constructed based on causality between time series. Then, the graph was clustered, and, feature selection was performed based on the clustering. Finally, the Vector Error Correction Model (VECM) was used to forecast the target variable. The evaluation is done against a benchmark consisting of the ARIMA model on the target variable, the VECM model with all the predictors, a feature selection method (Y. Sun et al., 2014), and a selection of dimension reduction methods. Proposed model outperforms other methods on evaluated datasets.

The feature selection method presented in (Przymus, Hmamouche, Casali, & Lakhal, 2017) is also based on causality for multivariate time series. Authors present approach that is based on a variant of random walk with restarts on a directed causality graphs. Proposed approach yields competitive results compared to other well established approaches. Under mild assumption that a single node is sufficient to compute the causality for two variables and fit a forecasting model for one variable, authors show that all the necessarily steps are scalable.

Shrinkage Methods

As was mentioned above, in a model containing a large number of predictors, many of them may have a minor or no effect on the model's product. Such variables can distort the effect of more significant variables.

One approach is to minimize (shrink) the impact of irrelevant variables by setting the coefficients close to 0. Thus, a model is fitted using all p predictors and regularization on the coefficient estimates (e.g. some of the coefficients are pushed towards 0). Shrinking the coefficient estimates can significantly reduce their variance.

The Ridge regression is a shrinkage method proposed in (Hoerl & Kennard, 1970). It aims to adapt a regularized logistic regression technique to supervised learning problems where the number of input features is very large. A common way to write the Ridge regression is:

$$\sum_{i=1}^{n}\left(y_i - \beta_0 - \sum_{j}^{p}\beta_j x_{i,j}\right) + \lambda\sum_{j=1}^{p}\beta_j^2 = RSS + \lambda\sum_{j=1}^{p}\beta_j^2$$

where RSS is the Residual Sum of Squares, $x_{i,j}$ are predictor variables, Y_i are the respective response, $\lambda\sum_{j=1}^{p}\beta_j^2$ is a shrinkage penalty, and λ is a tuning parameter. Optimizing this term has the effect of shrinking the estimated beta coefficients towards 0.

Naturally, when $\lambda = 0$, the penalty term has no effect. The selection of an appropriate value for λ is important and can be done using, for example, cross validation. One significant problem of Ridge regression is that the penalty term will never force any of the coefficients exactly to 0. Thus, all p predictors will be included in the final model (but some with coefficients close to 0).

A more modern alternative is the Least Absolute Shrinkage and Selection Operator (LASSO) method (Tibshirani, 1994). The LASSO works in a similar way as Ridge regression, with one exception, it uses a different penalty term, which enforces some of the coefficients to be exactly equal to 0. Therefore, non-zero coefficients can be used for variable selection, as only those are considered important by the model.

The Lasso coefficients minimize the quantity:

$$\sum_{i=1}^{n}\left(y_i - \beta_0 - \sum_{j}^{p}\beta_j x_{i,j}\right) + \lambda\sum_{j=1}^{p}\left|\beta_j\right| = RSS + \lambda\sum_{j=1}^{p}\left|\beta_j\right|.$$

The major difference between Lasso and Ridge regression is the penalty used, the former penalizes using $\ell 1$ norm and the later using $\ell 2$ norm. As a result, Lasso may force some coefficients exactly to 0 if the tuning parameter λ is large enough.

When two predictors are highly correlated, the $\ell 2$ regularization will keep both predictors, and at the same time, it will shrink the corresponding coefficients jointly by a small amount. While $\ell 1$ regularization will choose only one of the two predictors. Thus, $\ell 1$ penalty allows reduction of the effect of overfitting.

Lasso and Ridge regression can be extended to work with Vector autoregressive model.

Consider a k-dimensional time series $\left(y_1, \cdots, y_k\right)$ containing n observations, and suppose we are interested in forecasting the variable y_k. The VAR model in this case can be expressed as follows:

$$y_k\left(t\right) = a_0 + \sum_{i=1}^{p}\left(a_{1,i}y_1\left(t-i\right) + \cdots + a_{k,i}y_k\left(t-i\right)\right) + u\left(t\right),$$

where $A = \left[a_0, a_{1,1}, \cdots a_{k,p}\right]$ are the parameters of the model, and $u\left(t\right)$ is a vector of size $n-p$ representing the error terms.

The classical estimation of the parameters A is generally performed using the least squares (LS) method which seeks to minimize the sum of squares of u(t). This method has some drawbacks in the presence of many variables. The objective functions of the vector autoregressive model via Lasso and Ridge regression are more flexible, and can be expressed respectively as follows:

$$\min_{a_0, a_{1,1}, \cdots, a_{k,p}}\left(\sum_{t=p+1}^{n}\left(y_k\left(t\right) - a_0 - \sum_{l=1}^{k}\sum_{j=1}^{p}a_{l,j}y_l\left(t-j\right)\right)^2 + \sum_{l=1}^{k}\sum_{j=1}^{p}\lambda\left|a_{l,j}\right|\right),$$

$$\min_{a_0, a_{1,1}, \cdots, a_{k,p}}\left(\sum_{t=p+1}^{n}\left(y_k\left(t\right) - a_0 - \sum_{l=1}^{k}\sum_{j=1}^{p}a_{l,j}y_l\left(t-j\right)\right)^2 + \sum_{l=1}^{k}\sum_{j=1}^{p}\lambda\left(a_{l,j}\right)^2\right).$$

- λ is a tuning parameter.
- $\lambda\left|a_{l,j}\right|$ and $\lambda(a_{l,j})^2$ are the shrinkage penalties associated to Lasso and Ridge regression respectively.

A great deal of research has been dedicated to exploring shrinkage based methods in the context of time series forecasting. A Lasso based method was proposed in (Bai & Ng, 2008) to select a subset of predictors. The subset obtained was used in the construction of factors in dynamic factor models.

Other variants of Lasso were proposed in (J. Li & Chen, 2014), namely Lasso regression, Elastic Net regressions (ENET) and Group-Lasso regression (G-Lasso). Proposed approach succeeded in eliminating irrelevant predictors from the predictive model. The predictive accuracy of the resulting forecasts was higher than the accuracy of various dynamic factor models. According to the authors of this study, Lasso and Ridge regression can be employed when forecasting with a large number of predictors.

Least Angle Regression (LARS) is another shrinkage method, proposed in (Efron, Hastie, Johnstone, & Tibshirani, 200404). The selection process of the LARS algorithm produces a ranking of predictors. The total level of shrinkage is controlled by the number of selected variables. The variant of LARS method proposed in (Gelper & Croux, 2008) was used to construct a model for forecasting industrial production growth. The model was evaluated in two applications. The first task was to select predictors to forecast aggregate industrial production growth in the United States based on a total of 131 potential predictors. As a comparison authors followed the procedure described in (J. Stock & Watson, 2002) for forecasting US industrial production growth. The second application involved prediction of industrial production growth in Belgium based on 75 time series measuring European countries economic indicators. The TS-LARS (Time Series LARS) method was applied to identify the most important sentiment indicators for predicting growth of Belgian industrial production. The authors of this study illustrate that, unlike DFM, TS-LARS incorporates both the response variable and the forecast horizon in the forecast model setup. What is more, the model obtained by TS-LARS is easily understandable in terms of the original predictors while the factors extracted through DFM are hard to interpret.

Various other shrinkage methods were applied in order to improve forecasting precision. One of these approaches, the Adaptive Jump Selection (AJS) method, was proposed in (Ren, Xiao, & Zhang, 2013). The author of this research investigated both lag order selection and variable selection. The method was applied to a macroeconomic time series dataset containing 2 years of monthly observations. The proposed approach added to the VAR lag order selection literature a new two-step shrinkage method based on the adaptive forward selection idea.

Similarly, in (Korobilis, 2013) a general shrinkage representation based on hierarchical prior distributions is proposed. In this case, forecasting was realized on the basis of 129 variables measuring quarterly macroeconomic conditions in the U.S. The target variable is treated as the dependent variable and the remaining 128 variables enter the regression as the matrix of standardized exogenous predictors which are subject to shrinkage. The results obtained illustrate that, for particular data series, hierarchical shrinkage dominates factor model forecasts in terms of mean absolute error.

Another shrinkage approach, that allows a comparison of forecasting methods with DFM, was proposed in (J. H. Stock & Watson, 2012). The exploited dataset consisted of 143 variables, spanning 49 years and measuring quarterly U.S. macroeconomic performance. A shrinkage representation of the forecasting methods (Bagging, BMA, pretest...) was given. The estimation of the shrinkage parameters for those methods was handled by minimizing the mean square error. For most series, the shrinkage forecasts were inferior to the DFM forecasts.

Some findings from (J. H. Stock & Watson, 2012) were confirmed in (Jiang et al., 2017). For example, new results support the statement that there is little to no improvement in forecast accuracy when the number of predictors exceeds 20-40 variables for Australian dataset (Jiang et al., 2017).

At the same time, authors of (Jiang et al., 2017) highlighted that methods that perform well in (J. H. Stock & Watson, 2012) on US dataset do not necessarily work well with the Australian dataset (containing 151 variables). Hence, in contrast to the US data, the dynamic factor model does not retain its good forecast performance for the Australian economy.

This supports the intuitive hypothesis that performance of existing models will highly depend on data, and that wide portfolio of methods should be evaluated first in order to find the best performing method for given target variable.

In (Carriero, Kapetanios, & Marcellino, 2011), bayesian shrinkage methods were used as an alternative to factor models for forecasting macroeconomic time series. The stochastic volatility was included for two types of forecasts: point and density forecast.

DISCUSSION

While in most cases the goal is the construction of a robust multivariate forecasting model (this was discussed in the previous subsections), there are some cases where information about relationship between the observed variables is also important (Shmueli, 2010).

Approaches based on feature selection highlight the relationships in the most straightforward way, as they select only the most influential variables, and sometimes, with additional ranking of influence. Then, we have LASSO and LARS based approaches, where some insights about the relationships can be also extracted. As coefficients of unrelated variables will be set to 0, and other coefficients may be analyzed in order to gain more insights. Other approaches will make this task more and more complicated, leaving us with problem of interpreting the coefficients of forecasting or dimension reduction model, or interpreting weights and architecture of an artificial neural network.

SCALABILITY

For large datasets, accuracy is not the only criteria that should be considered, as means of effective computation of such methods are also important. Yet, this aspect did not receive enough attention in the literature. In this section, we will look at previously described methods and discuss them in terms of scalability. We will also briefly address popular trend of utilizing hardware accelerated computational nodes in scalable environments by pointing possible solutions. As some of presented state of the art approaches share some of the underling (e.g. DFM and two step approaches) we decided to discuss the scalability of common parts together. Thus, in first subsection we discuss common aspects of the first phase of DFMs, and methods based on feature selection and dimension reduction. Then in next subsection we discuss scalability of forecasting models.

Pre-Forecasting Step

The goal of this step is to reduce the number of used variables in the forecasting step, and this can be achieved by different means. Fortunately, large number of approaches found in the literature, will be based on widely known algorithms that are scalable or can be computed on a GPU. Thus, we will shortly describe them and point the reader to the source publications. In cases where no such works exist we will discuss the possible scalable solution.

We will start the discussion with algorithms that are common for both dynamic factor models and two steps approaches that use dimension reduction. As a reminder, the underlying goal is to find a transformation that projects the data into a lower dimensional space. Please note, that in case of multivariate time series forecasting the data will usually be dense, and this aspect has to be taken into account when searching for scalable algorithms.

One of most popular approaches for dimension reduction are methods based on principal component analysis (PCA) and Canonical Correlation Analysis (CCA).

In (Chu et al., 2007), a parallel programing framework is proposed based on map-reduce. The authors tackle the parallelization of some machine learning algorithms including PCA. The idea is that many statistical models can easily benefit from multi-cores programming utilizing a unified methodology, taking advantage of their summation form.

Efficient scalable map reduce implementation of PCA and CCA for sparse data were proposed in (Elgamal, Yabandeh, Aboulnaga, Mustafa, & Hefeeda, 2015) and (Lopez-Paz, Sra, Smola, Ghahramani, & Schölkopf, 2014).

In the case of dense data, it is better to use scalable versions of Probabilistic PCA (Tipping & Bishop, 1999) or Incremental PCA (Weng, Zhang, & Hwang, 2003), both variants are known to be scalable (Elgamal & Hefeeda, 2015).

Another viable option is to use algorithms that can be utilized in scalable heterogeneous computing environments with hardware accelerators like GPU cards. High-performance PCA algorithms for GPU that outperform CPU version for this problem can be used (Andrecut, 2009; Jošth et al., 2012).

Factor analysis (FA) is another practical dimension reduction technique that is often used in dynamic factor model. Several works discussed scalability of this algorithm. In (D. Chen, Hu, Wang, Zomaya, & Li, 2017), a parallel framework was proposed to scale factor analysis for multidimensional data. In another work (Hinrich et al., 2016), a probabilistic algorithm was proposed that, under some sparsity constraints is capable of finding components similar to those obtained with independent component analysis (ICA). A viable alternative is also the parallel factor analysis (PARAFAC) that works in scalable GPGPU supported computing environments (Chen et al., 2015).

Another group of methods that use pre-forecasting step will use feature selection algorithms. We will start by discussing causality based feature selection approaches (Y. Sun et al., 2014) and (Hmamouche et al., 2017).

Both approaches use the Granger causality test (Granger, 1980). To calculate the Granger causality test, two forecasting models have to be computed: an univariate model on target variable and a bivariate VAR model with a target variable and one additional predictor. Then, Granger causality is computed by comparing forecasting accuracy between univariate model and bivariate model (usually followed by significance test).

We will assume that fitting both models can be done on a single node. In cases, when the number of observations per time series is huge and fitting forecasting model exceeds capabilities of a single node, please refer to the scalable forecasting models described in the next section.

The basic building block in the case of (Y. Sun et al., 2014) and (Hmamouche et al., 2017) is scalable computation of Granger causality for set of tuples $G = (T \times P) \setminus \Delta$, where P is the set of predictors, $T \subset P$ the set of target variables, and $\Delta = (t, p) \in T \times P : t = p$. Thus, we have to compute univariate models for variables in P and bivariate models for tuples in G. This is trivially scalable as all models can be computed independently. Finally, the results should be grouped by target variable and simple statistical tests of accuracy computed for univariate model on variable $t \in T$, and bivariate model (t, p) (simple task in map reduce approach).

The algorithm proposed in (Y. Sun et al., 2014) requires computation of set $G = ((P \times T) \cup (T \times P)) \setminus \Delta$ using the previously described building block. The one additional step is to leave only such tuples (t, p) where granger causality significantly differs from granger causality of tuple (p, t).

The algorithm presented in (Hmamouche et al., 2017), uses the granger causality graph, thus, it requires computation of set $G = (P \times P) \setminus \Delta$. The results are gathered in a matrix, then, the Partitioning Around Medoids (PAM) method is applied. When the matrix is very large, scalable clustering algorithms could be used (like k-medoids and other methods investigated in (Babu, n.d.) and (Y. Wu et al., 2015).

It is also worth to mention that some of the methods described in the shrinkage section could be also used as feature selection methods, for example see LARS-EN described in next section.

Forecasting Step

In general, we can remark that the VAR model is scalable, because its resolution is generally reduced to a multiple regression task. Scalability of multiple regression is feasible, some algorithms based on matrix decomposition were investigated and implemented for this problem (X. Wu, Zhu, Wu, & Ding, 2014), (Rehab & Boufares, 2015).

Forecasting models that are applying neural networks use layers typically found in modern deep learning frameworks. For example, neural network models discussed earlier, use mostly fully connected feed forward networks with back propagation. Some models include some additional transformations that also could be easily build around existing frameworks. Thanks to renaissance in deep learning, a variety of high performance frameworks for heterogeneous distributed environments (multiple nodes with CPU and GPU) exists, like (D. Chen et al., 2015) and (Abadi et al., 2016), thus, making it easier than ever to reimplement those models in a scalable and heterogeneous way.

Scalability of Shrinkage Methods

Scalability of shrinkage methods was studied in several works. In (Frandi, Ñanculef, Lodi, Sartori, & Suykens, 2016), authors studied the practical advantages of using Frank–Wolfe algorithm in solving the Lasso regression problem on high dimensional datasets. Authors supported their claims with experiments, they used a dataset containing large number of variables, between hundred thousand and few millions variables, and have shown very good performance suitable for a single node.

Several works studied the scalability of shrinkage methods and their feasibility for high dimensional time series. In the context of high-dimensional multivariate time series, new network estimation techniques were proposed in (Barigozzi, Lippi, & Luciani, 2016). The proposed approach was based on graph theory in order to handle with the correlation structure. The proposed algorithm "The NETS network estimation" was founded on a two-step LASSO procedure. The results were illustrated on a financial network showing large connected components and a number of companies that are not connected to any other node.

In (Hallac, Leskovec, & Boyd, 2015), it was argued that general convex optimization solvers do not scale well. On the other hand, scalable solvers are often specialized to deal with narrow class of problems. To solve optimization problems, scalable general algorithms are needed. In this work, a network LASSO was proposed. It is a generalization of the group LASSO to a network setting that allows the simultaneous clustering and optimization on graphs. To evaluate the proposed approach, several types of applications were studied such as; binary classification, predicting housing prices, and event detection in time series data.

The importance of variable pre-selection before factor estimation was studied in (Kuzin, Marcellino, & Schumacher, 2013). In fact, LARS-EN (Least-Angle Regression with Elastic Net) algorithm was used in order to preselect the variables. The LARS-EN is capable of removing irrelevant regressors and allowing for shrinkage simultaneously. Results have shown that richness of data can be a burden for factor forecasting, and only careful preselection of variables may help exploiting the extra information from the large and heterogeneous dataset. In their experimental study, authors used a large set of about 500 time series.

CONCLUSION

Multivariate time series forecasting represents a special type of problem where both the past observations of the target variable and past observations of other variables have to be considered. In this paper, we discuss two main aspects of modeling "big data" multivariate time series, the number of observations, and the number of predictors involved.

When handling high-dimensional time series, the number of observations is the leaser problem, while, the number of variables is the greater problem. The argumentation behind is that time series are generally processed in 'rolling windows', which allows easy division of the problem to scalable sub problems. For cases, where rolling window is not a solution (or the size of the window is "big") we point to scalable forecasting models designed for this problem.

The greater problem lies in the number of observed variables. This challenges the classical machine learning and multivariate forecasting approaches. Thus, the use of scalable approaches that allow to reduce the impact of high dimensionality of input is crucial.

In this chapter, we provide a survey of forecasting models specific to high-dimensional time series, in terms of the number of features. We discuss the main prediction models used to forecast time series, starting from univariate models that forecast a variable based on its historic data, and multivariate models that use many variables.

We review the most relevant approaches that handle the problem of using multivariate models in the case of many predictors variables, e.g., DFMs models, basically designed to model multivariate time series, and two-step process, such as methods based on dimension reduction or feature selection. Then we discuss usage of shrinkage methods in multivariate forecasting. Finally, we discuss those approaches in terms of scalability.

From our literature review one observation is present in several works that models may struggle to fit good quality models if too many predictors are used (J. H. Stock & Watson, 2012), (Jiang et al., 2017), (Hallac, Leskovec, & Boyd, 2015), (Kuzin, Marcellino, & Schumacher, 2013). Furthermore, for (J. H. Stock & Watson, 2012) and (Jiang et al., 2017) macroeconomy datasets we have empirical evidence that using more than 20-40 predictor variables (from around 150) will not improve (or even can degrade) the quality of forecasts. Of course, this is not a general rule, but it supports the general intuition that using too many predictors may be counterproductive. Thus, while most of described approaches are feasible (sometimes with some extra research work) for scalable environments, not all of them will be able to give reasonable models when facing high dimension of the data. Thus, DFMs, dimension reduction models, and those shrinkage models that do not set coefficients exactly to 0 may struggle in such cases. Thus, we suggest, using a hierarchical approach, where some of the models are used to pre-group the data into hierarchy of variables.

REFERENCES

Abadi, M., Agarwal, A., Barham, P., Brevdo, E., Chen, Z., Citro, C., … Zheng, X. (2016). *TensorFlow: Large-Scale Machine Learning on Heterogeneous Distributed Systems*. Retrieved from http://arxiv.org/abs/1603.04467

Abraham, A., Nath, B., & Mahanti, P. K. (2001). Hybrid Intelligent Systems for Stock Market Analysis. In *Computational Science - ICCS 2001* (pp. 337–345). Berlin: Springer; doi:10.1007/3-540-45718-6_38

Akita, R., Yoshihara, A., Matsubara, T., & Uehara, K. (2016). Deep learning for stock prediction using numerical and textual information. In *Computer and Information Science (ICIS), 2016 IEEE/ACIS 15th International Conference on* (pp. 1–6). IEEE. 10.1109/ICIS.2016.7550882

Andrecut, M. (2009). Parallel GPU Implementation of Iterative PCA Algorithms. *Journal of Computational Biology*, *16*(11), 1593–1599. doi:10.1089/cmb.2008.0221 PMID:19772385

Babu, M. C. K., & Nagendra, P. (n.d.). Survey on Clustering on the Cloud by UsingMap Reduce in Large Data Applications. *International Journal of Engineering Trends and Technology*. Retrieved from http://www.ijettjournal.org/archive/ijett-v21p275

Bai, J., & Ng, S. (2008). Forecasting economic time series using targeted predictors. *Journal of Econometrics*, *146*(2), 304–317. doi:10.1016/j.jeconom.2008.08.010

Barigozzi, M., Lippi, M., & Luciani, M. (2016). *Non-stationary dynamic factor models for large datasets*. Retrieved from https://papers.ssrn.com/sol3/papers.cfm?abstract_id=2756940

Beyer, M. A., & Laney, D. (2012). *The importance of 'big data': a definition*. Stamford, CT: Gartner.

Box, G. (2013). Box and Jenkins: Time Series Analysis, Forecasting and Control. In *A Very British Affair* (pp. 161–215). Palgrave Macmillan UK. doi:10.1057/9781137291264_6

Carriero, A., Kapetanios, G., & Marcellino, M. (2011). Forecasting large datasets with Bayesian reduced rank multivariate models. *Journal of Applied Econometrics, 26*(5), 735–761. doi:10.1002/jae.1150

Chen, D., Hu, Y., Wang, L., Zomaya, A. Y., & Li, X. (2017). H-PARAFAC: Hierarchical Parallel Factor Analysis of Multidimensional Big Data. *IEEE Transactions on Parallel and Distributed Systems, 28*(4), 1091–1104. doi:10.1109/TPDS.2016.2613054

Chen, D., Li, X., Wang, L., Khan, S. U., Wang, J., Zeng, K., & Cai, C. (2015). Fast and Scalable Multi-Way Analysis of Massive Neural Data. *IEEE Transactions on Computers, 64*(3), 707–719. doi:10.1109/TC.2013.2295806

Chu, C.-t., Kim, S. K., Lin, Y.-a., Yu, Y., Bradski, G., Olukotun, K., & Ng, A. Y. (2007). Map-Reduce for Machine Learning on Multicore. In P. B. Schölkopf, J. C. Platt, & T. Hoffman (Eds.), Advances in Neural Information Processing Systems. MIT Press. Retrieved from http://papers.nips.cc/paper/3150-map-reduce-for-machine-learning-on-multicore.pdf

Dalto, M., Matuško, J., & Vašak, M. (2015). Deep neural networks for ultra-short-term wind forecasting. In *Industrial Technology (ICIT), 2015 IEEE International Conference on* (pp. 1657–1663). IEEE. 10.1109/ICIT.2015.7125335

Duan, Y., Lv, Y., & Wang, F.-Y. (2016). Travel time prediction with LSTM neural network. In *Intelligent Transportation Systems (ITSC), 2016 IEEE 19th International Conference on* (pp. 1053–1058). IEEE.

Efron, B., Hastie, T., Johnstone, I., & Tibshirani, R. (2004). Least angle regression. *Annals of Statistics, 32*(2), 407–499. doi:10.1214/009053604000000067

Elgamal, T., & Hefeeda, M. (2015). *Analysis of PCA Algorithms in Distributed Environments*. Retrieved from http://arxiv.org/abs/1503.05214

Elgamal, T., Yabandeh, M., Aboulnaga, A., Mustafa, W., & Hefeeda, M. (2015). sPCA: Scalable Principal Component Analysis for Big Data on Distributed Platforms. In *Proceedings of the 2015 ACM SIGMOD International Conference on Management of Data* (pp. 79–91). New York: ACM. 10.1145/2723372.2751520

Fan, J., Han, F., & Liu, H. (2014). Challenges of Big Data analysis. *National Science Review, 1*(2), 293–314. doi:10.1093/nsr/nwt032 PMID:25419469

Frandi, E., Ñanculef, R., Lodi, S., Sartori, C., & Suykens, J. A. K. (2016). Fast and scalable Lasso via stochastic Frank–Wolfe methods with a convergence guarantee. *Machine Learning, 104*(2-3), 195–221. doi:10.100710994-016-5578-4

García, S., Ramírez-Gallego, S., Luengo, J., Benítez, J. M., & Herrera, F. (2016). Big data preprocessing: Methods and prospects. *Big Data Analytics*, *1*(1), 9. doi:10.118641044-016-0014-0

Gelper, S., & Croux, C. (2008). *Least angle regression for time series forecasting with many predictors*. Retrieved from https://lirias.kuleuven.be/handle/123456789/164224

Geweke, J. (1977). The dynamic factor analysis of economic time series. *Latent variables in socio-economic models.*

Ghaderi, A., Sanandaji, B. M., & Ghaderi, F. (2017). *Deep Forecast: Deep Learning-based Spatio-Temporal Forecasting*. ArXiv Preprint ArXiv:1707.08110.

Granger, C. W. J. (1980). Testing for causality. *Journal of Economic Dynamics & Control*, *2*, 329–352. doi:10.1016/0165-1889(80)90069-X

Hallac, D., Leskovec, J., & Boyd, S. (2015). Network Lasso: Clustering and Optimization in Large Graphs. *KDD: Proceedings / International Conference on Knowledge Discovery & Data Mining. International Conference on Knowledge Discovery & Data Mining*, *2015*, 387–396. doi:10.1145/2783258.2783313 PMID:27398260

Hinrich, J. L., Nielsen, S. F. V., Riis, N. A. B., Eriksen, C. T., Frøsig, J., Kristensen, M. D. F., … Mørup, M. (2016). *Scalable Group Level Probabilistic Sparse Factor Analysis*. Retrieved from http://arxiv.org/abs/1612.04555

Hirata, T., Kuremoto, T., Obayashi, M., Mabu, S., & Kobayashi, K. (2017). *Forecasting Real Time Series Data using Deep Belief Net and Reinforcement Learning*. Academic Press.

Hmamouche, Y., Casali, A., & Lakhal, L. (2017). A Causality based feature selection approach for multivariate time series forecasting. Paper presented at *The International Conference on Advances in Databases, Knowledge, and Data Applications*, Barcelona, Spain.

Hoerl, A. E., & Kennard, R. W. (1970). Ridge Regression: Biased Estimation for Nonorthogonal Problems. *Technometrics*, *12*(1), 55–67. doi:10.1080/00401706.1970.10488634

Jiang, B., Athanasopoulos, G., Hyndman, R. J., Panagiotelis, A., & Vahid, F. (2017). *Macroeconomic forecasting for Australia using a large number of predictors* (Monash Econometrics and Business Statistics Working Paper No. 2/17). Monash University, Department of Econometrics and Business Statistics. Retrieved from https://ideas.repec.org/p/msh/ebswps/2017-2.html

Johansen, S. (1991). Estimation and Hypothesis Testing of Cointegration Vectors in Gaussian Vector Autoregressive Models. *Econometrica, 59*(6), 1551–1580. doi:10.2307/2938278

Jošth, R., Antikainen, J., Havel, J., Herout, A., Zemčík, P., & Hauta-Kasari, M. (2012). Real-time PCA calculation for spectral imaging (using SIMD and GP-GPU). *Journal of Real-Time Image Processing, 7*(2), 95–103. doi:10.100711554-010-0190-5

Kaastra, I., & Boyd, M. (1996). Designing a neural network for forecasting financial and economic time series. *Neurocomputing, 10*(3), 215–236. doi:10.1016/0925-2312(95)00039-9

Koprinska, I., Rana, M., & Agelidis, V. G. (2015). Correlation and instance based feature selection for electricity load forecasting. *Knowledge-Based Systems, 82*, 29–40. doi:10.1016/j.knosys.2015.02.017

Korobilis, D. (2013). Hierarchical shrinkage priors for dynamic regressions with many predictors. *International Journal of Forecasting, 29*(1), 43–59. doi:10.1016/j.ijforecast.2012.05.006

Kuzin, V., Marcellino, M., & Schumacher, C. (2013). Pooling Versus Model Selection for Nowcasting Gdp with Many Predictors: Empirical Evidence for Six Industrialized Countries. *Journal of Applied Econometrics, 28*(3), 392–411. doi:10.1002/jae.2279

Li, J., & Chen, W. (2014). Forecasting macroeconomic time series: LASSO-based approaches and their forecast combinations with dynamic factor models. *International Journal of Forecasting, 30*(4), 996–1015. doi:10.1016/j.ijforecast.2014.03.016

Lopez-Paz, D., Sra, S., Smola, A., Ghahramani, Z., & Schölkopf, B. (2014). *Randomized Nonlinear Component Analysis.* Retrieved from http://arxiv.org/abs/1402.0119

Mushtaq, R. (2011). *Augmented Dickey Fuller Test (SSRN Scholarly Paper No. ID 1911068)*. Rochester, NY: Social Science Research Network. Retrieved from https://papers.ssrn.com/abstract=1911068

Pena, D. (2009). Dimension reduction in time series and the dynamic factor model. *Biometrika, 96*(2), 494–496. doi:10.1093/biomet/asp009

Przymus, P., Hmamouche, Y., Casali, A., & Lakhal, L. (2017). Improving multivariate time series forecasting with random walks with restarts on causality graphs. In *2017 IEEE International Conference on Data Mining Workshops (ICDMW)* (pp. 924–931). IEEE.

Rahulgargiit. (2016). *Acceleration of Full-Brain Autoregressive Modelling using GPUs*. Retrieved June 28, 2017, from https://eklavyaweb.wordpress.com/2016/05/15/acceleration-of-full-brain-autoregressive-modelling-using-gpus/

Rehab, M. A., & Boufares, F. (2015). *Scalable Massively Parallel Learning of Multiple Linear Regression Algorithm with MapReduce. In 2015 IEEE Trustcom/BigDataSE* (Vol. 2, pp. 41–47). ISPA; doi:10.1109/Trustcom.2015.560

Ren, Y., Xiao, Z., & Zhang, X. (2013). Two-step adaptive model selection for vector autoregressive processes. *Journal of Multivariate Analysis*, *116*, 349–364. doi:10.1016/j.jmva.2013.01.004

Shen, F., Chao, J., & Zhao, J. (2015). Forecasting exchange rate using deep belief networks and conjugate gradient method. *Neurocomputing*, *167*, 243–253. doi:10.1016/j.neucom.2015.04.071

Shmueli, G. (2010). To Explain or to Predict? *Statistical Science*, *25*(3), 289–310. doi:10.1214/10-STS330

Stock, J., & Watson, M. W. (2002). Forecasting Using Principal Components from a Large Number of Predictors. *Journal of the American Statistical Association*, *97*(460), 1167–1179. doi:10.1198/016214502388618960

Stock, J. H., & Watson, M. (2011). Dynamic Factor Models. In *Oxford Handbook on Economic Forecasting*. Oxford University Press. doi:10.1093/oxfordhb/9780195398649.013.0003

Stock, J. H., & Watson, M. W. (2012). Generalized Shrinkage Methods for Forecasting Using Many Predictors. *Journal of Business & Economic Statistics*, *30*(4), 481–493. doi:10.1080/07350015.2012.715956

Sun, Y., Li, J., Liu, J., Chow, C., Sun, B., & Wang, R. (2014). Using causal discovery for feature selection in multivariate numerical time series. *Machine Learning*, *101*(1-3), 377–395. doi:10.100710994-014-5460-1

Thielbar, M., & Dickey, D. A. (2011). *Neural Networks for Time Series Forecasting: Practical Implications of Theoretical Results*. Academic Press.

Tibshirani, R. (1994). Regression Shrinkage and Selection Via the Lasso. *Journal of the Royal Statistical Society. Series B. Methodological*, *58*, 267–288.

Tipping, M. E., & Bishop, C. M. (1999). Probabilistic Principal Component Analysis. *Journal of the Royal Statistical Society. Series B, Statistical Methodology*, *61*(3), 611–622. doi:10.1111/1467-9868.00196

Ward, J. S., & Barker, A. (2013). *Undefined By Data: A Survey of Big Data Definitions*. Retrieved from http://arxiv.org/abs/1309.5821

Weng, J., Zhang, Y., & Hwang, W.-S. (2003). Candid covariance-free incremental principal component analysis. *IEEE Transactions on Pattern Analysis and Machine Intelligence*, *25*(8), 1034–1040. doi:10.1109/TPAMI.2003.1217609

Whittle, P. (1953). The Analysis of Multiple Stationary Time Series. *Journal of the Royal Statistical Society. Series B. Methodological*, *15*(1), 125–139.

Wlodarczyk, T. W. (2012). Overview of Time Series Storage and Processing in a Cloud Environment. In *4th IEEE International Conference on Cloud Computing Technology and Science Proceedings* (pp. 625–628). IEEE. 10.1109/CloudCom.2012.6427510

Wu, X., Zhu, X., Wu, G. Q., & Ding, W. (2014). Data mining with big data. *IEEE Transactions on Knowledge and Data Engineering*, *26*(1), 97–107. doi:10.1109/TKDE.2013.109

Wu, Y., Zhu, Y., Huang, T., Li, X., Liu, X., & Liu, M. (2015). Distributed Discord Discovery: Spark Based Anomaly Detection in Time Series. In *2015 IEEE 17th International Conference on High Performance Computing and Communications* (pp. 154–159). IEEE. 10.1109/HPCC-CSS-ICESS.2015.228

Wutsqa, D. U. (2008). The Var-NN Model for Multivariate Time Series Forecasting. *MatStat*, *8*(1), 35–43. Retrieved from http://research.binus.ac.id/publication/C12DAA42-899B-4DF3-BA44-4DD770B220C2/the-var-nn-model-for-multivariate-time-series-forecasting/

Yoon, H., & Shahabi, C. (2006). Shahabi: Feature Subset Selection on Multivariate Time Series with Extremely Large Spatial Features Data Mining Workshops. In *ICDM Workshops 2006. Sixth IEEE International Conference on*. IEEE. 10.1109/ICDMW.2006.81

Zhang, G. P. (2003). Time series forecasting using a hybrid ARIMA and neural network model. *Neurocomputing*, *50*, 159–175. doi:10.1016/S0925-2312(01)00702-0

Zhong, X., & Enke, D. (2017). Forecasting daily stock market return using dimensionality reduction. *Expert Systems with Applications*, *67*, 126–139. doi:10.1016/j.eswa.2016.09.027

Chapter 7
Exploring Multiple Dynamic Social Networks in Computer-Mediated Communications:
An Experimentally Validated Ecosystem

O. Isaac Osesina
Aware Inc., USA

John P. McIntire
United States Air Force, USA

M. Eduard Tudoreanu
University of Arkansas at Little Rock, USA

Paul R. Havig
United States Air Force, USA

Eric E. Geiselman
United States Air Force, USA

ABSTRACT

This chapter discusses concepts and tools for the exploration and visualization of computer-mediated communication (CMC), especially communication involving multiple users and taking place asynchronously. The work presented here is based on experimentally validated social networks (SN) extraction methods and consists of a diverse number of techniques for conveying the data to a business analyst. The chapter explores a large number of contexts ranging from direct social network graphs to more complex geographical, hierarchical, and conversation-centric approaches. User validation studies were conducted for the most representative techniques, centered both on extracting and on conveying of CMC data. The chapter examines methods for automatically extracting social networks, which is determining who is communicating with whom across different CMC channels. Beyond the network, the chapter focuses on the end-user discovery of topics and on integrating those with geographical, hierarchical, and user data. User-centric, interactive visualizations are presented from a functional perspective.

DOI: 10.4018/978-1-5225-4963-5.ch007

INTRODUCTION

Ease of analysis and exploration of the big data generated through computer-mediated communication (CMC) is significant to practitioners like network analysts, business and marketing experts, researchers, intelligence analysts, first responders, as it determines their ability to exploit the vast amount of data available through the different modern CMC platforms like microblog (Twitter), social media (Facebook, internet relay chat), instant messaging,(Instagram) etc. In order to empower users to take advantage of the wealth of information transmitted and stored within the CMC platforms, research into concepts and tools for efficient analysis, exploration and visualization of digital communications is essential. A diverse number of techniques for analyzing and conveying the information to a business analyst (and other practitioners) via a large number of contexts ranging from direct social network graphs to more complex geographical, hierarchical, and conversation centric approaches along with the results of their experiments are presented in this chapter.

Modern internet access and the ubiquity of smart phones have greatly increased (and perhaps altered) the dynamics of human communication; the variety and the currency of subjects, diversity and population of participants, multiplicity and intensity of opinions are difficult to envision in the absence CMC. Furthermore, access to the simultaneous engagement of users in multiple interactions via different CMC systems and applications like microblog, chats, messaging applications, and online social networking offers practitioners a rich virtual environment to better understand the complex dynamics of human communications. Although, these CMC archives along with their metadata like time, geographic location, and device identifiers provide practitioners like social network analysts, business and marketing experts, researchers, intelligence analysts, first responders with a wealth of information for analyzing different aspects of human interactions; the volume and diversity of available data presents the challenge of efficient of exploration and analysis for the purpose of extracting and presenting information of interest from the data. The challenge of extracting actionable information from CMC systems is still an active research topic. Methods for extracting situational awareness for tweets (Verma et al., 2011) as well as identification and categorization of disaster-related tweets Stowe et al. (2016) are some of the related works in this domain.

This chapter explores the above described challenge in the context of big data and under two broad objectives; namely, analysis and visualization. The nature of big data dictates that design choices for various techniques focus on simplicity of processing, where priority is given to analysis techniques that run fast and visualizations that present simple relationships and allow the user to navigate in the large expanse of relationships provided by big data. The CMC data analysis category includes methods for automatic analysis of actors, their social network structures as well as discussion topics across CMC channels. Visualization methods for social network structures along with the results of a study to examine their task-based effectiveness are also presented. In addition, visualization techniques for contexts and keywords in a multi-speaker, multi-topic, quasi-synchronous CMC system are discussed and experimented.

The objectives of this chapter are:

- Present methods for extracting the social network from multi-user communication;
- Present a set of visualization tools ranging from simple, explicit node-link representations, to complex, continuous, interactive visualizations that show the network implicitly in the context of additional data;
- Explore the effectiveness of both the social network (SN) extraction methods and representative visualizations.

BACKGROUND

Sociologists have long been interested in the study of social networks in the understanding of the complex relationship patterns between and among individuals as well as groups (Freeman, 2004). The related work section is divided into two namely: interaction network extraction and interaction visualization. In the former, works related to the identification and analysis of communication patterns and social network are presented, while the later focuses on research about visualizing communication interactions.

Social Network Extraction From CMC Data

For years, researchers have been interested in CMC data for understanding the evolution of online communities (Krikorian & Ludwig, 2002), promoting pro-social behaviors (Burkhalter & Smith, 2004), increasing social consciousness/encouraging user participation (Kelly, Sung, & Farnham, 2002), improving user interaction/increasing satisfaction (Viégas, 2005), and more recently for online abuse detection (Papegnies, Labatut, Dufour, & Linares, 2017).

Netscan (Smith M., 1999), a CMC analysis tool which reveals insights into the structure and characteristics of online communities, has been extensively studied and used for extracting different types of social network information. Burkhalter and Smith's (2004) study of Netscan revealed the use of SN information for member "typification," status, and group comparison. Smith, Farnham and Drucker (2000) studied the similarities between spatial and physical interactions using Netscan.

Also, Krikorian and Kiyomiya (2002) developed the newsgroup death model for determining the decline of online communities and detection of cliques based on asynchronous user interactions (Krikorian & Ludwig, 2003). Conversation Map (Sack, 2000) analyzed CMC information for revealing member centrality, conversation groups, and citation patterns within Usenet newsgroups. Rosen, Woelfel, Krikorian and Barnett (2003) illustrated the use of semantic analysis to determine groups and organizational patterns within an online educational universe. Shin, et al. (Shin, Xu, & Kim, 2008) exploited online social relationships for the discovery of power users within virtual communities.

The inference problem (Choudhury, Hofman, Mason, & Watts, 2010) is that, for many social media platforms, "real" social ties are not directly observable and must be extracted or inferred by observing communication events in social networks. For instance, being a "friend" with someone on FaceBook does not necessarily imply true friendship, or a strong social network link. The level of challenge in inferring social networks from CMC depends on the properties of the medium used. In a medium such as email, inferring social networks may be easier since observed events (e.g., Tom emails Jerry) are clearly defined and likely to represent a social network link. However such links are not clearly defined in multiuser chatrooms. Tyler, Wilkinson and Huberman (2003) as well as Diesner, Frantz and Carley (2005) explored methods for analyzing social network within e-mails. Mobile phone logs were also used to analyze friendship. (Eagle, Pentland, & Lazer, 2009). Since social links do not already exist in multi-user chatroom data, these methods cannot be directly applied to inferring links in chatroom logs.

Mutton (2004) introduced several approaches for extracting/inferring SN links within internet chat, two of which are implemented in the present work: (1) temporal proximity of messages and (2) direct addressing of users. This chapter additionally implements message content via keyword-based similarity to infer whether two individuals are talking about the same topic (are in the same conversation). As discussed above, there are a variety of potential uses and applications for social network data in CMC, but this research focuses primarily on inferring/extracting links between interacting users and obtaining an overview of the conversation content.

Visualization of CMC Interaction

Information visualization is a mature field of study with thousands of solutions developed for a wide range of audiences and tasks. This section focuses on those techniques that are the closest to the end-user visualizations developed or adapted in this chapter for the purposes of showing CMC data. The most obvious type of technique will look at simple representation of networks and graphs. Then, this section focuses on visualizations that can augment the social network and topic data with contextual perspectives: geographic information system (GIS) visualization and chatroom views.

Assuming one has access to a social network and knowledge of its members and their links, the question arises as to how to utilize this information. Often, the answer is to visualize it (make a picture of the data network). This can be difficult in practice, so previous researchers have tried to shed light on useful ways to portray network (node-link) graphs Ghoniem, Fekete, & Castagliola (2004) (2005) (Okoe, Jianu, & Kobourov, 2017). For instance, a series of experiments, Purchase et al. (2002), and Ware et al. (2002) suggested that node-link diagrams should minimize link crossings and avoid using bends, kinks, or turns in the links, in order to improve graph reading performance; otherwise, it makes little difference for graph readability how a node-link diagram is portrayed. They found little relation between graph aesthetics and performance (in terms of "understanding" a graph). They also found (as have many others) that node-link diagrams simply do not handle the problem of *scaling* very well: as the underlying networks get bigger (above 20 to 30 nodes), the graphs are more difficult (or sometimes impossible) to understand and/or use.

Ghoniem, Fekete, & Castagliola (2004) examined user performance on node-link versus matrix-based network visualizations. They tested performance on seven generic graph-based tasks while manipulating the size and density (connectivity) of the networks. For networks larger than about 20 nodes, they found, matrix-based visualizations were better for most tasks (the one exception being a path-finding task, such as "find the shortest path between nodes A and B," which was better when using node-link diagrams). Their results suggest that matrix-based visualizations should work well for large network datasets on a variety of network tasks, and their use should be encouraged despite observers' relative unfamiliarity with this visualization method. Later in this chapter, similar work is replicated and extended in several key aspects of such as the use of heat maps (as opposed to binary displays) in the matrices and luminance/color-varying links in the network diagrams. Such non-binary displays of network structure should, theoretically, allow more information to be portrayed to users about the underlying network data, at least regarding the "strength" of connections between nodes.

Geographical visualization has been used as a background for combining additional, textual information, to form a geovisualization mashup. Based on Google Earth, to mine latent spatio-temporal data (Wood, Dykes, Slingsby, & Clarke, 2007), the placement of words on the map is either through icons that are labelled and may require user interaction to open and read multiple pieces of information residing at a given coordinate, or through tag clouds or tag maps. The tag clouds being generated without regard of the tag's geo-coordinate lacks a precise positioning on the map, and again requires interaction to zoom into the right area, which is different from the BuzzVizz, the approach presented in this chapter. Mashup@GIS (Feng, Gan, &

Yang, 2009) was developed as a prototype that combines data and system functions to create a more secure and diverse application, but their focus is on displaying additional symbols, such as charts, at a certain geolocation. A similar data integration tool (Batty, Hudson-Smith, Milton, & Crooks, 2010) incorporates user friendly map manipulation, MapTube, as a way of visualizing spatial data. These concepts are GIS-centric in that they lack the ability to engage a user in analysing his/her spatial environment against real-time data sources, especially unstructured text. The need to improve awareness for electrical grid operators is recognized by Moses (Moses, 2007) in his mashup that allows users to view data in a hierarchal structure. That approach does not focus on unstructured text. Tomaszewski's research on disaster relief allows a user to visualize his/her surroundings by blending a Virtual Globe (implemented via Google Earth) with a context based application that relies on RSS feed content from web publications (Tomaszewski, 2010). TwitterStand (Sankaranarayanan, Samet, Teitler, Lieberman, & Sperling, 2009) attempts to address the low data quality of Twitter by creating a graphical news processing system that spots news based on a Twitter user's geographic location, but the systems data source is limited to only those users deemed reliable (T.V. stations, reporters, and recognized bloggers).

In the chatroom visualization arena, Neumann and colleagues (Neumann, Tat, Zuk, & Carpendale, 2006; Neumann, Tat, Zuk, & Carpendale, 2007) used unique characteristics of individuals' typing styles in a chatroom to provide an artistic rendering/visualization of the chat. The goal was to improve social consciousness and personalize interaction. PeopleGarden is a visualization that facilitates the analysis of virtual forums (Xiong & Donath, 1999). It uses flowers, petals, and pistil-like circles to represent users, their postings, and response quantification respectively. *Conversation threading* is the concept of somehow re-structuring disjointed and hard-to-follow conversations that occur on digital communications platforms, largely due to media type and interaction methods like asynchronicity of speakers (think of following a conversation over lengthy email exchanges, in a blog, or in a streaming chat format with multiple speakers). Conversation threading aids SN analysis by improving the usability, navigability, and understandability of conversations and topics under discussion. Smith et al. (Smith, Farnham, & Drucker, 2000) studied automated conversational threading within chat in an attempt to restore the natural turn-taking structure of spoken communication which is often disjointed in chat syntax. Researchers (Rohall, Gruen, Moody, & Kellerman, 2001) performed similar threading work using email CMC in order to counter the disjointedness that is sometimes present in lengthy email exchanges. Apart from the example of conversation threading, social network analysis of communication platforms has other important uses. For instance, Angluin, Aspnes and Reyzin (2010) used information about illness outbreaks from the Center for Disease Control to infer the underlying real-world social networks of patients to help identify, track, and contain spreading illness outbreaks. Abbasi & Chen (2008) describe a CMC analysis and visualization system, and showed how it could be used to understand the social network dynamics during an unfolding business scandal (Enron use case). Similarly, intelligence analysts utilize social media records to reconstruct or infer social networks for law enforcement and terrorism investigations.

EXTRACTING SOCIAL NETWORKS FROM CMC DATA

A social network (SN) is a structure that describes a set of individuals/actors and their interdependencies or interactions. This information is popularly represented by a graph structure where the nodes and their links or edges represent actors and interdependencies, respectively. CMC data generated on platforms such like IRC, Twitter, Instagram, Google Handouts, and Slack are a challenging category of big-data not only due to their variety, velocity and volume, but to the (semi-) unstructured nature of the content. The analysis or moderation of this data when done by human is expensive and often limited in scope. In order to operationalize and analyze this data researchers aim to characterize the nature of the interactions contained in this data in terms of relationship dynamics and material subjects. An approach to achieving this aim is to infer, detect, or otherwise extract the social network connections (links) between the actors (nodes). The extraction and visualization of this information is expected to contribute to the ease of distilling valuable information from large volumes of textual communication datasets (Albinsson & Morin, 2002). The effectiveness of this analysis has been researched for applications such as situational awareness (McIntire, Osesina, & Craft, 2011), online abuse detection (Papegnies, Labatut, Dufour, & Linares, 2017), behavior analysis (Tavassoli & Zweig, 2015) (Shin, Xu, & Kim, 2008).

The methods described in this section focus primarily on SN extraction methods for multi-user asynchronous data commonly found in chatrooms or user review sections of e-commerce websites. Other CMC applications that support direct messaging with explicit social network(s) revealing interactions among individual actors, e.g., e-mail, the use of the @ character in Twitter, or "reply to" comments on a social media post are not directly discussed. In an asynchronous multi-user chat environment like IRC channels or slack teams, the social networks of the actors and the different sub-communities (based on sub-topics of discussion) are not readily available or apparent, but might be analyzed or inferred based on communication patterns and content. Three independent methods for inferring and extracting social network within such a quasi-synchronous CMC environment are discussed. All the methods described herein have been developed by the authors.

Response-Time Analysis (RTA)

Response-time analysis uses the temporal distance between messages to infer of a later message being a response to earlier message(s) with the assumption of a normative ideal of alternating turns between and among users.

The distribution of natural delay and the likelihood that messages by other users are responses to a specific preceding message are used to estimate a probability that two or more people are in communication. The distribution pattern of the time between related messages within the chatroom can be determined by analyzing sample of the messages or expert knowledge. Figure 1 shows the relative frequency of response for the first 1.5 million chat messages in the MusicBrainz chat log (McIntire, Osesina, & Craft, 2011). The likelihood of a message being a response to any of its preceding can be determined based on their relative time difference. To facilitate the calculation of response probability, a mathematical distribution similar to the manually obtained response-time distribution is used. For example, the log-logistic function can be substituted for the response time distribution in Figure 1. Hence, the probability of response for a message can be calculated using its probability density function:

$$f\left(t\right)=\frac{\left(\beta/\alpha\right)\left(t/\alpha\right)^{\beta-1}}{\left(1+\left(t/\beta\right)\right)^{2}}. \quad (1)$$

t: is the time interval between the messages under examination
α: is the median response time.
β: is the shape parameter indicating its skewness

Naïve calculation of the relationship (message and response) between *all messages* quickly results in a combinatorial explosion; a known problem with this broad approach. In order to limit the number of calculations performed to a manageable number, probabilities of response are calculated for only messages that fall within what is termed a conversation cycle. A conversation cycle contains a message and all of its *possible* responses, and it starts with a user's message and contains all the message sequence (from other users) posted before the user's own next message. For example, in an IRC channel, a conversation cycle for a user starts when they post a message and ends just prior to their next message (Figure 2).

Figure 1. Relative frequencies of message response times for the first 1.5 million messages in the MusicBrainz dataset compared with the log logistics function where α=12 seconds and β=2. Such a distribution can be obtained for any dataset via analysis of samples or expert-knowledge

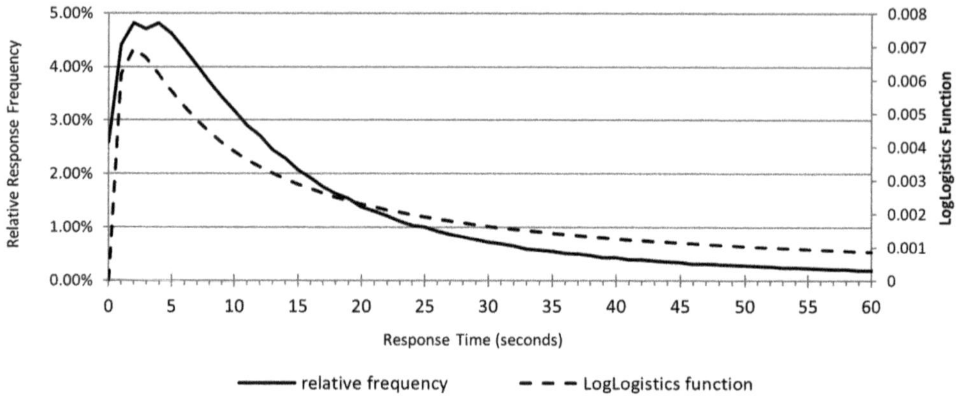

Figure 2. An example of a conversation cycle for user "_rob" (between 00:23:21 and 00:41:34)

3/1/2006	00:23:21	<_rob> one last little thing and then I am taking a break
3/1/2006	00:24:02	<yeti> later folks
3/1/2006	00:24:06	<organism> organism has joined #musicbrainz
3/1/2006	00:24:20	<yeti> yeti has quit
3/1/2006	00:38:34	<teleMan__> teleMan__ has quit
3/1/2006	00:38:42	<SenRepa> SenRepa has joined #musicbrainz
3/1/2006	00:39:57	<SenRepa> * SenRepa angryly removes and throws away all "extra" buttons on his keyboard for things like mute
3/1/2006	00:40:31	<SenRepa> after accidentally opening 30 FireFoxes
3/1/2006	00:40:52	<JetPower> i dont use those buttons
3/1/2006	00:41:19	<SenRepa> neither do i
3/1/2006	00:41:34	<SenRepa> my moniter pressed them
3/1/2006	00:42:00	<_rob> * _rob goes to take break

The total level of interaction (weight) among users is determined by the cumulative probabilities from multiple conversation cycles (Figure 3). Assuming that $g_{A\rightarrow B}(i) = f(t; i)$ represents the probability of user B responding to user A in the *i-th* conversation cycle, the total level of interaction of user A towards user B ($w_{A\rightarrow B}$) can be calculated as the sum of $g_{A\rightarrow B}$ for all conversation cycles of user A. The interactions of user B directed towards user A can also be calculated in the same manner by reversing the position of A and B. The average of these interactions ($w_{A\leftrightarrow B}$) is a non-directional interaction level between the two users. By iteratively analyzing the interactions for each user (egocentric), this method constructs the entire social network.

Figure 3. Example of a discontinuous interaction weight function. w = w(k) + w(k+1) + w(k+2)

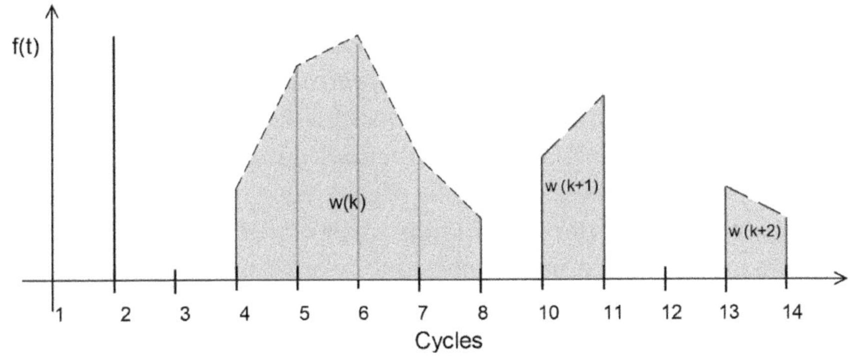

$$Interaction\ weight\left(w_{A\rightarrow B}\right)=\sum_{i=0}^{\infty}g\left(i\right).$$

An advantage of this method is its use of system time, hence it is not directly prone to user generated noise and the conversation language or domain. However, the determination of the delay distribution within a dataset (in the absence of expert knowledge) involves manually perusing chat messages.s a result, it is subject to sampling and analyst bias as different samples may yield different distribution patterns, and analysts may disagree on any particular message being a response to a reference message. Also, to be effective, this method requires the resolution of the timestamp recorded for each message to be in a similar range as the median response time. For example, if the median time is in the order of seconds, the time stamp resolution must at least be in the order of seconds. It is important to note that the distribution in Figure 1 was obtained by analyzing a subset of the MusicBrainz dataset. As such it may not be applicable to different dataset; however the calculations of response probability and conversation cycles are generalizable.

Word Context Usage Analysis (WCUA)

Word context usage analysis infers SN links among users based on keywords contained in their messages. *Keywords* are operationally-defined as the highest frequency words in the entire user generated chat messages after stop-words removal, and are assumed to be most informative of the conversation content (Jones, 1972; Dalianis, et al., 2004). This analysis can be approached from a couple of independent but complementary perspectives namely: (i) identification topics/sub-topics under conversation (communities) by creating links among keywords in the same message, (ii) identification of actors engaged in the different topics/sub-topics by creating links among actors utilizing common keywords.

Given the unavailability or unreliability of explicit sub-topics indicators in asynchronous chat environment, the identification of the different sub-topics under engagement must be inferred via other methods such as the messages exchange among actors. An easy and straight forward way to achieve this is by creating links among keywords used in each message, where the edges among the keywords indicate the relative frequency of co-occurrence. Similar frequency of keyword usage between users is more indicative of a link compared to relative skewness in usage. Graph invariant measures such as betweenness and centrality can then be used to identify the sub-graphs and their corresponding keywords representing different sub-topics. Although more sophisticated techniques, such as topic modeling based on language, domain and semantic knowledge, can be substituted for the above described bag-of-words approach, the keyword graph is a simple and efficient first approach.

Identification of the actors involved in these engagements is also an important for building an accurate SN because it provides a holistic view of the interaction dynamics. The bag-of-keywords used by individual users is compared to that of other users and links are created among user with intersecting keyword(s). The relative frequency of each keyword usage suggests the level of participation of users in the community. In addition, the use of weights to signify the level of importance of various keywords may also provide stronger indicators of users engaged in topics of interest.

The two components of WCUA, keywords and actors, are integrated together as shown in the representation of Figure 4. The nodes represent topics/sub-topics created by clustering keywords, and those include a sub-graph based on actors' usage of each keyword. Edges represent the co-occurrence of words in messages. In addition to providing information for keyword disambiguation and helping to identify correlated or seemingly disjointed conversations, WCUA provides information about user interactions across various topics.

Direct Addressing Analysis (DAA)

DAA, is one of the simplest methods for extracting interaction links among internet chatroom users. It infers the intended message recipient by identifying the screen name (username/nickname) referenced in the message, a.k.a. direct addressing (Mutton, 2004). Because it is used by the message owner to enhance the clarity of the intended recipient, it provides strong evidence for extracting SN relations in asynchronous multi-user communication. On the other hand, because users do not always explicitly indicate intended message recipient this way, the number of

Figure 4. Word context graph showing links among keywords used in the same message

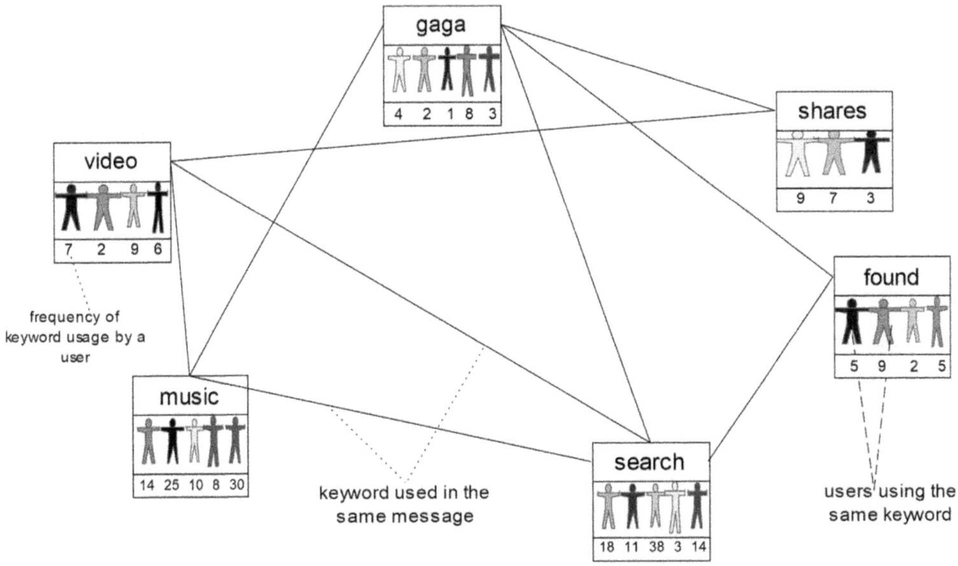

links extracted using this method can be expected to be relatively low. Furthermore, because it is directly dependent on user input, this method is prone to errors resulting from typographical mistakes and analysis of variations of the recipient's screen name (user name). On many modern CMC applications, the common denotation of intended recipient is the use of '@' followed by the recipient's identifier, as shown in the example below:

<Rob> Is the download complete?

…

<John> @Rob, yes.

Hybrid SN Link Extraction

A hybrid approach may be best in providing the right combination of the strengths and unique features of individual methods. For example, the keyword usage analysis can be used to provide context for links extracted using RTA (Figure 5). Also, due to the independence of the methods from one another, that is their probability of correctly extracting a link is statistically independent of each other, connections that appear likely in more than one method, have a higher certainty of being correct than anything an individual method can provide alone. These SN graph of each of the three methods (RTA, WCUA, and DAA) can be combined either by assigning

Figure 5. Example of a SN derived through the hybrid method

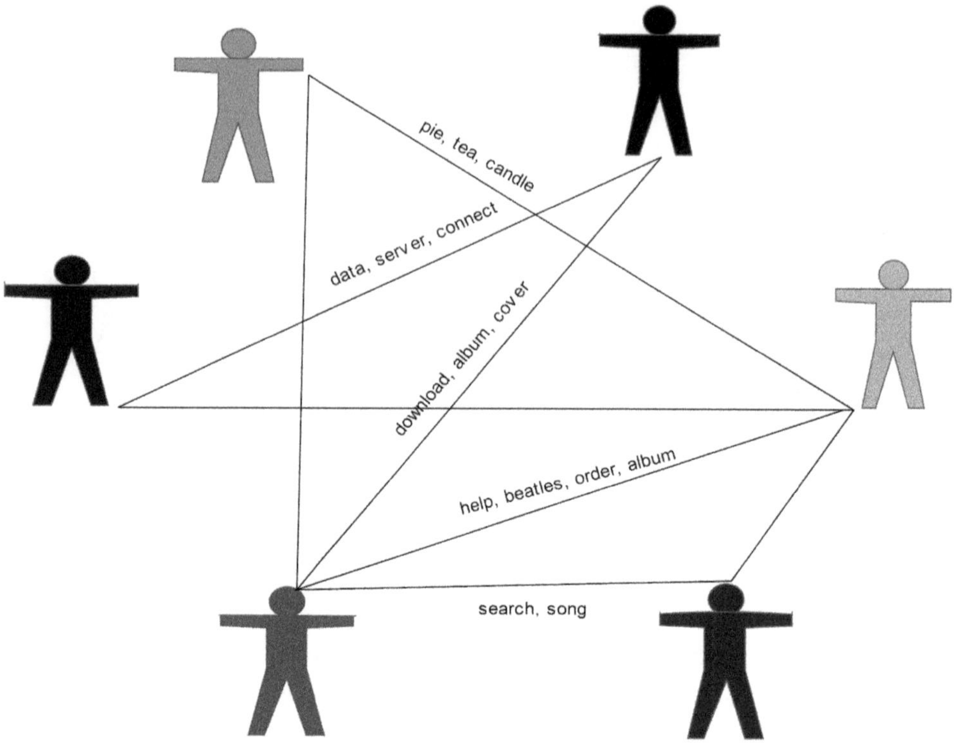

weights to identified links depending on the method or by averaging the results of all the methods. The weights can be based on intuition, expert-knowledge, or statistical analysis.

The experiments described in later sections of this chapter employed the relative F-measure of each method to determine the weights assigned to links identified by the corresponding method. In other words, the empirically measured performance of all the methods using F-measure was obtained, and the weight of a method is that method's F-measure divided by the sum of all the F-measures.

EXPERIMENTS IN SOCIAL NETWORK EXTRACTION

The SN extraction methods, response-time analysis, direct addressing analysis, word context usage analysis, and hybrid, are validated through experimental means. To provide realistic data, the study is using a freely available public chat dataset with over 14 million messages. This chatroom called "MusicBrainz" (http://chatlogs.

musicbrainz.org/musicbrainz/) is primarily used to discuss music and computer related topics. The data contains messages exchanged by users over the course of several years. While reporting on this dataset, the screen names of users were anonymized to protect users' identities. The data was collected via a web crawler which stored the entire information of each message including content such as user's screen name, date and time it was sent, and message text. During the analysis, system-generated messages (e.g., "Tom has logged on") were generally omitted.

This dataset is ideal for this experiment because it contains asynchronous interactions among several users engaging in both single and multiple concurrent conversations. Additionally, the chat message timestamps are at the same resolution as the median response time for the dataset (seconds as seen in Figure 1).

The performance of the SN extraction methods under experiment is judged in reference to the so called ground truth. In order to assess the performance of SN extraction methods, the links identified by each analysis is compared to a set of SN links known to be correct (ground truth). The curation of the ground truth can be done using an automatic method with known performance or it can be done manually. The ground truth in this experiment was curated through a manual process. A manageable subset of the dataset (3 continuous days: 1 – 3 June, 2006) was manually perused independently by different members of the group, the intended recipient(s) of each message was recorded, and the interaction weights between users were obtained from the count of sender and recipient. The manually identified links by the different group members were compared and found to have a reliability of 0.99 (Cronbach's alpha) and Pearson correlation of 0.90. The final set of ground truth data consists only of SN links extracted during both sets of manual scoring (any links with disagreement were discarded). Also, the interaction weights are taken as the average of the different manual curations.

Results

The correlation between SN links contained in the ground truth and those identified by the extraction methods was computed with the assumption that a strong correlation indicates a high performance (relative to the ground truth) and weak correlations indicates the opposite. Spearman's rank (using the link weights) and Pearson's standard correlations (using the number of links) were employed in this analysis.

From an information retrieval perspective, the ability of each method to identify links within the dataset (Singhal, 2001) was examined, but the weight of interaction was not considered. Three metrics, recall, precision and F-measure were computed. *Recall* measures the performance of the method in retrieving all possible links, and

Table 1. Social Network Link Retrieval Measurements

Measure	RTA	WCUA	DAA
Precision	0.73	1.0	**0.99**
Recall	0.92	**0.97**	0.47
F-measure	0.82	**0.98**	0.63

precision measures the accuracy of the retrieved links (Cleverdon, 1967). F-measure (Kandefer & Shapiro, 2009) uses both the recall and precision to form a combined score of accuracy for each individual extraction method.

The data for the Hybrid SN method is obtained by weighting the F-measure of each of the three methods using their relative F-measures which yield weights of 0.34, 0.40, and 0.26 for RTA, WCUA and DAA respectively.

As illustrated in Figure 6, RTA has the worst performance for link retrieval precision. This can be attributed to its more aggressive nature in identifying links, hence prone to more false positives. This may be mitigated using heuristics like introducing a minimum number of conversation cycles in which other users must appear in order to accept their message(s) as likely response(s). DAA on the other hand has perfect precision on the when it identifies a link, but fails to identify many

Figure 6. Link retrieval performance for SN extraction methods

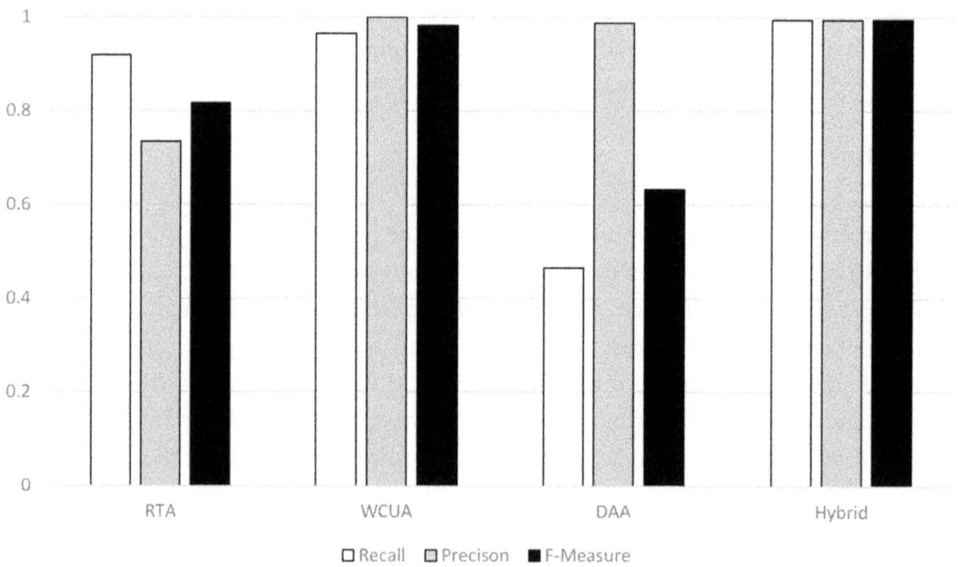

links. Despite the simplicity of using keywords to identify possible interactions among actors, WCUA exhibited the best performance of the three in terms of its ability to identify a substantial number of correct links.

While identifying links among users is important, identifying the strength (weight) of the link can also be useful. Figure 7 shows the correlations between the link weights estimated by the discussed link extraction methods and the ground truth; where link weight is the measured as the number of communication between users. As shown in Figure 6, RTA method is the most effective in link strength (weight) estimation when compared with the ground truth. Due to the infrequent use of direct addressing, the DAA method is unable to extract many links, hence its worst correlation performance.

In both link weights correlation and information retrieval analysis, the hybrid method outperforms the individual methods as it is able to proportionally combine their individual strengths and mitigate their weaknesses. While the three extraction methods described above are generalizable, same cannot be said for the specific results reported on the MusicBrainz dataset for various reasons. In the RTA method, the time-response distribution used for calculating probabilities is derived directly from a sample of the dataset hence may not be applicable to other datasets. Also, given the importance of this distribution it is obvious that the RTA method can only be as effective as the accuracy of the modeling of its time-response distribution. The WCUA can be enhanced by the analysis of synonyms and aliases in order to identify and relate words that may otherwise have been missed. While this enhancement did not appear to cause degradation to the analysis of the MusicBrainz dataset, it may be critical for other datasets.

Figure 7. Link Weights Correlation performance for SN extraction methods

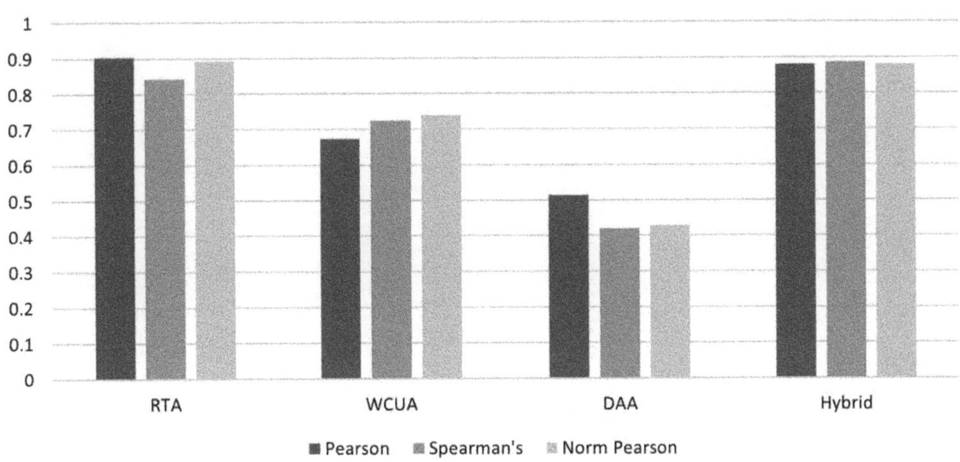

VISUALIZATION OF COMPUTER-MEDIATED COMMUNICATION

The ability to interactively visualize CMC information has been identified as important for statistical benchmarks, increasing social consciousness and interaction, improving educational interactions, and improving usability, navigability, and understanding of conversations and topics under discussion (McIntire, Osesina, & Craft, 2011). This part of the chapter explores first representations that present the social network explicitly as a graph. Following an assessment of the explicit network visualization, the chapter moves onto visual representations that convey the SN in the context of other information, in particular GIS, hierarchical, and chat views.

Social Network Visualization Experiments

Two traditional network visualization techniques were compared in the context of presenting a social network to the end-user:

1. Node-link diagram (Figure 8);
2. Adjacency matrix with a heat-map (Figure 9).

In both visualizations, connection (link) strength is represented by color/intensity (redundantly coded), with corresponding legends shown below both visualizations. In designing this experiment, only factors that can be manipulated on both visualization

Figure 8. Node-link network diagram visualization

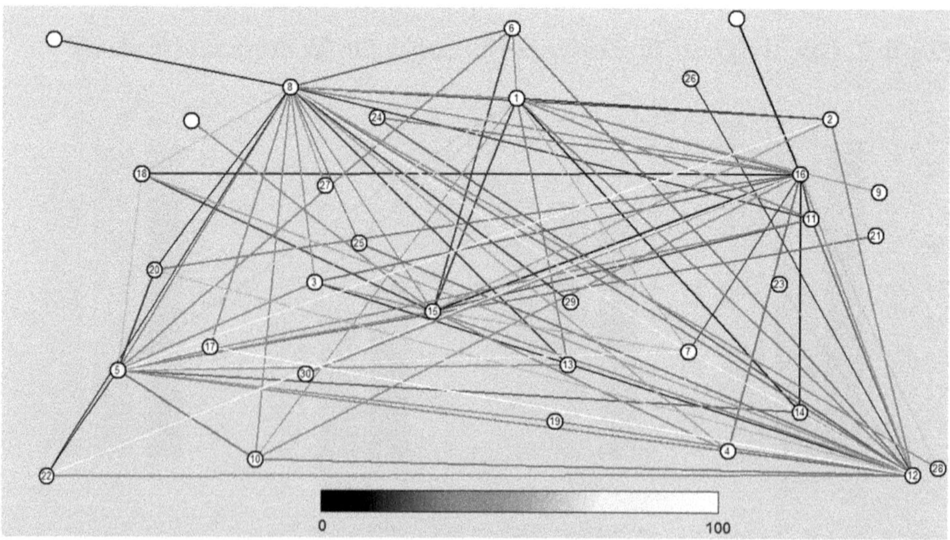

Figure 9. Adjacency matrix heat map visualization

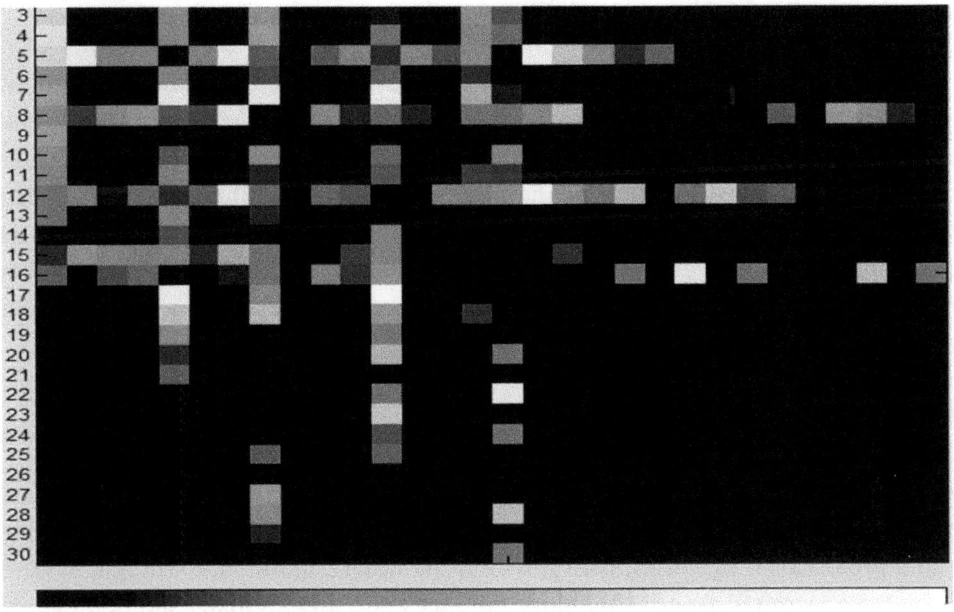

stimuli were considered. For example, on both stimuli, color denotes the strength of the link. It may be argued that the link/edge thickness better conveys strength on the node-link diagram, however translating this representation to the adjacency matrix with a heat-map is not trivial. Furthermore, some sophisticated arrangement of the nodes may afford better clarity, and interactivity such as highlighting of edges of selected nodes in the node-link stimuli, however for fair comparison, comparable ordering must be considered for the other visualization. In order to avoid the potential perpetuity of this balancing pursuit, the decision was made to use a representative layout (from multiple random spatial layouts) that minimized clutter/overlap layout algorithm was selected for the node-link diagram and the use lexicographical ordering for the nodes for the adjacency matrix.

Their effectiveness in performing following tasks was evaluated:

1. **Link Finding:** The speed and accuracy of determining whether two given nodes have a direct link.
2. **Link Strength/Weight Estimation:** Where a link has been identified between two nodes, the strength/weight of the link between two nodes is to be estimated.
3. **Node Connectivity Estimation:** Identification of the five nodes that were the most densely interconnected with the other nodes (had the most links directly connected to them).

4. **Node Finding:** The speed and accuracy of determining whether two given nodes have direct link to a common node.

Knowledge about the differential effectiveness of network data visualizations can be important for many areas of academia, applied sciences, the military, and the public. Participants were randomly assigned to complete the first three tasks using the matrix visualization or the node-link diagram stimulus; and the other visualization was chosen for the fourth task. This design resulted in a between-subjects experimental design where each participant was exposed to both visualizations, but performed different tasks with each. Task categories were performed in the order presented above from (i) to (iv).

Participants

A total number of 20 volunteers participated; 14 males and 6 females. The inclusion criteria were normal or corrected-to-normal visual acuity (self-reported as having had a professional eye examination within the last 12 months). Participants were volunteers recruited from active duty military and DoD civilians and contractors from the 711th Human Performance Wing at Wright-Patterson Air Force Base. Recruitment was conducted by word of mouth and/or email inquiries. Potential volunteers were asked if they would like to participate in a brief study on network visualizations; a short verbal description was provided and a copy of the Informed Consent Document was available for perusal. There was no restriction based on age or gender, nor any need to use these as limiting criteria. Total testing time for each participant lasted no more than 20 minutes, although there were no formal time limits for completion of the tasks. No compensation specific to this activity was provided to participants.

Equipment and Stimuli

Two possible visual stimuli were used: a node-link network diagram and a connectivity (or adjacency) matrix with a heat map (color/intensity is redundantly mapped to the link weights, with lighter colors indicating stronger links). The node-link network diagram consisted of 30 numbered nodes connected by weighted links/edges (again, with color/intensity being mapped to the link weights), as shown in Figure 8. Following Purchase et al.'s (2002) graph aesthetics findings (layout methods had little effect on performance as long as link bending and/or crossings were minimized); no specific graph layout algorithm was used for this visualization. After multiple randomized spatial iterations, a representative layout that minimized clutter/overlap of the links and nodes was selected. The adjacency matrix heat map displayed the same network data as the node-link diagram, and used the same color-coding scheme (to represent link weights), albeit in a different visual form. Row and column numbers indicated corresponding nodes, and were arranged in numerical order along both axes, thus the matrix was symmetrical due to this arrangement as shown in Figure 9. Stimuli were presented via a laptop computer with a 15-inch LCD monitor. A stopwatch was used by the experimenter to record task completion times, and participants recorded their responses using paper forms and a pen/pencil.

Results and Analysis

All of significance tests were conducted using two-tailed Welch's t-tests assuming unequal variances, with a significance level of alpha = 0.05.

1. **Link Finding:** 15 test items were used for this task. The matrix visualization resulted in significantly faster task completion times (faster by 56%) than the node-link visualization (t=4.90, p=.001). It also resulted in less variable task completion times (standard deviation of 34 seconds versus 92 seconds). No difference on accuracy was detected across both visualizations (96% for the matrix, 94% for the node-link; t=0.37, p=.721), however the node-link exhibited greater variability in accuracy (standard deviation of 12% versus 4% for the matrix visualization). A summary of the findings is depicted in Figure 10.
2. **Link Strength/Weight Estimation:** Using a range of 0 – 100, participants were asked to indicate the apparent strength of the connection between two nodes. Participants' accuracy was comparable in across the visualization types (±6.74 for the matrix, ±6.19 for the network; t=0.71, p=.494). Variability of judgment accuracy, as measured by standard deviation, was slightly larger for the node-link visualization at 1.84 versus 1.34 for the matrix visualization.
3. **Node Connectivity Estimation:** This task was not timed. Participants were instructed to indicate the five nodes with the most densely connectivity i.e. most links directly connected to it. They were instructed to guess the most connected nodes by visual estimation instead of counting the links by hand. The difference between the two visualization types in terms of accuracy was non-significant (t=1.38, p=.197) but the trend appeared to favor the matrix visualization (93%) versus the network visualization (87%). Variability in accuracy was comparable across the visualizations (9.6 for the matrix versus 9.4 for the node-link visualization, in units of standard deviation).
4. **Node Finding:** For each participant, the visualization type was changed from the previous tasks. The matrix visualization resulted in significantly faster completion times (faster by 45%) than the node-link visualization (t=3.03, p=.013). Variability in task completion times was slightly higher when using

Figure 10. Left: Total task completion times (in seconds) on the link-finding task for the matrix visualization and the node-link visualization. Error bars represent +/- one standard deviation from the mean. Right: Task accuracy on the link-finding task.

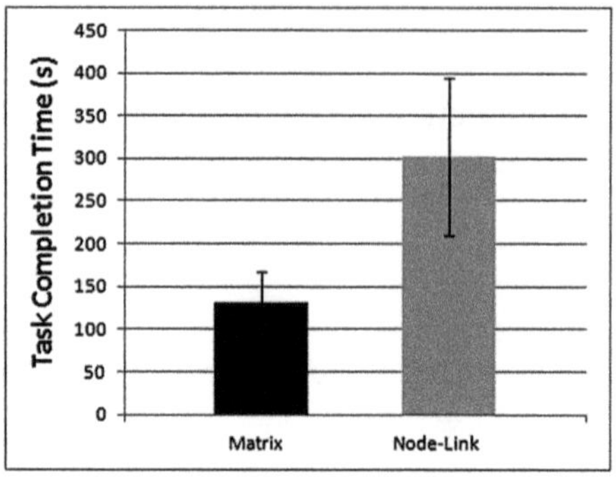

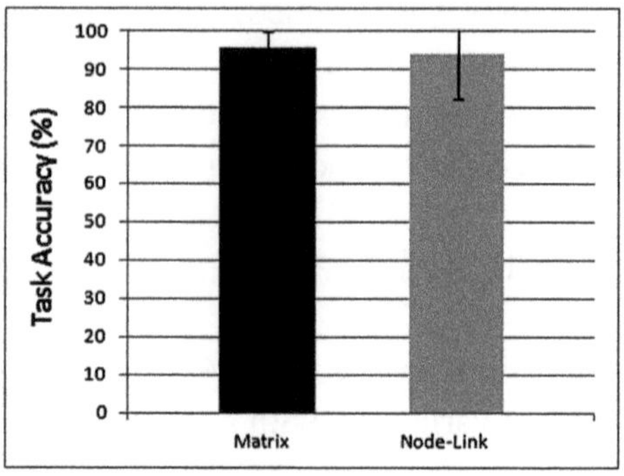

the matrix visualization compared to the node-link visualization (99 versus 92 units of standard deviation, respectively). Accuracy appeared slightly better with the node-link visualization (95%) versus the matrix visualization (86%) but this difference was non-significant (t=1.00, p=.340). However, variability in accuracy was noticeably higher for the matrix visualization at 27 units of standard deviation versus the node-link's 7 units.

Summary of Findings

Overall, the matrix visualization generally proved the more effective (see summary in Table 2). It resulted in 56% faster task completion times on the link-finding task, and 45% faster task completion times on the node-finding task, both of which were

Table 2. A comparative summary of performance measurements Note: the matrix visualization resulted in better performance for 4 of the 6 measurements, 2 of which were statistically significant at the alpha=.05 level

Task	Measure	Matrix w/ Heat Map	Node-link Diagram
Link Strength	Accuracy	±6.74 units	±6.19 units
Node Connectivity	Accuracy	93%	87%
Node-finding	Time	158 s (alpha≤.05)	286 s
	Accuracy	86%	95%
Link-finding	Time	133 s (alpha≤.05)	303 s
	Accuracy	96%	94%

statistically significant differences. Also, it resulted in slightly higher accuracy on the link-finding task, node interconnection judgment task, and the link strength judgment task, but these differences were statistically non-significant. Accuracy for the node-finding task was poorer for the matrix visualization, but again this difference was non-significant. In terms of consistency of measures, the matrix view resulted in lower standard deviations for the link-finding task completion times (34 versus 92), for the link-finding task accuracy (4 versus 12), and for the link strength judgments (1.34 versus 1.84). The opposite pattern was observed, in which the node-link visualization resulted in more consistent measures, for the node interconnection judgments (9.4 versus 9.6), for the node-finding task completion times (92 versus 99), and for the node-finding accuracy (7 versus 27).

This work confirms and extends the experimental research by Ghoniem et al. (2004; 2005). For those interested particularly in this topic, an up-to-date effort by Okoe et al. (2017) reviews recent work, and pits node-link versus matrix representations against each other on a suite of representative network analysis tasks. These researchers note that node-link diagrams can appear more compact and work well for sparse networks, and they again confirm that node-link diagrams are especially beneficial for path-tracing or path-following tasks. They also argue that node-link diagrams tend to work best for determining overall network connectivity, understanding topological distances and structure, and facilitating user interactivity. Matrix representations were beneficial for dense networks, by eliminating occlusion and connection ambiguity problems, and for conducting simple visual searches for particular links or nodes. Which visualization method should be recommended depends upon the network data under study and the tasks to be performed, as each has its own unique set of advantages and disadvantages.

Context-Enhanced Visualization of Computer-Mediated Communication

In addition to presenting CMC information as interplay between of social networks dynamics and topics/sub-topics of engagement as discussed in the previous section, CMC can be integrated into other environments that allow the user to draw additional insights. These environments, or contexts, serve to increase and improve the utility of data and the information contained therein. Such tools may help to easily identify topics (and consequently actors) of interest within a dataset composed of heterogeneous types of information. This section presents both novel visualization designs and an experiment aiming to quantify the value added by one of these visualizations. Each of the designs included here operates within a different context with a different overall purpose, yet they all contain information extracted from CMC big data sources.

BuzzVizz

BuzzVizz visualization tool exploits the logical linkage between the non-spatial textual data and Geographical Information System (GIS). It facilitates the integration of multiple, heterogeneous data sources in an easily navigable and comprehensible format. This proof of concept visualization system combines information from Twitter and World Wind (a GIS-based, Google Earth-like application developed by NASA), to provide near real-time geographical situational-awareness easily consumable by practitioners such as first responders, regional administrators, marketers, etc.

Like other unstructured textual information, messages broadcasted on Twitter (a.k.a., tweets) may contain explicit or implicit geographical references which indicate among other things the origin of the message, location of an event, or subject of the message. BuzzVizz uses this information for linking individual message to geographical location(s) and logically displays the keywords that are most prevalent as close as possible to the location in the context. A unique feature of BuzzVizz is its ability to allow users to sift through millions of messages in a short amount of time by simply performing the traditional maneuvers of zoom and pan on a digital map. In other words, as the user moves to locations of interest on the map, the system generates the appropriate queries to retrieve messages associated to geographical locations in focus on the map. It uses a simple word frequency analysis to identify keywords associated to different locations on the map. When a large area is displayed, tweets from many locations within that area are aggregated and displayed. When the user drills down, (zooms in on the map), fewer locations are included in the map view and consequently fewer tweets are part of the aggregation. Thus, tweets are assigned to locations, locations to areas on the map, and all tweets for an area are analyzed and displayed within that area's boundaries. The GIS software breaks down each zoom level into a number of rectangular tiles, and BuzzVizz computes the word frequency analysis for each of these tiles (areas). The normal behavior of the GIS software, where overviews have large tiles and zoomed-in views have small tiles is taken advantage by BuzzVizz to achieve different levels of aggregation.

The display is layered and behaves in a manner similar to place names on a map giving the user a summary of the topics tweeted over an area Figure 11. A complementary layer presents the principal user ID of the accounts tweeting in the area in focus in a similar manner to how topics are presented. As the user zooms in, the higher level of words disappears, and a new, more detailed layer is rendered. The opposite is true for zooming out. Because keywords must be spread out to be visible (for example, not all Chicago keywords or users can be placed exactly on top of Chicago), the location of keywords/users at national or continental views of the map appears less precisely than at lower levels. However, drilling down towards an area renders the keywords or users closer to their computed origin and also filters out topics from places not currently on the map. The layer dynamics can be configured through the same mechanisms as those of other GIS layers. This concept of information fusion and visualization is envisioned for multi-tiered situational awareness giving different level of user appropriate information granularity.

The visualization also allows users to pinpoint the exact location from which a specific keyword was tweeted. This is done interactively by "mousing-over" any keyword or username, which prompts the system to display a spread layer with cones placed at the exact locations that have tweets containing the hovered keyword/user (see the red keyword and cone in Figure 11). While the keyword and user layers, the words displayed on top of the map, provide a logical link from locations to topics, the spread layer, the cones place at various places, provide information in the opposite direction: from topics to locations.

We examined three techniques for arranging keywords associated to an area. The first technique relies on random placement; the second uses geometric patterns, such as concentric circles (see Figure 3) or grids; and the third uses weighted-average placement of keywords. The first two techniques are computationally inexpensive, with the second being able to also convey the relative importance of the terms by, for example, placing the most important term in the center and using a pre-defined ordered placement after that. The third technique requires the use of either forces or virtual "bungee cords" to pull a keyword in its final position. The anchor points for the forces or cords are the location of the queries associated with the keyword (e.g., the cities in which the keyword is tweeted). This approach is similar to MonkEllipse (Hsu, et al., 2004), and it will result in popular/widespread keywords appearing in the center of the area because they are "pulled" in multiple directions towards most places in that area. The averaged-position may also lead to overlap, and requires an extra overlap-reducing step in which keywords lying on top of each other are spread around

Three techniques for arranging keywords associated to an area were examined, but the simplest one was chosen given the requirements of big data. The first uses random placement; the second uses geometric patterns, such as concentric circles (as shown in Figure 11) or grids; and the third uses weighted-average placement of keywords. The first two techniques are computationally inexpensive, with the second being able to also convey the relative importance of the terms; for example, placing the most important term in the center and using a pre-defined ordered placement after that. The third technique requires the use of either forces or virtual "bungee cords" to pull a keyword in its final position. The anchor points for the forces or cords are the location of the queries associated with the keyword (e.g., the cities in which the keyword is tweeted). This approach is similar to MonkEllipse (Hsu, Inman, McColgin, & Stamper, 2004), and it will result in popular/widespread keywords appearing in the center of the area because they are "pulled" in multiple directions towards most places in that area. The second method was chosen for its simplicity and relatively light computation requirements.

BuzzVizz also provides cues about the age of various Twitter topics in each geographic area. As the topics get older, that is no new tweets about that topic have been posted in a while, the size of the font decreases until it finally disappears. Even on a static view, such as the snapshot in Figure 11, this is useful to further identify topics that are separated in time. More importantly this allows the user to play an animation that shows how topics evolved over time (and over each geographical region in the view). New topics begin in a large font, and stay large as long as more tweets are posted. As they age, they become smaller and smaller until they are no longer in the animation. Standard, play and pause controls are provided next to map Figure 11.

Figure 11. BuzzVizz with temporal controls shown in the lower left corner. Twitter keywords of different sizes show how much time has elapsed since that word was last tweeted in a particular area. The mouse is hovering over the red "women" keyword, and the spread layer shows the origin (red cone) of the tweet .The concentric red circles illustrate the layout algorithm for the keywords in the lower-right tile only and do not appear in the visualization.

TreeBuzz

The second proof of concept visualization is the implementation of a Twitter layer on top of a tree visualization (Figure 12). This visualization allows an analyst to easily examine the topics that correspond to various branches of a hierarchical structure, such as departments in a large organization, or national or international sporting leagues. The tree structure is external to the CMC data (for example the organization of a multinational department store), just as the GIS information was external in the case of BuzzVizz. It automatically categorizes the Twitter information using the hierarchical structure provided in the tree, thereby helping the user to easily determine what is being tweeted for different facets of the concept contained in the tree. TreeMaps (Shneiderman, 1992) are considered for representing the underlying hierarchical structure because they have clear separation of space dedicated to various nodes in the tree, that is they are space-filling. Keywords extracted from tweets are displayed, just as for BuzzVizz, on top of the existing TreeMap by changing the text orientation and placing them inside each tree node that is large enough to hold additional text. Clicking on a branch of the tree results in only that branch being shown, a typical TreeMap behavior. As such, the users can drill-down and see more detailed information relating to that branch only. Conversely, zooming out of a branch displays more comprehensive information, which includes multiple branches situated at the same level.

Figure 12. Twitter layer on a TreeMap

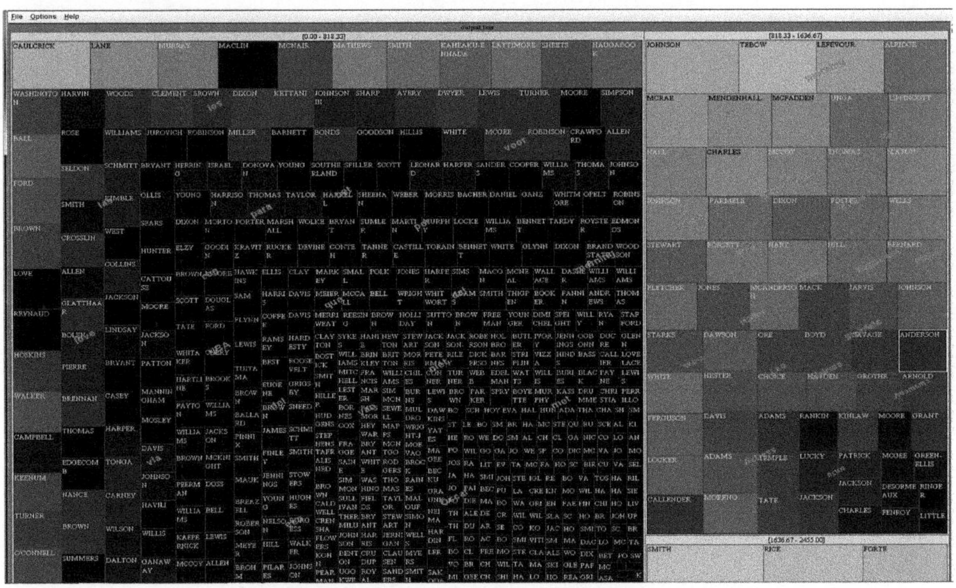

The proper use of color contrast is important in this visualization as keywords may be difficult to distinguish against the background colors. Original TreeMaps often use different colors to encode an additional data attribute (external to the CMC data; for example the amount of sales at each store), and the solution for TreeBuzz is to vary the color of the keywords as they are drawn on top of the nodes in order to contrast with the TreeMap nodes' background.

MagnetChat

This visualization prototype is designed to help users to interactively analyze topics or users of interest within a CMC environment, especially an asynchronous, multi-user CMC environment. It consists of three main panels as shown in Figure 13. The left panel displays chatroom conversations, where conversation start time and length can be interactively and continuously modified via the zoom function, with the shorter lengths allowing the user to read individual posts, and the longer lengths

Figure 13. MagnetChat visualization showing the actual conversation and user relationships. The rectangles are magnets, and the circles are dust representing usernames. Magnets can be moved and they attract dust/users differently based on the strength of the SN link. The size of the dust is proportional to the number of posts currently in the detailed chat

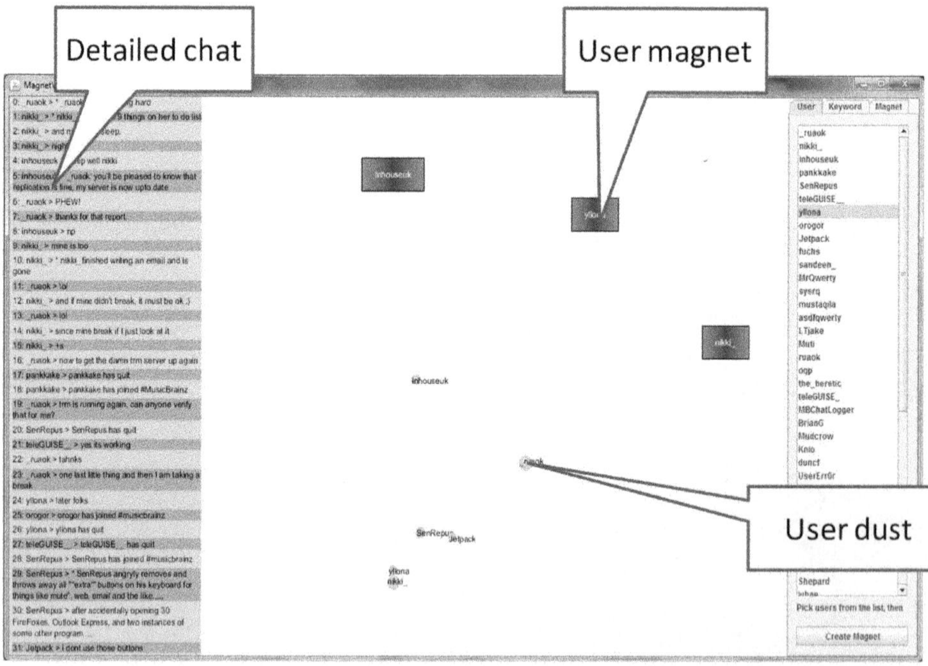

aggregating data about many posts. The main panel displays the result of the SN link extraction analysis in the context of conversations within the specified time window. The links are not explicitly shown to avoid clutter and stay within the simplicity requirement for big data, but they can be inferred as the attraction force between a "magnet" and nodes ("dust") in the SN. The SN link allows the exploration of basic relationships among keywords as well as among users. The right panel allows the selection of keywords and user names of interest for further analysis.

MagnetChat employs a Dust-and-Magnet (Soo Yi, Melton, Stasko, & Jacko, 2005) metaphor to explore the link graph, and a zoomable interface (Bederson, Grosjean, & Meyer, 2004) to allow smooth continuous zooming. The visualization (Figure 13) allows the user to select a portion of the conversation to be considered (left panel). The right panel performs magnet management, which includes adding and removing keyword or user magnets from the center panel. Magnets are in effect performing queries and filtering on the SN link graph. Both the conversation and magnet panels can be continuously panned and zoomed. The novelty of MagnetChat approach consists in the new way of using dust-and-magnet for relational (SN graph) rather than multivariate data (Soo Yi, Melton, Stasko, & Jacko, 2005), in the use of two independent graphs, username and keyword, in the same view, and in using the chatroom conversation as a way to integrate and filter information.

The conversation (right) panel can be continuously panned and zoomed. Panning only takes places horizontally and is essentially scrolling through the conversation. Zooming out groups individual posts when they become too small to read (Figure 14), with only the start time being displayed at higher zoom levels. The size of the dust is continuously adjusted as the conversation panel is being scrolled or zoomed. The size of the dust (circles in middle panel) is proportional to the number of times a username posts or a keyword occurs in the timeframe covered by the conversation panel.

The dust-and-magnet panel allows simultaneous display of both keywords dust and magnets and user dust and magnets (Figure 15). The attraction of the two types of network (keyword and user) works independent of each other when magnets are shaken; i.e., shaking a user magnet only attracts user dust and does not move keyword dust and vice-versa. The panel can be smoothly zoomed in and out, and the user can pan around the area. Dust that is too close together can be distinguished either by zooming in closer or by activating a random shake function for the dust via a single right-click. The shaking in this tool is just moving dust around randomly, and it is different than the shake function in (Soo Yi, Melton, Stasko, & Jacko, 2005).

The following tasks have been designed into the MagnetChat, although as with any user-centric endeavor, some may not be obvious to some users:

Figure 14. The conversation panel has been zoomed out, thus covering a longer time period and making reading individual posts impossible. Some users have been posting a lot during this time, and thus the circles representing them are larger.

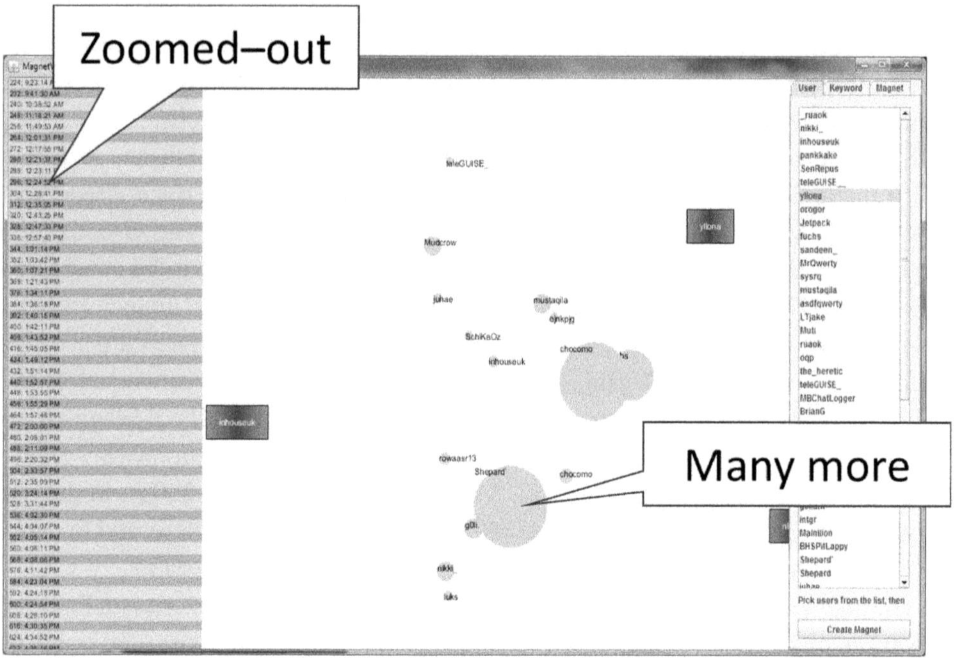

- Read individual posts in the conversation panel;
- Focus on particular usernames or keywords by creating a magnet via the right-side panel;
- Determine the strength of relationships (from the overall SN link graph) between a selected username or keywords and other users or keywords, respectively, via magnet grabbing and shaking. The dust moves towards the magnet at varying speed that is proportional to the strength of the link in the SN graph. MagnetChat also includes an option to just click and hold a magnet instead of continuously shaking it;
- See a user's or topic distribution over a chosen time period via brushing over dust, which will highlight the lines in the conversation (left) panel;
- See related usernames or keywords and their prevalence during a given period of time via scrolling and zooming of the conversation (left) panel. Dust will appear and disappear to show whether the topic or user occurs in any posts in the current period of time covered by the conversation panel. The dust will change size proportional to its frequency in the current time period;

Figure 15. MagnetChat shows both the username (blue) and keywords (green) graphs in the same panel. Zooming as well as a shake command can disambiguate dust that is close together.

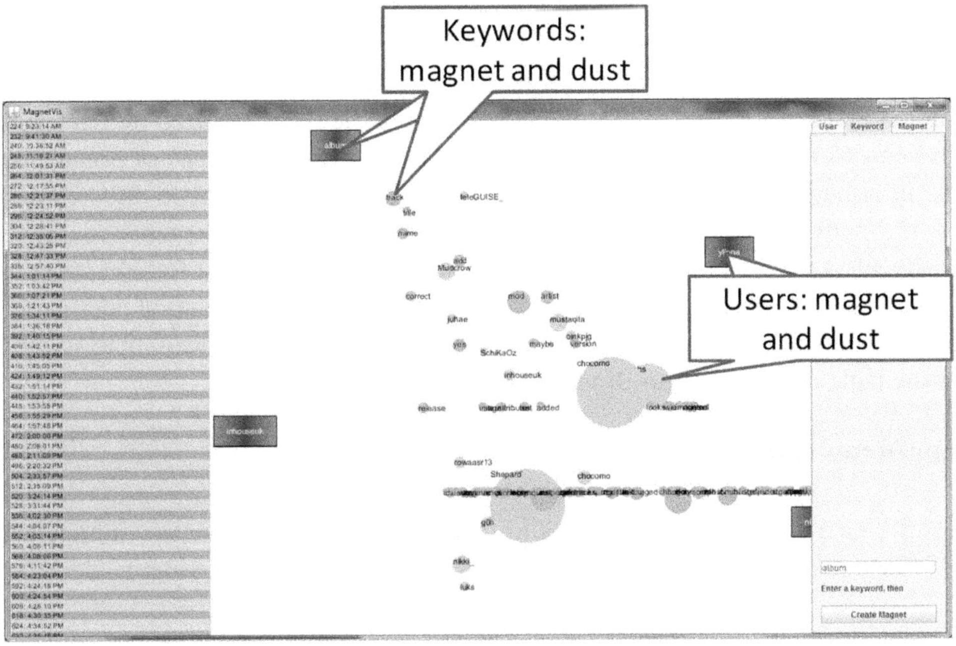

- See relationships between keywords and users via brushing over lines in the conversation (left) panel which will highlight the dust related to that line period in the magnet (center) panel.

Experimental Validation

An empirical study of the effectiveness of BuzzVizz is described in this section. Studies of TreeBuzz and MagnetChat have not been conducted. The empirical study design was influenced by theoretical examination and demonstration feedback obtained from several hours of informal interaction with potential users of BuzzVizz. The goals of the study include a better evaluation of the capabilities of BuzzVizz and a better insight on improving its efficiency. Additionally, the study took into account whether the believability of one source of information influences the credibility of other sources of information within the same visualization and whether it creates a "blind spot" preventing the critical examination of other information source(s). More precisely, whether a map, which is considered credible by users, can influence the manner in which users perceive aggregated Twitter data.

Given that absolute user metrics are not common in the measurement of the quality of visualizations, comparative analysis was used in the evaluation. To avoid bias towards BuzzVizz and have a strong point of comparison, a table platform was designed to specifically answer the questions presented to participants in the study. The simplest possible representation of the Twitter keywords was via a clear and concise table conveying the tweet-based buzz (Figure 16). Tweets relating to the United States were used in the study; hence the table was organized by US states and city. Sorting was employed in the table as an advanced means of organizing the information, but that was not applicable to BuzzVizz. The basic tasks chosen for the study involved information about entire states because the table could not easily allow access to portions of a state's data. It is possible that BuzzVizz could perform better on tasks that span portions of a state due to the natural contiguous presentation of locations in the same region on the map, but this was not examined as the table is at an obvious disadvantage.

About the Dataset

Twitter data was collected for a set of 711 cities spanning the entire continental US. Two different sets of tweets were collected one week apart using a cluster of

Figure 16. The table platform used in the study. Three columns show the city name, state abbreviation, and a set of Twitter keyword. A magnified inset is provided for the reader.

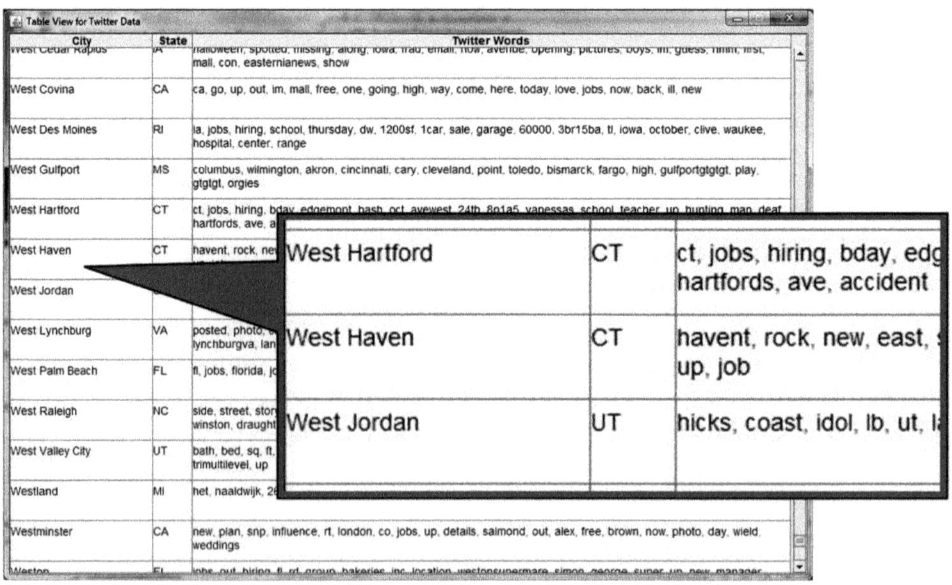

computers which allows all cities to be queried within the same hour. The tweets were processed and a set of keywords ordered by frequency were generated for each city. Approximately 700,000 tweets per day are associated with the 711 cities. Based on the limited real estate available for displaying words on a map (Osesina, Bartley, & Tudoreanu, 2010), only the 20 most frequent words within the tweets associated to any particular location or region are displayed in the visualization. In order to ensure the comparability of the results of the two platforms, the same 20 keywords are also presented in the table.

Equipment and Stimuli

The study was computer based, and a custom testing environment was developed in Java to present instructions, randomize platforms (table or map) and data, and collect answers and time parameters. The study tasks and visualization applications were designed such that only a single section of the questions was displayed at any particular time and also the visualization required for the task was automatically started by the testing software. Users were allowed to revisit or skip questions using "Previous" and "Next" buttons respectively.

Participants

All the 22 volunteers who participated in the study were university students over 18-years old; 80% were between 18 and 30 years old. The numbers of participants in undergraduate and graduate studies were evenly divided. 50% of the participants were in Information Technology related fields, 27% in the Arts, Humanities and Social Sciences, and the rest were in either Science and Mathematics or Business.

Procedure

Participants were given a brief tutorial on the study environment (BuzzVizz usage) along with guidelines on completing the study. Then the testing environment was started on a computer, and participants had unlimited time to perform the tasks.

The study was structured in a 5-part survey estimated to require approximately 60 minutes. Part 1 of the survey contained 9 brief background questions, including where did the participants obtain their daily news. Parts 2, 3, and 4 asked participants to relate Twitter keywords to news headlines. In Part 2, summarize headlines, participants were asked to determine possible news headlines based on the Twitter keywords displayed in BuzzVizz or table. The questions referred to particular cities and regions, given as a list of states (using two letter abbreviations). After determining a possible headline, participants were also asked to indicate on a scale of 1 to 5 (with 1 being low confidence) their confidence in the headline being an actually event that occurred in that region or city (to measure believability).

In Part 3, participants were asked to choose which regions and cities correspond to a given headline, i.e., the exact opposite of Part 2. Part 4 of the survey asked participants to list the keywords common to cities in a specified region. The dataset on Part 3 and 4 also contained a set of injected keywords meant to form a regional headline. The reason for this approach is the lack of regional headlines, affecting multiple cities, in the original, captured tweets. Two sets of injected keywords were added to 30% of the cities in one of the region. One of the headlines given to the participants was real while the other was one of the injected keyword sets.

The cities and regions were randomly chosen by the testing software. Two cities and two regions were included in each of the Parts 2 and 3, and a single region made the subject of Part 4. The testing software ran Parts 2, 3, and 4 twice, once for BuzzViz and once for the table. The order was chosen at random by the testing software. The software also ensured that participants would not encounter the same dataset and city or region more than once, thus no Twitter knowledge transfer was possible.

Part 5, similar to a post-questionnaire, requested participants to answer a series of feedback questions based on their experience during the survey. Questions asked included a subjective comparison of BuzzVizz and table on the ease of summarizing headlines, confidence in their performance, ease of navigation, ease of finding a city or region, and platform preference.

Results and Analysis

As previously stated all the participants are university students in both undergraduate and graduate categories. The study indicated a substantial proportion (82%) of the participants receive their news via Internet with 68% following news events on at least a weekly basis. This is a surprisingly large number of people who seem to get most or all of their news not from traditional media but through the internet; however, this is in line with very recent research which shows a similar shift, especially with the younger generation of news media consumers (Pew Research Center, 2016).

On the other hand, only a fraction (17%) of those who follow news via the internet use Twitter as a major source on at least weekly basis. Also, when asked about the reputation of both sources of information, 55% of respondents viewed Twitter as a reputable source of information compared to 95% for NASA World Wind.

Four geographically contiguous regions denoted by (lists of states) and four cities were used for Parts 2, 3 and 4 of the study. Given that real Twitter data whose news content is not known a priori, headlines in participants' responses were independently verified by two members of the evaluation team as correct if they appeared in a traditional news outlet and were recorded by LexisNexis. Furthermore, since determining all the news headlines available in each location covered on the map (continental US) is prohibitive, the analysis considered total number of correct and unique news headlines generated by all the participants (χ) as the total number of "real" news headlines contained within the data within each of the specified locations. Participants' evaluation was thus based on an adjusted score. For example, if a participant summarized 2 correct headlines (where a maximum of 4 is allowed) for a specified location and the total number of correct headlines summarized by all the participants (for the same location), χ=3, then the adjusted score for the task is 2/3.

$$Adjusted\ Score = \frac{\#\,of\ correct\ solutions}{maximum\ \#\ of\ possible\ solutions}$$

For the tasks of listing keywords, Part 4, the number of artificially injected keywords is the maximum number of possible solutions.

Bi-dimensional examination of the results shows little difference between BuzzViz and the table, hence performing statistical analysis to determine which visualization platform has an overall better performance was forgone and only the absolute values for the results are presented.

In the regional versus city tasks, there was no significant difference (2%) in the overall accuracy of performing both tasks on either visualization. Contrary to the hypothesis that regional tasks can be solved more accurately on a map compared to a table (due to contiguity), and that city tasks are vice-versa, it was observed that the opposite happened. In terms of duration of performing both tasks, the table also appears generally more efficient than the map (27%) as shown in Figure 17.

Although more research will be required in order to fully explain the reason for this observation, this chapter surmises that there aren't many tweets containing information of a regional nature in the dataset used for the experiment. For Part 4 - List Keywords, where the keywords were artificially injected, the map performs significantly (50%) better than the table (Figure 18). In other tasks where real tweet data is used, similar accuracy is observed between the two platforms. In addition to the higher accuracy achieved on the map for the keywords listing task, there is also better time performance for the task on the same visualization tool (8%). A final explanation for poor performance may be participants' geographical knowledge of the area considered in the study and proficiency in using the map visualization.

Overall, the table is 27% faster than the map. However as can be seen in Figure 19, in general there is significant reduction in the amount of time taken by participants from one task to the next, which may indicate increasing familiarity to the tasks

Figure 17. Adjusted Score and timing comparison on the two visualization tools

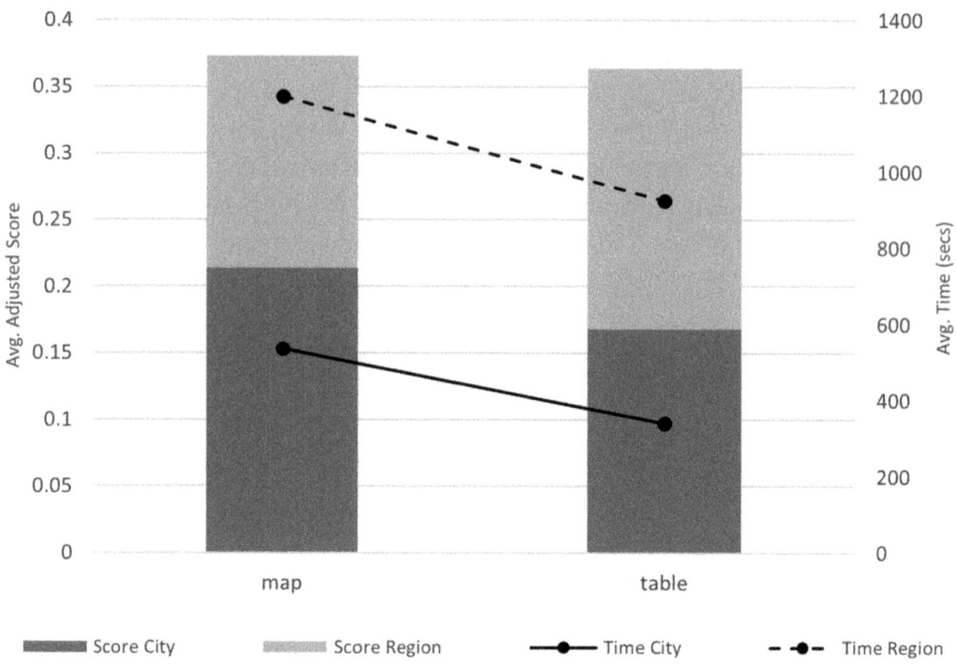

Figure 18. Performance by task category

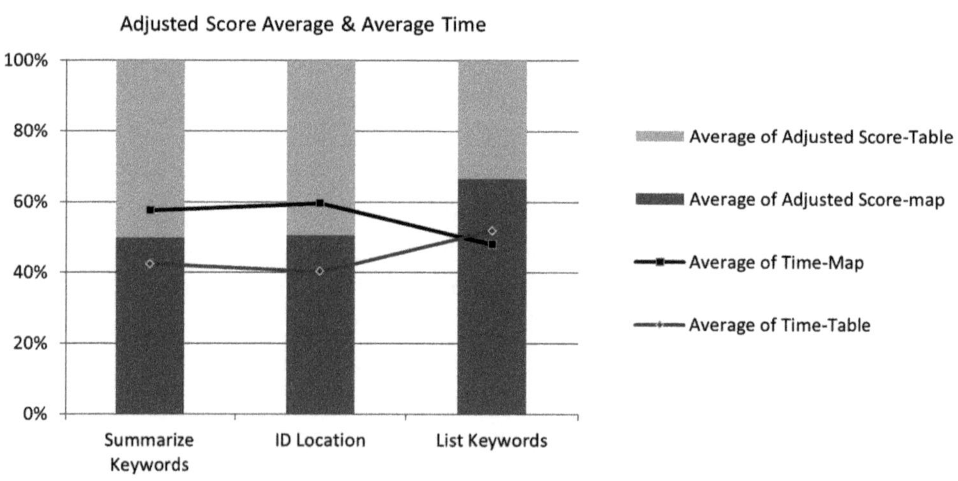

and visualization. The average amount of time taken for the initial tasks on the table was less than that on the map, possibly due to the simplicity and supposed relative familiarity of users to the table. Also, the time performance on the map was higher (albeit slightly) for the last two tasks which may indicate familiarity with visualization

Figure 19. Average participant learning curve

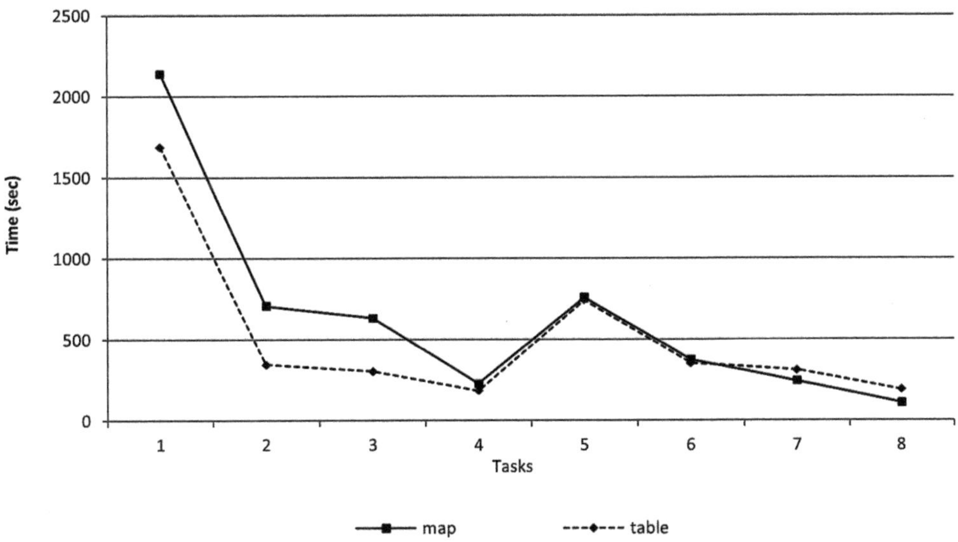

tool. In total, efficiency on table and map visualizations increased by 89% and 95% respectively. The reason spike in duration at Task 5 is not entirely clear. However, one can suppose it to be due to the phenomena of visualization novelty and/or task difficulty. Visualization novelty refers to the fact that tasks 1 and 5 are the first tasks in either platforms (map or table), hence the start of a new type of learning. Task difficulty refers to both task 1 and 5 involving the identification of headlines, which may be relatively more difficult.

The next analysis compared the reputation of Twitter information expressed by the participants in Part 1 of the study to their belief in the summarized headlines generated from the visualization. Although only 55% of the participants initially indicated trust in Twitter information, the average believability indicated for summarized headlines is 74% (3.7 out of 5). Table 1 indicates that participants' skepticism of Twitter information is not transferred to the visualization tool despite that they were told that the keywords in the visualization originated from Twitter; 86% of the visualization believability responses indicated 3 or higher out of 5. The believability responses for the map and table are almost identical (map = 3.75 and table = 3.72) suggesting that the blending of the information sources rather than the visualization is responsible for participants' relatively high confidence in the final information product.

Tables 3 and 4 summarize broad comparison of the performance of the map and table presentations based on tasks categories (Part 2, 3, and 4) as well as region versus city.

Table 3. Subjective assessment of the information product and its component

Believability (Visualization)	**High (2.6-5)**	37%	49%
	Low (1-2.5)	2%	12%
		Low (No)	**High (Yes)**
		Reputation (Twitter Information)	

Table 4. Broad comparison between the Table and Map visualizations

	Average of Adjusted Score	Average of Time	Average of Believability Scale
Region	Table	Table	Table
City	Map	Table	Map
Summarize	Same	Table	Map
Find Place	Map	Table	
List Keywords	Map	Map	

Overall, the map and the table visualizations appear to have the equal efficiencies. The map leads on accuracy and believability while the table holds a substantial lead on the time performance. However, if the learning curve is taken in to consideration (Figure 19), the time performance advantage enjoyed by the table is expected to be diminished over time.

Subjective preference of the users is summarized in Table 5. Overall, BuzzVizz was the preferred platform. Participants were split down the middle on which platforms, BuzzVizz or the table, makes it easier to find headlines. The same fifty-fifty split occurs for which platform inspires more confidence. Interestingly, more people find the table useful in locating cities and states than BuzzVizz (14 versus 8), yet a majority of participants prefer navigation in BuzzVizz rather than in the

Table 5. Counts of tasks categories of better performance

Visualization	Average of Adjusted Score	Average of Time	Average of Believability Scale	Σ Performance
Map	3.5	1	2	6.5
Table	1.5	4	1	6.5

Table 6. Distribution of participants' preference on visualization

	Map View	Table View
Ease of Summarizing Headlines	11	11
Confident in Responses	11	11
Ease of Navigation	13	9
Ease of Locating Cities/States	8	14
Task Platform Preference	14	8

table (13 versus 9). This may be a good indication that some participants find it easier to look for a textual city name alphabetically in a table than to find it location by scanning a potentially unfamiliar map.

CONCLUSION

This chapter addressed how to exploit information contained in big data generated from computer-mediated communication systems such as chatrooms, instant messaging, social media, and micro-blogs. The topic was viewed from two main perspectives; (i) analysis of the users (participants) and social dynamics (ii) analysis of the subjects (contents) of conversation. Due to the nature of big data, the simplicity-of-processing principle was employed in many design decisions of the techniques and tools presented in this chapter.

In the former perspective, methods for extracting social networks using temporal information and content of exchanged messages were introduced and their effectiveness measured using ground-truth data of IRC chat logs. The effectiveness measured were the user's degree (number of other users interacted with) and the strength (number of messages exchanged with other users) as depicted in the link-retrieval and link-weights correlation statistics respectively. It was observed that the different methods exhibit strengths that can be harmonized via a hybrid method in which the contribution of the different methods results in an overall best performance. In addition, a study of the best visualization techniques of social networks was performed between node-link diagram and adjacency matrix with a heat-map. The study was carefully designed such that neither of the visualization technique is given undue advantage; hence enhancements that cannot be applied to both methods were avoided. The study measured the speed and accuracy of determining degree and strength of nodes and links respectively. Tasks on the adjacency matrix with a heat-map showed statistically significant faster speed, however no differences were detected in terms of accuracy.

In the latter perspective, methods for integrating and jointly visualizing data from different environments are explored. The advantage of using already familiar visualization for exploring new data or to introduce new data that provide additional context are embodied in the geographical views of BuzzVizz, to heat map and more esoteric and complex in the form of TreeMap and the zoomable interface panels of MagnetChat. The description and prototyping of these visualizations was done using Twitter and internet relay chat (IRC) log data, however data from other forms of multi-user virtual environments such as WhastApp groups or Slack channels can also be employed. Results of a user study of the BuzzVizz was also presented, which revealed the transfer of user perspectives and experience with GIS data to the CMC information.

REFERENCES

Abbasi, A., & Chen, H. (2008). *Writeprints: A stylometric approach to identity-level identification and similarity detection in cyberspace. ACM Transactions on Information Systems.*

Albinsson, P.-A., & Morin, M. (2002). Visual Exploration of Communication in Command and Control. Academic Press. doi:10.1109/IV.2002.1028769

Angluin, D., Aspnes, J., & Reyzin, L. (2010). Inferring social networks from outbreaks. *21st International Conference, ALT 2010*, 104-118.

Batty, M., Hudson-Smith, A., Milton, R., & Crooks, A. (2010). Map Mashups, Web 2.0 and the GIS Revolution. *Annals of GIS*, *16*(1), 1–13. doi:10.1080/19475681003700831

Bederson, B. B., Grosjean, J., & Meyer, J. (2004). Toolkit design for interactive structured graphics. *IEEE Transactions on Software Engineering*, *30*(8), 535–546. doi:10.1109/TSE.2004.44

Burkhalter, B., & Smith, M. (2004). Inhabitants' uses and reactions to Usenet social accounting data. *Springer-Verlag*.

Choudhury, M. D., Hofman, J., Mason, W., & Watts, D. J. (2010). Inferring Relevant Social Networks from Interpersonal Communication. In *Proceedings of the 19th International Conference on World Wide Web* (pp. 301-310). Raleigh, NC: ACM. 10.1145/1772690.1772722

Cleverdon, C. (1967). The Cranfield tests on index language devices. *Aslib Proceedings*, *19*(6), 173–192. doi:10.1108/eb050097

Dalianis, H., Hassel, M., De Smedt, K., Liseth, A., Lech, T. C., & Wedekind, J. (2004). Porting and evaluation of automatic summarization. In Nordisk Sprogteknologi (pp. 107-121). Academic Press.

Diesner, J., Frantz, T. L., & Carley, K. M. (2005). Communication Networks from the Enron Email Corpus "It's Always About the People. Enron is no Different". *Computational & Mathematical Organization Theory*, *11*(3), 201–208. doi:10.100710588-005-5377-0

Eagle, N., Pentland, A. & Lazer, D. (2009). Inferring friendship network structure by using mobile phone data. *Proceedings of the National Academy of Sciences*, 106, 15274-15278. 10.1073/pnas.0900282106

Feng, X., Gan, L., & Yang, J. (2009). User-driven GIS Software Reuse Solution Based on SOA and Web 2.0 Concept. In *2nd International Conference on Computer Science and Information Technology* (pp. 5-9). Beijing: IEEE.

Freeman, L. C. (2004). The development of social network analysis: a study in the sociology of science. Vancouver, Canada Empirical Press.

Ghoniem, M., Fekete, J. D., & Castagliola, P. (2004). A comparison of the readability of graphs using node-link and matrix-based representations. In *IEEE Symposium on Information Visualization* (pp. 17-24). IEEE. 10.1109/INFVIS.2004.1

Ghoniem, M., Fekete, J.-D., & Castagliola, P. (2005). On the readability of graphs using node-link and matrix-based representations: A controlled experiment and statistical analysis. *Information Visualization*, *4*(2), 114–135. doi:10.1057/palgrave.ivs.9500092

Hsu, T.-W., Inman, L., McColgin, D., & Stamper, K. (2004). MonkEllipse: Visualizing the History of Information Visualization. In *IEEE Symposium on Information Visualization* (pp. r9-r9). IEEE.

Jones, K. S. (1972). A statistical interpretation of term specificity and its application in retrieval. *The Journal of Documentation*, *28*(1), 11–21. doi:10.1108/eb026526

Kandefer, M., & Shapiro, S. (2009). An F-Measure for Context-based Information Retrieval. *9th International Symposium on Logical Formalizations of Commonsense Reasoning*, 79-84.

Kelly, S. U., Sung, C., & Farnham, S. (2002). Designing for Improved Social Responsibility, User Participation and Content in On-Line Communities. *Proceedings of CHI*. 10.1145/503376.503446

Krikorian, D., & Kiyomiya, T. (2002). Bona fide groups as self-organizing systems: Applications to electronic newsgroups groups, Group communication in context: Studies of bona fide. *Lawrence Erlbaum.*

Krikorian, D., & Ludwig, G. (2002). Groupscope: Data mining tools for online communication networks. *22nd Annual Sunbelt Social Network Conference.*

Krikorian, D., & Ludwig, G. (2003). Advances in network analysis: Over-time visualization, dual-mode relations, and clique detection methods. *23rd Annual Sunbelt Social Network Conference.*

McIntire, J., Osesina, O. I., & Craft, M. (2011). Development of Visualizations for Social Network Analysis of Chatroom Text. *International Symposium on Collaborative Technologies and Systems.* 10.1109/CTS.2011.5928741

Moses, C. (2007). *New Visualization Technology to Enhance Situational Awareness for System Operators.* Tampa, FL: IEEE. doi:10.1109/PES.2007.386010

Mutton, P. (2004). Inferring and Visualizing Social Networks on Internet Relay Chat. In *Proceedings of the Information Visualisation, Eighth International Conference* (pp. 35-43). IEEE Computer Society. 10.1109/IV.2004.1320122

Neumann, P., Tat, A., Zuk, T., & Carpendale, S. (2006). Personalizing Typed Text Through Visualization. In *Proc. Compendium of InfoVis* (pp. 138–139). Los Alamitos, CA: IEEE Computer Society.

Neumann, P., Tat, A., Zuk, T., & Carpendale, S. (2007). KeyStrokes: Personalizing Typed Text with Visualization. In K. Museth, T. Möller, & A. Ynnerman (Eds.), *Eurographics/IEEE-VGTC Symposium on Visualization* (pp. 43–50). Academic Press.

Okoe, M., Jianu, R., & Kobourov, S. (2017). Revisited Network Representations. *25th Symposium on Graph Drawing (GD).*

Osesina, O. I., Bartley, C., & Tudoreanu, M. E. (2010). Mapping realities: The co-visualization of geographic and non-spatial textual information. *International Conference on Modeling, Simulation, and Visualization Methods*, 10-16.

Papegnies, E., Labatut, V., Dufour, R., & Linares, G. (2017). *Graph-based Features for Automatic Online Abuse Detection.* Le Mans: Statistical Language and Speech Processing. doi:10.1007/978-3-319-68456-7_6

Pew Research Center. (2016). *How Americans get their news.* Retrieved May 15, 2017, from http://www.journalism.org/2016/07/07/pathways-to-news/

Purchase, H. C., Carrington, D., & Allder, J.-A. (2002). Empirical evaluation of aesthetics-based graph layout. *Journal of Empirical Software Engineering*, *7*(3), 233–255. doi:10.1023/A:1016344215610

Rohall, S. L., Gruen, D., Moody, P., & Kellerman, S. (2001). Email visualizations to aid communications. *Proceedings of the IEEE Symposium on Information Visualization.*

Rosen, D., Woelfel, J., Krikorian, D., & Barnett, G. A. (2003). Procedures for Analyses of Online Communities. *Journal of Computer-Mediated Communication*, *8*(4).

Sack, W. (2000). Discourse Diagrams: Interface Design for Very Large Scale Conversations. *Proceedings of HICSS*. 10.1109/HICSS.2000.926717

Sankaranarayanan, J., Samet, H., Teitler, B. E., Lieberman, M. D., & Sperling, J. (2009). TwitterStand: News in Tweets. In *Proceedings of the 17th ACM SIGSPATIAL International Conference on Advances in Geographic Information Systems*. Seattle, WA: ACM.

Shin, H., Xu, Z., & Kim, E.-Y. (2008). *Discovering and Browsing of Power Users by Social Relationship Analysis in Large-Scale Online Communities. In Web Intelligence and Intelligent Agent Technology*. IEEE.

Shneiderman, B. (1992). Tree visualization with tree-maps: 2-d space-filling approach. *ACM Transactions on Graphics*, *11*(1), 92–99. doi:10.1145/102377.115768

Singhal, A. (2001). Modern Information Retrieval: A Brief Overview. *A Quarterly Bulletin of the Computer Society of the IEEE Technical Committee on Data Engineering*, *24*(4), 35–42.

Smith, M. (1999). Invisible crowds in cyberspace: Measuring and mapping the social structure of USENET. In *Communities in cyberspace: Perspectives on new forms of social organization*. London: Routledge Press.

Smith, M., Farnham, S., & Drucker, S. (2000). *The social life of small graphical chat spaces*. ACM SIG CHI. doi:10.1145/332040.332477

Soo Yi, J., Melton, R., Stasko, J., & Jacko, J. A. (2005). Dust & magnet: Multivariate information visualization using a magnet metaphor. *Information Visualization*, *4*(4), 239–256. doi:10.1057/palgrave.ivs.9500099

Stowe, K., Paul, M., Palmer, M., Palen, L., & Anderson, K. (2016). Identifying and Categorizing Disaster-Related Tweets. *The Fourth International Workshop on Natural Language Processing for Social Media*, 1-6.

Tavassoli, S., & Zweig, K. A. (2015). *Analyzing the activity of a person in a chat by combining network analysis and fuzzy logic. In Advances in Social Networks Analysis and Mining*. IEEE/ACM.

Tomaszewski, B. (2010). Situation Awareness and Virtual Globes: Applications for Disaster Management. *Computers & Geosciences*, *37*(1).

Tyler, J. R., Wilkinson, D. M., & Huberman, B. A. (2003). *Email as spectroscopy: Automated discovery of community structure within organizations. In Communities and Technologies* (pp. 81–96). Kluwer.

Verma, S., Vieweg, S., Corvey, W. J., Palen, L., Martin, J. H., Palmer, M., . . . Anderson, K. M. (2011). Natural Language Processing to the Rescue? Extracting "Situational Awareness" Tweets During Mass Emergency. *Fifth International AAAI Conference on Weblogs and Social Media*.

Viégas, F. B. (2005, September). *Revealing individual and collective pasts: Visualizations of online social archives.* Massachusetts Institute of Technology.

Ware, C., Purchase, H. C., Colpoys, L., & McGill, M. (2002). Cognitive measurements of graph aesthetics. *Journal of Information Visualization*, *1*(2), 103–110. doi:10.1057/palgrave.ivs.9500013

Wood, J., Dykes, J., Slingsby, A., & Clarke, K. (2007). Interactive Visual Exploration of a Large Spatio-Temporal Dataset: Reflections on a Geovisualization Mashup. *IEEE Transactions on Visualization and Computer Graphics*, *13*(6), 1176–1183. doi:10.1109/TVCG.2007.70570 PMID:17968062

Xiong, R., & Donath, J. (1999). PeopleGarden: Creating data portraits for users. *Proceedings of UIST*.

KEY TERMS AND DEFINITIONS

BuzzVizz: A visualization tool that shows the social network and its topics implicitly in the context of a layered map, or more generally of geographical information system (GIS) layers. Its goal is to provide a view of the topics discussed and/or users posting messages over various geographical areas.

Chatroom: A multi-user communication platform in which each post from a user is seen by everyone in that room. This chapter takes a more general view of the chatroom to include not only IRC communication, but also online comments sections for products and news as well as review sections for websites of e-commerce.

Computer-Mediated Communication (CMC): Tools based on computers and networking that allow people to send textual information to other people. Examples include IRC, Twitter, Facebook, text messaging, website-based comments and reviews.

Direct Addressing Analysis (DAA): A method of extracting the social network from computer-mediated communication that can be used when a user specifically mentioned another user ID in their posts.

Hybrid Link Extraction: A composite method of extracting the social network from computer-mediated communication that is based on a combination of multiple social networks extracted via other methods such as direct addressing analysis, response-time analysis, or word context usage analysis.

MagnetChat: A visualization tool that allows the user to determine the overall relationships between selected users or topics while providing the ability to move continuously through the conversation from individual posts to weeks at a time.

Response-Time Analysis (RTA): A method of extracting the social network from computer-mediated communication that is based on analyzing the time difference between user posts.

Social Network (SN): A graph whose nodes are user IDs and links represent binary relationships between these users. Often the links have different levels of strength corresponding to the level of interactions between pairs of users.

TreeBuzz: A visualization tool that provides an implicit view of the social network and topics combined with hierarchical data.

Word Context Usage Analysis (WCUA): A method of extracting the social network from computer-mediated communication that determines important words that appear in user's posts and relies on those words to find relationships between users.

Chapter 8
Analysis of Operation Performance of Blast Furnace With Machine Learning Methods

Kuo-Wei Hsu
National Chengchi University, Taiwan

Yung-Chang Ko
China Steel Corporation, Taiwan

ABSTRACT

Although its theoretical foundation is well understood by researchers, a blast furnace is like a black box in practice because its behavior is not always as expected. It is a complex reactor where multiple reactions and multiple phases are involved, and the operation heavily relies on the operators' experience. In order to help the operators gain insights into the operation, the authors do not use traditional metallurgy models but instead use machine learning methods to analyze the data associated with the operation performance of a blast furnace. They analyze the variables that are connected to the economic and technical performance indices by combining domain knowledge and results obtained from two fundamental feature selection methods, and they propose a classification algorithm to train classifiers for the prediction of the operation performance. The findings could assist the operators in reviewing as well as improving the guideline for the operation.

DOI: 10.4018/978-1-5225-4963-5.ch008

1. INTRODUCTION

Business intelligence is not a single technology but comprises multiple technologies, whose collaborative use is to efficiently and effectively utilize available data in decision-making for business or, more generally, all kinds of operations in all kinds of organizations. Likewise, big data is not a single technology but comprises multiple technologies. It comes with the same fundamental concept, which is utilization of data in decision-making, but big data is more concerned with various issues relevant to data. These issues are not only on the quantity of data but also on the characteristics and quality of data.

We generalize big data for business intelligence as the action that addresses data issues and performs data analysis to support decision-making and further to improve business. In this chapter, we present an application of machine learning to the operation of a blast furnace. From the big data perspective, we address the following V's:

- **Volume:** The data that we use us is a collection of samples that are sampled in different rates and processed in a daily basis for five years; the processed data is small, but the raw data is not.
- **Variety:** The data is collected from multiple sources; it is in a traditional format, but its contents are of high variety so that non-traditional data processing is required.
- **Veracity:** The data is collected from different systems designed for different functions and with different capabilities; the quality varies from one part of the data to another part so that robust analysis is required.
- **Value:** The methods presented in this chapter can assist the operators in having insights into the operation data, and the insights would be potentially valuable from the business perspective; the methods could be core components in an operation decision support system for blast furnaces.

A blast furnace is a manufacturing facility to achieve economies of scale in metal production. It is a tall and big structure in which raw materials are heated to a very high temperature in order to smelt metal and reduce raw material to molten metal. Blast furnaces have been used and studied for centuries (Geerdes, Chaigneau, & Kurunov, 2015; Peacey & Davenport, 2016), and they play an important role in the modern metal production (Zhou, Cheng, Wang, & Jiang, 2017). Each blast furnace is a complex system. The theories that support the operation of a blast furnace are well developed and well understood; however, in practice, how the blast furnace performs is not always as planned and how it reacts to the operation adjustment is not always as expected. The quality of raw materials has a significant impact on the operation of a blast furnace. Some small differences inside the blast furnace or in raw materials would possibly lead to differences not negligible in the quality and/or quantity of the produced metal. Raw materials with sufficient quality would assist the operators in obtaining the steady operation of a blast furnace and reaching the predetermined production target. The steady supply of raw materials with sufficient quality is one of the key factors that enable a blast furnace toward the steady production of hot metal. Competition in the industry has been the driving force behind the more efficient production. If the operators could know more about how the quality of raw materials influences the operation performance, they would have a better chance of achieving the better hot metal productivity with less cost, which corresponds to the better business performance. For example, if the quality of raw materials could be downgraded but still meet the requirement while at the same time, the quality of the product could be maintained, then the production cost would be reduced (and the competitive advantage would be obtained). The benefit of such cost reduction would be great especially when the blast furnace is not fully loaded. Therefore, it is of high value to have better understanding on the relationship between the quality of raw materials and the operation performance of a blast furnace. In addition, the operators would like to know more about how operation parameters would affect the operation performance. For example, it is valuable to know the impact of the operation of hot blast on the productivity.

The quality of raw materials and operation parameters are independent variables, and they are together viewed as the input; the economic and technical performance indices are dependent variables, and they are individually viewed as the output. The objective of our work is to investigate the relationship between the independent variables (input) and the dependent variables (output). To achieve the objective, a type of approaches that one can use is to use theory-based numerical analysis to develop mathematical models to simulate the operation of a blast furnace. This type of approaches starts with some theory, makes an assumption on the process that generates data, develops a model, and finally collects data to evaluate the model. Examples of the papers related to this type of approaches include Azadeh & Ghaderi (2006), Chu, Guo, Shen, Yagi, & Nogami, (2007), da Rocha, Guilherme, de Castro, Sazaki, & Yagi (2013), Danloy, Mignon, Munnix, Dauwels, & Bonte (2001), de Castro, de Mattos Araújo, da Mota, Sasaki, & Yagi (2013), de Castro, Nogami, & Yagi (2002), Harvey & Gheribi (2014), Jindal, Pujari, Sandilya, & Ganguly (2007), Nogami, Chu, & Yagi (2006), Shen, Guo, Chew, Austin, & Yu (2015), Ueda, Natsui, Nogami, Yagi, & Ariyama (2010), Yang, Zhou, & Yu (2015),

Zhang et al. (2014). Usually, the assumption made by these types of approaches are so strong that the developed model is hardly applicable to most of the situations with which the operators have to deal; it is a shortcoming of this type of approach (Zeng, Gao, & Su, 2010). Another type of approach that one can use to achieve the goal is to use statistical methods or techniques to analyze the relationship between the two types of variables mentioned above. Usually, this type of approach is has a relatively small number of variables, each of which represents a property of raw materials or an operation parameter; the number of variables considered by this type of approach is so small that the relationship obtained from the related analysis would be of little value to the operators. This type of approach cannot analyze data of high complexity. An example is a linear regression model. However, it is difficult to use simple statistical techniques to model the relationships between variables in a blast furnace (Dhond, Gupta, & Vadhavkar, 2000). Researchers have proposed advanced regression models, such as those presented in Faleiro, Velloso, de Castro, & Sampaio (2013) and Tang, Zhuang, & Jiang (2009). Even so, these approaches are still based on strong assumptions.

The approach used in our work and presented in this chapter is driven by data. The data that we use is neither generated by simulation nor collected from an experimental blast furnace in a lab. We use the actual data collected from an operating blast furnace. We analyze the data generated by the blast furnace from 2008 to 2012. The approach does not make a strong assumption on the underlying data generation process, which is looked-for but is not obtainable. For example, it does not assume that there exists a linear relationship between the quality of raw materials and the productivity. The approach requires opinions from domain experts, and thus could be viewed as a kind of knowledge-based approach.

The raw data is big. We consider statistics of raw values rather than raw values themselves, and this greatly reduces the technical difficulty of processing the raw data and that of analyzing the processed data. There are hundreds of variables in the raw data. With the help from domain experts, we consider 66 variables and three performance indices, which are the productivity, coke rate, and permeability resistance. The first is an economic index; the second and third are technical performance indices. In Table 1, we compare this chapter to the selected related work. Please note that the definition of productivity in Ghosh & Majumdar, (2011) is different from that in this chapter.

Data-driven approaches have been discussed by researchers, such as Chakraborti, & Saxén (2007), Pettersson, Zhou, Yuan, Wang, & Chai (2015), Saxén & Pettersson (2007), Saxén, Gao, & Gao (2013), Xu et al., (2016), Chen, Liu, Wang, Zhao, &

Table 1. A comparison between this chapter and the selected related work

Paper	Target	Task
(Zeng et al., 2010)	silicon content	time series analysis, regression
(Dhond et al., 2000)	hot metal temperature, silicon content	regression
(Tang et al., 2009)	silicon content	regression
(Faleiro et al., 2013)	charcoal consumption	regression
(Luo, Liu, & Zhao, 2005)	silicon content	regression
(Sun, Yin, Wu, & Tu, 2006)	state of blast furnace	classification
(Ghosh & Majumdar, 2011)	productivity	classification, regression
(Wang & Liu, 2011)	silicon content	feature selection, regression
(Jian, Shen, & Song, 2012)	changing trend of silicon content	feature selection, classification
(Xu, Hua, Tang, & Guan, 2016)	silicon content	regression
(Hua, Wu, Li, & Guan, 2017)	silicon content	regression
This chapter	productivity, coke rate, permeability resistance	feature selection, classification

Wang (2017), and the value of using data mining in the modern manufacturing environment has also been discussed by researchers such as Choudhary, Harding, & Tiwari, (2009), Harding, Shahbaz, & Kusiak (2006). Nevertheless, our approach is original (since we could not find the same approach in the literature).

Our contributions are as follows: First, we propose a method that uses clustering to help determine class labels, which are necessary for classification. This method can be applied in situations where class labels are not clearly pre-defined. Second, we propose a method that combines domain knowledge and results given by two fundamental feature selection methods. This can be a reference method to whoever cannot obtain satisfactory results from a single feature selection method. Third, we propose a classification algorithm that can train a subspace ensemble of Bayesian classifiers, and this algorithm is suitable for cases in which stable classification performance is preferred. This chapter would be beneficial to practitioners as well as researchers, as it provides a real-world application and new methods.

The remainder of this chapter is organized as follows: In Section 2, we will discuss why and how we model the problem of analyzing the operation performance of a blast furnace as a series of machine learning problems, and we will formally define each of them. In Sections 3, we will provide a detailed description of how we process the data according to the problem definitions. In Sections 4 and 5, we will discuss in detail our methods for the selection of influential variables and for the prediction of the operation performance, respectively. In Section 6, we will present the results of our analysis. Finally, in Section 7, we will conclude this chapter.

2. PRELIMINARIES

A blast furnace is a metallurgical furnace, and it smelts the iron ore as well as produces hot metal, which will be further processed into steel. One of the essential issues regarding the operation of a blast furnace is to have better understanding on the relationship between the quality of raw materials and its operation performance. The operators would like to know what the level of the influence on the production would be when there is a small change in the level of quality of raw materials. In addition, it is critical to understand more about the relationship between the set of operation parameters and the operation performance of a blast furnace. The operators would like to know in more detail about how using a different set of operation parameters and raw materials with a different level of quality would affect the production.

Machine learning is to algorithmically explore as well as learn the relationships between variables in the data, such as feature selection, and the relationships between data samples, such as classification. Feature selection is to select the independent variables that can facilitate the learning task. Knowledge about the independent variables that are necessary to describe the dependent variable is valuable for domain experts (Kommenda, Kronberger, Feilmayr, & Affenzeller, 2011). If there is a dependent numeric variable defined in the data, and the task is to train a model that can map the values of the independent variables to the value of the dependent variable, then it is classification. Machine learning is an important part of big data analysis.

The first step of our approach to analyzing the data is to perform data processing, whose goal is mainly to filter and transform the content of data. Subsequently, we perform feature selection and then build a model for classification. We define the original format of the data as follows.

Definition 1: In the given data set D containing N data samples, a data sample contains a date field, a vector, and a target field. The vector of the i-th data sample is $x_i = (v_1(i), \ldots, v_M(i))$, where $1 \leq i \leq N$, $1 \leq j \leq M$, and non-missing $v_j(i) \in R$ is the value that x_i takes on the j-th independent variable or feature, while $v_j(i)$ could be null or missing; $v_j = \{v_j(i), 1 \leq i \leq N\}$. The target field is associated with a performance index.

In data processing, we use the values of the date field to help us fill missing values and to remove data during shutdown. We consider the three performance indices separately. Each is an independent variable, which is originally numeric.

Before labeling, we have to transform an independent numeric variable into a categorical variable holding class labels. Each class label represents the level of a performance index. We use clustering to assist in the determination of the class labels. After data processing is done, we have a new data set, as defined below.

Definition 2: The data set D returned by data processing is of size N, in which a data sample contains a vector and a class label. In D, which will be used in feature selection, the vector of the i-th data sample is $x_i = (v_1(i), \ldots, v_M(i))$, where $1 \leq i \leq N$ (which is smaller than that in Definition 1), $1 \leq j \leq M$, and $v_j = \{v_j(i), 1 \leq i \leq N\} = [0, 1]$ (meaning that each feature is normalized); the i-th data sample is also with the class label $y_i \in \{c_l, 1 \leq l \leq K\}$.

Data processing reduces the size of the original data set, while feature selection reduces the dimension of the original data set. After feature selection is done, we have another new data set, whose definition is as follows.

Definition 3: The data set D returned by feature selection is of size N, in which the i-th data sample contains $x_i = (v_1(i), \ldots, v_M(i))$, where $1 \leq i \leq N$ (which equal to that in Definition 2), $1 \leq j \leq M$ (which is smaller than that in Definition 2), and $v_j = \{v_j(i), 1 \leq i \leq N\} = [0, 1]$; the i-th data sample is also with the class label $y_i \in \{c_l, 1 \leq l \leq K\}$ (where K is equal to that in Definition 2).

Given the data set defined in Definition 3, we can use a classification algorithm to build a model for classification of the levels of the productivity, coke rate, or permeability resistance. These are performance indices in which the operators of a blast furnace are interested. The following is the general definition for a classification algorithm.

Definition 4: Given a data set where there are an input space $X = \{x_i, 1 \leq i \leq N\}$ (where N is equal to that in Definition 3), which is a set of vectors associated with data samples, and given an output space $Y = \{c_l, 1 \leq l \leq K\}$ (where N is equal to those in Definitions 2 and 3), which is the set of the determined class labels, a classification algorithm is to learn from the data to build (or train) a function that maps X to Y, or f: $X \rightarrow Y$, and the function is a classification model or classifier.

3. DATA PROCESSING

3.1 Data Description

We analyze the data collected from the sensors installed in an operating blast furnace and from the manufacturing-related information systems. There are many sensors, and their sampling rates would be in minutes or seconds. The raw data collected from the sensors would be at the level of terabyte (TB). There are several manufacturing-related information systems, and they would generate data in a daily or hourly basis. The raw data collected from the manufacturing-related information systems would be at the level of gigabyte (GB). We consider variables and values in the daily reports about the operation of the blast furnace. More specifically, we use daily averages of variables.

There are hundreds of variables in the raw data. With the help from domain experts, we consider 66 variables, excluding the three performance indices, among hundreds of variables in the raw data. Among the 66 variables (input), 62 are directly acquired from the daily reports in which we (and the operators) are interested, and four are derived from some variables in the daily reports. Among the 66 variables, nine are with reference to operation parameters, and 57 are in relation to properties of raw materials. Properties of raw materials include physical and chemical properties of coke and sinter. Viewed as the target (output), the economic and technical performance indices are the productivity, coke rate, and permeability resistance. These three are the target or dependent variables that we consider and analyze separately. Those 66 variables are independent variables (or features considered in feature selection and classification), as listed below:

- **Operation Parameters:** Blast volume (BV), blast temperature (BT), blast moisture (BM), pulverized coal injection (PCI), and five others
- **Physical Properties of Coke:** Eight regarding the sizes, coke strength after reaction (CSR), MS, M10, M40, and reactivity
- **Physical Properties of Sinter:** Seven regarding the sizes, MS, reduction disintegration index (RDI), and three others
- **Chemical Properties of Coke:** The percentages for FE, CAO, AL_2O_3, MGO, TIO_2, SIO_2, ash, and six others
- **Chemical Properties of Sinter:** The percentages for FEO, CAO, AL_2O_3, MGO, TIO_2, SIO_2, basicity ratio B2, and eight others
- **Derived Features Regarding the Consumption of Raw Materials:** Sinter, pellet, and lump ore ratios, and the sum of sinter and pellet ratios

Details are confidential. Some variables shall not be revealed.

3.2 Workflow

For practitioners and researchers, in most of machine learning projects, the initial yet critical step is data processing. Figure 1 presents the workflow of data processing that we propose.

The first step is to fill missing values. If there is a missing value on a feature on some date, we simply find the closest date whose value is not missing and use the value. We first look for the closest date backward, and if it does not exist, then we perform the search from the date having the missing value forward.

The second step is to derive features. We derive four variables from the consumption of raw materials recorded in the data, and they are sinter ratio, pellet ratio, lump ore ratio, and the sum of the first two.

The third step is to remove data during shutdown. When a blast furnace shuts down for maintenance, the sensor readings may not be accurate and therefore the data is abandoned. We remove the data during shutdown, and additionally we remove the data for one day before and after shutdown in order to ensure the quality of the data.

The fourth step is to remove outliers. We define an outlier as a data sample in which there is at least a feature having a value either too high or too low. This definition is different from that used in Faleiro et al. (2013), where data samples collected during shutdown are viewed as outliers. We use domain knowledge to define a proper range of values that each feature could take. We would not attempt to modify outliers but simply remove them, and we make no attempt to understand what causes the outliers.

The fifth step, also the last step, is to normalize the data. The domain of a variable or feature is composed of all values that could possibly be taken by the feature. For some features, their domains are large, while for some others, their domains are small. The features of large domains may dominate the calculation in feature selection and training classifiers, and they may cover the features of small domains. The importance of a feature cannot be determined by the size of its domain. Features could have small domains and still be important, but they would be in the shadow

Figure 1. Workflow of data processing

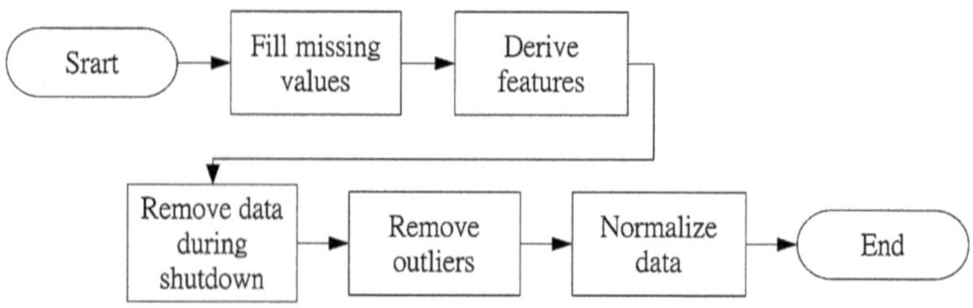

of those features having large domains if we use together features having different sizes of domains in the calculation. As a result, we apply normalization to all features. Here, normalization means a linear transformation that maps the minimum and maximum values of the original domain of a feature to 0 and 1, respectively; it maps the original domain of a feature to the unit interval [0, 1], as in Tang et al. (2009) and Xu et al. (2016) but not Pettersson et al. (2007), where normalization is actually standardization.

Equation 1, shown below, is to normalize the value that the i-th data sample in a data set takes on the j-th feature or the j-th independent variable. In the equation, v_j is the domain of the j-th feature, superscripts are used to distinguish between the original value and the normalized value, and min and max are respectively to find the minimum and maximum values in the domain of a feature.

$$v_j^{normalized}\left(i\right) = \frac{v_j^{original}\left(i\right) - \min\left(v_j\right)}{\max\left(v_j\right) - \min\left(v_j\right)} \tag{1}$$

3.3 Label Determination

We need labeled data samples in order to do feature selection and classification. Nevertheless, how to assign labels depends on the goal and the target of the analysis, such as the blast furnace that provides the data. Every blast furnace is unique in its design and construction, and it is distinct from others in some way. Furthermore, the setting of the main problem studied in this chapter is new, and the determination of the class labels could be somewhat subjective, so we need a method that can help us determine the class labels in a less subjective and more objective manner. The determination of the class labels would and perhaps should not be totally objective, because it requires more or less domain knowledge to tackle the main problem studied in this chapter.

We propose to determine the class labels with the help of clustering. It is original. We first use the expectation-maximization algorithm (EM) to partition the data set into groups or clusters such that the distance between two data samples in the same group is smaller than that between two in different groups. When doing clustering, we use all features but not a target, which holds the values that will be transformed into the class labels. Subsequently, we consider the dependent variable, and we average its values for each group. Then, we sort these average values, and we calculate the middle value for each such pair of adjacent average values. These middle values are points of separation, or they are boundaries used to differentiate data samples of classes, that is, to distinguish the data samples belonging to one class from those belonging to another class. Figure 2 illustrates the idea of using the clustering result to suggest class boundaries. In the figure, the left and right sides correspond to low and high values of the dependent variable in consideration, respectively. For a dependent variable representing a performance index, the class boundaries are used with domain knowledge to segment its domain to generate levels for its values. The segmentation is different from discretization in their objectives.

The following presents the pseudocode for using clustering to determine class labels. It shows the aforementioned steps in an algorithmic way, and it corresponds to Definition 2.

Input: A data set D consisting of N data samples (with N numeric target values) and M features, as described in Definition 1; the number of classes, K
Output: A list of K-1 points of separation
Procedure:

```
Set the number of clusters to K and apply the EM algorithm to the data set
Initialize A, a list of K elements
For i = 1 to K
        Get the target values corresponding to the data records that belong to the i-th cluster returned by the EM algorithm
        A[i] = average value of the target values gotten previously
End for
Initialize B, a list of K-1 elements
For i = 1 to K-1
        B[i] = (A[i]+A[i+1])/2
End for
Return B
```

Figure 2. Illustration of using the clustering result to suggest class boundaries

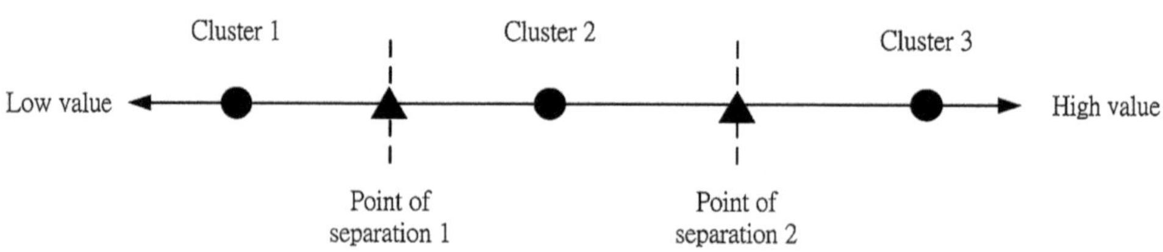

A dependent variable is a class, and a level is a label. Labeling means label assignment. After having the labels for a class, we assign a label to every data sample. Then, we can do feature selection and classification on the data.

In (Ghosh & Majumdar, 2011), the authors consider a binary classification task for modeling blast furnace productivity, and they use the median value of productivity as a threshold to assign a class label, high or low productivity, to every data sample.

4. FEATURE SELECTION

4.1 Fundamental Methods

Feature selection is to automatically or semi-automatically assess all the features in a given data set and select some of them such that the classification model built upon the selected features performs better than does that built upon all the features. Some features might have a negative impact on classification. Two fundamental methods to feature selection include the one based on information gain and the one based on correlation between features: The former assesses and sorts the capability of separating classes for each feature, while the latter aims to find a group of features such that the ratio of the feature-class correlation to the feature-feature correlation is as large as possible. Overall, feature selection is not a trivial task (Kommenda et al., 2011).

Feature selection based on information gain assesses features individually. It uses the distribution of the class labels to calculate the expected information. For each feature, it calculates the entropy first and then subtracts the entropy from the expected information to obtain the information gain; the larger is the information gain value of a feature, the better is the capability of a feature to separate one class from the others. Finally, all the features are sorted according to their information gain values. This method implicitly selects features. Features having low information gain values are disregarded. This is usually done by comparing the information gain value of each feature with a threshold, while how to set the threshold requires domain knowledge and how to use the threshold is not the concern of this method.

Correlation-based feature selection assesses features collectively, and it explicitly selects features by returning a group of features, which is a subset of the given feature set. The features in such a group are considered as a whole and their order has no meaning. In the beginning, this method calculates the feature-class correlation by first calculating correlation between each feature in a group and the class and then aggregating the correlation values. This correlation indicates how well the group of features classifies the given data samples; the larger it is, the better is the group of features. Furthermore, this method calculates the feature-feature correlation by first calculating correlation for each feature pair in a group and then aggregating the correlation values. This correlation indicates how dependent the features in a group are on each other or how independent a feature is of any other; the lower it is, the better is the group of features. A set of dependent features is of little value and could be a problem for some algorithms used to build classification models. In the end, this method searches for a group corresponding to a large ratio of the feature-class correlation to the feature-feature correlation. The search is usually performed in a greedy manner.

These two feature selection methods are not new, but we propose a new way to use them together with domain knowledge.

4.2 The Proposed Method

We consider operation parameters and properties of raw materials separately. There are two main reasons for doing this. First, they are different types of features in nature. Second, considering them separately could avoid that some unobvious yet important features are covered by those dominant yet obvious features. Furthermore, we utilize the aforementioned methods as procedural units. The first method, feature selection based on information gain, is used to calculate the helpfulness of each operation parameter and the usefulness of each property of raw materials. Furthermore, the second method, correlation-based feature selection, is used to find proper subset of operation parameters and separately to find a proper subset of properties of raw materials.

We propose a method to combine the results to complete feature selection for our analysis, as presented below. It corresponds to Definition 3. Initially, the data set is randomly partitioned into 10 equal-sized subsets. Next, we iteratively leave one subset and apply correlation-based feature selection to the combination the other subsets. A combination of subsets is used just once. Finally, we take the union of the groups of features returned by correlation-based feature selection. As a result, we select operation parameters according to the result given by correlation-based feature selection. Considering the features for the sizes of coke and sinter, we select those having the largest information gain values. Considering other features for physical and chemical properties of coke and sinter, we select those having information values larger than 0.1, or we select those having information values smaller than 0.1 but in the result given by correlation-based feature selection. For the derived features, we select sinter ratio, pellet ratio, and lump ore ratio, since the fourth derived feature is the sum of the first two and is less useful than either one.

Input: A data set D consisting of N data samples (with N class labels) and M features, as described in Definition 2

Output: A list of features
Procedure:

```
1.        Initialize a set R
2.        Initialize G, a list of M elements
3.        For each feature
4.                Calculate its information gain for the
class, and put the result in G
5.        End for
6.        Initialize a set H
7.        Apply correlation-based feature selection to D, and
put the result in H
8.        For each feature corresponding to an operation
parameter
9.                If it is in H then put it in R
10.        End for
11.        Consider the features for the sizes of coke and
sinter, check G and put the one with the largest information
gain in R
12.        For each of other features corresponding to
physical and chemical Properties of coke and sinter
13.                If its information gain > 0.1 then put it
in R
14.                Else if it is in H then put it in R
15.        End for
16.        Return R
```

5. CLASSIFICATION

The glass-box classification algorithms are used to train classifiers for the discovery of hidden patterns that later would be examined by domain experts and accordingly transformed into knowledge. Examples include those able to build Bayesian classifiers.

We propose a classification algorithm to predict the levels of the three performance indices. The following presents its pseudocode. It corresponds to Definition 4. The proposed classification algorithm uses a subspace method to train an ensemble composed of Bayesian classifiers. Here, the term space means a feature space, and a subspace is a space composed of a subset of the whole feature set. An ensemble is a group of classifiers, and itself is a classifier. To train an ensemble is to train these classifiers by using a base classification algorithm with training data. We use an ensemble method to enhance the stability of the classification model trained by using the base classification algorithm of the ensemble. When it is given a data sample that needs to be classified, an ensemble passes the data sample as inputs to the classifiers that it contains, and then it collects as well as aggregates the individual outputs or labels from them to produce the final output or label. The classifiers contained in an ensemble need to be different, and we achieve this by manipulating the feature space.

The core of the proposed classification algorithm is Bayesian classification algorithm, one of the top 10 data mining algorithms (Wu et al., 2008), and the shell of the proposed method is a procedure similar to Random Subspace Method (Ho, 1998). Bayesian classifiers represent a probabilistic approach to classification problems, while they are simple but often effective (Domingos & Pazzani, 1996; Yager, 2006). For example, it has been applied to the data for tax audit selection (Hsu, Pathak, Srivastava, Tschida, & Bjorklund, 2015). Bayesian classifiers are based on the assumption that features are independent of each other. Dependent features could have negative effect on the performance of Bayesian classifiers. However, Bayesian classification algorithm is still widely used in various applications (Wu et al., 2008), and this is partly because the negative effect brought by dependent features may be canceled out (Zhang, 2004). Moreover, we use the procedure similar to that used in Random Subspace Method (Ho, 1998) to introduce differences to the classifiers contained in an ensemble, while we remove the random component to make the resulting ensemble not probabilistic but deterministic, as requested by the users.

As presented in the following, for a given data set consisting of N data samples and M features, we generate M data sets each of which consists of N data samples and M-1 features. Such a data set is a training data set. We leave out a feature to create a subspace when generating a training data set, and we create M distinct subspaces each of which is used to vertically partition the given data set. These subspaces are distinct from each other, because no two are exactly the same. Since the partition is not done horizontally, the number of data samples in a training data set is N, which is the number of data samples in the given data set. Then, we train a Bayesian classifier upon a training data set, so we will have M Bayesian classifiers in the end, and no two are trained by using the same training data set. As presented below, for a given data sample that we want to classify, we use the M Bayesian classifiers to have M labels, each of which is given by a Bayesian classifier, and we use majority voting to aggregate these M labels to produce the final label for the given data sample.

Input: A data set D consisting of N data samples (with N class labels) and M features, as described in Definition 2

Output: An ensemble composed of M Bayesian classifiers

Procedure:

```
1.        Initialize a set R
2.        For i= 1 to M
3.                Discard the i-th feature and create a
training data set consisting of the N                data
samples and M-1 features
4.                Train a Bayesian classifier with the
training data set created previously
5.                Add the  Bayesian classifier trained
previously to R
6.        End for
7.        Return R
```

The above is about how the proposed classification algorithm trains an ensemble, while the following is about how the trained ensemble is used to classify a data sample.

Input: A data sample consisting of M features
Output: A class label
Procedure:

```
1.        Initialize P to be an array whose number of elements
is the number of classes,        K (which is stored in the
ensemble)
2.        For i = 1 to M
3.                Discard the i-th feature and create a data
record having M-1 features
4.                Pass the data sample created previously to
the i-th Bayesian classifier
5.                Get the class probabilities from the
classifier and put them in an array T
6.                For j = 1 to K
7.                        Accumulate P by doing P[j] = P[j] +
T[j]
8.                End for
9.        End for
10.        Find the largest element in P and return the class
label corresponding to its index
```

Because the characteristics of the data usually change from time to time, the users often have to replace the employed classifier with one retrained by using a different set of parameters or by using a different classification algorithm. Even so, the users sometimes observe variances in the quality of the predictions. Such variances would be a source of the uncertainty. As time passes, the uncertainty would hinder the users from the employment of the classifier. Therefore, in practice, it is more important to have a classification algorithm that can train classifiers having stable classification performance than to have one that gives classifiers sometimes showing high precision but sometimes not; moreover, the users would be less satisfied with a classification algorithm that gives classifiers showing high precision for some performance index but not others. Furthermore, in practice, a classification algorithm having fewer parameters that need to be tuned is preferable to one having more parameters and demanding the use of an additional procedure to obtain the optimal set of parameters. However, the optimality usually holds only for the training data or, more generally, for some combinations of the data samples. For example, an artificial neural network trained to predict the states of a blast furnace would perform well for normal states but not for abnormal states (Lin, Yue, Zhao, & Li, 2009).

6. RESULTS

We implement the aforementioned methods and algorithm with the help of WEKA (Hall et al., 2009).

6.1 Data Processing

We consider three levels or class labels for each of the productivity, coke rate, and permeability resistance. They are low (L), medium (M), and high (H). The class boundaries suggested by the clustering result are reported in Table 2. The actual class boundaries used as points of separation to distinguish classes and determine class labels are different from those reported in Table 2. The actual values are confidential, but they are close to those suggested by the clustering result.

Table 2. The class boundaries suggested by the clustering result

Performance Index	Suggested Class Boundaries
Productivity	7755, 8219
Coke rate	326, 334
Permeability resistance	0.28, 0.29

We generate three data sets from the original data set after processing it, and each data set is for a performance index, which is the productivity, coke rate, or permeability resistance. Because the change in the demand and supply during 2010 and 2012, the blast furnace that provides the data was sometimes operated in a way somewhat different from how it is generally operated. So, we pay extra attention to the data collected from 2010 to 2012.

For productivity, the percentage of the data samples being labeled as H in 2008-2012 is lower than 50%, while that in 2010-2012 is slightly higher than 50%; for coke rate, the percentage of data samples being labeled as H in 2008-2012 is much higher than that in 2010-2012, while the percentage of data samples being labeled as L in 2008-2012 is much lower than that in 2010-2012; for permeability resistance, the majority of the data samples in 2008-2012 are those labeled as L, while that in 2010-2012 are data samples labeled as M. These observations tell us that there exist certain changes in the distributions of the class labels in different time frames.

6.2 Feature Selection

The result for feature selection reported in Table 3, where a selected variable is marked with an asterisk.

In the end, we discover 43, 35, and 44 variables important for the prediction of the levels of the productivity, coke rate, and permeability resistance, respectively. Most of these variables are important for all the three performance indices, while some of these variables are exclusively important for some performance index. Combined with the observations that we have in the previous subsection, we can see that the prediction tasks for the three performance indices are different and that having a classification algorithm working stably for them is difficult.

For operation parameters, BV plays an important role in the prediction of the levels of the productivity and permeability resistance, and BT is essential in predicting the levels of the permeability resistance. PCI is related to fuel injection, so it is associated with the coke rate. All the things in a blast furnace have to be permeable so that heated gas could pass through and be diffused, and thus BV and BT are relevant to the permeability resistance.

For physical properties of coke, M40, M10, and reactivity are essential for all, while MS and CSR are essential for all but the coke rate; large, medium, and small sizes have significant impacts on the prediction tasks for the productivity, coke rate, and permeability resistance, respectively. Coke has to be in the form of large particle, and it has to be solid so that it would not be totally crushed by the raw materials above it. Our result suggests that the effect of medium-sized and small-sized coke in the raw materials should not be neglected. Moreover, for physical properties of sinter, MS is essential for all, and RDI is essential for all but the productivity; small size

Table 3. The result given by the proposed feature selection method

Group	Variable	Productivity	Coke Rate	Permeability Resistance
Operation parameters	BV	*		*
	BT			*
	BM			
	PCI		*	
	5 others	2	1	4
Physical properties of coke	8 regarding the sizes	large	medium	small
	MS	*		*
	M40	*	*	*
	M10	*	*	*
	reactivity	*	*	*
	CSR	*		*
Physical properties of sinter	7 regarding the sizes	medium	small	medium
	MS	*	*	*
	RDI		*	*
	3 others	3	1	2
Chemical properties of coke	FE%			
	CAO%	*	*	*
	AL2O3%	*	*	*
	MGO%	*	*	*
	TIO2%	*		*
	SIO2%	*	*	
	ASH%	*	*	*
	6 others	5	4	5
Chemical properties of sinter	FEO%	*	*	*
	CAO%	*	*	*
	AL2O3%	*	*	*
	MGO%	*	*	*
	TIO2%		*	
	SIO2%	*	*	*
	B2	*	*	*
	8 others	8	6	8
Derived variables	sinter ratio	*	*	*
	pellet ratio	*	*	*
	lump ore ratio	*	*	*
	sinter ratio plus pellet ratio			

is essential for the coke rate, and medium size is essential for the productivity and permeability resistance. Levels of sizes for sinter are different from those for coke.

For chemical properties of coke, most variables are important in predicting the levels of all; the percentage of TIO_2 is essential for the prediction tasks for the productivity and permeability resistance, but not the coke rate; the percentage for SIO_2 is essential for the prediction task for the coke rate, but not the productivity and permeability resistance. Moreover, for chemical properties of sinter, most variables play an important role in the prediction of all the three performance indices; the percentage of TIO_2 is essential only for the coke rate.

6.3 Classification

We evaluate the trained classifiers by using precision, a widely-used measure. Precision is defined as the proportion of correct outputs (for data samples whose class labels are correctly classified) to total outputs given by a classifier. It indicates that when a classifier classifies a data sample as some class, how likely the data sample actually belongs to that class.

Equation 2, shown below, is to calculate the weighted average of precision values achieved by a classifier. It is used because we take into account the distribution of the class labels. In theequation, k is the number of classes, n_i is the number of data samples that belong to the i-th class, N is the number of data samples, p_i is the precision that the classifier achieves for the i-th class, and P is the weighted average of precision values.

$$P = \frac{1}{N}\sum_{i=1}^{k}\left(n_i \times p_i\right) \tag{2}$$

We compare the proposed classification algorithm to the decision tree construction algorithm C4.5 (Quinlan, 1993) and sequential minimal optimization (SMO) (Hastie & Tibshirani, 1998; Keerthi, Shevade, Bhattacharyya, & Murthy, 2001; Platt, 1999), a type of support vector machine (SVM). We use polynomial and radial basis function (RBF) kernels. C4.5 and SVM are also among top 10 data mining algorithms (Wu et al., 2008). We additionally consider multilayer perceptron (MLP), a type of artificial neural network (ANN). For these algorithms, we use the parameters recommended by the toolkit.

Bayesian classifiers, decision trees, support vector machines, and artificial neural networks, are used in the applications related to this chapter, as reviewed in (Köksal, Batmaz, & Testik, 2011). An example for Bayesian classifiers is (Perzyk, Biernacki, & Kochański, 2005); examples for SVM (and its variants) include (An,

Yang, Zhou, Wang, & Pan, 2015; Ghosh & Majumdar, 2011; Jian et al., 2012; Liu, Wang, Mo, & Zhao, 2011; Tian & Wang, 2010; Wang & Liu, 2011; Wang, Zhang, Gao, & Lu, 2006; Xu et al., 2016); examples (and its variants) for ANN include (Chen, 2001; Dhond et al., 2000; Lin et al., 2009; Perzyk et al., 2005; Pettersson et al., 2007; Radhakrishnan & Mohamed, 2000; Sun et al., 2006; Yuan et al., 2015).

CART (classification and regression tree) (Breiman, Friedman, Stone, & Olshen, 1984) is another decision tree construction algorithm on the list of top 10 data mining algorithms (Wu et al., 2008). However, CART is not very different from C4.5, as the difference in the provided classifications between SVMs with different kernels would sometimes be larger than that between C4.5 and CART (Hsu & Srivastava, 2012). So, we consider C4.5 only.

The proposed classification algorithm uses the normalized data, while the others use the preprocessed but not normalized data. This is because, for example, SMO and MLP normalize data by themselves.

We use 10-fold cross-validation to evaluate as well as compare the classification algorithms. The classification performance given by the proposed classification algorithm is reported in Table 4.

Compared to the classification performance achieved by using a single Bayesian classifier, the ensemble of Bayesian classifiers trained by the proposed classification algorithm achieves better classification performance on all the data sets except on for the productivity for 2010-2012. Using a single Bayesian classifier is unstable and thus would probably suffer more from overfitting, because the range of the values for its classification performance is between 0.61 and 0.8. Using an ensemble indeed stabilizes the use of Bayesian classification. The proposed classification algorithm is specifically effective in predicting the levels of the permeability resistance, because it outperforms others on the two corresponding data sets. C4.5 ranks the first for the prediction of the levels of the coke rate, and it is followed by MLP for 2008-

Table 4. The classification performance in the weighted average of precision values achieved by the considered classification algorithms

	Productivity		Coke Rate		Permeability Resistance	
	2008-2012	**2010-2012**	**2008-2012**	**2010-2012**	**2008-2012**	**2010-2012**
The proposed method	0.78	0.77	0.77	0.78	0.71	0.7
Single Bayesian	0.75	0.8	0.67	0.75	0.61	0.61
C4.5	0.79	0.78	0.87	0.88	0.68	0.63
SMO (polynomial)	0.8	0.82	0.81	0.86	0.7	0.68
SMO (RBF)	0.69	0.55	0.65	0.55	0.55	0.52
MLP	0.8	0.74	0.84	0.84	0.66	0.66

2012 and by SMO with polynomial kernel for 2010-2012. SMO with RBF kernel does not perform well on all the data sets. The classifiers trained by the proposed classification algorithm provide values ranging from 0.7 to 0.78, which is relatively stable compared to those provided by C4.5, SMO with polynomial kernel, SMO with RBF kernel, and MLP. If the goal is to make prediction on the data collected in a specific time frame for a specific performance index, one can run evaluation and use the classification algorithm that trains the best classifier. However, this limits the usefulness of the system, and the problem caused by overfitting would gradually diminish its usefulness. If the system is required to be applicable to the data sets for different targets with different distributions and still achieve the same level of classification performance, the proposed classification algorithm would be an ideal option.

7. CONCLUSION

A blast furnace is a reactor in which complex physical and chemical processes are involved. The operators of a blast furnace view it as a black box because how it would react to the operation adjustment is not completely predictable. The operators usually operate blast furnaces according to their experience. For that reason, the more the operators know about the practical reactions of a blast furnace to the operation adjustment, the better they could operate it. Some metallurgy models are proposed for such a purpose. However, the actual data is hardly fit for most of the models, especially those built upon simulation.

We adopt a data-driven approach, and we use machine learning methods to analyze the actual data collected from an operating blast furnace during a period of five years. The approach can also be categorized as a knowledge-based approach. Unlike most of the related papers where the data contains a small number of variables connected to an economic or technical performance index, the data that we use contains 66 variables connected to three performance indices, including the productivity, coke rate, and permeability resistance. Therefore, the complexity of our analysis is higher than that of those that we could find in the literature.

In data processing, we propose to use clustering to help determine class labels. For analyzing the variables that are connected to the economic and technical performance indices, we incorporate domain knowledge with results obtained from two fundamental feature selection methods. In the end, we discover 43, 35, and 44 variables important for the prediction of the levels of the productivity, coke rate, and permeability resistance, respectively. For predicting the operation performance of the blast furnace, or more precisely, for predicting the levels of the three performance indices, we propose a classification algorithm that is able to train classifiers having stable classification performance.

Our findings could help the operators of a blast furnace review as well as improve the guideline for the operation. Furthermore, our work could assist in the operation and resource planning for blast furnaces.

REFERENCES

An, R., Yang, C., Zhou, Z., Wang, L., & Pan, Y. (2015). Comparison of different optimization methods with support vector machine for blast furnace multi-fault classification. *IFAC-PapersOnLine*, *48*(21), 1204–1209. doi:10.1016/j.ifacol.2015.09.690

Azadeh, A., & Ghaderi, S. F. (2006). Optimization of an automatic blast furnace through integrated simulation modeling. *Journal of Computational Science*, *2*(4), 382–387. doi:10.3844/jcssp.2006.382.387

Breiman, L., Friedman, J., Stone, C. J., & Olshen, R. A. (1984). *Classification and regression trees*. New York, NY: Chapman & Hall.

Chen, J. (2001). A predictive system for blast furnaces by integrating a neural network with qualitative analysis. *Engineering Applications of Artificial Intelligence*, *14*(1), 77–85. doi:10.1016/S0952-1976(00)00062-2

Chen, L., Liu, Q. L., Wang, L. Q., Zhao, J., & Wang, W. (2017). Data-driven Prediction on Performance Indicators in Process Industry: A Survey. *Acta Automatica Sinica*, *6*, 8.

Choudhary, A. K., Harding, J. A., & Tiwari, M. K. (2009). Data mining in manufacturing: A review based on the kind of knowledge. *Journal of Intelligent Manufacturing*, *20*(5), 501–521. doi:10.100710845-008-0145-x

Chu, M. S., Guo, X. Z., Shen, F. M., Yagi, J. I., & Nogami, H. (2007). Numerical analysis of blast furnace performance under charging iron-bearing burdens with high reducibility. *Journal of Iron and Steel Research International*, *14*(2), 13–19. doi:10.1016/S1006-706X(07)60020-X

da Rocha, E. P., Guilherme, V. S., de Castro, J. A., Sazaki, Y., & Yagi, J. I. (2013). Analysis of synthetic natural gas injection into charcoal blast furnace. *Journal of Materials Research and Technology*, *2*(3), 255–262. doi:10.1016/j.jmrt.2013.02.015

Danloy, G., Mignon, J., Munnix, R., Dauwels, G., & Bonte, L. (2001). Blast furnace model to optimize the burden distribution. In *Proceedings of the 60th Ironmaking Conference* (pp. 37-48). Academic Press.

de Castro, J. A., de Mattos Araújo, G., da Mota, I. D. O., Sasaki, Y., & Yagi, J. I. (2013). Analysis of the combined injection of pulverized coal and charcoal into large blast furnaces. *Journal of Materials Research and Technology*, *2*(4), 308–314. doi:10.1016/j.jmrt.2013.06.003

de Castro, J. A., Nogami, H., & Yagi, J. I. (2002). Three-dimensional multiphase mathematical modeling of the blast furnace based on the multifluid model. *ISIJ International*, *42*(1), 44–52. doi:10.2355/isijinternational.42.44

Dhond, A., Gupta, A., & Vadhavkar, S. (2000). Data mining techniques for optimizing inventories for electronic commerce. In *Proceedings of the 6th ACM SIGKDD International Conference on Knowledge Discovery and Data Mining* (pp. 480-486). ACM. 10.1145/347090.347188

Domingos, P., & Pazzani, M. (1996). Beyond independence: Conditions for the optimality of the simple bayesian classifier. In *Proceedings of the 13th International Conference on Machine Learning* (pp. 105-112). Academic Press.

Faleiro, R. M. R., Velloso, C. M., de Castro, L. F. A., & Sampaio, R. S. (2013). Statistical modeling of charcoal consumption of blast furnaces based on historical data. *Journal of Materials Research and Technology*, *2*(4), 303–307. doi:10.1016/j.jmrt.2013.04.002

Geerdes, M., Chaigneau, R., & Kurunov, I. (2015). *Modern Blast Furnace Ironmaking: An Introduction*. IOS Press.

Ghosh, A., & Majumdar, S. (2011). Modeling blast furnace productivity using support vector machines. *International Journal of Advanced Manufacturing Technology*, *52*(9), 989–1003. doi:10.100700170-010-2786-0

Hall, M., Frank, E., Holmes, G., Pfahringer, B., Reutemann, P., & Witten, I. H. (2009). The WEKA data mining software: An update. *ACM SIGKDD Explorations Newsletter*, *11*(1), 10–18. doi:10.1145/1656274.1656278

Harding, J. A., Shahbaz, M., & Kusiak, A. (2006). Data mining in manufacturing: A review. *Journal of Manufacturing Science and Engineering*, *128*(4), 969–976. doi:10.1115/1.2194554

Harvey, J. P., & Gheribi, A. E. (2014). Process simulation and control optimization of a blast furnace using classical thermodynamics combined to a direct search algorithm. *Metallurgical and Materials Transactions. B, Process Metallurgy and Materials Processing Science*, *45*(1), 307–327. doi:10.100711663-013-0004-9

Hastie, T., & Tibshirani, R. (1998). Classification by pairwise coupling. In Advances in Neural Information Processing Systems (pp. 507-513). Academic Press. doi:10.1214/aos/1028144844

Ho, T. K. (1998). The random subspace method for constructing decision forests. *IEEE Transactions on Pattern Analysis and Machine Intelligence*, *20*(8), 832–844. doi:10.1109/34.709601

Hsu, K. W., Pathak, N., Srivastava, J., Tschida, G., & Bjorklund, E. (2015). Data mining based tax audit selection: a case study of a pilot project at the minnesota department of revenue. *Real World Data Mining Applications*, 221-245.

Hsu, K. W., & Srivastava, J. (2012). Improving bagging performance through multi-algorithm ensembles. *Frontiers of Computer Science*, *6*(5), 498–512.

Hua, C., Wu, J., Li, J., & Guan, X. (2017). Silicon content prediction and industrial analysis on blast furnace using support vector regression combined with clustering algorithms. *Neural Computing & Applications*, *28*(12), 4111–4121.

Jian, L., Shen, S., & Song, Y. (2012). Improving the solution of least squares support vector machines with application to a blast furnace system. *Journal of Applied Mathematics*.

Jindal, A., Pujari, S., Sandilya, P., & Ganguly, S. (2007). A reduced order thermo-chemical model for blast furnace for real time simulation. *Computers & Chemical Engineering*, *31*(11), 1484–1495. doi:10.1016/j.compchemeng.2006.12.015

Keerthi, S. S., Shevade, S. K., Bhattacharyya, C., & Murthy, K. R. K. (2001). Improvements to Platt's SMO algorithm for SVM classifier design. *Neural Computation*, *13*(3), 637–649. doi:10.1162/089976601300014493

Köksal, G., Batmaz, İ., & Testik, M. C. (2011). A review of data mining applications for quality improvement in manufacturing industry. *Expert Systems with Applications*, *38*(10), 13448–13467. doi:10.1016/j.eswa.2011.04.063

Kommenda, M., Kronberger, G., Feilmayr, C., & Affenzeller, M. (2011). Data mining using unguided symbolic regression on a blast furnace dataset. In *Proceedings of European Conference on the Applications of Evolutionary Computation* (pp. 274-283). Springer. 10.1007/978-3-642-20525-5_28

Lin, Z., Yue, Y., Zhao, H., & Li, H. (2009). Judging the states of blast furnace by ART2 neural network. In *Proceedings of the 6th Sixth International Symposium on Neural Networks* (pp. 857-864). Springer Berlin/Heidelberg. 10.1007/978-3-642-01216-7_91

Liu, L. M., Wang, A. N., Mo, S. H. A., & Zhao, F. Y. (2011). Multi-class classification methods of cost-conscious LS-SVM for fault diagnosis of blast furnace. *Journal of Iron and Steel Research International, 18*(10), 1733–23. doi:10.1016/S1006-706X(12)60016-8

Luo, S. H., Liu, X. G., & Zhao, M. (2005). Prediction for silicon content in molten iron using a combined fuzzy-associative-rules bank. In *Proceedings of International Conference on Fuzzy Systems and Knowledge Discovery* (pp. 667-676). Springer. 10.1007/11540007_82

Nogami, H., Chu, M., & Yagi, J. I. (2006). Numerical analysis on blast furnace performance with novel feed material by multi-dimensional simulator based on multi-fluid theory. *Applied Mathematical Modelling, 30*(11), 1212–1228. doi:10.1016/j.apm.2006.03.013

Peacey, J. G., & Davenport, W. G. (2016). *The iron blast furnace: theory and practice*. Elsevier.

Perzyk, M., Biernacki, R., & Kochański, A. (2005). Modeling of manufacturing processes by learning systems: The naïve Bayesian classifier versus artificial neural networks. *Journal of Materials Processing Technology, 164*, 1430–1435. doi:10.1016/j.jmatprotec.2005.02.043

Pettersson, F., Chakraborti, N., & Saxén, H. (2007). A genetic algorithms based multi-objective neural net applied to noisy blast furnace data. *Applied Soft Computing, 7*(1), 387–397. doi:10.1016/j.asoc.2005.09.001

Platt, J. C. (1999). Fast training of support vector machines using sequential minimal optimization. In B. Schölkopf, C. J. C. Burges, & A. J. Smola (Eds.), *Advances in kernel methods: support vector learning* (pp. 185–208). Cambridge, MA: MIT Press.

Quinlan, J. R. (1993). *C4.5: programs for machine learning*. San Mateo, CA: Morgan Kaufmann Publishers.

Radhakrishnan, V. R., & Mohamed, A. R. (2000). Neural networks for the identification and control of blast furnace hot metal quality. *Journal of Process Control, 10*(6), 509–524. doi:10.1016/S0959-1524(99)00052-9

Saxén, H., Gao, C., & Gao, Z. (2013). Data-driven time discrete models for dynamic prediction of the hot metal silicon content in the blast furnace—A review. *IEEE Transactions on Industrial Informatics*, *9*(4), 2213–2225. doi:10.1109/TII.2012.2226897

Saxén, H., & Pettersson, F. (2007). Nonlinear prediction of the hot metal silicon content in the blast furnace. *ISIJ International*, *47*(12), 1732–1737. doi:10.2355/isijinternational.47.1732

Shen, Y., Guo, B., Chew, S., Austin, P., & Yu, A. (2015). Three-dimensional modeling of flow and thermochemical behavior in a blast furnace. *Metallurgical and Materials Transactions*, *46*(1), 432–448. doi:10.100711663-014-0204-y

Sun, T., Yin, Y., Wu, S., & Tu, X. (2006). ART2-Based Approach to Judge the State of the Blast Furnace. In *Proceedings of the 6th International Conference on Intelligent Systems Design and Applications* (Vol. 1, pp. 118-122). IEEE. 10.1109/ISDA.2006.108

Tang, X., Zhuang, L., & Jiang, C. (2009). Prediction of silicon content in hot metal using support vector regression based on chaos particle swarm optimization. *Expert Systems with Applications*, *36*(9), 11853–11857. doi:10.1016/j.eswa.2009.04.015

Tian, H., & Wang, A. (2010). A novel fault diagnosis system for blast furnace based on support vector machine ensemble. *ISIJ International*, *50*(5), 738–742. doi:10.2355/isijinternational.50.738

Ueda, S., Natsui, S., Nogami, H., Yagi, J. I., & Ariyama, T. (2010). Recent progress and future perspective on mathematical modeling of blast furnace. *ISIJ International*, *50*(7), 914–923. doi:10.2355/isijinternational.50.914

Wang, A., Zhang, L., Gao, N., & Lu, H. (2006). Fault diagnosis of blast furnace based on improved SVMs algorithm. In *Proceedings of the 6th International Conference on Intelligent Systems Design and Applications* (Vol. 1, pp. 825-828). IEEE. 10.1109/ISDA.2006.150

Wang, Y., & Liu, X. (2011). Prediction of silicon content in hot metal based on SVM and mutual information for feature selection. *Journal of Information and Computational Science*, *8*(16), 4275–4283.

Wu, X., Kumar, V., Ross Quinlan, J., Ghosh, J., Yang, Q., Motoda, H., ... Zhou, Z. H. (2008). Top 10 algorithms in data mining. *Knowledge and Information Systems*, *14*(1), 1–37. doi:10.100710115-007-0114-2

Xu, X., Hua, C., Tang, Y., & Guan, X. (2016). Modeling of the hot metal silicon content in blast furnace using support vector machine optimized by an improved particle swarm optimizer. *Neural Computing & Applications, 27*(6), 1451–1461. doi:10.100700521-015-1951-7

Yager, R. R. (2006). An extension of the naive Bayesian classifier. *Information Sciences, 176*(5), 577–588. doi:10.1016/j.ins.2004.12.006

Yang, W. J., Zhou, Z. Y., & Yu, A. B. (2015). Discrete particle simulation of solid flow in a three-dimensional blast furnace sector model. *Chemical Engineering Journal, 278*, 339–352. doi:10.1016/j.cej.2014.11.144

Yuan, M., Zhou, P., Li, M. L., Li, R. F., Wang, H., & Chai, T. Y. (2015). Intelligent multivariable modeling of blast furnace molten iron quality based on dynamic AGA-ANN and PCA. *Journal of Iron and Steel Research International, 22*(6), 487–495. doi:10.1016/S1006-706X(15)30031-5

Zeng, J. S., Gao, C. H., & Su, H. Y. (2010). Data-driven predictive control for blast furnace ironmaking process. *Computers & Chemical Engineering, 34*(11), 1854–1862. doi:10.1016/j.compchemeng.2010.01.005

Zhang, H. (2004). The optimality of naive Bayes. In *Proceedings of the 17th International FLAIRS Conference*. AAAI Press.

Zhang, J., Qiu, J., Guo, H., Ren, S., Sun, H., Wang, G., & Gao, Z. (2014). Simulation of particle flow in a bell-less type charging system of a blast furnace using the discrete element method. *Particuology, 16*, 167–177. doi:10.1016/j.partic.2014.01.003

Zhou, D. D., Cheng, S. S., Wang, Y. S., & Jiang, X. (2017). The production and development of large blast furnaces in China during 2015. *Ironmaking & Steelmaking, 44*(5), 351–358. doi:10.1080/03019233.2016.1210915

Zhou, P., Yuan, M., Wang, H., & Chai, T. (2015). Data-driven dynamic modeling for prediction of molten iron silicon content using ELM with self-feedback. *Mathematical Problems in Engineering*.

Compilation of References

Abadi, M., Agarwal, A., Barham, P., Brevdo, E., Chen, Z., Citro, C., … Zheng, X. (2016). *TensorFlow: Large-Scale Machine Learning on Heterogeneous Distributed Systems*. Retrieved from http://arxiv.org/abs/1603.04467

Abbasi, A., & Chen, H. (2008). *Writeprints: A stylometric approach to identity-level identification and similarity detection in cyberspace. ACM Transactions on Information Systems.*

Abidi, L., Cérin, C., Geldwerth-Feniger, D., & Lafaille, M. (2015). *Cloud Computing for e-Sciences at Université Sorbonne Paris Cité*. Taormina, Italy: Advances in Service-Oriented and Cloud Computing - Workshops of ESOCC.

Abidi, L., Saad, W., & Cérin, C. (2017). A Deployment System for highly Heterogeneous and Dynamic Environments. *International Conference on High Performance Computing & Simulation*, Genoa, Italy. 10.1109/HPCS.2017.98

Abouzeid, A., Bajda-Pawlikowski, K., Abadi, D., Rasin, A., & Silberschatz, A. (n.d.). *HadoopDB: An Architectural Hybrid of MapReduce and DBMS Technologies for Analytical Workloads*. Retrieved from http://www.vldb.org/pvldb/2/vldb09-861.pdf

Abraham, A., Nath, B., & Mahanti, P. K. (2001). Hybrid Intelligent Systems for Stock Market Analysis. In *Computational Science - ICCS 2001* (pp. 337–345). Berlin: Springer; doi:10.1007/3-540-45718-6_38

Abu-Mustafa, Y., Magdon-Ismail, M., & Lin, H. T. (2012). *Learning from data: a short course.* AMLbooks.

Adams, R. P., & MacKay, D. J. (2007). *Bayesian online changepoint detection.* arXiv preprint arXiv:0710.3742

Aggarwal, C., Bhuiyan, M., & Hasan, M. (2014). Frequent Pattern Mining Algorithms: A Survey. In C. Aggarwal & J. Han (Eds.), *Frequent Pattern Mining*. Cham: Springer. doi:10.1007/978-3-319-07821-2_2

Agrawal, R., Mannila, H., Srikant, R., Toivonen, H., & Verkamo, A. I. (1996). Fast discovery of association rules. In *Advances in Knowledge Discovery and Data Mining* (pp. 307–328). AAAI/MIT Press.

Agrawal, R., & Srikant, R. (2014). *Fast algorithms for mining association rules.* VLDB.

Ahmad, S., & Purdy, S. (2016). *Real-Time Anomaly Detection for Streaming Analytics.* arXiv preprint arXiv:1607.02480

Akbani, R., Kwek, S., & Japkowicz, N. (2004, September). Applying support vector machines to imbalanced datasets. In *European conference on machine learning* (pp. 39-50). Springer. 10.1007/978-3-540-30115-8_7

Akdogan, A., Shahabi, S., & Demiryurek, U. (2014). ToSS-it: A Cloud-based Throwaway Spatial Index Structure for Dynamic Location Data. *International Conference on Mobile Data Management.* 10.1109/MDM.2014.37

Akita, R., Yoshihara, A., Matsubara, T., & Uehara, K. (2016). Deep learning for stock prediction using numerical and textual information. In *Computer and Information Science (ICIS), 2016 IEEE/ACIS 15th International Conference on* (pp. 1–6). IEEE. 10.1109/ICIS.2016.7550882

Albinsson, P.-A., & Morin, M. (2002). Visual Exploration of Communication in Command and Control. Academic Press. doi:10.1109/IV.2002.1028769

Alfaro-Almagro, F., Jenkinson, M., Bangerter, N. K., Andersson, J. L. R., Griffanti, L., Douaud, G., ... Smith, S. M. (2018). Image processing and Quality Control for the first 10, 000 brain imaging datasets from UK Biobank. *NeuroImage, 166*, 400–424. doi:10.1016/j.neuroimage.2017.10.034 PMID:29079522

Ammar, K., Elsayed, A., Sabri, M., & Terry, M. (2015). BusMate: Understanding Mobility Behavior for Trajectory-based Advertising. *International Conference on Mobile Data Management.* 10.1109/MDM.2015.71

Amplab. (2018). *Amplap UC Berkeley.* Retrieved from https://amplab.cs.berkeley.edu/tag/spark/

Andrecut, M. (2009). Parallel GPU Implementation of Iterative PCA Algorithms. *Journal of Computational Biology, 16*(11), 1593–1599. doi:10.1089/cmb.2008.0221 PMID:19772385

Angluin, D., Aspnes, J., & Reyzin, L. (2010). Inferring social networks from outbreaks. *21st International Conference, ALT 2010*, 104-118.

An, R., Yang, C., Zhou, Z., Wang, L., & Pan, Y. (2015). Comparison of different optimization methods with support vector machine for blast furnace multi-fault classification. *IFAC-PapersOnLine, 48*(21), 1204–1209. doi:10.1016/j.ifacol.2015.09.690

Armbrust, M., Xin, R. S., Lian, C., Huai, Y., Liu, D., Bradley, J. K., ... Zaharia, M. (2015, May). Spark sql: Relational data processing in spark. In *Proceedings of the 2015 ACM SIGMOD International Conference on Management of Data* (pp. 1383-1394). ACM. 10.1145/2723372.2742797

Arnold, P., & Rahm, E. (2014). Enriching ontology mappings with semantic relations. *Data & Knowledge Engineering, 93*, 1–18. doi:10.1016/j.datak.2014.07.001

Asch, M., & Moore, T. (2018). *Big Data and Extreme-Scale Computing: Pathways to Convergence.* Retrieved from http://www.exascale.org/bdec/sites/www.exascale.org.bdec/files/whitepapers/bdec2017pathways.pdf

Auer, S., Berners-Lee, T., Bizer, C., Capadisli, S., Heath, K., & Lehmann, J. (2017). *Workshop on Linked Data on the Web co-located with 26th International World Wide Web Conference (WWW 2017). CEUR Workshop Proceedings.* CEUR-WS.org.

Azadeh, A., & Ghaderi, S. F. (2006). Optimization of an automatic blast furnace through integrated simulation modeling. *Journal of Computational Science, 2*(4), 382–387. doi:10.3844/jcssp.2006.382.387

Baader, F., Calvanese, D., McGuinness, D., Nardi, D., & Patel-Schneider, P. (2003). *The Description Logic Handbook: Theory, Implementation, and Applications.* Cambridge University Press.

Babu, K., Ranabothu, N., & Kumar, N. (2013). Achieving k-anonymity Using Improved Greedy Heuristics for Very Large Relational Databases. *Trans. Data Priv., 6*(1), 1–17.

Babu, M. C. K., & Nagendra, P. (n.d.). Survey on Clustering on the Cloud by UsingMap Reduce in Large Data Applications. *International Journal of Engineering Trends and Technology.* Retrieved from http://www.ijettjournal.org/archive/ijett-v21p275

Bai, J., & Ng, S. (2008). Forecasting economic time series using targeted predictors. *Journal of Econometrics, 146*(2), 304–317. doi:10.1016/j.jeconom.2008.08.010

Bao, J., He, T., Ruan, S., Li, Y., & Zheng, Y. (2017). *Planning Bike Lanes based on Sharing-Bike's Trajectories.* SIGKDD. doi:10.1145/3097983.3098056

Barigozzi, M., Lippi, M., & Luciani, M. (2016). *Non-stationary dynamic factor models for large datasets.* Retrieved from https://papers.ssrn.com/sol3/papers.cfm?abstract_id=2756940

Batty, M., Hudson-Smith, A., Milton, R., & Crooks, A. (2010). Map Mashups, Web 2.0 and the GIS Revolution. *Annals of GIS, 16*(1), 1–13. doi:10.1080/19475681003700831

Bayer, R., & McCreight, E. (1970). Organization and Maintenance of Large Ordered Indices. *ACM SIGFIDET Workshop on Data Description, Access and Control.* 10.21236/AD0712079

Beck, G., Duong, T., Azzag, H., & Lebbah, M. (2016). Distributed mean shift clustering with approximate nearest neighbours. *International Joint Conference on Neural Networks.* 10.1109/IJCNN.2016.7727595

Bederson, B. B., Grosjean, J., & Meyer, J. (2004). Toolkit design for interactive structured graphics. *IEEE Transactions on Software Engineering, 30*(8), 535–546. doi:10.1109/TSE.2004.44

Behrens, M. (2014). Understanding Encryption – Symmetric, Asymmetric, & Hashing. *Atomic Spin.* Retrieved from https://spin.atomicobject.com/2014/11/20/encryption-symmetric-asymmetric-hashing/

Benbernou, S., & Ouziri, M. (2017). Enhancing Data Quality by Cleaning Inconsistent Big RDF Data. IEEE Big Data conference, Boston, MA. doi:10.1109/BigData.2017.8257913

Benbernou, S., Huang, X., Ouziri, M. (2017). Semantic-based and Entity-Resolution Fusion to Enhance Quality of Big RDF Data. *IEEE Transaction on Big Data.*

BenchSys. (2016). Retrieved from https://www.benchsys.com/

Bengio, Y. (2009). Learning deep architectures for AI. *Foundations and trends® in Machine Learning, 2*(1), 1-127.

Bengio, Y., Ducharme, R., Vincent, P., & Jauvin, C. (2003). A neural probabilistic language model. *Journal of Machine Learning Research, 3*(Feb), 1137–1155.

Bentounsi, M. (2015). *Business Process as a Service - BPaaS: Securing Data and Services* (PhD Thesis). Sorbonne Paris Cité - Université Paris Descartes, France.

Bentounsi, M., & Benbernou, S. (2016). Secure complex monitoring event processing. *NCA, 2016*, 392–395.

Bentounsi, M., Benbernou, S., & Atallah, M. J. (2016). Security-aware Business Process as a Service by hiding provenance. *Computer Standards & Interfaces, 44*, 220–233. doi:10.1016/j.csi.2015.08.011

Beres, D. (2016). *Microsoft Chat Bot Goes On Racist, Genocidal Twitter Rampage.* Retrieved from https://www.huffingtonpost.com/entry/microsoft-tay-racist-tweets_us_56f3e678e4b04c4c37615502

Beyer, K. S., & Ramakrishnan, R. (1999). Bottom-up computation of sparse and iceberg cubes. In A. Delis, C. Faloutsos, & S. Ghandeharizadeh (Eds.), *Special Interest Group on Management of Data (SIGMOD) Conference* (pp. 359–370). ACM Press. doi:10.1145/304182.304214

Beyer, M. A., & Laney, D. (2012). *The importance of 'big data': a definition.* Stamford, CT: Gartner.

Bhansali, R. J. (2002). Multi-Step Forecasting. *A Companion to Economic Forecasting*, 206-221.

Bhattacharya, I., & Getoor, L. (2017). Entity Resolution. Encyclopedia of Machine Learning and Data Mining, 402-408.

Bird, S., Klein, E., & Loper, E. (2009). *Natural language processing with Python: analyzing text with the natural language toolkit.* O'Reilly Media, Inc.

Bishop, C. (2007). Pattern Recognition and Machine Learning (2nd ed.). Springer.

Boehm, C., & Krebs, F. (2004). The k-Nearest Neighbour Join: Turbo Charging the KDD Process. *Knowledge and Information Systems, 6*(6), 728–749. doi:10.100710115-003-0122-9

Bonchi, F., & Lucchese, C. (2004). On closed constrained frequent pattern mining. In K. Morik & R. Rastogi (Eds.), *ICDM* (pp. 35–42). IEEE Computer Society.

Bordes, A., Ertekin, S., Weston, J., & Bottou, L. (2005). Fast kernel classifiers with online and active learning. *Journal of Machine Learning Research*, *6*(Sep), 1579–1619.

Box, G. (2013). Box and Jenkins: Time Series Analysis, Forecasting and Control. In A Very British Affair (pp. 161–215). Palgrave Macmillan UK. doi:10.1057/9781137291264_6

Box, G. E., Jenkins, G. M., Reinsel, G. C., & Ljung, G. M. (2015). *Time series analysis: forecasting and control*. John Wiley & Sons.

Bradford, C. (2014). *5 Common Encryption Algorithms and the Unbreakables of the Future – StorageCraft*. StorageCraft Technology Corporation. Available: http://www.storagecraft.com/blog/5-common-encryption-algorithms/

Brain Initiative. (n.d.). *What is the Brain Initiative?* Retrieved from https://www.braininitiative.nih.gov/

Breiman, L., Friedman, J., Stone, C. J., & Olshen, R. A. (1984). *Classification and regression trees*. New York, NY: Chapman & Hall.

Brenner, J. (2014). Nations everywhere are exploiting the lack of cybersecurity. *Washington Post*. Retrieved from www.washingtonpost.com/opinions/joel-brenner-nations-everywhere- are-exploiting-the-lack-of-cybersecurity/2014/10/24/1e6e4b70-5b85-11e4-b812- 38518ae74c67_story.html

Brockwell, P. J., & Davis, R. A. (2013). *Time series: theory and methods*. Springer Science & Business Media.

Brodersen, K. H., Gallusser, F., Koehler, J., Remy, N., & Scott, S. L. (2015). Inferring causal impact using Bayesian structural time-series models. *The Annals of Applied Statistics*, *9*(1), 247–274. doi:10.1214/14-AOAS788

Buchin, M., Dodge, S., & Speckmann, B. (2014). Similarity of Trajectories taking into account geographic context. *Journal of Spatial Information Science*.

Bukhari, A. C., Krauthammer, M., & Baker, C. J. O. (2014). Sebi: An architecture for biomedical image discovery, interoperability and reusability based on semantic enrichment. *Proceedings of the 7th International Workshop on Semantic Web Applications and Tools for Life Sciences*.

Buneman, P., Khanna, S., & Tan, W. C. (2000, December). Data provenance: Some basic issues. In *International Conference on Foundations of Software Technology and Theoretical Computer Science* (pp. 87-93). Springer.

Burdick, D., Calimlim, M., Flannick, J., Gehrke, J., & Yiu, T. (2005). *Mafia: A maximal frequent itemset algorithm*. Academic Press.

Burdick, D., Calimlim, M., Flannick, J., Gehrke, J., & Yiu, T. (2005, November). MAFIA: A maximal frequent itemset algorithm. *IEEE Transactions on Knowledge and Data Engineering*, *17*(11), 1490–1504. doi:10.1109/TKDE.2005.183

Burkhalter, B., & Smith, M. (2004). Inhabitants' uses and reactions to Usenet social accounting data. *Springer-Verlag*.

Cao Huu, Q. (2017). *Policy-based usage control for trustworthy data sharing in smart cities* (PhD Thesis). Telecom & Management Sud, Paris, France.

Carriero, A., Kapetanios, G., & Marcellino, M. (2011). Forecasting large datasets with Bayesian reduced rank multivariate models. *Journal of Applied Econometrics*, *26*(5), 735–761. doi:10.1002/jae.1150

Casali, A., Cicchetti, R., & Lakhal, L. (2003). Cube lattices: A framework for multidimensional data mining. *Proceedings of the 2003 Society for Industrial and Applied Methods (SIAM) International Conference on Data Mining*. Retrieved from https://epubs.siam.org/doi/pdf/10.1137/1.9781611972733.35

Casali, A., Nedjar, S., Cicchetti, R., & Lakhal, L. (2007). Convex Cube: Towards a Unified Structure for Multidimensional Databases. In R. Wagner, N. Revell, & G. Pernul (Eds.), Lecture Notes in Computer Science: Vol. 4653. *Database and Expert Systems Applications. DEXA 2007*. Berlin: Springer. doi:10.1007/978-3-540-74469-6_56

Casali, A., Nedjar, S., Cicchetti, R., & Lakhal, L. (2009). Closed cube lattices. *Annals of Information Systems*, *3*, 145–164.

Cavoukian, A. (2009). *Privacy by Design: A Primer*. Retrieved from www.privacybydesign.ca/content/uploads/2013/10/pbd-primer.pdf

Cell Ontology. (n.d.). Retrieved from https://bioportal.bioontology.org/ontologies/CL

Chakka, P., Everspaugh, A., & Patel, J. (2003). *Indexing Large Trajectory Datasets With SETI*. CIDR.

Chaudhuri, S., Dayal, U., & Narasayya, V. (2011). An overview of business intelligence technology. *Communications of the ACM*, *54*(8), 88–98. doi:10.1145/1978542.1978562

Cheatham, M., Cruz, I. F., Euzenat, J., & Pesquita, C. (2017). Special issue on ontology and linked data matching. *Semantic Web*, *8*(2), 183–184. doi:10.3233/SW-160251

Chekol, M. W., & Pirrò, G. (2016). Containment of Expressive SPARQL Navigational Queries. *International Semantic Web Conference*.

Chen, L., Liu, Q. L., Wang, L. Q., Zhao, J., & Wang, W. (2017). Data-driven Prediction on Performance Indicators in Process Industry: A Survey. *Acta Automatica Sinica*, *6*, 8.

Chen, D., Hu, Y., Wang, L., Zomaya, A. Y., & Li, X. (2017). H-PARAFAC: Hierarchical Parallel Factor Analysis of Multidimensional Big Data. *IEEE Transactions on Parallel and Distributed Systems*, *28*(4), 1091–1104. doi:10.1109/TPDS.2016.2613054

Chen, D., Li, X., Wang, L., Khan, S. U., Wang, J., Zeng, K., & Cai, C. (2015). Fast and Scalable Multi-Way Analysis of Massive Neural Data. *IEEE Transactions on Computers*, *64*(3), 707–719. doi:10.1109/TC.2013.2295806

Chen, H., Chiang, R. H., & Storey, V. C. (2012). Business intelligence and analytics: From big data to big impact. *Management Information Systems Quarterly*, *36*(4).

Chen, J. (2001). A predictive system for blast furnaces by integrating a neural network with qualitative analysis. *Engineering Applications of Artificial Intelligence*, *14*(1), 77–85. doi:10.1016/S0952-1976(00)00062-2

Chen, L., & Lian, X. (2012). *Query Processing over Uncertain Databases*. Morgan & Claypool Publishers.

Chen, S., Ooi, B., Tan, K., & Nascimento, M. (2008). *ST2B-tree: A Self-tunable Spatio-temporal B+-tree Index for Moving Objects*. SIGMOD. doi:10.1145/1376616.1376622

Choudhary, A. K., Harding, J. A., & Tiwari, M. K. (2009). Data mining in manufacturing: A review based on the kind of knowledge. *Journal of Intelligent Manufacturing*, *20*(5), 501–521. doi:10.100710845-008-0145-x

Choudhury, M. D., Hofman, J., Mason, W., & Watts, D. J. (2010). Inferring Relevant Social Networks from Interpersonal Communication. In *Proceedings of the 19th International Conference on World Wide Web* (pp. 301-310). Raleigh, NC: ACM. 10.1145/1772690.1772722

Chu, C.-t., Kim, S. K., Lin, Y.-a., Yu, Y., Bradski, G., Olukotun, K., & Ng, A. Y. (2007). Map-Reduce for Machine Learning on Multicore. In P. B. Schölkopf, J. C. Platt, & T. Hoffman (Eds.), Advances in Neural Information Processing Systems. MIT Press. Retrieved from http://papers.nips.cc/paper/3150-map-reduce-for-machine-learning-on-multicore.pdf

Chu, M. S., Guo, X. Z., Shen, F. M., Yagi, J. I., & Nogami, H. (2007). Numerical analysis of blast furnace performance under charging iron-bearing burdens with high reducibility. *Journal of Iron and Steel Research International*, *14*(2), 13–19. doi:10.1016/S1006-706X(07)60020-X

Chu, X., Ilyas, I. F., & Koutris, P. (2016). Distributed data deduplication. *Proceedings of the VLDB Endowment International Conference on Very Large Data Bases*, *9*(11), 864–875. doi:10.14778/2983200.2983203

Cicchetti, R., Lakhal, L., Nedjar, S., Novelli, N., & Casali, A. (2011). Summarizing datacubes: Semantic and syntactic approaches. In D. Taniar & L. Chen (Eds.), *Integrations of Data Warehousing, Data Mining and Database Technologies - Innovative Approaches* (pp. 19–39). Information Science Reference. doi:10.4018/978-1-60960-537-7.ch002

Cios, K. J., Swiniarski, R. W., Pedrycz, W., & Kurgan, L. A. (2007). Unsupervised learning: clustering. In Data Mining (pp. 257-288). Springer US. doi:10.1007/978-0-387-36795-8_9

Cleverdon, C. (1967). The Cranfield tests on index language devices. *Aslib Proceedings*, *19*(6), 173–192. doi:10.1108/eb050097

Coates, A., Baumstarck, P., Le, Q., & Ng, A. Y. (2009, October). Scalable learning for object detection with GPU hardware. In *Intelligent Robots and Systems, 2009. IROS 2009. IEEE/RSJ International Conference on* (pp. 4287-4293). IEEE. 10.1109/IROS.2009.5354084

Cohen, W. W., & Sarawagi, S. (2004, August). Exploiting dictionaries in named entity extraction: combining semi-markov extraction processes and data integration methods. In *Proceedings of the tenth ACM SIGKDD international conference on Knowledge discovery and data mining* (pp. 89-98). ACM. 10.1145/1014052.1014065

Collobert, R., & Weston, J. (2008, July). A unified architecture for natural language processing: Deep neural networks with multitask learning. In *Proceedings of the 25th international conference on Machine learning* (pp. 160-167). ACM. 10.1145/1390156.1390177

Collobert, R., Weston, J., Bottou, L., Karlen, M., Kavukcuoglu, K., & Kuksa, P. (2011). Natural language processing (almost) from scratch. *Journal of Machine Learning Research, 12*(Aug), 2493–2537.

Colom, R., Karama, S., Jung, R. E., & Haier, R. J. (2010). Human intelligence and brain networks. *Dialogues in Clinical Neuroscience, 12*(4), 489. PMID:21319494

Crawford, K., & Schultz, J. (2014). Big Data and Due Process: Toward a Framework to Redress Predictive Privacy Harms. *Boston College Law Review. Boston College. Law School, 55*(1), 93–128.

Cryer, J. D., & Chan, K. S. (2008). *Time series analysis: with applications in R*. Springer Science & Business Media. doi:10.1007/978-0-387-75959-3

CUMULUS. (n.d.). Retrieved from https://cumulus.parisdescartes.fr/

da Rocha, E. P., Guilherme, V. S., de Castro, J. A., Sazaki, Y., & Yagi, J. I. (2013). Analysis of synthetic natural gas injection into charcoal blast furnace. *Journal of Materials Research and Technology, 2*(3), 255–262. doi:10.1016/j.jmrt.2013.02.015

Dalianis, H., Hassel, M., De Smedt, K., Liseth, A., Lech, T. C., & Wedekind, J. (2004). Porting and evaluation of automatic summarization. In Nordisk Sprogteknologi (pp. 107-121). Academic Press.

Dalto, M., Matuško, J., & Vašak, M. (2015). Deep neural networks for ultra-short-term wind forecasting. In *Industrial Technology (ICIT), 2015 IEEE International Conference on* (pp. 1657–1663). IEEE. 10.1109/ICIT.2015.7125335

Danloy, G., Mignon, J., Munnix, R., Dauwels, G., & Bonte, L. (2001). Blast furnace model to optimize the burden distribution. In *Proceedings of the 60th Ironmaking Conference* (pp. 37-48). Academic Press.

DBPedia. (n.d.). Retrieved from http://wiki.dbpedia.org/

de Castro, J. A., de Mattos Araújo, G., da Mota, I. D. O., Sasaki, Y., & Yagi, J. I. (2013). Analysis of the combined injection of pulverized coal and charcoal into large blast furnaces. *Journal of Materials Research and Technology, 2*(4), 308–314. doi:10.1016/j.jmrt.2013.06.003

de Castro, J. A., Nogami, H., & Yagi, J. I. (2002). Three-dimensional multiphase mathematical modeling of the blast furnace based on the multifluid model. *ISIJ International*, *42*(1), 44–52. doi:10.2355/isijinternational.42.44

De Gooijer, J. G., & Hyndman, R. J. (2006). 25 years of time series forecasting. *International Journal of Forecasting*, *22*(3), 443–473. doi:10.1016/j.ijforecast.2006.01.001

Dean, J., Corrado, G., Monga, R., Chen, K., Devin, M., Mao, M., . . . Ng, A. Y. (2012). Large scale distributed deep networks. In Advances in neural information processing systems (pp. 1223-1231). Academic Press.

Dean, J., & Ghemawat, S. (2004). Mapreduce: Simplified data processing on large clusters. *Conference on Symposium on Operating Systems Design & Implementation.*

Devens, R. (1865). Cyclopædia of Commercial and Business Anecdotes, Volume 1. D. Appleton

Dhond, A., Gupta, A., & Vadhavkar, S. (2000). Data mining techniques for optimizing inventories for electronic commerce. In *Proceedings of the 6th ACM SIGKDD International Conference on Knowledge Discovery and Data Mining* (pp. 480-486). ACM. 10.1145/347090.347188

Diesner, J., Frantz, T. L., & Carley, K. M. (2005). Communication Networks from the Enron Email Corpus "It's Always About the People. Enron is no Different". *Computational & Mathematical Organization Theory*, *11*(3), 201–208. doi:10.100710588-005-5377-0

Ding, H., Trajcevski, G., & Scheuermann, P. (2008). Efficient Similarity Join of Large Sets of Moving Object Trajectories. *International Symposium on Temporal Representation and Reasoning*. 10.1109/TIME.2008.25

Dittrich, J., Blunschi, L., & Vaz Salles, M. A. (2009). Indexing Moving Objects Using Short-Lived Throwaway Indexes. *International Symposium on Advances in Spatial and Temporal Databases*. 10.1007/978-3-642-02982-0_14

Dittrich, J., Blunschi, L., & Vaz Salles, M. A. (2011). Movies: Indexing moving objects by shooting index images. *GeoInformatica*, *15*(4), 727–767. doi:10.100710707-011-0122-y

Domingos, P., & Pazzani, M. (1996). Beyond independence: Conditions for the optimality of the simple bayesian classifier. In *Proceedings of the 13th International Conference on Machine Learning* (pp. 105-112). Academic Press.

Domingos, P. (2012). A few useful things to know about machine learning. *Communications of the ACM*, *55*(10), 78–87. doi:10.1145/2347736.2347755

Dong, G., & Li, J. (1999). Efficient mining of emerging patterns: Discovering trends and differences. In Knowledge Discovery and Data Mining (pp. 43–52). Academic Press.

Dong, G., & Li, J. (2005). Mining border descriptions of emerging patterns from dataset pairs. *Knowledge and Information Systems*, *8*(2), 178–202. doi:10.100710115-004-0178-1

Dong, X. L., & Srivastava, D. (2015). *Big Data Integration. Synthesis Lectures on Data Management*. Morgan & Claypool Publishers.

Données publiques. (n.d.). Retrieved from https://donneespubliques.meteofrance.fr/

Dorigo, M., & Gambardella, L. M. (2016, January). Ant-Q: A reinforcement learning approach to the traveling salesman problem. *Proceedings of ML-95, Twelfth Intern. Conf. on Machine Learning*, 252-260.

Duan, Y., Lv, Y., & Wang, F.-Y. (2016). Travel time prediction with LSTM neural network. In *Intelligent Transportation Systems (ITSC), 2016 IEEE 19th International Conference on* (pp. 1053–1058). IEEE.

Duong, T., Beck, G., Azzag, H., & Lebbah, M. (2016). Nearest neighbour estimators of density derivatives, with application to mean shift clustering. *Pattern Recognition Letters*, *80*, 224–230. doi:10.1016/j.patrec.2016.06.021

Durbin, R., Eddy, S. R., Krogh, A., & Mitchison, G. (1998). *Biological sequence analysis: probabilistic models of proteins and nucleic acids*. Cambridge University Press. doi:10.1017/CBO9780511790492

Eagle, N., Pentland, A. & Lazer, D. (2009). Inferring friendship network structure by using mobile phone data. *Proceedings of the National Academy of Sciences*, 106, 15274-15278. 10.1073/pnas.0900282106

Efron, B., Hastie, T., Johnstone, I., & Tibshirani, R. (2004). Least angle regression. *Annals of Statistics*, *32*(2), 407–499. doi:10.1214/009053604000000067

Eiben, C. B., Siegel, J. B., Bale, J. B., Cooper, S., Khatib, F., Shen, B. W., ... Baker, D. (2012). Increased Diels-Alderase activity through backbone remodeling guided by Foldit players. *Nature Biotechnology*, *30*(2), 190–192. doi:10.1038/nbt.2109 PMID:22267011

Eickhoff, C. (2014). Crowd-Powered Experts: Helping Surgeons Interpret Breast Cancer Images. *ECIR Workshop on Gamification for Information Retrieval*. 10.1145/2594776.2594788

Elgamal, T., & Hefeeda, M. (2015). *Analysis of PCA Algorithms in Distributed Environments*. Retrieved from http://arxiv.org/abs/1503.05214

Elgamal, T., Yabandeh, M., Aboulnaga, A., Mustafa, W., & Hefeeda, M. (2015). sPCA: Scalable Principal Component Analysis for Big Data on Distributed Platforms. In *Proceedings of the 2015 ACM SIGMOD International Conference on Management of Data* (pp. 79–91). New York: ACM. 10.1145/2723372.2751520

Elwood, S., & Leszczynski, A. (2011). Privacy reconsidered: New representations, data practices, and the geoweb. *Geoforum*, *42*(1), 6–15. doi:10.1016/j.geoforum.2010.08.003

Emrich, T., Kriegel, H., Mamoulis, N., Renz, & Züfle, M. (2012a). Querying Uncertain Spatio-Temporal Data. *IEEE International Conference on Data Engineering*.

Emrich, T., Kriegel, H., Mamoulis, N., Renz, & Züfle, M. (2012b). Indexing Uncertain Spatio-Temporal Data. *CIKM.*

Engle, C., Lupher, A., Xin, R., Zaharia, M., Franklin, M. J., Shenker, S., & Stoica, I. (2012): Shark: fast data analysis using coarse-grained distributed memory. *SIGMOD Conference*, 689-692. 10.1145/2213836.2213934

Engle, R. F., & Yoo, B. S. (1987). Forecasting and testing in co-integrated systems. *Journal of Econometrics, 35*(1), 143–159. doi:10.1016/0304-4076(87)90085-6

European Data Protection Supervisor. (2014). *Privacy and competitiveness in the age of big data: The interplay between data protection, competition law and consumer protection in the Digital Economy.* Retrieved from secure.edps.europa.eu/EDPSWEB/webdav/shared/Documents/Consultation/Opinions/2014/14-03-26_competitition_law_big_data_EN.pdf

Evelson, B., & Norman, N. (2008). *Topic overview: Business intelligence.* Forrester Research.

Faleiro, R. M. R., Velloso, C. M., de Castro, L. F. A., & Sampaio, R. S. (2013). Statistical modeling of charcoal consumption of blast furnaces based on historical data. *Journal of Materials Research and Technology, 2*(4), 303–307. doi:10.1016/j.jmrt.2013.04.002

Fang, Y., Cao, J., Wang, J., Peng, Y., & Song, W. (2012). Htpr*-tree: An efficient index for moving objects to support predictive query and partial history query. *International Conference on Web-Age Information Management.* 10.1007/978-3-642-28635-3_3

Fan, J., Han, F., & Liu, H. (2014). Challenges of Big Data analysis. *National Science Review, 1*(2), 293–314. doi:10.1093/nsr/nwt032 PMID:25419469

Fe-Fei, L. (2003, October). A Bayesian approach to unsupervised one-shot learning of object categories. In *Computer Vision, 2003. Proceedings. Ninth IEEE International Conference on* (pp. 1134-1141). IEEE. 10.1109/ICCV.2003.1238476

Feng, X., Gan, L., & Yang, J. (2009). User-driven GIS Software Reuse Solution Based on SOA and Web 2.0 Concept. In *2nd International Conference on Computer Science and Information Technology* (pp. 5-9). Beijing: IEEE.

Firmani, D., Saha, B., & Srivastava, D. (2016). *Online Entity Resolution Using an Oracle.* PVLDB.

Foaf. (n.d.). Retrieved from http://www.foaf-project.org/

Forbes, S. A., Beare, D., Gunasekaran, P., Leung, K., Bindal, N., Boutselakis, H., ... Kok, C. Y. (2014). COSMIC: Exploring the world's knowledge of somatic mutations in human cancer. *Nucleic Acids Research, 43*(D1), D805–D811. doi:10.1093/nar/gku1075 PMID:25355519

Forman, G., & Cohen, I. (2004, September). Learning from little: Comparison of classifiers given little training. In *European Conference on Principles of Data Mining and Knowledge Discovery* (pp. 161-172). Springer. 10.1007/978-3-540-30116-5_17

Frandi, E., Ñanculef, R., Lodi, S., Sartori, C., & Suykens, J. A. K. (2016). Fast and scalable Lasso via stochastic Frank–Wolfe methods with a convergence guarantee. *Machine Learning*, *104*(2-3), 195–221. doi:10.100710994-016-5578-4

Freeman, L. C. (2004). The development of social network analysis: a study in the sociology of science. Vancouver, Canada Empirical Press.

Friedman, J., Hastie, T., & Tibshirani, R. (2001). The elements of statistical learning (Vol. 1). New York: Springer.

Fritz, M. H. Y., Leinonen, R., Cochrane, G., & Birney, E. (2011). Efficient storage of high throughput DNA sequencing data using reference-based compression. *Genome Research*, *21*(5), 734–740. doi:10.1101/gr.114819.110 PMID:21245279

Fukunaga, K., & Hostetler, L. (1975). The estimation of the gradient of a density function, with applications in pattern recognition. *IEEE Transactions on Information Theory*, *21*(1), 32–40. doi:10.1109/TIT.1975.1055330

Fung. (2010). *Introduction to privacy-preserving data publishing: concepts and techniques.* Chapman & Hall/CRC.

Fuster, G. G., & Scherrer, A. (2015). *Big Data and smart devices and their impact on privacy.* Committee on Civil Liberties, Justice and Home Affairs (LIBE), Directorate-General for Internal Policies, European Parliament. Retrieved from http://www.europarl.europa.eu/RegData/etudes/STUD/2015/536455/IPOL_STU(2015)5364 55_EN.pdf (last accessed 4 November 2015)

Gaber, M. M., Zaslavsky, A., & Krishnaswamy, S. (2005). Mining data streams: A review. *SIGMOD Record*, *34*(2), 18–26. doi:10.1145/1083784.1083789

Ganter, B., & Wille, R. (1999). *Formal Concept Analysis: Mathematical Foundations.* Berlin: Springer-Verlag Berlin Heidelberg. doi:10.1007/978-3-642-59830-2

Garcia Seco de Herrera, A., Foncubierta-Rodriguez, A., Markonis, D., Schaer, R., & Müller, H. (2014). Crowdsourcing for medical image classification. *Annual congress SGMI.*

García, S., Ramírez-Gallego, S., Luengo, J., Benítez, J. M., & Herrera, F. (2016). Big data preprocessing: Methods and prospects. *Big Data Analytics*, *1*(1), 9. doi:10.118641044-016-0014-0

Garland, M., & Kirk, D. (2010). Understanding Throughput-oriented Architectures. *Communications of the ACM*, *53*(11), 58–66. doi:10.1145/1839676.1839694

Gedik, B., & Liu, L. (2004). MobiEyes: Distributed Processing of Continuously Moving Queries on Moving Objects in a Mobile System. *EDBT*, 67–87.

Geerdes, M., Chaigneau, R., & Kurunov, I. (2015). *Modern Blast Furnace Ironmaking: An Introduction.* IOS Press.

Gelper, S., & Croux, C. (2008). *Least angle regression for time series forecasting with many predictors.* Retrieved from https://lirias.kuleuven.be/handle/123456789/164224

Geweke, J. (1977). The dynamic factor analysis of economic time series. *Latent variables in socio-economic models*.

Ge, Y., Xiong, H., Zhou, Z., Ozdemir, H., Yu, J., & Lee, K. (2010). Top-Eye: top-k evolving trajectory outlier detection. *International Conference on Information and Knowledge Management*.

Ghaderi, A., Sanandaji, B. M., & Ghaderi, F. (2017). *Deep Forecast: Deep Learning-based Spatio-Temporal Forecasting*. ArXiv Preprint ArXiv:1707.08110.

Ghahramani, Z. (2015). Probabilistic machine learning and artificial intelligence. *Nature*, *521*(7553), 452–459. doi:10.1038/nature14541 PMID:26017444

Ghoniem, M., Fekete, J. D., & Castagliola, P. (2004). A comparison of the readability of graphs using node-link and matrix-based representations. In *IEEE Symposium on Information Visualization* (pp. 17-24). IEEE. 10.1109/INFVIS.2004.1

Ghoniem, M., Fekete, J.-D., & Castagliola, P. (2005). On the readability of graphs using node-link and matrix-based representations: A controlled experiment and statistical analysis. *Information Visualization*, *4*(2), 114–135. doi:10.1057/palgrave.ivs.9500092

Ghose, A. (2017). *Tap: Unlocking the Mobile Economy*. Cambridge, MA: MIT Press.

Ghosh, A., & Majumdar, S. (2011). Modeling blast furnace productivity using support vector machines. *International Journal of Advanced Manufacturing Technology*, *52*(9), 989–1003. doi:10.100700170-010-2786-0

Giovanni, T. (2012). *OpenNebula 3 Cloud Computing*. Packt Publishing Limited.

Goodfellow, I., Pouget-Abadie, J., Mirza, M., Xu, B., Warde-Farley, D., Ozair, S., . . . Bengio, Y. (2014). Generative adversarial nets. In Advances in neural information processing systems (pp. 2672-2680). Academic Press.

Goodfellow, I., Bengio, Y., & Courville, A. (2016). *Deep learning*. MIT Press.

Gottfredson, L. S. (2004). Intelligence: Is it the epidemiologists' elusive" fundamental cause" of social class inequalities in health? *Journal of Personality and Social Psychology*, *86*(1), 174–199. doi:10.1037/0022-3514.86.1.174 PMID:14717635

Gouda, K., & Zaki, M. J. (2005). Genmax: An efficient algorithm for mining maximal frequent itemsets. *Data Mining and Knowledge Discovery*, *11*(3), 223–242. doi:10.100710618-005-0002-x

Gowanlock, M., Casanova, H. (2014). Distance Threshold Similarity Searches on Spatiotemporal Trajectories using GPGPU. *HiPC*.

Gowanlock, M., & Casanova, H. (2016). Distance threshold similarity searches: Efficient Trajectory Indexing on the GPU. *IEEE Transactions on Parallel and Distributed Systems*, *27*(9), 2533–2545. doi:10.1109/TPDS.2015.2500896

Granger, C. W. J. (1980). Testing for causality. *Journal of Economic Dynamics & Control*, *2*, 329–352. doi:10.1016/0165-1889(80)90069-X

Gray, J., Chaudhuri, S., Bosworth, A., Layman, A., Reichart, D., Venkatrao, M., ... Pirahesh, H. (1997). Data cube: A relational aggregation operator generalizing group-by, cross-tab, and sub totals. *Data Mining and Knowledge Discovery*, *1*(1), 29–53. doi:10.1023/A:1009726021843

Grid5000: Home. (2017). Retrieved from https://www.grid5000.fr/mediawiki/index.php/Grid5000:Home

Guo, X., Yin, Y., Dong, C., Yang, G., & Zhou, G. (2008, October). On the class imbalance problem. In *Natural Computation, 2008. ICNC'08. Fourth International Conference on* (Vol. 4, pp. 192-201). IEEE 10.1109/ICNC.2008.871

Güting, R., Behr, T., & Xu, J. (2010). Efficient K-nearest Neighbor Search on Moving Object Trajectories. *The VLDB Journal*, *19*(5), 687–714. doi:10.100700778-010-0185-7

Güting, R., & Schneider, M. (2005). *Moving Objects Databases*. Morgan Kaufmann Publishers.

Gu, Y., Lo, A., & Niemegeers, I. (2009). A survey of indoor positioning systems for wireless personal networks. *IEEE Communications Surveys and Tutorials*, *11*(1), 13–32. doi:10.1109/SURV.2009.090103

Halevy, A., Rajaraman, A., & Ordille, J. (2006, September). Data integration: the teenage years. In *Proceedings of the 32nd international conference on Very large data bases* (pp. 9-16). VLDB Endowment.

Hallac, D., Leskovec, J., & Boyd, S. (2015). Network Lasso: Clustering and Optimization in Large Graphs. *KDD: Proceedings / International Conference on Knowledge Discovery & Data Mining. International Conference on Knowledge Discovery & Data Mining*, *2015*, 387–396. doi:10.1145/2783258.2783313 PMID:27398260

Hall, M., Frank, E., Holmes, G., Pfahringer, B., Reutemann, P., & Witten, I. H. (2009). The WEKA data mining software: An update. *ACM SIGKDD Explorations Newsletter*, *11*(1), 10–18. doi:10.1145/1656274.1656278

Hamilton, J. D. (1994). *Time series analysis* (Vol. 2). Princeton, NJ: Princeton University Press.

Han, J., Pei, J., Dong, G., & Wang, K. (2001). *Efficient computation of iceberg cubes with complex measures. In Proceedings of Special Interest Group on Management of Data (SIGMOD)* (pp. 1–12). ACM.

Harding, J. A., Shahbaz, M., & Kusiak, A. (2006). Data mining in manufacturing: A review. *Journal of Manufacturing Science and Engineering*, *128*(4), 969–976. doi:10.1115/1.2194554

Harvey, A. C. (1990). *Forecasting, structural time series models and the Kalman filter*. Cambridge University Press. doi:10.1017/CBO9781107049994

Harvey, J. P., & Gheribi, A. E. (2014). Process simulation and control optimization of a blast furnace using classical thermodynamics combined to a direct search algorithm. *Metallurgical and Materials Transactions. B, Process Metallurgy and Materials Processing Science*, *45*(1), 307–327. doi:10.100711663-013-0004-9

Hastie, T., & Tibshirani, R. (1998). Classification by pairwise coupling. In Advances in Neural Information Processing Systems (pp. 507-513). Academic Press. doi:10.1214/aos/1028144844

Hastie, T., Tibshirani, R., & Friedman, J. (2009). Overview of supervised learning. In *The elements of statistical learning* (pp. 9–41). Springer New York. doi:10.1007/978-0-387-84858-7_2

Heaton, J. (2016). Comparing Dataset Characteristics that Favor the Apriori, Eclat or FP-Growth Frequent Itemset Mining Algorithms. *Proceeding of the IEEE SoutheastCon*, 1-7. 10.1109/SECON.2016.7506659

Hendawi, A., & Mokbel, M. (2012). Predictive Spatio-temporal Queries: A Comprehensive Survey and Future Directions. *ACM International Workshop on Mobile Geographic Information Systems*. 10.1145/2442810.2442828

He, Y., Tan, H., Luo, W., Feng, S., & Fan, J. (2014). Mr-dbscan: A scalable mapreduce-based dbscan algorithm for heavily skewed data. *Frontiers of Computer Science*, *8*(1), 83–99. doi:10.100711704-013-3158-3

Heyes, C. (2012). New thinking: The evolution of human cognition. *Philosophical Transactions of the Royal Society of London. Series B, Biological Sciences*, *367*(1599), 2091–2096. doi:10.1098/rstb.2012.0111 PMID:22734052

He, Z., Kraak, M., Huisman, O., Ma, X., & Xiao, J. (2013). Parallel indexing technique for spatio-temporal data. *ISPRS Journal of Photogrammetry and Remote Sensing*, *78*(0), 116–128. doi:10.1016/j.isprsjprs.2013.01.014

Hill, N., Hussein, I., Davis, K., Ma, E., Spivey, T., Ramey, A., ... Runstadler, J. (2017). Reassortment of Influenza A Viruses in Wild Birds in Alaska before H5 Clade 2.3.4.4 Outbreaks. *Emerging Infectious Diseases*, *23*(4), 654–657. doi:10.3201/eid2304.161668 PMID:28322698

Hinrich, J. L., Nielsen, S. F. V., Riis, N. A. B., Eriksen, C. T., Frøsig, J., Kristensen, M. D. F., … Mørup, M. (2016). *Scalable Group Level Probabilistic Sparse Factor Analysis*. Retrieved from http://arxiv.org/abs/1612.04555

Hinton, G. E., & Sejnowski, T. J. (Eds.). (1999). *Unsupervised learning: foundations of neural computation*. MIT Press.

Hirata, T., Kuremoto, T., Obayashi, M., Mabu, S., & Kobayashi, K. (2017). *Forecasting Real Time Series Data using Deep Belief Net and Reinforcement Learning*. Academic Press.

Hmamouche, Y., Casali, A., & Lakhal, L. (2017). A Causality based feature selection approach for multivariate time series forecasting. Paper presented at *The International Conference on Advances in Databases, Knowledge, and Data Applications*, Barcelona, Spain.

Hochreiter, S., & Schmidhuber, J. (1997). Long short-term memory. *Neural Computation*, *9*(8), 1735–1780. doi:10.1162/neco.1997.9.8.1735 PMID:9377276

Hoerl, A. E., & Kennard, R. W. (1970). Ridge Regression: Biased Estimation for Nonorthogonal Problems. *Technometrics*, *12*(1), 55–67. doi:10.1080/00401706.1970.10488634

Ho, T. K. (1998). The random subspace method for constructing decision forests. *IEEE Transactions on Pattern Analysis and Machine Intelligence*, *20*(8), 832–844. doi:10.1109/34.709601

Howe, B., Franklin, M. J., Haas, L. M., Kraska, T., & Ullman, J. D. (2017). *Data Science Education: We're Missing the Boat, Again.* ICDE.

Hsu, K. W., Pathak, N., Srivastava, J., Tschida, G., & Bjorklund, E. (2015). Data mining based tax audit selection: a case study of a pilot project at the minnesota department of revenue. *Real World Data Mining Applications*, 221-245.

Hsu, K. W., & Srivastava, J. (2012). Improving bagging performance through multi-algorithm ensembles. *Frontiers of Computer Science*, *6*(5), 498–512.

Hsu, T.-W., Inman, L., McColgin, D., & Stamper, K. (2004). MonkEllipse: Visualizing the History of Information Visualization. In *IEEE Symposium on Information Visualization* (pp. r9-r9). IEEE.

Hua, C., Wu, J., Li, J., & Guan, X. (2017). Silicon content prediction and industrial analysis on blast furnace using support vector regression combined with clustering algorithms. *Neural Computing & Applications*, *28*(12), 4111–4121.

Hyndman, R. J., Athanasopoulos, G., Razbash, S., Schmidt, D., Zhou, Z., Khan, Y., ... Wang, E. (2015). Forecast: Forecasting functions for time series and linear models. *R Package Version, 6*(6), 7.

Hyndman, R. J., & Khandakar, Y. (2007). *Automatic time series for forecasting: the forecast package for R (No. 6/07)*. Monash University, Department of Econometrics and Business Statistics.

Indyk, P., & Motwani, R. (1998). Approximate nearest neighbors: Towards removing the curse of dimensionality. *Annual ACM Symposium on Theory of Computing*. 10.1145/276698.276876

Irshad, H., Montaser-Kouhsari, L., Waltz, G., Bucur, O., Nowak, J. A., Dong, F., ... Beck, A. H. (2015). Crowdsourcing image annotation for nucleus detection and segmentation in computational pathology: Evaluating experts, automated methods, and the crowd. *Pacific Symposium on Biocomputing*, 294. PMID:25592590

Jackson, P. C. (1985). *Introduction to artificial intelligence*. Courier Corporation.

Jacox, E. H., & Samet, H. (2007). Spatial join techniques. *ACM Transactions on Database Systems*, *32*(1), 7, es. doi:10.1145/1206049.1206056

Jagadish, H. V., Gehrke, J., Labrinidis, A., Papakonstantinou, Y., Patel, J. M., Ramakrishnan, R., & Shahabi, C. (2014). Big data and its technical challenges. *Communications of the ACM*, *57*(7), 86–94. doi:10.1145/2611567

Japkowicz, N. (2000, July). Learning from imbalanced data sets: a comparison of various strategies. In AAAI workshop on learning from imbalanced data sets (Vol. 68, pp. 10-15). AAAI.

Jensen, C., Lin, D., & Ooi, B. (2004). *Query and Update Efficient B+-tree Based Indexing of Moving Objects*. VLDB. doi:10.1016/B978-012088469-8.50068-1

Jensen, C., Lu, H., & Yang, B. (2009). Indexing the Trajectories of Moving Objects in Symbolic Indoor Space. *International Symposium on Advances in Spatial and Temporal Databases*. 10.1007/978-3-642-02982-0_15

Jensen, C., & Pakalnis, S. (2007). *TRAX: Real-world Tracking of Moving Objects*. VLDB.

Jiang, B., Athanasopoulos, G., Hyndman, R. J., Panagiotelis, A., & Vahid, F. (2017). *Macroeconomic forecasting for Australia using a large number of predictors* (Monash Econometrics and Business Statistics Working Paper No. 2/17). Monash University, Department of Econometrics and Business Statistics. Retrieved from https://ideas.repec.org/p/msh/ebswps/2017-2.html

Jian, L., Shen, S., & Song, Y. (2012). Improving the solution of least squares support vector machines with application to a blast furnace system. *Journal of Applied Mathematics*.

Jindal, A., Pujari, S., Sandilya, P., & Ganguly, S. (2007). A reduced order thermo-chemical model for blast furnace for real time simulation. *Computers & Chemical Engineering*, *31*(11), 1484–1495. doi:10.1016/j.compchemeng.2006.12.015

Johansen, S. (1991). Estimation and Hypothesis Testing of Cointegration Vectors in Gaussian Vector Autoregressive Models. *Econometrica*, *59*(6), 1551–1580. doi:10.2307/2938278

Jones, K. S. (1972). A statistical interpretation of term specificity and its application in retrieval. *The Journal of Documentation*, *28*(1), 11–21. doi:10.1108/eb026526

Jošth, R., Antikainen, J., Havel, J., Herout, A., Zemčík, P., & Hauta-Kasari, M. (2012). Real-time PCA calculation for spectral imaging (using SIMD and GP-GPU). *Journal of Real-Time Image Processing*, *7*(2), 95–103. doi:10.100711554-010-0190-5

Jr, R. J. B. (1998). Efficiently mining long patterns from databases. In L. M. Haas & A. Tiwary (Eds.), *Proceedings of Special Interest Group on Management of Data (SIGMOD) Conference* (pp. 85–93). ACM Press.

Judd, K., & Mees, A. (1995). On selecting models for nonlinear time series. *Physica D. Nonlinear Phenomena*, *82*(4), 426–444. doi:10.1016/0167-2789(95)00050-E

Kaastra, I., & Boyd, M. (1996). Designing a neural network for forecasting financial and economic time series. *Neurocomputing*, *10*(3), 215–236. doi:10.1016/0925-2312(95)00039-9

Kaelbling, L. P., Littman, M. L., & Moore, A. W. (1996). Reinforcement learning: A survey. *Journal of Artificial Intelligence Research*, *4*, 237–285.

Kandefer, M., & Shapiro, S. (2009). An F-Measure for Context-based Information Retrieval. *9th International Symposium on Logical Formalizations of Commonsense Reasoning*, 79-84.

Kantz, H., & Schreiber, T. (2004). *Nonlinear time series analysis* (Vol. 7). Cambridge university press.

Keerthi, S. S., Shevade, S. K., Bhattacharyya, C., & Murthy, K. R. K. (2001). Improvements to Platt's SMO algorithm for SVM classifier design. *Neural Computation*, *13*(3), 637–649. doi:10.1162/089976601300014493

Kelly, S. U., Sung, C., & Farnham, S. (2002). Designing for Improved Social Responsibility, User Participation and Content in On-Line Communities. *Proceedings of CHI*. 10.1145/503376.503446

Kendall, M. G., & Ord, J. K. (1990). *Time-series* (Vol. 296). London: Edward Arnold.

Khalilian, M., & Mustapha, N. (2010). *Data stream clustering: Challenges and issues*. arXiv preprint arXiv:1006.5261

Kirchgässner, G., & Wolters, J. (2007). *Introduction to modern time series analysis*. Springer Science & Business Media. doi:10.1007/978-3-540-73291-4

Kitchin, R. (2015). Data-driven, networked urbanism. *Programmable City Working Paper 14*. Retrieved from http://ssrn.com/abstract=2641802

Kitchin, R. (2014a). The real-time city? Big data and smart urbanism. *GeoJournal*, *79*(1), 1–14. doi:10.100710708-013-9516-8

Kitchin, R. (2014b). *The Data Revolution: Big Data, Open Data, Data Infrastructures and Their Consequences*. London: Sage.

Kittur, A., Chi, E. H., & Suh, B. (2008). Crowdsourcing user studies with mechanical turk. SIGCHI conference on human factors in computing systems, Florence, Italy. doi:10.1145/1357054.1357127

Köksal, G., Batmaz, İ., & Testik, M. C. (2011). A review of data mining applications for quality improvement in manufacturing industry. *Expert Systems with Applications*, *38*(10), 13448–13467. doi:10.1016/j.eswa.2011.04.063

Kommenda, M., Kronberger, G., Feilmayr, C., & Affenzeller, M. (2011). Data mining using unguided symbolic regression on a blast furnace dataset. In *Proceedings of European Conference on the Applications of Evolutionary Computation* (pp. 274-283). Springer. 10.1007/978-3-642-20525-5_28

Koprinska, I., Rana, M., & Agelidis, V. G. (2015). Correlation and instance based feature selection for electricity load forecasting. *Knowledge-Based Systems*, *82*, 29–40. doi:10.1016/j.knosys.2015.02.017

Korobilis, D. (2013). Hierarchical shrinkage priors for dynamic regressions with many predictors. *International Journal of Forecasting*, *29*(1), 43–59. doi:10.1016/j.ijforecast.2012.05.006

Krautheim, F. J. (2009). Private Virtual Infrastructure for Cloud Computing. *Proceedings of the 2009 conference on Hot topics in cloud computing HotCloud'09*, Article No. 5.

Krikorian, D., & Kiyomiya, T. (2002). Bona fide groups as self-organizing systems: Applications to electronic newsgroups groups, Group communication in context: Studies of bona fide. *Lawrence Erlbaum*.

Krikorian, D., & Ludwig, G. (2002). Groupscope: Data mining tools for online communication networks. *22nd Annual Sunbelt Social Network Conference.*

Krikorian, D., & Ludwig, G. (2003). Advances in network analysis: Over-time visualization, dual-mode relations, and clique detection methods. *23rd Annual Sunbelt Social Network Conference.*

Kumar, A., Dyer, S., Kim, J., Li, C., Leong, P. H. W., Fulham, M. J., & Feng, D. (2016). Adapting content-based image retrieval techniques for the semantic annotation of medical images. *Computerized Medical Imaging and Graphics*, *49*, 37–45. doi:10.1016/j.compmedimag.2016.01.001 PMID:26890880

Kuzin, V., Marcellino, M., & Schumacher, C. (2013). Pooling Versus Model Selection for Nowcasting Gdp with Many Predictors: Empirical Evidence for Six Industrialized Countries. *Journal of Applied Econometrics*, *28*(3), 392–411. doi:10.1002/jae.2279

Kyung-Hoon, H., Haejun, L., & Duckjoo, C. (2012). *Medical Image Retrieval: Past and Present.* Healthc Inform Research.

Lakshmanan, L. V. S., Pei, J., & Han, J. (2002). Quotient cube: How to summarize the semantics of a data cube. *Proceedings of VLDB '02 the 28th international conference on Very Large Data Bases,* 778-789.

Leal, E., Gruenwald, L., Zhang, J., & You, S. (2015). TKSimGPU: A Parallel Top-K Trajectory Similarity Query Processing Algorithm for GPGPUs. *IEEE International Conference on Big Data*. 10.1109/BigData.2015.7363787

LeCun, Y., & Bengio, Y. (1995). Convolutional networks for images, speech, and time series. The handbook of brain theory and neural networks, 3361(10), 1995

LeCun, Y., Bengio, Y., & Hinton, G. (2015). Deep learning. *Nature*, *521*(7553), 436–444. doi:10.1038/nature14539 PMID:26017442

LeCun, Y., Bottou, L., Bengio, Y., & Haffner, P. (1998). Gradient-based learning applied to document recognition. *Proceedings of the IEEE*, *86*(11), 2278–2324. doi:10.1109/5.726791

Lee, J., Han, J., & Whang, K. (2007). Trajectory Clustering: A Partition-and Group Framework. *SIGMOD Conference.*

Lee, V., Kim, C., Chhugani, J., Deisher, M., Kim, D., Nguyen, A., ... Dubey, P. (2010). Debunking the 100x gpu vs. cpu myth: An evaluation of throughput computing on cpu and gpu. *SIGARCH Computer Architecture News*, *38*(3), 451–460. doi:10.1145/1816038.1816021

Leifman, G., Swedish, T., Roesch, K., & Raskar, R. (2015). *Leveraging the Crowd for Annotation of Retinal Images*. EMBC. doi:10.1109/EMBC.2015.7320185

Lessl, M., Bryans, J. S., Richards, D., & Asadullah, K. (2011). Crowd sourcing in drug discovery. *Nature Reviews. Drug Discovery*, *10*(4), 241–242. doi:10.1038/nrd3412 PMID:21455221

Li, J., & Chen, W. (2014). Forecasting macroeconomic time series: LASSO-based approaches and their forecast combinations with dynamic factor models. *International Journal of Forecasting, 30*(4), 996–1015. doi:10.1016/j.ijforecast.2014.03.016

Lin, Z., Yue, Y., Zhao, H., & Li, H. (2009). Judging the states of blast furnace by ART2 neural network. In *Proceedings of the 6th Sixth International Symposium on Neural Networks* (pp. 857-864). Springer Berlin/Heidelberg. 10.1007/978-3-642-01216-7_91

Liu, L. M., Wang, A. N., Mo, S. H. A., & Zhao, F. Y. (2011). Multi-class classification methods of cost-conscious LS-SVM for fault diagnosis of blast furnace. *Journal of Iron and Steel Research International, 18*(10), 1733–23. doi:10.1016/S1006-706X(12)60016-8

Li, W., Mahadevan, V., & Vasconcelos, N. (2014). Anomaly detection and localization in crowded scenes. *IEEE Transactions on Pattern Analysis and Machine Intelligence, 36*(1), 18–32. doi:10.1109/TPAMI.2013.111 PMID:24231863

Li, Z., Ji, M., Lee, J., Tang, L., Yu, Y., Han, J., & Kays, R. (2010). *MoveMine: Mining Moving Object Databases*. SIGMOD. doi:10.1145/1807167.1807319

Lloyd, S. P. (1982). Least squares quantization in PCM. *IEEE Transactions on Information Theory, 28*(2), 129–137. doi:10.1109/TIT.1982.1056489

Lopez, M. M., & Kalita, J. (2017). *Deep Learning applied to NLP*. arXiv preprint arXiv:1703.03091

Lopez-Paz, D., Sra, S., Smola, A., Ghahramani, Z., & Schölkopf, B. (2014). *Randomized Nonlinear Component Analysis*. Retrieved from http://arxiv.org/abs/1402.0119

Louppe, G. (2014). *Understanding random forests: From theory to practice*. arXiv preprint arXiv:1407.7502

Luhn, H. P. (1958). A business intelligence system. *IBM Journal of Research and Development, 2*(4), 314–319. doi:10.1147/rd.24.0314

Luo, J., Wu, M., Gopukumar, D., & Zhao, Y. (2016). Big Data Application in Biomedical Research and Health Care: A Literature Review. *Biomedical Informatics Insights, 8*, BII.S31559. doi:10.4137/BII.S31559 PMID:26843812

Luo, S. H., Liu, X. G., & Zhao, M. (2005). Prediction for silicon content in molten iron using a combined fuzzy-associative-rules bank. In *Proceedings of International Conference on Fuzzy Systems and Knowledge Discovery* (pp. 667-676). Springer. 10.1007/11540007_82

Lyon, D. (2014). Surveillance, Snowden, and Big Data: Capacities, consequences, critique. *Big Data and Society, 1*(2), 1–13. doi:10.1177/2053951714541861

Ma, C., & Lu, H. (2013). KSQ: Top-K Similarity Query on Uncertain Trajectories. *IEEE Transactions on Knowledge and Data Engineering*.

Manning, C. D., & Schütze, H. (1999). *Foundations of statistical natural language processing*. MIT Press.

Mao, M., Peng, Y., & Spring, M. (2010). *An adaptive ontology mapping approach with neural network based constraint satisfaction*. J. Web Sem.

Ma, Q., Yang, B., Qian, W., & Zhou, A. (2009). Query Processing of Massive Trajectory Data Based on MapReduce. *International Workshop on Cloud Data Management*. 10.1145/1651263.1651266

Mavandadi, S., Dimitrov, S., Feng, S., Yu, F., Sikora, U., Yaglidere, O., ... Ozcan, A. (2012). Distributed Medical Image Analysis and Diagnosis through Crowd-Sourced Games: A Malaria Case Study. *PLoS One*, *7*(5), e37245. doi:10.1371/journal.pone.0037245 PMID:22606353

Mayhew, A. (2001). File Distribution Efficiencies: cfengine Versus rsync. *Proceedings of the 15th Conference on Systems Administration LISA*, 273-276.

McCallum, A., & Jensen, D. (2003). A note on the unification of information extraction and data mining using conditional-probability, relational models. *Computer Science Department Faculty Publication Series*, 42.

McIntire, J., Osesina, O. I., & Craft, M. (2011). Development of Visualizations for Social Network Analysis of Chatroom Text. *International Symposium on Collaborative Technologies and Systems*. 10.1109/CTS.2011.5928741

McKinney, W., Perktold, J., & Seabold, S. (2011). Time series analysis in Python with statsmodels. *Jarrodmillman. Com*, 96-102.

Meng, X., Bradley, J., Yavuz, B., Sparks, E., Venkataraman, S., Liu, D., ... Xin, D. (2016). Mllib: Machine learning in apache spark. *Journal of Machine Learning Research*, *17*(1), 1235–1241.

Michalewicz, Z., Schmidt, M., Michalewicz, M., & Chiriac, C. (2006). *Adaptive business intelligence*. Springer Science & Business Media.

Mokbel, M., Ghanem, T., & Aref, W. (2003). Spatio-temporal access methods. *A Quarterly Bulletin of the Computer Society of the IEEE Technical Committee on Data Engineering*, *26*(2), 40–49.

Morfonios, K., & Ioannidis, Y. E. (2006). Cure for cubes: Cubing using a rolap engine. In *Proceedings of 32nd International Conference on Very Large Data Bases* (pp. 379–390). ACM Digital Library.

Morfonios, K., Konakas, S., Ioannidis, Y. E., & Kotsis, N. (2007). Rolap implementations of the data cube. *ACM Computing Surveys*, *39*(4), 12, es. doi:10.1145/1287620.1287623

Moses, C. (2007). *New Visualization Technology to Enhance Situational Awareness for System Operators*. Tampa, FL: IEEE. doi:10.1109/PES.2007.386010

Müller, H., Michoux, N., Bandon, D., & Geissbuhler, A. (2004). A review of content-based image retrieval systems in medical applications. Clinical benefits and future directions. *International Journal of Medical Informatics*, *73*(1), 1–23. doi:10.1016/j.ijmedinf.2003.11.024 PMID:15036075

Murphy, K. P. (2012). *Machine Learning: A Probabilistic Perspective*. Cambridge, MA: The MIT Press.

Murphy, M. H. (2015). The introduction of smart meters in Ireland: Privacy implications and the role of privacy by design. *Dublin University Law Journal, 38*(1).

Mushtaq, R. (2011). *Augmented Dickey Fuller Test (SSRN Scholarly Paper No. ID 1911068)*. Rochester, NY: Social Science Research Network. Retrieved from https://papers.ssrn.com/abstract=1911068

Mutton, P. (2004). Inferring and Visualizing Social Networks on Internet Relay Chat. In *Proceedings of the Information Visualisation, Eighth International Conference* (pp. 35-43). IEEE Computer Society. 10.1109/IV.2004.1320122

Namiot, D. (2015). On big data stream processing. *International Journal of Open Information Technologies, 3*(8), 48–51.

Nanni, L., Fantozzi, C., & Lazzarini, N. (2015). Coupling different methods for overcoming the class imbalance problem. *Neurocomputing, 158*, 48–61. doi:10.1016/j.neucom.2015.01.068

Nasr, G. E., & Badr, C. (2003). Buc algorithm for iceberg cubes: Implementation and sensitivity analysis. In I. Russell, & S. M. Haller (Eds.), *FLAIRS Conference* (pp. 255–260). AAAI Press.

National Cancer Institute Thesaurus. (n.d.). Retrieved from https://bioportal.bioontology.org/ontologies/NCIT

Nedjar, S., Casali, A., Cicchetti, R., & Lakhal, L. (2009). Emerging cubes: Borders, size estimations and lossless reductions. *Information Systems, 34*(6), 536–550. doi:10.1016/j.is.2009.03.001

Nedjar, S., Casali, A., Cicchetti, R., & Lakhal, L. (2010). Reduced representations of emerging cubes for olap database mining. *International Journal of Business Intelligence and Data Mining, 4*(3-4), 267–300.

Nedjar, S., Cicchetti, R., & Lakhal, L. (2011). Extracting semantics in olap databases using emerging cubes. *Information Sciences, 181*(10), 2036–2059. doi:10.1016/j.ins.2010.12.022

Nedjar, S., Lakhal, L., & Cicchetti, R. (2013). Emerging data cube representations for olap database mining. In G. Dong & J. Bailey (Eds.), *Contrast Data Mining* (pp. 109–128). CRC Press.

Nentwig, M., Hartung, M., Ngomo, A. N., & Rahm, E. (2017). A survey of current Link Discovery frameworks. *Semantic Web.*

Neumann, P., Tat, A., Zuk, T., & Carpendale, S. (2007). KeyStrokes: Personalizing Typed Text with Visualization. In K. Museth, T. Möller, & A. Ynnerman (Eds.), *Eurographics/ IEEE-VGTC Symposium on Visualization* (pp. 43–50). Academic Press.

Neumann, P., Tat, A., Zuk, T., & Carpendale, S. (2006). Personalizing Typed Text Through Visualization. In *Proc. Compendium of InfoVis* (pp. 138–139). Los Alamitos, CA: IEEE Computer Society.

Nguyen-Dinh, L., Aref, W., & Mokbel, M. (2010). Spatio-Temporal Access Methods: Part 2 (2003 - 2010). *A Quarterly Bulletin of the Computer Society of the IEEE Technical Committee on Data Engineering*, *33*(2), 46–55.

Nguyen, T. B., Wang, S., Anugu, V., Rose, N., McKenna, M., Petrick, N., ... Summers, R. M. (2012). Distributed human intelligence for colonic polyp classification in computer-aided detection for CT colonography. *Radiology*, *262*(3), 824–833. doi:10.1148/radiol.11110938 PMID:22274839

Ni, J., & Ravishankar, C. (2005). PA-tree: A Parametric Indexing Scheme for Spatio-temporal Trajectories. *International Conference on Advances in Spatial and Temporal Databases*, 254–272. 10.1007/11535331_15

Nogami, H., Chu, M., & Yagi, J. I. (2006). Numerical analysis on blast furnace performance with novel feed material by multi-dimensional simulator based on multi-fluid theory. *Applied Mathematical Modelling*, *30*(11), 1212–1228. doi:10.1016/j.apm.2006.03.013

Okoe, M., Jianu, R., & Kobourov, S. (2017). Revisited Network Representations. *25th Symposium on Graph Drawing (GD)*.

Oniśko, A., Druzdzel, M. J., & Wasyluk, H. (2001). Learning Bayesian network parameters from small data sets: Application of Noisy-OR gates. *International Journal of Approximate Reasoning*, *27*(2), 165–182. doi:10.1016/S0888-613X(01)00039-1

Osesina, O. I., Bartley, C., & Tudoreanu, M. E. (2010). Mapping realities: The co-visualization of geographic and non-spatial textual information. *International Conference on Modeling, Simulation, and Visualization Methods*, 10-16.

Pagel, M. (2017). Q&A: What is human language, when did it evolve and why should we care? *BMC Biology*, *15*(1), 64. doi:10.118612915-017-0405-3 PMID:28738867

Papegnies, E., Labatut, V., Dufour, R., & Linares, G. (2017). *Graph-based Features for Automatic Online Abuse Detection*. Le Mans: Statistical Language and Speech Processing. doi:10.1007/978-3-319-68456-7_6

Pavlo, A., Paulson, E., Rasin, A., Abadi, D., DeWitt, D., Madden, S., & Stonebraker, M. (2009). *A comparison of approaches to large-scale data analysis. In Special Interest Group on Management of Data (SIGMOD)* (pp. 165–178). ACM.

Peacey, J. G., & Davenport, W. G. (2016). *The iron blast furnace: theory and practice*. Elsevier.

Pearl, J. (2003). Causality: Models, reasoning, and inference. *Econometric Theory*, *19*(675-685), 46

Pearl, J. (2018). *Theoretical Impediments to Machine Learning With Seven Sparks from the Causal Revolution*. arXiv preprint arXiv:1801.04016

Pei, K., Cao, Y., Yang, J., & Jana, S. (2017). *Towards Practical Verification of Machine Learning: The Case of Computer Vision Systems*. arXiv preprint arXiv:1712.01785

Pei, J., Han, J., & Lakshmanan, L. V. S. (2004). Pushing convertible constraints in frequent itemset mining. *Data Mining and Knowledge Discovery*, *8*(3), 227–252. doi:10.1023/B:DAMI.0000023674.74932.4c

Pelanis, M., Šaltenis, S., & Jensen, C. (2006). Indexing the past, present, and anticipated future positions of moving objects. *ACM Transactions on Database Systems*, *31*(1), 255–298. doi:10.1145/1132863.1132870

Pena, D. (2009). Dimension reduction in time series and the dynamic factor model. *Biometrika*, *96*(2), 494–496. doi:10.1093/biomet/asp009

Perzyk, M., Biernacki, R., & Kochański, A. (2005). Modeling of manufacturing processes by learning systems: The naïve Bayesian classifier versus artificial neural networks. *Journal of Materials Processing Technology*, *164*, 1430–1435. doi:10.1016/j.jmatprotec.2005.02.043

Peters, S. (2015). Smart Cities' 4 Biggest Security Challenges. *InformationWeek: Dark Reading*. Retrieved from http://www.darkreading.com/vulnerabilities---threats/smart-cities-4-biggest-security-challenges/d/d-id/1321121

Pettersson, F., Chakraborti, N., & Saxén, H. (2007). A genetic algorithms based multi-objective neural net applied to noisy blast furnace data. *Applied Soft Computing*, *7*(1), 387–397. doi:10.1016/j.asoc.2005.09.001

Pew Research Center. (2016). *How Americans get their news*. Retrieved May 15, 2017, from http://www.journalism.org/2016/07/07/pathways-to-news/

Platt, J. C. (1999). Fast training of support vector machines using sequential minimal optimization. In B. Schölkopf, C. J. C. Burges, & A. J. Smola (Eds.), *Advances in kernel methods: support vector learning* (pp. 185–208). Cambridge, MA: MIT Press.

Przymus, P., Hmamouche, Y., Casali, A., & Lakhal, L. (2017). Improving multivariate time series forecasting with random walks with restarts on causality graphs. In *2017 IEEE International Conference on Data Mining Workshops (ICDMW)* (pp. 924–931). IEEE.

Purchase, H. C., Carrington, D., & Allder, J.-A. (2002). Empirical evaluation of aesthetics-based graph layout. *Journal of Empirical Software Engineering*, *7*(3), 233–255. doi:10.1023/A:1016344215610

Qi, H., & Snyder, W. E. (1999). Content-based image retrieval in picture archiving and communications systems. *Journal of Digital Imaging*, *12*(S1), 81–83. doi:10.1007/BF03168763 PMID:10342174

Quinlan, J. R. (1993). *C4.5: programs for machine learning*. San Mateo, CA: Morgan Kaufmann Publishers.

Raddick, M. J., Bracey, G., Gay, L. G., Lintott, C. J., Cardamone, C., Murray, P., Schawinski, K., Szalay, A. S., & Vandenberq, J. (2013). *Galaxy Zoo: Motivations of Citizen Scientists*. Academic Press.

Radford, A., Metz, L., & Chintala, S. (2015). *Unsupervised representation learning with deep convolutional generative adversarial networks.* arXiv preprint arXiv:1511.06434

Radhakrishnan, V. R., & Mohamed, A. R. (2000). Neural networks for the identification and control of blast furnace hot metal quality. *Journal of Process Control*, *10*(6), 509–524. doi:10.1016/S0959-1524(99)00052-9

Radiology Lexicon. (n.d.). Retrieved from https://bioportal.bioontology.org/ontologies/RADLEX

Raghunathan, B. (2013). *The Complete Book of Data Anonymization: From Planning to Implementation.* CRC Press.

Raghupathi, W., & Raghupathi, V. (2014). *Big data analytics in healthcare: promise and potential.* Health Information Science and Systems.

Rahulgargiit. (2016). *Acceleration of Full-Brain Autoregressive Modelling using GPUs.* Retrieved June 28, 2017, from https://eklavyaweb.wordpress.com/2016/05/15/acceleration-of-full-brain-autoregressive-modelling-using-gpus/

Raina, R., Madhavan, A., & Ng, A. Y. (2009, June). Large-scale deep unsupervised learning using graphics processors. In *Proceedings of the 26th annual international conference on machine learning* (pp. 873-880). ACM. 10.1145/1553374.1553486

Ranu, S., Deepak, P., Telang, A., Deshpande, P., & Raghavan, S. (2015). Indexing and Matching Trajectories under Inconsistent Sampling Rates. *IEEE International Conference on Data Engineering*. 10.1109/ICDE.2015.7113351

Rehab, M. A., & Boufares, F. (2015). *Scalable Massively Parallel Learning of Multiple Linear Regression Algorithm with MapReduce. In 2015 IEEE Trustcom/BigDataSE* (Vol. 2, pp. 41–47). ISPA; doi:10.1109/Trustcom.2015.560

Ren, Y., Xiao, Z., & Zhang, X. (2013). Two-step adaptive model selection for vector autoregressive processes. *Journal of Multivariate Analysis*, *116*, 349–364. doi:10.1016/j.jmva.2013.01.004

Rohall, S. L., Gruen, D., Moody, P., & Kellerman, S. (2001). Email visualizations to aid communications. *Proceedings of the IEEE Symposium on Information Visualization.*

Rosen, D., Woelfel, J., Krikorian, D., & Barnett, G. A. (2003). Procedures for Analyses of Online Communities. *Journal of Computer-Mediated Communication*, *8*(4).

RosettaHub. (n.d.). Retrieved from http://www.rosettahub.com

Ross, K. A., & Srivastava, D. (1997). Fast computation of sparse datacubes. *Proceedings of the 23rd International Conference on Very Large Data Bases*, 116–125.

Russell, S., & Norvig, P. (1995). *Artificial Intelligence: A modern approach.* Englewood Cliffs, NJ: Prentice-Hall.

Sabherwal, R. (2007). Succeeding with business intelligence: Some insights and recommendations. *Cutter Benchmark Review*, *7*(9), 5–15.

Sack, W. (2000). Discourse Diagrams: Interface Design for Very Large Scale Conversations. *Proceedings of HICSS*. 10.1109/HICSS.2000.926717

Sallam, R. L., Richardson, J., Hagerty, J., & Hostmann, B. (2011). *Magic quadrant for business intelligence platforms*. Stamford, CT: Gartner Group.

Šaltenis, S., Jensen, C., Leutenegger, S., & Lopez, M. (2000). *Indexing the Positions of Continuously Moving Objects*. SIGMOD. doi:10.1145/342009.335427

Samarati, P., & Sweeney, L. (1998). Generalizing data to provide anonymity when disclosing information (abstract). In *Proceedings of the seventeenth ACM SIGACT-SIGMOD-SIGART symposium on Principles of database systems (PODS '98)*. ACM. 10.1145/275487.275508

Samet, H. (1984). The quadtree and related hierarchical data structures. *ACM Computing Surveys*, *16*(2), 187–260. doi:10.1145/356924.356930

Samovskiy, D. (2010). *The Rise of DevOps*. Retrieved from http://www.somic.org/2010/03/02/the-rise-of-devops/

Sankaranarayanan, J., Samet, H., Teitler, B. E., Lieberman, M. D., & Sperling, J. (2009). TwitterStand: News in Tweets. In *Proceedings of the 17th ACM SIGSPATIAL International Conference on Advances in Geographic Information Systems*. Seattle, WA: ACM.

Santucci, G. (2013). Privacy in the Digital Economy: Requiem or Renaissance? *Privacy Surgeon*. Retrieved from www.privacysurgeon.org/blog/wp-content/uploads/2013/09/Privacy-in-the-Digital-Economy-final.pdf

Sarawagi, S., & Bhamidipaty, A. (2002, July). Interactive deduplication using active learning. In *Proceedings of the eighth ACM SIGKDD international conference on Knowledge discovery and data mining* (pp. 269-278). ACM. 10.1145/775047.775087

Saxén, H., Gao, C., & Gao, Z. (2013). Data-driven time discrete models for dynamic prediction of the hot metal silicon content in the blast furnace—A review. *IEEE Transactions on Industrial Informatics*, *9*(4), 2213–2225. doi:10.1109/TII.2012.2226897

Saxén, H., & Pettersson, F. (2007). Nonlinear prediction of the hot metal silicon content in the blast furnace. *ISIJ International*, *47*(12), 1732–1737. doi:10.2355/isijinternational.47.1732

Schölkopf, B., & Smola, A. J. (2002). *Learning with kernels: support vector machines, regularization, optimization, and beyond*. MIT Press.

Scott, S. L. (2017). bsts: Bayesian Structural Time Series. *R package version 0.6. 2*.

Sebastiani, F. (2002). Machine learning in automated text categorization. *ACM Computing Surveys*, *34*(1), 1–47. doi:10.1145/505282.505283

Serrano, E., Blas, F.J.G., Carretero, J., & Desco, M. (2017). Medical Imaging Processing on a Big Data platform using Python: Experiences with Heterogeneous and Homogeneous Architectures. *IEEE/ACM CCGRID*, 830-837.

Shanahan, J. G., & Dai, L. (2015). Large scale distributed data science using apache spark. In *Proceedings of the 21th ACM SIGKDD International Conference on Knowledge Discovery and Data Mining* (pp. 2323-2324). ACM. 10.1145/2783258.2789993

Shen, F., Chao, J., & Zhao, J. (2015). Forecasting exchange rate using deep belief networks and conjugate gradient method. *Neurocomputing*, *167*, 243–253. doi:10.1016/j.neucom.2015.04.071

Shen, Y., Guo, B., Chew, S., Austin, P., & Yu, A. (2015). Three-dimensional modeling of flow and thermochemical behavior in a blast furnace. *Metallurgical and Materials Transactions*, *46*(1), 432–448. doi:10.100711663-014-0204-y

Sherer, J. A., Le, J., & Taal, A. (2015, July). Big Data Discovery, Privacy, and the Application of Differential Privacy Mechanisms. *Comput. Internet Lawyer*, *32*(7), 10–16.

Shindler, M., Wong, A., & Meyerson, A. W. (2011). Fast and accurate k-means for large datasets. In Advances in neural information processing systems (pp. 2375-2383). Academic Press.

Shin, H., Xu, Z., & Kim, E.-Y. (2008). *Discovering and Browsing of Power Users by Social Relationship Analysis in Large-Scale Online Communities. In Web Intelligence and Intelligent Agent Technology*. IEEE.

Shmueli, G. (2010). To Explain or to Predict? *Statistical Science*, *25*(3), 289–310. doi:10.1214/10-STS330

Shneiderman, B. (1992). Tree visualization with tree-maps: 2-d space-filling approach. *ACM Transactions on Graphics*, *11*(1), 92–99. doi:10.1145/102377.115768

Shvaiko, P., & Euzenat, J. (2013). Ontology Matching: State of the Art and Future Challenges. *IEEE Trans. Knowl. Data Eng.*

Šidlauskas, D., Ross, K., Jensen, C., & Šaltenis, S. (2011). Thread-level Parallel Indexing of Update Intensive Moving-object Workloads. *International Conference on Advances in Spatial and Temporal Databases*. 10.1007/978-3-642-22922-0_12

Šidlauskas, D., Šaltenis, S., & Jensen, C. (2012). *Parallel Main-memory Indexing for Moving-object Query and Update Workloads*. SIGMOD. doi:10.1145/2213836.2213842

Siemens. (2018). Retrieved from https://www.plm.automation.siemens.com/fr/products/teamcenter/

Silva, L. A., Costa, C., & Oliveira, J. L. (2012). A PACS archive architecture supported on cloud services. *International Journal of Computer Assisted Radiology and Surgery*, *7*(3), 349–358. doi:10.100711548-011-0625-x PMID:21678039

Silver, D., & Hassabis, D. (2016). *AlphaGo: Mastering the ancient game of Go with Machine Learning*. Research Blog.

Silvestri, C., Lettich, F., Orlando, S., & Jensen, C. S. (2014). GPU-Based Computing of Repeated Range Queries over Moving Objects. *International Conference on Parallel, Distributed and Network-Based Processing*. 10.1109/PDP.2014.27

Singhal, A. (2001). Modern Information Retrieval: A Brief Overview. *A Quarterly Bulletin of the Computer Society of the IEEE Technical Committee on Data Engineering*, *24*(4), 35–42.

Sis4web. (n.d.). Retrieved from http://www.sisncom.com/IMG/pdf/sis4web.pdf

Sismanis, Y., Deligiannakis, A., Roussopoulos, N., & Kotidis, Y. (2002). Dwarf: shrinking the petacube. Special Interest Group on Management of Data (SIGMOD) Conference, 464–475. doi:10.1145/564691.564745

Slaney, M., & Casey, M. (2008). Locality-sensitive hashing for finding nearest neighbors. *IEEE Signal Processing Magazine*, *25*(2), 128–131. doi:10.1109/MSP.2007.914237

Smedley, D., Schubach, M., Jacobsen, J. O., Köhler, S., Zemojtel, T., Spielmann, M., ... Haendel, M. A. (2016). A whole-genome analysis framework for effective identification of pathogenic regulatory variants in Mendelian disease. *American Journal of Human Genetics*, *99*(3), 595–606. doi:10.1016/j.ajhg.2016.07.005 PMID:27569544

Smith, M. (1999). Invisible crowds in cyberspace: Measuring and mapping the social structure of USENET. In *Communities in cyberspace: Perspectives on new forms of social organization*. London: Routledge Press.

Smith, M., Farnham, S., & Drucker, S. (2000). *The social life of small graphical chat spaces*. ACM SIG CHI. doi:10.1145/332040.332477

Sonntag, D., Wennerberg, P., & Zillner, S. (2010). Applications of an Ontology Engineering Methodology. *AAAI Spring Symposium: Linked Data Meets Artificial Intelligence*.

Soo Yi, J., Melton, R., Stasko, J., & Jacko, J. A. (2005). Dust & magnet: Multivariate information visualization using a magnet metaphor. *Information Visualization*, *4*(4), 239–256. doi:10.1057/palgrave.ivs.9500099

Spark Packages. (2015). Retrieved from https://spark-packages.org

Spirtes, P. (2010). Introduction to causal inference. *Journal of Machine Learning Research*, *11*(May), 1643–1662.

Stillwell, M., & Coutinho, J. G. F. (2015). A DevOps approach to integration of software components in an EU research project. *Proceedings of the 1st International Workshop on Quality-Aware DevOps*. 10.1145/2804371.2804372

Stock, J. H., & Watson, M. (2011). Dynamic Factor Models. In *Oxford Handbook on Economic Forecasting*. Oxford University Press. doi:10.1093/oxfordhb/9780195398649.013.0003

Stock, J. H., & Watson, M. W. (2012). Generalized Shrinkage Methods for Forecasting Using Many Predictors. *Journal of Business & Economic Statistics*, *30*(4), 481–493. doi:10.1080/07350015.2012.715956

Stock, J., & Watson, M. W. (2002). Forecasting Using Principal Components from a Large Number of Predictors. *Journal of the American Statistical Association*, *97*(460), 1167–1179. doi:10.1198/016214502388618960

Stonebraker, M., Bruckner, D., Ilyas, I. F., Beskales, G., Cherniack, M., Zdonik, S. B., . . . Xu, S. (2013, January). Data Curation at Scale: The Data Tamer System. CIDR.

Stowe, K., Paul, M., Palmer, M., Palen, L., & Anderson, K. (2016). Identifying and Categorizing Disaster-Related Tweets. *The Fourth International Workshop on Natural Language Processing for Social Media*, 1-6.

Stumme, G., Taouil, R., Bastide, Y., Pasquier, N., & Lakhal, L. (2002). Computing iceberg concept lattices with titanic. *Data & Knowledge Engineering*, *42*(2), 189–222. doi:10.1016/S0169-023X(02)00057-5

Sun, J., Tao, Y., Papadias, D., & Kollios, G. (2006). Spatio-temporal join selectivity. *Information Systems*, *31*(8), 793–813. doi:10.1016/j.is.2005.02.002

Sun, T., Yin, Y., Wu, S., & Tu, X. (2006). ART2-Based Approach to Judge the State of the Blast Furnace. In *Proceedings of the 6th International Conference on Intelligent Systems Design and Applications* (Vol. 1, pp. 118-122). IEEE. 10.1109/ISDA.2006.108

Sun, Y., Li, J., Liu, J., Chow, C., Sun, B., & Wang, R. (2014). Using causal discovery for feature selection in multivariate numerical time series. *Machine Learning*, *101*(1-3), 377–395. doi:10.100710994-014-5460-1

Sutton, R. S., & Barto, A. G. (1998). Reinforcement learning: An introduction: Vol. 1. *No. 1*. Cambridge, MA: MIT press.

Sweeney, L. (2002). *K-anonymity: A model for protecting privacy*. Retrieved from https://epic.org/privacy/reidentification/Sweeney_Article.pdf

Szmit, M., & Szmit, A. (2012). Usage of modified Holt-Winters method in the anomaly detection of network traffic: Case studies. *Journal of Computer Networks and Communications*.

Tang, X., Zhuang, L., & Jiang, C. (2009). Prediction of silicon content in hot metal using support vector regression based on chaos particle swarm optimization. *Expert Systems with Applications*, *36*(9), 11853–11857. doi:10.1016/j.eswa.2009.04.015

Tan, H., Luo, W., & Ni, L. (2012). Clost: A hadoop-based storage system for big spatio-temporal data analytics. *ACM International Conference on Information and Knowledge Management*. 10.1145/2396761.2398589

Tao, Y., Papadias, D., & Sun, J. (2003). *The TPR*-tree: An Optimized Spatio-temporal Access Method for Predictive Queries*. VLDB. doi:10.1016/B978-012722442-8/50075-6

Tavassoli, S., & Zweig, K. A. (2015). *Analyzing the activity of a person in a chat by combining network analysis and fuzzy logic. In Advances in Social Networks Analysis and Mining*. IEEE/ACM.

Thielbar, M., & Dickey, D. A. (2011). *Neural Networks for Time Series Forecasting: Practical Implications of Theoretical Results*. Academic Press.

Tian, H., & Wang, A. (2010). A novel fault diagnosis system for blast furnace based on support vector machine ensemble. *ISIJ International*, *50*(5), 738–742. doi:10.2355/isijinternational.50.738

Tibshirani, R. (1994). Regression Shrinkage and Selection Via the Lasso. *Journal of the Royal Statistical Society. Series B. Methodological*, *58*, 267–288.

Tipping, M. E., & Bishop, C. M. (1999). Probabilistic Principal Component Analysis. *Journal of the Royal Statistical Society. Series B, Statistical Methodology*, *61*(3), 611–622. doi:10.1111/1467-9868.00196

Tomaszewski, B. (2010). Situation Awareness and Virtual Globes: Applications for Disaster Management. *Computers & Geosciences*, *37*(1).

Tong, H. (2011). Nonlinear time series analysis. In *International Encyclopedia of Statistical Science* (pp. 955–958). Springer Berlin Heidelberg. doi:10.1007/978-3-642-04898-2_411

Trajcevski, G., Yaagoub, A., & Scheuermann, P. (2011). Processing (Multiple) Spatio-temporal Range Queries in Multicore Settings. *International Conference on Advances in Databases and Information Systems*. 10.1007/978-3-642-23737-9_16

Tsai, C. W., Lai, C. F., Chao, H. C., & Vasilakos, A. V. (2015). Big data analytics: A survey. *Journal of Big Data*, *2*(1), 21. doi:10.118640537-015-0030-3 PMID:26191487

Tsay, R. S., Peña, D., & Pankratz, A. E. (2000). Outliers in multivariate time series. *Biometrika*, *87*(4), 789–804. doi:10.1093/biomet/87.4.789

Turban, E., Sharda, R., Aronson, J. E., & King, D. (2008). *Business Intelligence: A Managerial Approach*. Upper Saddle River, NJ: Prentice Hall Press.

Turing, A. M. (1950). Computing machinery and intelligence. *Mind*, *59*(236), 433–460. doi:10.1093/mind/LIX.236.433

Tyler, J. R., Wilkinson, D. M., & Huberman, B. A. (2003). *Email as spectroscopy: Automated discovery of community structure within organizations. In Communities and Technologies* (pp. 81–96). Kluwer.

Ueda, S., Natsui, S., Nogami, H., Yagi, J. I., & Ariyama, T. (2010). Recent progress and future perspective on mathematical modeling of blast furnace. *ISIJ International*, *50*(7), 914–923. doi:10.2355/isijinternational.50.914

University of Indiana. (n.d.). *Harp Project*. Retrieved from http://salsaproj.indiana.edu/harp/

Verhoosel, J. P. C., Bekkum, M. V., & Evert, F. V. (2015). Ontology matching for big data applications in the smart dairy farming domain. *International Semantic Web Conference*.

Verma, S., Vieweg, S., Corvey, W. J., Palen, L., Martin, J. H., Palmer, M., . . . Anderson, K. M. (2011). Natural Language Processing to the Rescue? Extracting "Situational Awareness" Tweets During Mass Emergency. *Fifth International AAAI Conference on Weblogs and Social Media.*

Viégas, F. B. (2005, September). *Revealing individual and collective pasts: Visualizations of online social archives.* Massachusetts Institute of Technology.

W3C. (2004). *World Wide Web Consortium Issues RDF and OWL Recommendations.* Retrieved from https://www.w3.org/2004/01/sws-pressrelease.html.en

Wagner, R., Thom, M., Schweiger, R., Palm, G., & Rothermel, A. (2013, August). Learning convolutional neural networks from few samples. In *Neural Networks (IJCNN), The 2013 International Joint Conference on* (pp. 1-7). IEEE 10.1109/IJCNN.2013.6706969

Wang, J., Crawl, D., Purawat, S., Nguyen, M., & Altintas, I. (2015, October). Big data provenance: Challenges, state of the art and opportunities. In *Big Data (Big Data), 2015 IEEE International Conference on* (pp. 2509-2516). IEEE.

Wang, A., Zhang, L., Gao, N., & Lu, H. (2006). Fault diagnosis of blast furnace based on improved SVMs algorithm. In *Proceedings of the 6th International Conference on Intelligent Systems Design and Applications* (Vol. 1, pp. 825-828). IEEE. 10.1109/ISDA.2006.150

Wang, H., Zimmermann, R., & Ku, W. (2006). Distributed Continuous Range Query Processing on Moving Objects. *International Conference on Database and Expert Systems Applications.* 10.1007/11827405_64

Wang, Y., & Liu, X. (2011). Prediction of silicon content in hot metal based on SVM and mutual information for feature selection. *Journal of Information and Computational Science, 8*(16), 4275–4283.

Wang, Y., Zheng, Y., & Xue, Y. (2014). Travel Time Estimation of a Path using Sparse Trajectories. *KDD: Proceedings / International Conference on Knowledge Discovery & Data Mining. International Conference on Knowledge Discovery & Data Mining.*

Ward, J. S., & Barker, A. (2013). *Undefined By Data: A Survey of Big Data Definitions.* Retrieved from http://arxiv.org/abs/1309.5821

Ward, P., He, Z., Zhang, R., & Qi, J. (2014). Real-time continuous intersection joins over large sets of moving objects using graphic processing units. *The VLDB Journal, 23*(6), 1–21. doi:10.100700778-014-0358-x

Ware, C., Purchase, H. C., Colpoys, L., & McGill, M. (2002). Cognitive measurements of graph aesthetics. *Journal of Information Visualization, 1*(2), 103–110. doi:10.1057/palgrave.ivs.9500013

Watson, H. J., & Wixom, B. H. (2007). The current state of business intelligence. *Computer, 40*(9), 96–99. doi:10.1109/MC.2007.331

Weber, R. H., & Heinrich, U. I. (2012). *Anonymization: SpringerBriefs in Cybersecurity.* Springer. doi:10.1007/978-1-4471-4066-5

Wei, W., Lu, H., Feng, J., & Yu, J. X. (2002). Condensed cube: An efficient approach to reducing data cube size. *Proceedings of the 18th International Conference on Data Engineering*, 155–165.

Weng, J., Zhang, Y., & Hwang, W.-S. (2003). Candid covariance-free incremental principal component analysis. *IEEE Transactions on Pattern Analysis and Machine Intelligence*, *25*(8), 1034–1040. doi:10.1109/TPAMI.2003.1217609

Werner, G., Yang, S., & McConky, K. (2017). Time series forecasting of cyber attack intensity. In *Proceedings of the 12th Annual Conference on Cyber and Information Security Research* (p. 18). ACM. 10.1145/3064814.3064831

Whang, S. E., Marmaros, D., & Garcia-Molina, H. (2013). Pay-as-you-go entity resolution. *IEEE Trans. Knowl. Data Eng.*

Whittle, P. (1953). The Analysis of Multiple Stationary Time Series. *Journal of the Royal Statistical Society. Series B. Methodological*, *15*(1), 125–139.

Wikipedia. (n.d.). *Bulk synchronous parallel*. Retrieved from https://en.wikipedia.org/wiki/Bulk_synchronous_parallel

Wlodarczyk, T. W. (2012). Overview of Time Series Storage and Processing in a Cloud Environment. In *4th IEEE International Conference on Cloud Computing Technology and Science Proceedings* (pp. 625–628). IEEE. 10.1109/CloudCom.2012.6427510

Wolfson, O., Xu, B., Chamberlain, S., & Jiang, L. (1998). Moving objects databases: Issues and solutions. *International Conference on Scientific and Statistical Database Management.*

Wood, J., Dykes, J., Slingsby, A., & Clarke, K. (2007). Interactive Visual Exploration of a Large Spatio-Temporal Dataset: Reflections on a Geovisualization Mashup. *IEEE Transactions on Visualization and Computer Graphics*, *13*(6), 1176–1183. doi:10.1109/TVCG.2007.70570 PMID:17968062

Wu, Y., Zhu, Y., Huang, T., Li, X., Liu, X., & Liu, M. (2015). Distributed Discord Discovery: Spark Based Anomaly Detection in Time Series. In *2015 IEEE 17th International Conference on High Performance Computing and Communications* (pp. 154–159). IEEE. 10.1109/HPCC-CSS-ICESS.2015.228

Wutsqa, D. U. (2008). The Var-NN Model for Multivariate Time Series Forecasting. *MatStat*, *8*(1), 35–43. Retrieved from http://research.binus.ac.id/publication/C12DAA42-899B-4DF3-BA44-4DD770B220C2/the-var-nn-model-for-multivariate-time-series-forecasting/

Wu, X., Kumar, V., Ross Quinlan, J., Ghosh, J., Yang, Q., Motoda, H., ... Zhou, Z. H. (2008). Top 10 algorithms in data mining. *Knowledge and Information Systems*, *14*(1), 1–37. doi:10.100710115-007-0114-2

Wu, X., Zhu, X., Wu, G. Q., & Ding, W. (2014). Data mining with big data. *IEEE Transactions on Knowledge and Data Engineering*, *26*(1), 97–107. doi:10.1109/TKDE.2013.109

Xin, D., Han, J., Li, X., Shao, Z., & Wah, B. W. (2007). Computing iceberg cubes by top-down and bottom-up integration: The starcubing approach. *IEEE Transactions on Knowledge and Data Engineering*, *19*(1), 111–126. doi:10.1109/TKDE.2007.250589

Xin, D., Shao, Z., Han, J., & Liu, H. (2006). C-cubing: Efficient computation of closed cubes by aggregation-based checking. *Proceedings of the 22nd International Conference on Data Engineering (ICDE).*

Xiong, R., & Donath, J. (1999). PeopleGarden: Creating data portraits for users. *Proceedings of UIST.*

Xu, X., Hua, C., Tang, Y., & Guan, X. (2016). Modeling of the hot metal silicon content in blast furnace using support vector machine optimized by an improved particle swarm optimizer. *Neural Computing & Applications*, *27*(6), 1451–1461. doi:10.100700521-015-1951-7

Xu, Y., & Tan, G. (2014). Sim-tree: Indexing moving objects in large-scale parallel microscopic traffic simulation. *ACM Conference on Principles of Advanced Discrete Simulation.* 10.1145/2601381.2601388

Yager, R. R. (2006). An extension of the naive Bayesian classifier. *Information Sciences*, *176*(5), 577–588. doi:10.1016/j.ins.2004.12.006

Yang, B., Lu, H., & Jensen, C. (2010). Probabilistic Threshold K-Nearest Neighbor Queries over Moving Objects in Symbolic Indoor Space. *International Conference on Extending Database Technology*. 10.1145/1739041.1739083

Yang, C., Zhang, X., Zhong, C., Liu, C., Pei, J., Ramamohanarao, K., & Chen, J. (2014). A spatiotemporal compression based approach for efficient big data processing on cloud. *Journal of Computer and System Sciences*, *80*(8), 1563–1583. doi:10.1016/j.jcss.2014.04.022

Yang, W. J., Zhou, Z. Y., & Yu, A. B. (2015). Discrete particle simulation of solid flow in a three-dimensional blast furnace sector model. *Chemical Engineering Journal*, *278*, 339–352. doi:10.1016/j.cej.2014.11.144

Yang, Y., Saleemi, I., & Shah, M. (2013). Discovering motion primitives for unsupervised grouping and one-shot learning of human actions, gestures, and expressions. *IEEE Transactions on Pattern Analysis and Machine Intelligence*, *35*(7), 1635–1648. doi:10.1109/TPAMI.2012.253 PMID:23681992

Yiu, M., Tao, Y., & Mamoulis, N. (2008). The B^{dual}-Tree: Indexing Moving Objects by Space Filling Curves in the Dual Space. *The VLDB Journal*, *17*(3), 379–400. doi:10.100700778-006-0013-2

Yoon, H., & Shahabi, C. (2006). Shahabi: Feature Subset Selection on Multivariate Time Series with Extremely Large Spatial Features Data Mining Workshops. In *ICDM Workshops 2006. Sixth IEEE International Conference on.* IEEE. 10.1109/ICDMW.2006.81

Yuan, J., Zheng, Y., Zhang, C., Xie, W., Xie, X., Sun, G., & Huang, Y. (2010). T-drive: Driving Directions Based on Taxi Trajectories. *SIGSPATIAL International Conference on Advances in Geographic Information Systems*. 10.1145/1869790.1869807

Yuan, M., Zhou, P., Li, M. L., Li, R. F., Wang, H., & Chai, T. Y. (2015). Intelligent multivariable modeling of blast furnace molten iron quality based on dynamic AGA-ANN and PCA. *Journal of Iron and Steel Research International*, *22*(6), 487–495. doi:10.1016/S1006-706X(15)30031-5

Yu, Z., Liu, Y., Yu, X., & Pu, K. (2015). Scalable Distributed Processing of K-Nearest Neighbor Queries over Moving Objects. *IEEE Transactions on Knowledge and Data Engineering*, *27*(5), 1383–1396. doi:10.1109/TKDE.2014.2364046

Zaharia, M., Xin, R. S., Wendell, P., Das, T., Armbrust, M., Dave, A., ... Stoica, I. (2016). Apache Spark: A unified engine for big data processing. *Communications of the ACM*, *59*(11), 56–65. doi:10.1145/2934664

Zeng, J. S., Gao, C. H., & Su, H. Y. (2010). Data-driven predictive control for blast furnace ironmaking process. *Computers & Chemical Engineering*, *34*(11), 1854–1862. doi:10.1016/j.compchemeng.2010.01.005

Zerlang, J. (2017). GDPR: A milestone in convergence for cyber-security and compliance. *Network Security*, *6*(6), 8–11. doi:10.1016/S1353-4858(17)30060-0

Zhang, G. P. (2003). Time series forecasting using a hybrid ARIMA and neural network model. *Neurocomputing*, *50*, 159–175. doi:10.1016/S0925-2312(01)00702-0

Zhang, H. (2004). The optimality of naive Bayes. In *Proceedings of the 17th International FLAIRS Conference*. AAAI Press.

Zhang, J., Qiu, J., Guo, H., Ren, S., Sun, H., Wang, G., & Gao, Z. (2014). Simulation of particle flow in a bell-less type charging system of a blast furnace using the discrete element method. *Particuology*, *16*, 167–177. doi:10.1016/j.partic.2014.01.003

Zhang, J., You, S., & Gruenwald, L. (2012). U2STRA: High-Performance Data Management of Ubiquitous Urban Sensing Trajectories on GPGPUs. *City Data Management Workshop*. 10.1145/2390226.2390229

Zhang, R., Lin, D., Ramamohanarao, K., & Bertino, E. (2008). Continuous intersection joins over moving objects. *IEEE International Conference on Data Engineering*.

Zheng, Y., Xie, X., & Ma, W. (2010). GeoLife: A Collaborative Social Networking Service among User, Location and Trajectory. *A Quarterly Bulletin of the Computer Society of the IEEE Technical Committee on Data Engineering*, *33*(2), 32–39.

Zhong, X., & Enke, D. (2017). Forecasting daily stock market return using dimensionality reduction. *Expert Systems with Applications*, *67*, 126–139. doi:10.1016/j.eswa.2016.09.027

Zhou, D. D., Cheng, S. S., Wang, Y. S., & Jiang, X. (2017). The production and development of large blast furnaces in China during 2015. *Ironmaking & Steelmaking*, *44*(5), 351–358. doi:10.1080/03019233.2016.1210915

Zhou, P., Yuan, M., Wang, H., & Chai, T. (2015). Data-driven dynamic modeling for prediction of molten iron silicon content using ELM with self-feedback. *Mathematical Problems in Engineering*.

Zhou, Z. H. (2012). *Ensemble methods: foundations and algorithms*. CRC Press.

About the Contributors

Jérôme Darmont is full professor of computer science at the University of Lyon, France, and the director of the ERIC research center. He received his Ph.D. in 1999 from the University of Clermont-Ferrand II, France, and then joined the University of Lyon 2 as an associate professor. He became full professor in 2008. His research interests mainly relate to database and data warehouse performance (performance optimization, auto-administration, benchmarking, data lakes...) and cloud business intelligence (data security, query performance and cost, personal BI, big data analytics...). He is a member of several editorial boards and has served as a reviewer for numerous conferences and journals. Along with Torben Bach Pedersen, he initiated the VLDB Cloud Intelligence workshop series in 2012.

Sabine Loudcher is a full professor in Computer Science in a research lab of data science and business intelligence of the University of Lyon (France). She received her PhD degree in Computer Science from the University of Lyon in 1996 and since 2015, she is a full professor. From 2003 to 2012, she was the Assistant Director of the ERIC laboratory. Now, she leads a scientific axis of the Institute of Human Sciences of Lyon (MSH LSE) and she manages the Master of Digital Humanities of the University of Lyon (France). She carries out research on OLAP and Data Mining. She is more interested about data coming from documents or social networks. Her current work focuses on Graph OLAP, Text OLAP and Text Mining. She is involved in several projects especially in Digital Humanities with Social Sciences researchers.

* * *

Leila Abidi is PhD in computer science, her specialty is system distributed on a large scale. She defended her thesis in March 2015 at the University of Paris 13 and since then she is a research engineer at Sorbonne Paris for the IDV project (Life imaging project) for which she is responsible for setting up and managing a cloud computing platform. Website: http://lipn.univ-paris13.fr/~abidi/.

Rajendra Akerkar is leading Big Data research at Vestlandsforsking. His primary domain of activities is big data and semantic technologies with aim to combine strong theoretical results with high impact practical results. His recent research focuses on application of big data methods to real-world challenges such as urban mobility and emergency management, and social media analysis in a wide set of semantic dimensions. He has extensive experience in managing research and development projects funded by both industry and funding agencies, including the EU Framework Programs and the Research Council of Norway.

Hana Alouaoui is a research assistant at IUT Aix en Provence-Aix Marseille University. Member of DBA team at LIF laboratory. Previously, postdoctoral researcher at Icube laboratory at Strasbourg University. She received her PHD in computer science from ISG Tunisia. Her research interests include spatiotemporal knowledge discovery, future risks prediction, spatial data mining and time series forecasting.

Hanene Azzag is currently associate professor at the University of Paris 13 (France) and a member of machine learning team A3 in LIPN Laboratory. Her main research is in biomimetic algorithms, machine learning and visual data mining. In 2002 she gained an MSC (DEA) in Artificial Intelligence from Tours University. In 2005, after three years Tours Lab, she received her PhD degree in Computer Science from the University of Tours. She received the "Habilitation à Diriger des Recherches" (accreditation to lead research) degree in Computer Science from Paris 13 University in 2013.

Salima Benbernou is a Professor in Computer Science at université Sorbonne-Paris Cité -Paris Descartes. She is leading data intensive and knowledge oriented system group (diNo). Her interests are on the interplay of data management at scale and privacy. She is an associate editor at ACM TOS journal. Her research is supported by French national research organizations (CNRS, BPI, ANR) and European Commission.

Mehdi Bentounsi received a Ph.D. in Computer Science at Université Paris Descartes in 2015 and then joined Université Sorbonne Paris Cité as a postdoc for the IDV project. His research interests lie in the field of information security, privacy and databases with emphasis on data lifecycle management, privacy, and data security in cloud computing and untrusted environments.

Christophe Cérin has been a professor of computer science at the University of Paris 13, France since 2005. He initiated an infrastructure project related to big data and high performance computing for e-sciences for USPC (Université Sorbonne Paris Cité). At Paris13, he chairs the board for the cluster computing facility available to all campus scientists and also chairs the 'Expert Committee' in charge of recruiting and mentoring full time junior and senior professors in computer science. His industrial experience includes serving as local chair for the Dolphin and Wendelin projects related to Cloud and Big-Data. His previous industrial project was the Resilience project related to Cloud Computing where he was the local chair. His research focuses on High Performance Computing, including Grid Computing and he develops middleware, algorithms, tools and methods for distributed systems. His Web page at http://lipn.univ-paris13.fr/~cerin/ contains links to his publications list and educational activities.

Rosine Cicchetti is a full professor at the University of Aix-Marseilles (France) and former responsible and actual member of the database and machine learning research team at the Laboratory of Fundamental Computer Science (LIF) of Marseilles. She obtained the PhD in 1990 (University of Nice, France) and the Habilitation for Research Direction in 1996 (University of Aix-Marseilles). Her research topics encompass Databases, Data Mining, Data Warehousing, Statistical databases and Multidimensional Skylines.

Tarn Duong completed a Ph.D. in computational statistics in 2005. Since then he has been employed as a researcher at numerous university departments in Australia and in France. His research interests include Big Data Analysis for experimental sciences.

Philippe Garteiser graduated from Strasbourg University in Biology, Physics and Chemistry. He then got an engineering degree in bioengineering followed by a PhD in Bioengineering in the University of Oklahoma. Dr. Garteiser now holds a senior researcher position in the Center for Research on Inflammation (Inserm U1149, Paris). Philippe Garteiser is an executive member of the "Imageries Du Vivant" programme of the Sorbonne Paris Cité Universities.

Eric E. Geiselman is an Engineering Research Psychologist at the U.S. Air Force Research Laboratory's 711th Human Performance Wing, in the Airman Systems Directorate. He spent eight years as an airline pilot and eventually became a crew resource management instructor. He holds an MA in experimental psychology from the University of Dayton and is pursuing a doctorate in systems engineering at the Air Force Institute of Technology.

Le Gruenwald is a Professor, Dr. David W. Franke Professor, and Samuel Roberts Noble Foundation Presidential Professor in the School of Computer Science at The University of Oklahoma. She received her Ph.D. in Computer Science from Southern Methodist University, MS in Computer Science from the University of Houston, and BS in Physics from the University of Saigon. She worked for National Science Foundation as a Cluster Lead and Program Director of the Information Integration and Informatics cluster and a Program Director of the Cyber Trust program. Dr. Gruenwald's major research interests include Data Management, Data Mining, and Information Privacy and Security.

Paul Havig is a senior engineering research psychologist at the Air Force Research Laboratory's 711th Human Performance Wing. He received his BA in Psychology from the University of California at San Diego in 1989 and his PhD in Experimental Psychology from the University of Texas at Arlington in 1997. His major area of research is visual perception.

Youssef Hmamouche is PhD student interested in the fields of data mining and machine learning. His actual research focuses on prediction models and feature selection methods specific to forecasting time series with large number of variables.

Kuo-Wei (David) Hsu was an assistant professor in the Department of Computer Science at the National Chengchi University. He earned his Ph.D. degree from the Department of Computer Science and Engineering at the University of Minnesota. Prior to that, he worked as an Information Engineer in the National Taiwan University Hospital. He obtained his M.S. degree from the Department of Computer Science and Information Engineering at the National Taiwan University, and B.S. degree from the Department of Electrical Engineering at the National Chung Hsing University. His current research interests include data management and analysis.

Yung-Chang Ko is a scientist at the Iron & Steel Research & Development Department of China Steel Corporation. He received PHD in Mechanical Engineering from National Cheng Kung University. His professional achievements include heat transfer, gas and liquid combustion blast furnace iron making.

Lotfi Lakhal received the PhD degree in computer science and the Habilitation for Research Direction from the University of Nice-Sophia-Antipolis (France) respectively in 1986 and in 1991.He is a full professor at the University of Aix-Marseille - IUT of Aix en Provence and member of the Laboratory of Fundamental Computer Science (LIF) of Marseilles. His research interest includes Databases,

Formal Concept Analysis, Data Mining, Data Warehousing, Multidimensional Skylines and Time Series Forecasting.

Eleazar Leal is an assistant professor in the Department of Computer Science in the University of Minnesota Duluth. He received his Ph.D. in Computer Science at the University of Oklahoma. His research interests are: Spatial Databases, Stream Databases, Multicore and GPU Algorithms for Databases and Data Mining.

Mustapha Lebbah is currently Associate Professor at the University of Paris 13 and a member of Machine learning Team A3, LIPN. His main researches are centred on machine learning and data mining (Unsupervized Learning, Self-organizing map, Probabilistic and Statistic, scalable machine learning and data science). Graduated from USTO University where he received his engineer diploma in 1998. Thereafter, he gained an MSC (DEA) in Artificial Intelligence from the Paris 13 University in 1999. In 2003, after three year in RENAULT R&D, he received his PhD degree in Computer Science from the University of Versailles. He received the "Habilitation à Diriger des Recherches" (accreditation to lead research) degree in Computer Science from Paris 13 University in 2012. He is a member of the french group in "complex data mining", and Secretary for the French Classification Society since november 2012.

Mickaël Martin-Nevot currently prepare the Phd degree in computer science from the University of Aix-Marseille (France). He is an part-time assistant professor at the University of Aix-Marseille - IUT of Aix en Provence and is a member of the Laboratory of Fundamental Computer Science (LIF) of Marseilles. His research work concerns OLAP Mining and Data Warehousing.

John P. McIntire is an engineering research psychologist at the Air Force Research Laboratory 711th Human Performance Wing. He received his Ph.D. in human factors psychology from Wright State University in 2014. He specializes in vision-related human factors experimental research, including in visualization, depth perception, 3D vision, stereoscopic and 3D displays, display design, and user interface evaluation. Recently, he has worked on rapid innovation projects involving military installation security systems and dismounted soldier navigation technologies.

Prakhar Mehrotra is head of Data Science, Finance, Uber Technologies.

Sébastien Nedjar obtained the Phd degree in computer science from the University of Aix-Marseille (France) in 2009. He is an assistant professor at the University of Aix-Marseille - IUT of Aix en Provence and is a member of the Laboratory of Fundamental Computer Science (LIF) of Marseilles. His research work concerns OLAP Mining, Data Warehousing and Multidimensional Skylines.

Isaac Osesina is a research scientist at Aware Inc. Prior to joining Aware, he was a researcher at the University of Arkansas at Little Rock (UALR) Center for Advanced Research in Entity Resolution and Information Quality. He obtained his doctorate degree in Integrated Computing at the same institution. His current research areas include entity and identity resolution, named entity recognition, social network analysis and information visualization. His works are published in several international journals and conferences.

Mourad Ouziri is assistant professor at Paris Descartes University. His research interests concern the use of knowledge representation formalisms and reasoning mechanisms for efficient data management, especially in distributed environments. He develops approaches to manage data on the Web, semantic Web, data uncertainty and inconsistency, semantic heterogeneity, and privacy. Recently, his research focuses on managing big RDF data dealing with data quality in huge amounts of heterogeneous RDF data. The aim of this work is to develop suitable reasoning algorithms to make efficient data querying with respect to quality requirements. His application domains are related to big data, open data, crowdsourcing, privacy and social networks. In big data, his aim is to develop MapReduce and Spark-based inferences to combine company internal data with open data to improve data quality. In crowdsourcing, privacy and social networks domains, he developed a team-based approach to process crowdsourcing by involving members in social networks with respect to privacy. He has published his works in journals (ACM TWEB 2016 Transactions on the Web, ACM TOIT 2016 Transactions on Internet Technology, ML 2017 Machine Learning Journal), conferences (WISE – Web Information System Engineering) and workshops (DL – Description Logics).

Piotr Przymus received PhD from Faculty of Mathematics, Informatics, and Mechanics, University of Warsaw in the field of data mining and databases in 2014. Currently works at the LIF at Aix-Marseille University. His main scientific interests are: data mining, database systems, distributed and parallel programing and GPGPU computing.

Soror Sahri is associate professor at Université Paris Descartes (Sorbonne Paris Cité) and is a member of LIPADE (Laboratoire d'Informatique Paris Descartes). She received her PhD in computer science from Paris-Dauphine University, where she worked on scalable and Distributed databases. Actually, her main research concerns especially data management, data quality and distributed databases.

M. Eduard Tudoreanu, DSc, is Professor of Information Science at University of Arkansas Little Rock. Professor Tudoreanu has expertise in human-computer interaction, in advanced visualization of complex data, information quality, and in virtual reality. He worked on 2D and 3D visualization environments and has extensive experience in software development and user interface design. Professor Tudoreanu was the founding Technical Director of the Emerging Analytics Center. He has been teaching Human-Computer Interface (HCI) for the past ten years as well as Information Visualization for more than ten years. He has been the keynote speaker at ABSEL 2010, served as a panelist for the National Science Foundation, advisory panel for Missouri EPSCoR, and received grants from the G. W. Donaghey Foundation, National Science Foundation, Air Force Research Laboratory, NASA, US Department of Education, and Acxiom Corporation. He earned his Doctor of Science degree in Computer Science in 2002 from the Washington University in St. Louis.

Jianting Zhang is Associate Professor in Geographical Information System (GIS) and Computer Science at the City College of New York. He has broad research interests in geospatial technologies and their environmental and social-economic applications. Trained as both a geographer and a computer scientist, he is committed to the interdisciplinary research that crosses the boundary of computer science, information technologies and domain sciences, such as geography, ecology and transportation.

Index

I

K

L

M

N

O

P

Q

R

S

T

V

W

www.ingramcontent.com/pod-product-compliance
Ingram Content Group UK Ltd.
Pitfield, Milton Keynes, MK11 3LW, UK
UKHW051451290926
15471UKWH00008B/1148